HISTORY

OF THE

PRESBYTERIAN CHURCH

IN THE

UNITED STATES OF AMERICA.

BY

E. H. GILLETT,

AUTHOR OF "THE LIFE AND TIMES OF JOHN HUSS."

VOL. I.

PHILADELPHIA:
PRESBYTERIAN PUBLICATION COMMITTEE,
1334 CHESTNUT STREET.

NEW YORK: A. D. F. RANDOLPH, 683 BROADWAY.

PREFACE.

More than seventy years have elapsed since the attention of the General Assembly of the Presbyterian Church in the United States was called to the subject of preparing a history of the denomination in this country. In 1791, Rev. Drs. Witherspoon, McWhorter, and Green, and Rev. Messrs. William Graham, James Hall, and James Templeton, were appointed a committee "to devise measures for the collecting of materials necessary" to carry out the project. In accordance with the suggestions of their report, it was enjoined upon each Presbytery "strictly to order their members to procure all the materials for forming a history of the Presbyterian Church in this country, in the power of each member, and bring in the same to their Presbytery, and that the Presbyteries forward the said collection of materials to the next General Assembly."

In 1792, and in successive years till 1795, the subject was considered, and "delinquent Presbyteries" were called upon for their reports. But no further action was taken till 1804, when Dr. Green and Mr. Ebenezer Hazard were appointed, from the materials gathered, to write the history. Delinquent Presbyteries were again called upon to complete their narratives.

In 1813, Dr. Green and Mr. Hazard stated to the

Assembly that they had found it impracticable to go on with the work, and their request that the papers which they possessed might be transferred to Dr. Miller, who should be authorized and requested to complete the history, was granted. In 1819, Dr. Green was by vote of the Assembly associated with Dr. Miller in the preparation of the work. Their request, in 1825, to be discharged from the duty committed to them, was received with "unfeigned regret;" and although it was granted, the project of the preparation of the History was not abandoned. Measures were adopted "to insure the continuation and completion of the work with the least possible delay." A new committee, consisting of Drs. Green, Janeway, and Ely,[1] was appointed for this purpose.

Here, however, the matter was suffered to rest. It was left to individual enterprise and effort to investigate the history of the Church during different periods and in different localities. Works of great value for reference and authority in compiling a general history of the Church have thus been produced; and while important materials have been irrevocably lost by the lapse of time and past neglect, the task of preparing a connected history has in some respects been greatly facilitated.

In these circumstances, the Publication Committee of the Assembly judged, several years since, that the long-deferred project should be undertaken afresh. Nothing could be gained, and much might be lost,

---

[1] Upon Dr. Ely's resignation in 1836, Dr. Luther Halsey was appointed in his place.

by further delay. With each successive year matters of great value were passing to oblivion. Presbyterians, moreover, ignorant of the history of their own Church, and of its policy as illustrated by that history, might justly claim such information as would serve at once for the vindication of their own ecclesiastical preferences and the position of the denomination with which they were identified.

It was resolved, therefore, to take steps for the preparation of a work not too voluminous for popular perusal, yet sufficiently minute to combine a measure of local with general interest,—a work which should present an outline of the origin and progress of the Church, the methods and results of its efforts, and the spirit and policy by which those efforts have been directed.

Selected by the committee for the task of preparing such a work, I have endeavored to embody with historic impartiality the most important facts, accessible to diligent and faithful investigation, in the work which is now offered to the Church. The labor has been by no means a light one. Materials have been gathered from most diverse and unlooked-for sources. By correspondence, and by the examination of old records, letters, and narratives,—some of which must have slept unmolested on the files of Presbytery for more than half a century,—I have endeavored to supply the lack of other authorities; and in this I have been greatly aided by the most ready and efficient co-operation of numerous individuals who have cheerfully rendered their assistance. To some of them I have been indebted for valuable information which will be found in the notes, or has been incorporated in the body of the work.

But the labor, I need scarcely say, has been "a labor of love." Much of the history of the Church in this country has been hitherto buried in obscurity and neglect, and the exploration of it has been like the search for hidden treasures. Time-stained journals and moth-eaten volumes have possessed a rare charm when, like the "Catacombs," they have given back to us the memorials of a patience, toil, and fidelity which deserve an honor second only to that of the primitive disciples. Something of the gratification of one who lights upon the soiled and dust-covered masterpiece of a great painter, and who finds that by care and diligence he can restore its faded lineaments, has been afforded in recovering from an ever-deepening obscurity the features of those heroic pioneers of Christian effort to whom not only the Church, but the country and the world, are so deeply indebted. To enter as a partisan into such a field as this, would be a peculiar profanation of the sanctity of historic truth; and if any misrepresentations of the facts or aspects of the periods of controversy through which the Church has been called to pass are here to be found, they are at least not due either to any conscious design, or to any bias received from personal participation in the scenes of strife. Almost an entire generation has passed from the stage since the memorable conflict by which the Church was rent in sunder; and he who can now survey the period with other feelings than those of regret for human weakness, and sorrow for the causes of mutual alienation, must have a conscience which the old rust of controversy still gnaws or the zeal of partisanship still blinds. Yet there should be no ignoring of the historic position of the Church. If that reunion which is so confidently anticipated by many is ever consummated, it is wise that it should rest on a solid basis, and not be built upon either ignorance or misconception of the facts of history. This is apology enough for not passing over facts of which the historian himself would be gladly spared the detail.

In the preparation of the work, I have, as far as possible, availed myself of authorities contemporaneous with the facts narrated. Among these are to be classed the minutes of the Synod of New York and Philadelphia, and those of the General Assembly; those also of Synods and Presbyteries, so far as accessible; "The Literary and Theological Magazine," "New York Missionary Magazine," "Connecticut Evangelical Magazine," Annual Reports of the Connecticut Missionary Society from 1793 to 1820, "Assembly's Magazine," "Panoplist," "Christian Advocate," "Christian Spectator," "Biblical Repository," "Presbyterian Quarterly Review," "Princeton Review," "American Quarterly Register," "New York Observer," "New York Evangelist," "Christian Herald" (1816–21), "Presbytery Reporter," "Home Missionary," Reports of the different Domestic Missionary Societies, &c., besides files, more or less complete, of the various Presbyterian journals at the South and West.[1]

[1] New Orleans "True Witness," "Presbyterian Herald," "Southern Presbyterian," "North Carolina Presbyterian," "Central Christian Herald," &c.

Next in importance to these have been local histories, such as Prime's Long Island, Hotchkin's Western New York, Nevin's Churches of the Valley, Foote's Sketches of Virginia and North Carolina, Davidson's Kentucky, "Old Redstone," Bolton's History of Westchester County, Smyth's Second Church of Charleston, Macdonald's History of the Church of Jamaica, Riker's Newtown, Hoyt's Church of Orange, Stearns's Church of Newark, Hall's Church of Trenton, Eager's Orange County, Campbell's Tryon County, Munsell's Annals of Albany, Murray's Elizabethtown, Hewatt's History of South Carolina, History of Londonderry, Histories of Pittsburg, Cincinnati, Detroit, St. Louis, &c., Greenleaf's Churches of Maine, Greenleaf's Churches of New York City, Dwight's Travels, Reed's Christian Traveller, &c.

In biography, Dr. Sprague's Annals, so far as they have extended, have been invaluable and indispensable; although in some instances I have been constrained to differ from the views which they present. Very important materials also have been derived from such memoirs as those of Drs. Alexander, Green, J. H. Rice, Nesbit, Rodgers, Griffin, Cleland, Macurdy, Baldwin, Rowland, Baker, Holley, and Rev. Messrs. Badger, Christmas, Porter, Cornelius, Larned, Bruen, and others. Wilson's "Historical Almanac" has furnished information nowhere else accessible, and has proved of material service.

Among works of a more general historical character which have been profitably consulted, must be mentioned Prince's History, Felt's Ecclesiastical History of New England, Histories of the United

States by Grahame, Hildreth, and Bancroft, Historical Collections of the different States, made by individuals, Societies, or State authority in the form of "Documentary History," and numerous State histories, like Trumbull's Connecticut, Simms's South Carolina, Ramsay's Tennessee, &c., Dr. Green's History of Presbyterian Missions, Humphrey's Revival Sketches, and the well-known works of Hodge and Webster.

The list of historical and obituary discourses which I have been able to collect, or at least to consult, has exceeded my anticipations. I have had peculiarly favorable opportunities in this respect, and have thus been enabled to add not a little to that minuteness of detail which is often necessary to clothe and give life to the statistics,—the skeleton of history. A list of these it is not necessary here to insert, as probably they are not sufficiently accessible in any public collection to enable the reader to make reference to them.

Beside these, historical pamphlets, like that of the tour of Mills and Schermerhorn to the Southwest, and that narrating the scenes of revival in the Carolinas of 1802, or controversial pamphlets, like those of Dr. Ely, Messrs. Patterson, McCalla, &c., of Philadelphia, of Drs. Rice, Peters, Wilson, Beecher, and others, have fallen in my way and been sifted for facts.

Another class of works has not been overlooked, and has been, indeed, indispensable. To this belong Barnes's Trial, Barnes's Defence, Reports of the Presbyterian Church Case before the Civil Courts, Judd's History of the Division of the Presbyterian

Church, Crocker's Catastrophe of the Presbyterian Church, Wood's Old and New Theology, with others which it is needless to mention.

Some reference has been already made to manuscript and oral communications. But the manuscript History of the Secession of the Associated Presbyteries (1799–1818), by Dr. N. S. Prime, is worthy of special mention; and the files of the old Albany Presbytery—unexplored, perhaps, for half a century—afforded not only some of the original histories of churches ordered to be prepared by the General Assembly, but much other information of value. In the private library of the Stated Clerk of the General Assembly I obtained access to many works which I have met with nowhere else, and from friends in both branches of the Presbyterian Church I have received assistance and information to which I have been greatly indebted.

No one can be more sensible than myself of the imperfections of the work. Some of them, indeed, from the lack of materials, were inevitable. There are still gaps here and there, which remain, and in all probability will long remain, to be filled, while the assigned limits of the work[1] have precluded the insertion of much matter that had been already prepared. Such an undertaking as this gives us—and, after all corrections and additions, must still give us—only an approximation to a complete history. Yet, by sending the work forth, even in its present

[1] In repeated instances, instead of giving the full name of the ministers in the text, I have endeavored to save space by using only the surname. By a reference, however, to the Index, the full name may readily be found in nearly every instance.

form, a great want which our churches have long felt will, I trust, be supplied, and many facts, important in the history of the Church, which might otherwise have soon passed into oblivion, will be preserved. No one can thoughtfully peruse the story of the perils and hardships, the toils and achievements, of the fathers and pioneers of the Church, or linger over even the controversies and dissensions by which at times it has been rent, or, especially, regard the great work which it has nobly achieved, without deriving therefrom lessons of truth, wisdom, and love.

E. H. Gillett.

Harlem, New York City, April 11, 1864.

CONTENTS.

CHAPTER I.

FRANCIS MAKEMIE.

CHAPTER II.

THE FIRST PRESBYTERY, 1706–1715.

CHAPTER III.

THE SYNOD, 1717–1729.

CHAPTER VI.

THE PERIOD OF THE DIVISION, 1741–1758.

CHAPTER VII.

PRESBYTERIANISM IN VIRGINIA.

CHAPTER VIII.

THE SYNODS AND THEIR SCHOOLS.

CHAPTER XI.

ASSOCIATED PRESBYTERIES.

CHAPTER XII.

THE CAROLINAS—RISE AND PROGRESS OF THE CHURCH.

CHAPTER XIII.

"OLD REDSTONE," 1776–1793.

CHAPTER XIV.

GENERAL ASSEMBLY, 1789–1800.

CHAPTER XV.

NEW JERSEY AND PENNSYLVANIA, 1789–1800.

CHAPTER XVI.

MARYLAND AND VIRGINIA, 1789–1800.

CHAPTER XVII.

THE CAROLINAS, 1789–1800.

CHAPTER XVIII.

NEW YORK, 1789–1800.

CHAPTER XIX.

KENTUCKY, 1775–1800.

CHAPTER XXII.

PENNSYLVANIA, 1800–1820.

CHAPTER XXIII.

NEW JERSEY, 1800–1820.

THE HISTORY

OF THE

PRESBYTERIAN CHURCH

IN THE

UNITED STATES.

CHAPTER I.

FRANCIS MAKEMIE.

AMERICAN Presbyterianism, like American civilization, has derived its distinctive character from many and diverse influences. As we trace the course of its history we find it receiving tributaries from distant and varied sources, yet all blending in a current that flows in a channel of its own, and marked at every step by features peculiar to itself. Commingled in it, and made more or less homogeneous by it, we find the elements of English "dissent," Irish fervor, Scotch persistence, and Huguenot devotion. There is scarce a memorable event in the history of Protestantism in the Old World that does not assist to elucidate the character of its founders. It inherits alike the memories of the noble men who fell victims to the bigotry of Alva or Laud, or endured the brutal cruelty of Lauderdale or Jeffries. In the annals of the Genevan republic, the heroism of the Netherlands, the sufferings of the Huguenots,—culminating in the bloody St. Bartholomew,—the sterling conscientiousness of the Puritans, and the unswerving loyalty to Christ's crown and covenant evinced by the countrymen of John Knox, may be discerned the elements of that training which shaped the views and character of its founders.

Thus, without taking any other church on earth as its model, it was built up out of materials drawn from sources the most diverse, and into a structure that constitutes its own type. Even here it was modified by local influences,—sometimes constrained in the New World to renew the struggle which had become too familiar in the Old, and to protest against an intolerance which could not but revive memories of Acts of Conformity, bigoted proscription, or Claverhouse's dragoons. Yet ere long it was left unmolested, and, in a field broad enough to tax its utmost energies, was called to the task of competing with other denominations in the noble work of evangelizing a young and growing empire.

Although it was not till after the commencement of the eighteenth century that the Presbyterian Church in this country assumed an organized form, yet many of the elements that were finally assimilated and embodied in it had been long acclimated on these Western shores. The Plymouth Church conformed—almost as far as in its isolated position was possible—to the French Presbyterian type.[1] The early Synods of New England repeatedly and emphatically endorsed the importance of the eldership. The Synods themselves were the concession of public conviction to the necessity for a supervision of the churches which a state theocracy strove vainly to supply. Not a few of the leading minds of New England regretted and opposed

---

[1] Life of Brewster.

the tendencies upon which the churches were for many years steadily drifting towards a relaxation of church order and discipline, and it is scarcely surprising that they should have strongly favored the Presbyterian system, when they felt constrained, like Stone of Hartford, to define Congregationalism as "a speaking aristocracy in the face of a silent democracy," or to say of it, with the elder Edwards, "I have *long* been out of conceit of our unsettled, independent, confused way of church government in this land."

Nor were there wanting those, even in New England, who had been educated under the Presbyterianism of men like Owen and Baxter and Manton and Jacomb, but who with their liberal sympathies readily adopted the ecclesiastical usages of the land of their adoption. But as they went abroad,—some of them removing to Long Island and some to New York and New Jersey,—they just as liberally and readily acquiesced in the forms and methods of their new religious associations, and, like Burr of Newark and Dickinson of Elizabethtown,—without violating their convictions or sacrificing an iota of principle,—became the leaders in the ranks of the Presbyterian Church.

Thus, long before the first Presbytery was formed, quite a number of churches on Long Island and in New Jersey which subsequently became identified with the Presbyterian Church had been organized by the descendants of the Puritans, and mainly by New England men. In only one or two instances is it probable that the church was possessed of a Presbyterian organization; but their sympathies were one with Protestant Dissenters, whether in the mother country or its colonies. The New England Puritan affiliated readily with the "Scotch Independent," which in the lips of a Churchman was often a synonym for Presbyterian, and in the absence of that state supervision of the churches which constituted the administration of the "New England Theocracy," he felt the propriety and yielded to the expediency of an organization to which should be committed "the care of the churches."

By the year 1700 there must have been in the colonies of New York and New Jersey from ten to fifteen churches which were of a New England origin and type. It is more than possible that the church at Jamaica was organized as Presbyterian,[1] and if so it is probably the only one of them all entitled to claim this distinction until at least some years after the formation of the first Presbytery. Nor did it come into connection with Presbytery until some time subsequent to its organization.[2]

The man to whom the honor belongs of laying the foundations of the Presbyterian Church, as an organized body, in this country, is Francis Makemie. He was an Irishman,—born near Rathmelton, Donegal county, Ireland,—a student at one of the Scotch universities, and a licentiate of the Presbytery of Laggan in 1681. Three years later, after laboring a while in Barbadoes,[3] he organized the Presbyterian Church in Snow Hill, Maryland. Here, in the narrow neck of land between the Chesapeake and the ocean, sheltered by the mild

---

1 See Macdonald's Jamaica.

2 Macdonald's "History of the Presbyterian Church of Jamaica, L.I." (new and enlarged edition), published since the above was written, labors to show that the Jamaica Church is the oldest existing church of the Presbyterian name in America. He certainly renders this highly probable. And yet the church is spoken of by Vesey and others as one of Scotch Independents, and the fact that it stood in connection with no presbytery until after Macnish commenced his pastorate, forces us to regard it as Independent Presbyterian, and not an integral portion of "The Presbyterian Church in the United States" as already organized by the Presbytery at Philadelphia.

3 Foote's Sketches, First Series, p. 42.

laws of a colony founded by a Roman Catholic nobleman, the Presbyterian Church of America began its existence.[1]

It is probable, indeed, that other Presbyterian congregations had been gathered before this in other localities. But their condition must have been far from promising, and rarely could they have enjoyed the ordinances of the sanctuary. The population was sparse, and there were no "towns." Makemie notices it as "an unaccountable humor"[2] that no attempts were made to build them. The people were scattered like sheep in the wilderness, and a large portion of his labor was to search them out. Soon after he had commenced his ministry in Maryland, he found on Elizabeth River in Virginia "a poor desolate people" mourning the loss of their "dissenting ministers from Ireland," who had been removed by death the summer previous.[3] It was not long before quite a number of congregations were gathered in the region which he had selected as his field of labor. An itinerant missionary, and in reality the bishop of a primitive diocese, he journeyed from place to place, sometimes on the Eastern Shore of Maryland, sometimes in Virginia, and sometimes extending his journeys as far as South Carolina. To the extent of his ability he supplied the feeble churches, but he deeply felt the need of others to assist him. To obtain these was an object of paramount importance, and he spared no effort to attain it. With this end in view, he corresponded with ministers in London and in Boston. But he was not content with this. He broke away—we may be sure at a great sacrifice—from the pressing

[1] From 1649 to 1692, Maryland enjoyed perfect religious toleration. In the latter year the Episcopal was made the Established Church. The attempt to introduce this innovation was made in 1677, but defeated by Lord Baltimore.

[2] Sprague, iii. 2. [3] Ib. iii. 6.

calls around him that he might personally urge his appeals. He crossed the ocean and applied to the Independent and Presbyterian ministers of London for aid. He visited New England and consulted with Mather. Indefatigable in effort, clear-sighted and sagacious in his views, liberal in sentiment, fearless in the discharge of duty, and shrinking from no burden, his name needs no eulogy beyond the simple record of what he accomplished and endured.

Makemie had been but a few years in Maryland when the English Revolution took place. For the English Dissenter it secured some of his just rights, but its benefits were scarcely felt on this side of the ocean. Indeed, in Maryland it resulted in the establishment by law of the Episcopal Church. The principles of religious liberty were not to be vindicated here without a struggle, and the early history of the American Presbyterian Church rallies around it the sympathies of every friend of civil and religious freedom. The experience of Makemie in a New York prison, or before a royal judge, reminds us of Baxter and the abuse heaped upon him by the infamous Jeffries; while the history of the Virginia Dissenters is not unworthy a place by the side of that of the English Non-conformists of 1662.

Makemie in 1703–4 visited England and procured as fellow-laborers John Hampton and George Macnish.[1] They returned with him to Maryland,—sent out and sustained by the London Union of Presbyterian and Independent ministers. But when they reached Maryland it was to experience the intolerance that allowed that colony no longer the enviable reputation for religious freedom which it once enjoyed. The Episcopal had now become the Established Church, and no Dissenter was allowed to preach without a license. For

---

[1] Usually, but incorrectly, spelled McNish.

many years in New York, Virginia, Maryland, and South Carolina, the growth of the Presbyterian Church was checked by persecution and intolerance. We cannot do justice to the spirit of the first Presbyterian ministers and their noble vindication of religious liberty, without a brief review of the conditions of their fields of labor.

For a long period Virginia rivalled the mother country in the hardships with which she treated all but Episcopalians. The Established Church was exclusively tolerated and sustained by law, and every form of dissent was accounted obnoxious. For three-quarters of a century it was suppressed by the most rigid laws, and for another three-quarters of a century it was at best but barely tolerated, and in some cases altogether interdicted. In the earlier period the laws against those who did not conform were peculiarly rigid. By the Act of 1618, absentees from the parish church were punished by a fine and a night in the stocks, and for the third offence by being made slaves to the colony for a year and a day. In the revisal of 1642 the Act for Conformity was made more severe on ministers. The Governor and Council were directed to send away any who did not comply with this enactment. Nor was the law suffered to remain a dead letter.

There was already in Virginia a Puritan leaven long before the arrival of Makemie.[1] In 1607, Rev. Henry Jacobs fled with the celebrated John Robinson to Leyden. He subsequently returned to England and organized the first Congregational Church in that country in 1616. In 1624, he emigrated to Virginia[2]

[1] Prince's Chronology.

[2] In 1624 Henry Jacob, who had been the pastor of the Southwark Congregational Church, London, left his charge and removed to Virginia, where he died. The scene and duration of his labors are uncertain, but in 1642 (May 24) Richard Bennet, Daniel Gookin,

with thirty members of his congregation. He was succeeded in his labors in this country by Rev. Mr.

John Hyll, and others, to the number of seventy-one persons, wrote to the ministers of New England, speaking of themselves as "inhabitants of the county of the Upper Norfolk in Virginia," and as having prepared an address to the ministers in an appeal for help in the previous year. At the later date they speak of "the present incumbent" being determined to leave them, so that they are forced to provide for themselves. The county, they say, is of large extent, and it had been found necessary to divide it into three parts, each of which was willing to support a pastor. Philip Bennet was agent for the applicants, who desired to obtain three ministers, such as should on trial be found "faithful in pureness of doctrine and integrity of life."

The Virginia letters were read publicly, and a time was appointed to consider them. Phillips of Watertown, Tompson of Braintree, and Miller of Rowley, were designated. The first declined, and his colleague Knowles consented to take his place. Miller's health forbade his compliance. Knowles and Tompson set out, and at New Haven were joined by James, formerly of Charlestown. They were eleven weeks in reaching their destination; but when they reached their field of labor they were greatly encouraged.

Their labors were greatly prospered; but the authorities silenced them, and they returned in less than a year. But Thomas Harrison, the chaplain of the Governor, had been brought under their influence, and had adopted and begun to preach their evangelical views. Virginia renewed its application to Massachusetts for help. William Durand of Upper Norfolk wrote also to New Haven urging John Davenport (Felt, i. 515) to advance the sending of ministers to Virginia. He states that his friends had thought of applying in England for pastors, but had concluded that those of best qualifications were to be found in New England.

Knowles, Tompson,—whose wife died on the mission,—and James, had scarcely left Virginia when the Indians rose and massacred a large number of the settlers. A "mortal sickness" also prevailed, and the Governor likewise ordered those who would not conform to Episcopacy to leave the jurisdiction. Harrison was left alone,—pastor of a church at Nansemond gathered by the missionaries and composing "a large congregation,"—but in 1648 he also left for

Lathrop. Congregationalist Dissenters were thus introduced into Virginia at an early period.

In 1641, a gentleman from Virginia by the name of Bennet visited Boston with letters from Virginia residents to New England ministers, "bewailing their sad condition for want of the glorious gospel," and entreating that they might thence be supplied. The letters were openly read at Boston upon a lecture-day, and the subject was taken up in earnest. Tompson and Knowles, colleague-pastors at Watertown and Braintree, were selected for the mission, and on their way were joined by James of New Haven.

Their voyage was slow and difficult. They began "to suspect whether they had a clear call of God to the undertaking," but their success on their arrival soon dispelled their fears. The magistrates, indeed, gave them little encouragement, but from the people they received a warm welcome. In several parts of the country "there were many people brought home to God." But they were not long left unmolested. The Episcopal clergy were far from exemplary in the discharge of their duties.[1] They felt the rebuke of a better example, and at their instance, or at least with their sanction, the laws against dissent were enforced against the New England ministers. They were "discharged from public preaching in Virginia," but they continued their labors in private, "and did much good." They were at length, however, forced to leave.

In 1648, the Virginia Puritans were still numerous. About one hundred and eighteen were associated under

---

New England, and his people, to avoid persecution, thought of removing to the Bahamas. Thus "dissent" was rooted out of the colony just so far as intolerance could effect it.—*Felt's New England*, i. 216, 471–7, 487, 496, 515, 526–7; ii. 7.

[1] Bishop Meade's Churches of Virginia.

the pastoral care of Harrison, who had been the Governor's chaplain, but who, from the moment he showed a leaning to the Puritans, was looked upon with disfavor. He, too, withdrew to New England, and the congregations were scattered. During the time of Cromwell (about 1556), we still find traces of the Puritans. A certain people congregated into a church, calling themselves "Independents," was found to be "daily increasing," and "several consultations were had how to suppress and extinguish them." These consultations bore fruit. "The pastor was banished, next their other teachers," while of the people some were imprisoned or disarmed, till "they knew not in those straights how to dispose of themselves." It was estimated that the number of this class of Dissenters amounted at this period to about a thousand.

In 1662, the laws were made still more rigid against Non-conformists. The Quakers, as well as Puritans, experienced harsh treatment. It seems probable that, in spite of adverse legislation, quite a number of Presbyterian or Independent Dissenters still remained in the colony; but they were scattered and disorganized, and subject to many disabilities. It was in these circumstances that Makemie first visited the region. On the borders of Maryland, but within the Virginia line, was the place of his residence; yet it was ten years after the toleration edict of 1689 before he could procure a legal license to preach in Virginia. And even then he had no light difficulties to encounter. The spirit of the preceding period still survived, and for half a century longer Presbyterians were regarded with great disfavor.

Meanwhile, efforts were made, in the face of great difficulties and discouragements, to extend the Presbyterian Church in other directions.[1] The town of Ja-

[1] Ministers were sent from New England to New York, 1685, at

maica on Long Island had been largely settled by Presbyterians. In 1702, they numbered over a hundred families, "exemplary for all Christian knowledge and goodness." They had a church valued at six hundred pounds, and a parsonage at more than double that amount. In 1702, the town chose Presbyterian church-wardens and vestrymen, and settled as their pastor John Hubbard, a native of Ipswich, Mass., and a classmate of Andrews of Philadelphia. But High-Church intolerance was in the ascendency in the colony, and the Presbyterians were ejected to make room for the Episcopalians. Bartow, the church-missionary of West Chester, in Hubbard's absence, took possession of the church and began to read the Liturgy. Hubbard arrived, and, finding what was the state of things, withdrew, and assembled the congregation, who furnished themselves seats and benches from the church, in a neighboring orchard. Bartow meanwhile concluded his services, locked the door of the church, and gave the key to the sheriff. The people demanded it, but were refused. The Governor, Lord Cornbury, thanked Bartow for what he had done, but summoned Hubbard, with the heads of the congregation, before him, and forbade him any more to preach in the church.[1]

Nor was this all. He added meanness to injustice. During the great sickness of 1702, in New York, Cornbury entreated Hubbard, in a friendly manner, for the use of the parsonage. It was granted; but Cornbury requited the favor by putting the house, when he

---

the desire of Governor Andrews. Pierson and Bishop of Stamford wrote to I. Mather of Boston and Shepard of Charlestown, that they had conversed with the Governor, and that he expressed the wish that several plantations might be supplied with honest and able ministers, promising them encouragement.—*Felt, N. England,* ii. 679.

[1] See N. Y. Doc. Hist. and McDonald's Hist. of the Church of Jamaica.

vacated it, into the hands of the Churchmen. Without form or due course of law, he gave the sheriff a warrant to dispossess Hubbard of the glebe: this was surveyed out into lots, and leased for the benefit of the Episcopalians. The aggrieved party were "afraid to petition" for redress.

The Presbyterians of Bedford, in West Chester county, N.Y., had petitioned for a minister. The petition remained unanswered "until an abdicated Scotch Jacobite parson obtruded upon them, that insults intolerably over them, is consulted with." Such was the domineering and tyrannic style in which liberty of conscience was dealt with in the province of New York. "If a people want a minister, they must have a license to call one, whether from New England or Europe; a license to admit ministers to attend any ordination, and limited for number, and tied up from exercising their ministry without license, though in a transient manner; which has drove some out of the government, and deterred others from coming thereunto; which informs all, what liberty of conscience Dissenters do enjoy."

In what spirit the authorities of the colony would receive dissenting preachers from abroad may readily be surmised. In January, 1707, Makemie and Hampton, on their way to New England, doubtless to procure supplies for newly organized churches in their own neighborhood, passed through New York. Makemie proposed to preach in the Dutch church; but Lord Cornbury forbade him. In consequence of this, at the earnest request of a number of individuals, he preached a sermon at the house of William Jackson, in Pearl Street. The exercises were as public as possible. The doors were thrown open, and the sermon was printed. This was on Sunday, the 20th of January. The same day Hampton preached at Newtown, on Long Island, in the public meeting-house, offered by the inhabitants.

Here he was joined on Wednesday by Makemie, who by public appointment was to preach that day. But no sooner had he arrived than he and Hampton were both apprehended by the sheriff Cardale, acting under the authority of a warrant from Lord Cornbury.

The prisoners were taken before the Governor at Fort Anne, New York. Cornbury demanded of them how they dared preach under his government without a license. Makemie referred him to the Toleration Act of King William in 1689. He told them this did not extend to the American Plantations. Makemie replied that it was not a limited or local act, and adduced his certificates of license from courts of record in Maryland and Virginia. Worsted in the argument, Cornbury appealed to the act of Parliament directed, as he said, against *strolling preachers*, and told Makemie and Hampton that they were such. "There is not one word, my lord," said Makemie, "mentioned in any part of the law, against *travelling* or *strolling* preachers." To this the Governor could only reply, "*You shall not spread* your pernicious doctrines here." Makemie told him that the doctrines he taught were found in "our confession of faith," and challenged all the clergy of New York to show any thing false or pernicious in them, adding that he could make it appear that they were agreeable to the established doctrines of the Church of England. "But these Articles," replied the Governor, "you have not signed." "As to the *Articles of religion*," said Makemie, "I have a copy in my pocket, and am ready at all times to sign, *with those exceptions specified in the law*."

Upon this, the Governor charged him with preaching in a private house. Makemie replied that his lordship had denied him permission to preach in the Dutch church, and hence he had been necessitated to do as he had done; but he had preached "*in as public a manner as possible, with open doors.*"

Again Cornbury fell back upon his instructions, declaring none should preach without his license. Makemie replied that the law, and not his instructions, was the rule for him. He could not be guided by what he had never seen and perhaps never should see. "Promulgation," said he, "is the life of the law." The Governor then demanded that they should give bonds and security for good behavior and not to preach any more under his government. "For our behavior," said Makemie, "though we endeavor to live always so as to keep a conscience void of offence towards God and man, we are willing to give it; but to give bond and security to preach no more under your Excellency's government, if invited and desired by any people, *we neither can nor dare do.*" "Then you must go to jail," said the Governor. It was in vain that Makemie remonstrated. Lord Cornbury sat down to write out the necessary papers for their discharge from the custody of Cardale and their commitment in New York. While he was doing so, Hampton demanded of him a license, but it was peremptorily denied. Makemie moved that it was highly necessary that the law should be produced before their commitment, and offered to remunerate the attorney if he would produce the limiting clause of the act. But the motion was disregarded. In a contemptuous tone, the Governor asked Makemie if he knew law. "I do not," replied Makemie, "pretend to know law; but I pretend to know this particular law, having had sundry disputes thereon." He had quite a large collection of law-books in his library.

The copy of their commitment was made out. It was illegal in several respects. It was granted and signed by the Governor, and not by any sworn officers appointed and authorized by law. The queen's name or authority was not mentioned in it. No crime was alleged as a ground of commitment, and the direction to the sheriff to keep them safely was not, "*until they are delivered by due course of law*," but, "until further orders."

Thus Makemie and Hampton found themselves imprisoned with no prospect of immediate release. They petitioned the Governor for a knowledge of their crime, and, as they were strangers on their way to New England, and four hundred miles from their habitations, for "a speedy trial according to law," which they humbly conceived to be "the undoubted right and privilege of every English subject." To this petition a verbal but unsatisfactory reply was returned through the sheriff. They could not learn "the right way to have a trial." Petitioning to be admitted, in the custody of the sheriff, to make application to the Quarter Sessions in order to offer themselves "for qualification as the law directs," they were again rebuffed, and the messengers who presented the petition were severely threatened.

They now resolved "to trouble his Excellency with no more petitions," but presented their application to the Quarter Sessions. Their petition was looked at and handed about, but allowed no reading in open court. To the chief-justice, Roger Mompesson, they made application after an imprisonment of several weeks, and a writ of *habeas corpus* was granted. But when it was to be served, the sheriff told them he had a new mittimus, wherein their crime was specified, by which it was evident that for more than six weeks they had been subjected to false and illegal imprisonment. To complete the iniquity, the sheriff demanded the payment of twelve dollars for the commitment, and as much more for the return of the writ,—refusing, moreover, receipts for the money when it had been paid.

The case was now brought before the grand jury, and a true bill found against Makemie; for though Hampton was equally an offender, he was dropped from the indictment. The trial came on upon the 4th of June. The iniquity of the prosecution was abundantly shown, and after his attorneys had concluded their arguments, Makemie arose and spoke in his own defence. With great force of argument he vindicated himself from every charge, and showed himself more than a match for the prosecuting attorney. He showed great familiarity with the English laws bearing upon the subject of toleration, and effectually set aside the authority of the Governor's instructions as a rule of law. The jury brought in a verdict of *not guilty*, and solemnly declared that they believed the defendant innocent of any violation of law. Yet in spite of the verdict, and his own plea for moderate charges, the bill of costs which he was forced to pay amounted to more than eighty-three pounds.

Even after this, Makemie was not left unmolested. He narrowly escaped a second prosecution, based, if possible, on even weaker grounds than the first. A strange intolerance pursued him as a chief offender, but the object was to obstruct the preaching of all Presbyterian ministers. The Dutch and other Dissenters neither asked nor would receive a license; yet they were not disturbed. But any attempt of Presbyterian ministers to extend their Church was seriously obstructed.

Nor was New York the only province in which they had to encounter gross and severe intolerance. The statutes of Virginia, as we have already seen, were so framed as scarcely to recognize even the existence of the Toleration Act of 1689. In Maryland the petitions of Hampton and Macnish for licenses to preach in accordance with the act, were opposed by Episcopal influence. The vestry of the parish of Coventry appeared against them, encouraged, as is supposed, by Rev. Robert Keith, of Dividing Creek. The petitions were referred to the Governor and Council, and were finally granted, Mr. Hampton settling at Snow Hill. Still the hardships imposed upon Dissenters even in this colony, established originally on principles of equal liberty, but where the Episcopal Church was now established, were by no means light. A tax of forty pounds of tobacco was imposed on every "taxable," to meet the expense of building and repairing churches and supporting ministers. The meeting-houses of Dissenters were to be "unbarred, unbolted, and unlocked." The nature of the obstacles thrown in the way of the Presbyterians and other Dissenters may be judged from the character of the Episcopal clergy of that day in Virginia as well as Maryland,—the off-scouring of the English Church,—men, for the most part, according to Bishop Meade, far more worthy to be ejected from society than to lead or instruct the flock.

In the Carolinas, moreover, Presbyterians were made to feel the edge of intolerant legislation. During the troublous period from the Restoration to the Revolution (1660–1688) they had sought a shelter from persecution in a colony in which civil and religious rights were solemnly guaranteed to them. They had increased in numbers, and amounted in South Carolina to several thousands. But in 1703, by methods that savored of the brutality of Jeffries and the bigotry of James II., the Episcopal was made by law the established Church. Dissenters of all classes were taxed for its support, and those who did not conform were disfranchised. They who had left England for freedom of conscience were pursued by English intolerance across the ocean, and, in spite of their earnest remonstrance and appeal to Parliament, the yoke was fastened to their necks, and they were politically and socially degraded by a legislation which, to prop up Episcopacy, violated the solemn pledge in the faith of which they had become exiles from their native land.

Thus amid scenes of intolerance and persecution the Presbyterian Church in this country commenced its career. But it soon manifested, in the persons of its adherents, a vital energy that was to overbear obnoxious statutes and tyrannic legislation. The treatment which Makemie, Hubbard, Hampton, Macnish, and others experienced at the hands of royal Governors or servile judges, fitly links the history of American Presbyterianism with the memories of the English, Irish, and Scotch Dissenters under the reigns of the Stuarts.

CHAPTER II.

THE FIRST PRESBYTERY.

THE first Presbytery formed in this country dates from 1705 or 1706. The loss of the first leaf of the records leaves the precise time uncertain. Our first view of it is obtained from the minutes of a meeting, called probably at Freehold,[1] N.J., for the purpose of ordaining Mr. John Boyd. It consisted at this time of seven ministers, Francis Makemie, John Hampton, George Macnish, Samuel Davis, John Wilson, Jedediah An-

[1] The church at Freehold was organized about 1692, and John Boyd, who died in 1708, was the first minister. A charter of incorporation for this church, including those of Allentown and Shrewsbury, was obtained through the influence of Governor Belcher. (Hodge, i. 56.) The country around Upper Freehold was at that time a wilderness full of savages.—*Webster*, 323.

drews, and Nathaniel Taylor. Some of these men had been for many years laboring in their respective fields. In 1684, Makemie was performing the duties of pastor of the church at Snow Hill, which he had assisted to organize. He had been ordained an Evangelist in 1681,[1] and sent out by Laggan Presbytery, on the application of Colonel Stevens of Maryland, as a missionary to this country. For some time he labored in Barbadoes, and afterwards on reaching Maryland, "notwithstanding all obstacles, his hearers and congregations multiplied." It became, consequently, his great anxiety to obtain more laborers for the extensive and inviting field which was opened before him. With this object in view, he corresponded with Increase Mather of Boston,[2] and at length crossed the ocean and applied for aid to the Presbyterian Congregational Union of London, which Increase Mather had had a hand in forming.

His application was not in vain. "A respectable body of Dissenters in London[3] sent out, for the purpose of serving as evangelists in the middle and southern colonies of America, two itinerants for the space of two years."[4] These they undertook to support, engaging afterwards to send out others on the same conditions.

This was in 1704–5. Makemie returned in the fall of 1705 with the two ministerial brethren, "his associates,"[5] John Hampton and George Macnish. According to law, since the Toleration Act was designed to take effect in the colonies, they were entitled to the unmolested exercise of their ministry. Macnish commenced preaching at Monokin and Wicomico; Hampton, who had applied with him to Somerset Court to be qualified, meanwhile going north with Makemie to New York.

---

1 Foote's Sketches.
2 Webster, 297.
3 Miller's Life of Rodgers, 90.
4 Foote, 52.
5 Ibid. 53; Webster, 90.

Of the other members of the Presbytery, Samuel Davis was residing in Delaware as early as 1692, when that Quaker convert to Episcopacy, George Keith, visited him. John Wilson, as early as 1702, preached in the court-house at New Castle,[1] but, becoming dissatisfied, removed. In a few months, however, "finding it not for the better," he returned. He was doubtless one of those who gave Keith occasion to speak of Cotton Mather's "emissaries."[2]

Of these, Andrews also was accounted one. He was born at Hingham, Mass., in 1674, and graduated at Harvard in 1695. In 1698, at the instance of the "New England Doctors," if we are to regard the insinuations of Keith, he went to Philadelphia. The Quaker schism had opened the way for the commencement of religious services by Baptists, Presbyterians, and Episcopalians, and, as the latter withdrew from common services, the Baptists proposed to the Presbyterians that Mr. Andrews and his infant congregation should unite with them. The negotiation, however, proved futile, and in 1701 Andrews was ordained. His congregation was far from homogeneous. At the outset there were "nine Baptists and a few Independents in the town." There were, moreover, Scotch, Welsh, Swedish,[3] and New England elements. The prospect for the young congregation was far from promising. "The Presbyterians," says the Episcopal missionary Talbot, "have come a great way to lay hands on one another; but, after all,

---

[1] The Presbyterian church in New Castle is believed to be the continuation of the Dutch church which William Penn found in existence in 1683. Wilson probably commenced his labors here, continuing there till after the formation of the Presbytery.

[2] Prot. Hist. Col., i. 67.

[3] The Wicacoe (Swedish) church, near the navy-yard, was organized in 1675, by order of the general courts, held at New Castle in that year.—*Old Records, Vol. B.* F.

I think they had as good stay at home, for all the good they do. . . In Philadelphia one pretends to be a Presbyterian, and has a congregation to which he preaches." The prospect was but little better in 1703. "They have here," says Keith, "a Presbyterian meeting and minister, one called Andrews; but they are not like to increase here."

They did increase, however. Under the influence and labors of Andrews the heterogeneous mass began to coalesce. In 1705, five adults were baptized; in 1706, four more.

We have thus the elements which were to give to American Presbyterianism its earliest distinctive type, brought together in the first Presbytery. Makemie was a correspondent of Increase Mather, and an applicant for missionary aid to the Dissenters of London, composed of Presbyterians and Congregationalists. By them his two "associates," Hampton and Macnish, were supported for several years.[1] Andrews was a Massachusetts man, and Wilson, originally from Scotland, but an emigrant to Connecticut, was probably an emissary of the "New England Doctors." Taylor was settled on the Patuxent, over a congregation composed to a considerable extent of Independents; although the body consisted originally, according to tradition, of a colony of two hundred from Fifeshire. They arrived, with Taylor as their pastor, it is said, in 1690, and founded the church of Upper Marlborough. Davis can scarcely be taken into account: for fourteen years he had labored in Delaware

---

[1] Rev. *George Macnish* was undoubtedly a *Scotchman*. His name (which he wrote as above) indicates it; his descendants assert it; and Rev. Mr. Poyer of Jamaica, in a letter of April, 1714, to the society in England, styles him "a Scotch Independent preacher," and in another letter "an Independent North Britain preacher."
J. R.

before a Presbytery was formed,[1] and never attended its sessions afterwards, except upon a single occasion.[2]

Nor was the intrusion of the "emissaries" uncalled for. Keith had split the Quakers, and was itinerating over the whole land in behalf of Episcopacy. He preached at Boston, and Increase Mather felt called upon to print a refutation. Keith's answer was published at New York, and circulated in the Jerseys and in Philadelphia, where he preached with unwearied zeal. He needed, consequently, to be met on his own ground. Those among whom he scattered his peculiar doctrines were many of them in sympathy with Mather. According to Keith himself, "the people of East Jersey who are not Quakers are generally Independents, having originally come from New England." He thought that "the young generation might easily be brought off to the Church," if "the Church" was only set up among them.

There was indeed danger of this. In East and West Jersey, "except in two or three towns, there was no place of public worship of any sort." The people lived "very mean, like Indians." The difficulty was to get ministers of any kind. The Church of England was especially unfortunate in those whom she sent out. "We want a great many good ministers here in America," wrote Talbot;[3] "but we had better have none at all than such scandalous beasts as some make themselves,—not only the worst of ministers, but of men." Such as these were not wanted. "Those that we have to deal with," he continues, "are a sharp and inquisitive people: they are not satisfied with one doctor's opinion, but must have something that is authentic, if we hope to prevail with them."

---

[1] Webster, p. 311. [2] Dr. Hill.

[3] Epis. Hist. Col. xxxvii.

The zeal of Keith and Talbot was great. They were encouraged by the Society—then recently formed—for the Propagation of the Gospel in Foreign Parts. All the Episcopal clergy in the provinces north of Virginia were its missionaries.[1] In 1700, there were less than half a dozen of them in this part of the country, and only one in Pennsylvania. Before the first Presbytery was formed, there were five Episcopal congregations in that State; and in the course of two years the society in England sent out thirteen missionaries. Jealousy of New England stimulated Episcopal zeal. They were especially afraid lest—to use their own language—"Presbyterian ministers from New England would swarm into these countries and prevent the increase of the Church." The people showed themselves, as Talbot thought, only too ready to accept these "emissaries." "They send," he says, "to New England, and call any sorry young man, purely for want of some good honest clergyman of the Church of England."

At Woodbridge, N.J., in 1703, there was an "Independents' meeting-house," and Keith was glad of the chance to preach in it. This was one of the places named by Cockburn in 1685, in reference to the wants of which he says, writing to Scotland, "there is nothing discourages us more than want of ministers here. . . . They have a mind to bring them from Scotland." But along with the Scottish settlers in the troublous period of James II. there came also colonists from New England. Nearly half a century before, New Haven had shown extreme persistence in the resolution to sustain her claims to the territory. At every favorable opportunity, she had sent out loads of emigrants. Once the Dutch Governor at Manhattan had seized their vessel and

---

[1] Wilberforce, Hist. Epis. Church.

forced them to return. They applied to Cromwell for aid; but the Protector died too soon to help them. Yet they were not discouraged; and as soon as Dutch rule vanished from New Amsterdam, the often-defeated project was revived. That "sharp and inquisitive people" whom the Episcopal missionaries found it hard to deal with, poured in, and before the close of the seventeenth century the laws of the colony attested the presence of those who are called indifferently Independents and Presbyterians.[1] Indeed, notwithstanding the Scotch element, a very large proportion of the early settlers were from New England, although a considerable number of Quakers had here found refuge. Mather and the "New England Doctors" would have acted a part unworthy of themselves if they had lacked active sympathy with Presbyterians in the neighboring colonies. If they could have modelled their own Churches anew, they would have secured them the advantages of Synods and ruling elders.[2]

In Philadelphia, Andrews was greatly encouraged. The Episcopal missionaries were jealous of his progress. "There is," says Talbot (1705), "a new meeting-house built for Andrews, and almost finished, . . . which I am afraid will draw away great part of the Church, if there be not the greatest care taken of it." The first Presbytery met in that house. Andrews and Makemie were kindred spirits, and the Presbytery was the result of their co-operative councils. Each was a missionary, and felt the burden of care for the Churches. Makemie traversed the country to Boston, and crossed the ocean, to obtain ministers. Andrews could not so well leave his post, but he was scarcely less active. He went abroad on preaching-tours through the surrounding region, in Pennsylvania and the Jerseys

[1] Mulford's Hist. of New Jersey. [2] Pres. Quar. Rev., Jan. 1859.

Quite a number of congregations were gathered at various points, and ministers were needed to supply them. This was the subject of greatest anxiety to the Presbytery. They were little anxious whence they came, if they were only good men. They wrote to New England, Scotland, Ireland, and the Congregational and Presbyterian Union of London, to procure them. Evidently their ecclesiasticism was of no very rigid type. The argument for the Scotticism of the original Presbytery, drawn from the presumption that, if any considerable New England element was in union with it, it would have manifested itself in a form of government more or less allied to Congregationalism, is utterly invalid. The early ecclesiasticism of New England was largely Presbyterian.[1]

The correspondence of the Presbytery at this early

[1] The sympathy between the Presbyterian churches and New England was perfectly natural. Robinson (see "Life of Brewster") was a Presbyterian, and claimed that his church at Leyden was conformed to the rule of the French Presbyterian Church. In 1606, Brewster was chosen elder in Robinson's congregation, and in 1609 was made Robinson's assistant. He declined, however,—as only an elder,—to administer the ordinances, even when the church at Plymouth had no other teacher. Then the church at Plymouth was in reality a Presbyterian Church, with Brewster for its ruling elder.—*Prince's Chronology*, pp. 114, 120.

A permanent ruling eldership was accepted as a principle of church order by the early New England settlers. (Ib. 177.) Salem and Charlestown had ruling elders (263–311), Watertown and Boston. (358, 365, 409.) The office is distinctly recognized by the Synods of New England, at Cambridge, in 1646 and 1680; and at the latter date the *Westminster Confession* was adopted.—*Mather's Mag.* ii. 180, 207. The Synod of Connecticut, in 1708 (Saybrook Platform), adopted it. Even Eliot ordained elders at Martha's Vineyard.—*Mather*, i. 515.

Synods were held at Cambridge in 1637, 1649, 1657, 1679, 1680, and at Boston in 1662, all of which distinctly name ruling elders as officers in the Church.—*Mather*, ii. 192, 207, 238, 279, 289. This period throws light upon the liberal spirit by which it was animated. In 1708, a letter was written to certain ministers in Connecticut. It speaks of the object of the formation of the Presbytery,—"for the furthering and promoting the true interests of religion and godliness." It declares, "It is our universal desire to walk in the nearest union and fellowship with the churches in those parts where you inhabit, not knowing any difference in opinion so weighty as to inhibit such a proposal, nor doubting of your cordial assent thereto."

In 1709, a letter to Sir Edmund Harrison, an eminent Dissenter in London, states, "It is a sore distress and trouble to us, that we are not able to comply with the desires of sundry places crying unto us for ministers to deal forth the word of life unto them; therefore we most earnestly beseech you, in the bowels of the Lord, to intercede with the *ministers of London* and other well-affected gentlemen, to extend their charity

---

was the distinct feature of the organization adopted by the Synod in 1680, in accordance with "Heads of Agreement" in England, in the formation of which, in 1690, Dr. Increase Mather bore a distinguished part.—*Mather*, ii. 233, 235.

Thus at the formation of the first Presbytery there was no representation of such Congregationalism as that which prevails to-day on this continent; and the apparent laxness in the language of the Saybrook Platform is merely a copy of the "Heads of Agreement" of 1690 on this point.

There was no diversity, therefore, really, between the Irish Presbyterians and the New England "emissaries" in the matter of ecclesiastical sympathy. The doctrine and discipline of New England was regarded as identical with that of the Dissenters in Great Britain and the more southern provinces in this country. The founders of the Presbyterian Church were as anxious to procure ministers from New England as Mather was to send them. For them, help from this source was a matter of convenience and necessity, and they found those who joined them one with themselves in the matters of church order and discipline.

and pity to us, to carry on so necessary and glorious a work; otherwise many people will remain in a perishing condition as to spiritual things." There is no trace of Scotch jealousy or rigid ecclesiasticism in this epistle.[1]

In 1710, a letter was sent to the Presbytery of Dublin in response to their desire for a correspondence to "be settled and continued from time to time." It narrates briefly the efforts of Makemie with the ministers of London, and expresses the conviction that had they—"our friends at home"—been equally watchful and diligent as the Episcopal society in London, "our interest in most foreign plantations might have carried the balance." With saddened feelings, they confess the weakness of their numbers. In Virginia there was but one congregation, on Elizabeth River; "in Maryland only four, in Pennsylvania five, and in the Jerseys two, with some places of New York." The Presbytery request their friends in Dublin to raise the sum of sixty pounds to support for a year an itinerant minister whom they were to send out, at the same time informing them that they had exerted their influence to secure a similar favor from the ministers of London, "in the hands of Rev. Mr. Calamy."[1]

In the same year a letter was addressed to the Synod of Glasgow. It was invited by the assurance of a member of the Synod, of its "willingness to correspond with us in what concerns the advancement of the Mediator's interest in those regions where our lot is fallen." Of the Synod, the Presbytery, in view of the urgent demand for ministers, make a request similar to that which they had made to the Presbytery of Dublin.

---

[1] The London ministers to whom the letters were addressed were the very men who adopted the "Heads of Agreement" nineteen years before.

From London there came back a cheering response, for which the Presbytery expressed their gratitude in the warmest terms. In 1712, Thomas Reynolds engaged, for the ensuing year, to advance thirty pounds for missionary labor within the bounds of the Presbytery; promising, according to his capacity, to do what he could to serve them in after-years. "I should be glad," he says, "to be an instrument of disappointing any that can encourage no expectation from us." The aid was seasonable; it proved "the relief of some weak congregations," unable to maintain their own ministers.

From the time of its formation, the Presbytery continued steadily to increase in numbers and strength. At its meeting in 1706, John Boyd, a probationer from Scotland, was ordained, and commenced his labors in New Jersey at Freehold and Middletown. In 1708, "trials" were appointed to Mr. Joseph Smith (from New England), whose settlement was desired among them by the people of Cohansey. In 1710, John Henry and James Anderson were received; the first—invited, upon the death of Makemie, by his people, to succeed him—was from the Presbytery of Dublin; the last, settled first at New Castle and afterward in New York, was from Scotland. At the same meeting, Nathaniel Wade, who had been ordained and settled at Woodbridge, N.J., by the ministers of Fairfield county, previous to 1708, and Joseph Morgan, who, after several years of discouraging experience in West Chester county, N.Y., had settled in 1709 at Freehold, were received as members of the body.

Early in 1712, George Gillespie had been licensed by the Glasgow Presbytery. He came shortly after to New England, with letters from Principal Stirling to Cotton Mather. By the latter he was recommended to the divided people of Woodbridge, but finally settled at White Clay Creek, at the same time extending his care to the congregations of Red Clay, Lower Brandywine, and Elk River, in Delaware.[1]

The people of Patuxent applied the same year to friends in London to procure a pastor, and Daniel McGill was sent over. In the two following years the Presbytery was strengthened by the accession of four new members, Howell Powell,[2] Malachi Jones, Robert Witherspoon,[3] and David Evans,—all but Witherspoon (who was a Scotchman) from Wales.

In 1715, John Bradner, Hugh Conn, and Robert Orr were received. The first, from Scotland, was licensed and ordained in this country, and settled over the congregation of Cape May:[4] he afterwards removed to Goshen, N.Y., where he died.[5] Conn was a native of Ireland, but sent over by the "friends in London," and bore with him the cheering letter of Thomas Reynolds to the Presbytery. He was settled in Baltimore county, and became a member of the New Castle Presbytery. Orr was from Ireland or Scotland, and in 1715 accepted a call to Maidenhead and Hopewell.

Besides these, several others had joined the Presbytery, but the connection was transient or their position less important. The Presbytery had increased to such an extent that, in the judgment of its members, a division was demanded. The new Presbyteries would in-

---

1 His remains lie buried at the "Head of Christiana," where a marble slab commemorates his virtues.

2 Ordained at Cohansey, October 15, 1714.

3 Rev. Robert Witherspoon was ordained at Appoquinimy, now Drawyer's Church (Del.), May 13, 1714, and died in May, 1718.

4 Bradner preached first at Fairfield, N.J., afterwards at Cape May. These churches were *colonies* from New England.

Mr. Joseph Smith was probably the first minister at Cohansey, from Deerfield, Mass.; and the tradition is that that people brought their minister with them. The colony was from Fairfield, Conn. Mr. S. was a member of Presbytery in 1708.

5 Riker's Newtown.

deed be weak, but already there was assurance of their rapid growth. There were quite a number of ministers and churches whose distance rendered their connection with a single Presbytery, central to Philadelphia, unadvisable. Measures were already taken to establish a Presbyterian congregation in New York. A church had for many years been in existence at Newark, N.J., and in 1709 Jonathan Dickinson had been ordained at Elizabethtown by the ministers of Fairfield county, but had as yet formed no connection with Presbytery.

On Long Island quite a number of churches, known sometimes as Presbyterian and sometimes as Independent,[1] but formed on the New England model, were ready, through the influence of Macnish, who meanwhile had removed to Jamaica, to be organized into a Presbytery by themselves, and to receive under their care the churches and ministers that might be disposed to unite with them. Pumroy of Newtown had already (1715) united with the Presbytery, and in the following year a call from Southampton was presented to Samuel Gelston, accompanied by the assurance that the people were ready to place themselves under its care.

In these circumstances, Macnish and Pumroy were left to act according to their discretion, with regard to the formation of a Presbytery on Long Island. It was recommended to them "to use their best endeavors with the neighboring brethren that are settled there, which as yet join not with us, to join with them" in the erection of a Presbytery. The other members and churches of the original body were set off to form the three Presbyteries of Philadelphia, New Castle, and Snow Hill.

Thus, in ten years from the formation of the original

---

[1] Nearly all the early churches on Long Island and in New Jersey were colonies from New England.

Presbytery it had grown to a Synod. The period had been one marked also by general harmony, as well as by rapid growth. The ministers of the body were from Ireland, Scotland, London, Wales, and New England, and, laying aside all differences of minor importance, they had cheerfully and heartily co-operated on a basis broad enough to accommodate them all. As yet there were manifest no doctrinal diversities. All were Calvinists, and all cheerfully assented to, if they did not prefer, the Presbyterian form of government. The laborers in the field stood ready to welcome faithful fellow-laborers, from whatever quarter they might come. To the reverend brethren of the Church of Scotland, whom, said they, "we sincerely honor and affectionately esteem as fathers," they represented the desolate condition of the vacant places that had applied for ministers. To the Presbytery of Dublin, and to the ministers of London, they had likewise sent similar requests, and with the ministers of Boston, New Haven, and New England, generally, they were on the most friendly terms. To Connecticut they had sent expressly for aid, and were disappointed to find that the vacancies in that colony were so numerous as to defeat their expectations.

The necessity of a specific adoption of standards by the Presbytery does not yet seem to have occurred. The great body of the ministers, while they were yet few in number and drawn together by the urgent necessities of their common field, were evidently united in doctrinal sentiment. The most trying discussions of Presbytery were those which concerned variances between pastor and people,—as the case of Wade at Woodbridge,—the morals or the discretion of the ministers, as in the case of Van Vleck and Evans. Nor, when we regard the intimacy and mutual confidence of Andrews and Makemie, the last bequeathing his library to the former, one from New England and the other sustained and encouraged by the London ministers, can we feel that either they or their "associates" were in danger of error on the side of excessive strictness. Their moderation, indeed, was such that they were drawing towards them, as they were recommending the policy that would do it, the Congregationalists of Long Island.

With Drs. Miller and Hodge, against all the arguments of Dr. Green, we must hold to the strong improbability that the lost leaf of the records contained any specific standard for the adoption of members.

CHAPTER III.

THE SYNOD, A.D. 1717–1729.

UPON the division of the original Presbytery and the formation of the Synod, the Long Island Presbytery commenced its existence. It met and was constituted at Southampton, April 17, 1717, and its first work was the examination and ordination of Samuel Gelston, whose call to the Southampton church had been approved by the Presbytery of Philadelphia in the preceding year. The ministers who took part in the ordination undoubtedly composed the entire Presbytery.[1] They were George Macnish, who had removed to Jamaica in 1710, Samuel Pumroy, who was settled at Newtown, and George Phillips, who for twenty years had been laboring at Setauket. The churches under the care of the Presbytery had, most of them, been long in existence. Their membership was largely from New

---

[1] Prime's Long Island.

England, and their forms of worship and government were Congregational or Independent. The church at Southampton was gathered as early as 1640, when Abraham Pierson, afterwards the founder of the church at Newark, was its pastor. The church at Setauket enjoyed, as early as 1655, the labors of Rev. Nathaniel Brewster, a grandson of Elder Brewster of Mayflower memory. Newtown was settled by English emigrants in 1652, and in 1671 a house of worship was erected. It was not till 1724, seven years after the erection of the Presbytery, that the church was provided with ruling elders and became distinctly Presbyterian.[1] The first settlement of Jamaica was in 1656, and in 1663, by vote of the town, a meeting-house was erected. It was replaced by a stone edifice in 1690; but in 1702 the arbitrary authority of Lord Cornbury wrested it from the Presbyterians and placed it in the hands of the Episcopal rector.

But beside these churches under the care of the Presbytery, there was quite a number of others, composed largely of New England settlers in other parts of the island. Some of these, at a later period, became Presbyterian. The one at Southold was gathered in 1641. Emigrants from Lynn found their way to East Hampton in 1648, and were prompt in securing for themselves the privileges of public worship. Huntington was settled from New England in 1658, and soon after a church-edifice was erected. Hempstead enjoyed the labors of Rev. Richard Denton at the earliest period of its history, in 1644. A church was gathered at Bridgehampton in 1695, and at Mattituck in 1715.

Thus, at the period of the formation of the Presbytery there were at least ten or twelve churches, called indifferently Presbyterian or Independent, on

---

[1] Riker's Annals of Newtown.

the island. Several of them in the course of a few years became connected with that body, which embraced at first but the four churches of Jamaica, Newtown, Setauket, and Southampton. The church at Mattituck came into connection with the Presbytery in 1719, and some of the others invited at least its counsel and assistance. Only their own records, in the loss of others, can show the precise date at which they became distinctively Presbyterian.

Of the three other Presbyteries, the first to be noticed is that of Philadelphia. It numbered at its formation six ministers:—Andrews, at Philadelphia; Jones, at Abington; Powell, at Cohansey; Orr, at Maidenhead and Hopewell; Bradner, at Cape May; and Morgan, at Freehold. Of these, Bradner is said to have been from Scotland, and Orr from Ireland. Jones and Powell were Welshmen; Andrews and Morgan were from New England. The missionary field of this Presbytery was quite extended, and there were several congregations destitute of pastors.

The Presbytery of New Castle likewise numbered six ministers:—Anderson, at New Castle, Delaware; McGill, at Patuxent; Gillespie, at White Clay Creek; Evans, on the Welsh Tract; Witherspoon, at Appoquinimy; and Conn, in Baltimore county, Maryland. Here, with a single exception, all the members were from Scotland or Ireland.

The Presbytery of Snow Hill, which became absorbed in that of New Castle, numbered as members only Davis, Hampton, and Henry. The first still remained among the people with whom he had so long been connected without pastoral settlement, yet no longer serviceable in the pulpit. Hampton was settled at Snow Hill, and Henry was Makemie's successor at Rehoboth.

Here, at the commencement of the existence of Synod, were the nineteen ministers of whom it was composed, scattered at wide distances along the coast from Virginia to the eastern part of Long Island. The demand for new laborers in the field was greater than ever before, and new congregations were in process of formation at various points. In New York and its vicinity, the intolerance of Lord Cornbury and the intrusion of Episcopacy had discouraged the efforts of those who were now known as Dissenters. The treatment of Makemie was a warning to any from abroad who might propose to follow his example. Consequently, several years passed before measures were taken to form a Presbyterian congregation.

Meanwhile, however, discord had begun to spread in the ranks of what its friends were pleased to call, most unwarrantably, the Established Church. In 1693, the Assembly of the colony, at the instance of the Governor, and by what that devoted friend of Episcopacy, Colonel Lewis Morris, denominated his "artifice," made provision, by an act, for the maintenance of "one good sufficient Protestant minister" within the bounds of each town in the province where the people should desire it. The "one good and sufficient Protestant minister," according to the interpretation of Lord Cornbury and his zealous friends, could be no other than a clergyman of the Church of England. The congregations, however, were still entitled to the choice of vestrymen and churchwardens. The denial of this right would at once have opened the eyes and excited the indignation of the Assembly, who were almost to a man "Dissenters."

And now the door was opened for Episcopal aggression. It began at Jamaica, and continued there for more than thirty years. Indirectly the whole Episcopal Church in this country became a party. Poyer, the Jamaica incumbent, after the death of Urquart, who had succeeded Hubbell, was disposed, with the encouragement of the Governor, to prosecute his suit against the vestry, who had called Macnish, and put him in possession of the parsonage. But there was apprehension lest the case should go against the prosecutor. The judges, for the most part, were "dissenters," and would be disposed to do justice against Episcopal aggression. The decision would furnish a precedent, and every Episcopal incumbent would be left at the mercy of his vestry and churchwardens. Vesey of New York perceived the danger. He was a graduate of Harvard, and had been sent by Increase Mather[1] to "confirm the minds of those who had removed for their convenience from New England" to New York. His express mission, according to Episcopal accounts, was to counteract the influence of the chaplain of the forces sent out from England, and till 1697 he was "a dissenting preacher on Long Island." But he was bought over by Governor Fletcher by the offer of the Rectory of New York and a promised increase of stipend. From this time he was a zealous Churchman; and, in defence of his own views of the interest of the Church, he succeeded in bringing nearly all the Episcopal clergymen in New York and the neighboring provinces to join with him in dissuading Poyer from prosecuting his suit, and in sending to England representations prejudicial to the character and standing of Governor Hunter, who had succeeded Lord Cornbury.

Hence ensued a breach between the clergy and the Governor. Nor was this all. To promote more effectually his designs, Vesey converted his vestry into a close corporation, and adopted measures which divided the congregation into two hostile and embittered parties. He did not hesitate to designate his opponents as "schismatics," and by other opprobrious

---

[1] New York Hist. Col. iii. 438.

titles. Some of them withdrew, and worshipped in the chapel of the garrison.

This was in 1714. The document in which the aggrieved party tell their story contains several passages which were scored out of the original. Among these is one in which they say, "We have yet no dissenting congregation of English in the town, which, we fear, makes ours (the separated party) larger than it would be if there was one; and how deplorable a folly would it be to raise one out of our own dissensions!"

But those dissensions were not without their influence. The proceedings of Lord Cornbury—who closed his career as Governor in 1708, and was passed over by his creditors into the sheriff's hands—had created towards him a strong feeling of indignation and disgust. The proceedings of Vesey had rendered him unpopular with large numbers in his own parish. His course in regard to Poyer's suit had lost him the sympathy and respect of the Governor who had succeeded Cornbury, and thus, by the discord in the ranks of the "Established Church," the hopes of the Presbyterians were encouraged.

After Makemie's visit, and especially after the close of Cornbury's administration, they met, as opportunity afforded, in private dwellings. "They kept together, and continued, with few interruptions and with a gradual increase of their number, to meet for worship without a minister, until the year 1716, when John Nicoll, Patrick McKnight, Gilbert Livingston, Thomas Smith, and a few others, conceived the plan of forming themselves into a regular Presbyterian church and calling a stated pastor."[1] Measures were immediately taken at this fitting opportunity, when division pervaded the Episcopal ranks, and the persecuting power

[1] Life of Rodgers

of the Church was palsied, to carry out their design. In the summer of that year they extended a call to Anderson at New Castle, in Delaware. The commission of the Synod, to whom the case was referred, decided that Anderson ought to accept the call, and accordingly, in October, 1716, he removed to New York.

Here he was favorably received, and for three years, by the permission of the authorities, the infant congregation was allowed to occupy the City Hall for public worship. Meanwhile ground was purchased on Wall Street as a site for a church-edifice, and a building was erected in 1719. The necessary funds were procured in part from friends in the city, and in part from collections in Connecticut and in Scotland.

In 1720 a charter of incorporation was sought of the Governor and the Council; but the opposition of the vestry of Trinity Church defeated the application. The result was, that the fee simple of the property was vested in Anderson the pastor, and Nicoll, Liddle, and Ingliss, members of the congregation, and by them, in 1730, conveyed in due form of law to the Moderator and commission of the General Assembly of the Church of Scotland. Until 1766, no further efforts were made to secure a charter.

Anderson was a man of talents, learning, and piety, a graceful and popular preacher. But he had not long been settled before a portion of his congregation became dissatisfied. He was charged with a spirit of ecclesiastical domination and with improper interference in the temporal concerns of the Church. Livingston and Smith complained to Synod of his sermons, and, after hearing them read, that body expressed themselves as wishing that "they had been delivered in softer and milder terms in some passages." In 1721, a division took place, and a distinct society was formed, to which Jonathan Edwards preached fo the space of nine months. But the new congregation was too feeble to support a minister, and the future author of the "Inquiry into the Freedom of the Will" found difficulties in his way which determined him to seek another field of labor.

Anderson did not long continue in the pastorate at New York. In 1726 he accepted a call to New Donegal, in Pennsylvania, and was succeeded by Ebenezer Pemberton, under whose ministry the old divisions were healed. Pemberton was a native of Boston, and a graduate of Harvard College. His father was a clergyman, and the son, trained from his early years for the ministry, fulfilled in a diligent, faithful, and useful pastorate at New York the promise of his youth. He was "a man," says Smith,[1] "of polite breeding, pure morals, and warm devotion." His labors were eminently successful. He understood the character of the people he had to deal with better than Anderson. They were largely from New England. "As New England," says Colonel Morris, with a sneer which time has changed into eulogy, "was, excepting some families, the *scum* of the Old, so the greatest part of the English in this province was the scum of the New." But in Mr. Pemberton they were well united. For thirty years he exercised his ministry, and had the satisfaction to see the old house of worship replaced by a new and much larger edifice, and his congregation increased to twelve hundred or fourteen hundred souls.[2]

In 1717, Jonathan Dickinson united with the Philadelphia Presbytery. He had been ordained at Elizabethtown, N.J., by the ministers of Fairfield county, in 1708, and for nine years had labored over the extensive field embracing not only Elizabethtown, but Rahway, Westfield, Connecticut Farms, Springfield, and a part of

---

[1] Hist. of New York, i. 259.

[2] Ibid. 260.

Chatham. He was a native of Massachusetts, and a graduate of Yale College. With uncommon sagacity, calm judgment, and unshrinking firmness,—tempered, however, with the spirit of Christian forbearance and moderation,—he was well qualified to take a prominent part in the public concerns as well as controversies of the Church. For nearly forty years he continued in the exercise of the ministry; and the incidents of his life are interwoven with the history of Presbyterianism throughout the period of his career. His intellectual superiority and commanding influence made him the leader of the old Synod before the separation, and he was the acknowledged leader of the new Synod after the division had taken place.

The church at Newark, not yet connected with the Presbytery, but under the care of the venerable Prudden, and soon destined to enjoy the pastoral labors of President Burr, had already been in existence as an independent church for more than half a century. It was established in 1665 by the elder Pierson, who had previously removed from Lynn, Mass., to Southampton on Long Island, and thence to Branford, Conn., where he had formed a church.[1] On the union of the colonies of New Haven and Hartford, his opposition to the growing laxity of sentiment and his zeal for his own peculiar ecclesiastical views led him, with a large portion of his charge, to seek out a new place of settlement. His son was the first President of Yale College, and his grandson was for some years pastor at Woodbridge, N.J. The date of his ordination was almost

[1] Mr. Pierson is said to have been episcopally ordained, but to have been "equally displeased with the tyranny of Charles I. both in Church and State, and with the civil madness and religious enthusiasm which prevailed under Cromwell, and that he annexed himself to the party which were called Moderate Presbyterians." —*Mc Whorter's Hist. Discourses*, 1807.

contemporaneous with the organization of the Synod. It took place April 19, 1717.

From this period the number of ministers and congregations rapidly increased. Moses Dickinson, a brother of Jonathan, succeeded Orr in Hopewell and Maidenhead, in New Jersey, in 1718. Robert Cross, from Ireland, was installed at New Castle in the following year. Joseph Lamb, a graduate of Yale College, became pastor of Mattituck in 1717, and in 1719 his church united with the Presbytery of Long Island, by which he had been ordained. Samuel Young, from Armagh Presbytery, was appointed by the New Castle Presbytery to supply Drawyers, in Delaware, and shortly before his death, in 1721, took charge of a congregation that had been recently gathered about the branches of the Elk and was composed mainly of emigrants from Ireland. John Clement, who afterwards supplied Gloucester and Pilesgrove, and William Steward, who accepted a call to Monokin and Wicomico, were received in 1718.

In the ten years that followed, the membership of the Synod was largely increased. At the close of this period seven ministers had been received from New England, five from Scotland or Ireland, three from England and Wales, and several were licensed by the Presbyteries in this country. From New England came Webb of Newark (1720); the younger Dickinson of Maidenhead and Hopewell; Walton of Crosswicks, whose erratic course was as surprising as his eloquence; Parris of Cohansey; Hubbell of Westfield and Hanover, —including the present congregations of Morristown, Chatham, and Parsippany; Elmer of Fairfield in Cohansey, and Pemberton of New York. From England came John Orme, who settled with the congregation of Marlborough on Patuxent, and Robert Laing, who supplied Brandywine and White Clay. From Wales came Thomas Evans, who labored at Pencader; William McMillan and Adam Boyd—the former sent to supply the people of Virginia, and the latter settled at Octorara—were both ordained in this country. Boyd was commended by Cotton Mather, and both he and McMillan were connected with the New Castle Presbytery. Of the other ministers, Alexander Hutchinson was sent over by the Glasgow Presbytery in answer to the petition of the Synod, and settled at Bohemia Manor and Broad Creek. Thomas Craighead, who finally settled at Pequa, was the son of an Irish minister, but labored for some time in New England before he joined the Synod. Cotton Mather loved and esteemed him. In a letter to a friend he spoke of him as "of an excellent spirit and a great blessing to your plantation,"—"a man of singular piety, meekness, humility, and industry in the work of God." Joseph Houston, who settled at Elk River, was from Ireland, but had supplied the pulpit of Mr. Hillhouse, at New London, Conn., for several months previous to his uniting with the Synod. Archibald McCook and William Tennent were likewise from Ireland.

The first of these came over as a student, and was licensed by the New Castle Presbytery. His field of labor was Kent, in Delaware. It embraced Dover[1] (St. Jones) and Murthur Kill. Ten years previously, the destitution of the region had attracted the attention of Presbytery. Repeatedly they had been furnished with temporary supplies. Gelston, Cross, Hook, T. Evans, Steward, Hutchinson, and Finch had visited them; but McCook became in 1727 their first pastor.

But in some respects the most important name added to the Synod's list during the ten years from 1719 to 1729

---

[1] St. Jones is now *Dover*, on Jones', or anciently, St. Jones' Creek in St. Jones, now Kent county, Del.

was that of William Tennent. His influence upon the progress and prosperity of the Church entitles him to a rank second to no other. In learning, piety, and the wise forethought which he manifested in regard to provision for an educated ministry, he is entitled to the highest honor.

The Synod had increased during its career from 1717 to 1729 from about fifteen to nearly thirty members, and its congregations in a corresponding proportion. Its great anxiety was to make provision for the destitutions within its bounds. One of its first measures was the establishment of "a fund for pious uses." Letters were written to London, Dublin, and Glasgow, petitioning for aid. The claims of "many smaller places of lesser ability to maintain and support the interest of Christ among them" were urgently pressed, and "not altogether without success."

The obligation and necessity of effort on its own part were, moreover, clearly recognized. A letter was addressed to the several congregations within the bounds of Synod, earnestly enforcing the duty of making annual collections in behalf of the proposed funds. The response given was such as might have been expected in the feeble state of the churches. Many were unable to do any thing; but in 1719 the amount secured was more than twenty pounds; and the judicious expenditure of succeeding years was the means of accomplishing great and important results. The congregation at New York received material assistance from a part of the Glasgow collection, and several feeble churches or needy ministers received valuable aid.

To the Dissenting ministers of London the Synod gave in 1718 a full statement of their condition. They had "begun a small fund," they said; "but it is yet so small that little or nothing can be done with it." Their ministers numbered twenty-three, all of them settled or with prospects of settlement; yet there were still "many vacancies which either cry to us for help," or give ground of hope that, if they could be provided with an able and faithful ministry, "the happy effects of it would soon appear." A strong desire was expressed for "the honor and comfort of a yearly correspondence" with the London brethren, and help was craved "of all well-disposed Christians everywhere, especially, if possibly it can be, of the city of London." The Synod of Glasgow and Ayr, and Principal Stirling, received the hearty thanks of Synod for "their kindness to the interest of religion in these wilderness parts."

Attention was largely drawn at each annual meeting to the claims of destitute places within the Synod's bounds. McGill was sent on successive missions, first to Potomoke, in Virginia, and subsequently to Kent county, Delaware. Morehead was employed at Pilesgrove and Gloucester, and Octorara and Hanover were aided from the fund.

To secure more prompt action, and to settle matters claiming attention during the intervals of Synod, a commission was appointed in 1720. It was clothed "with the whole authority of the Synod," and the management of the fund was committed to its disposal. It is natural to suppose that for this body the ablest members of the Synod would be appointed; and it consisted, in fact, of Jones, Andrews, Macnish, Anderson, Dickinson, and Evans. Three of these were in the vicinity of New York, where their services were most likely to be required.

The troubles in the Church at New York led to repeated conferences with the ministers of Connecticut and the trustees of Yale College, by whom Edwards had been sent to supply the congregation which had separated from Anderson's. Each party seemed in earnest to restore peace, and the Synod expressed their thanks to the Connecticut ministers "for their concern about the interest of religion in New York." They closed their minute (1723), appointing a conference, with a recommendation that, in case of a successful issue, the committee should "treat with said ministers about a union with us, and empower them to concert and conclude upon any methods that may conduce to that end."

McGill and Cross were members, with Andrews, Phillips, Morgan, and Dickinson, of this committee, and McGill and Conn were appointed to write the letter in reply to the one which had been received from Connecticut, requesting the conference. Nothing could show more decisively the absence on the part of the Synod of all jealousy of New England influence, than this minute which contains the recommendation of union, and which seems to have been adopted without the utterance of the least dissent.

Indeed, on the subject of ecclesiastical authority—the only point in reference to which there had been, as yet, any serious division of sentiment—the Synod had harmonized during the previous year. Against the measure of 1721, Dickinson, Jones, Morgan, Pierson, Evans, and Webb, had entered their protest. The minute to which objection was taken, after stating that Presbyterian government and church discipline had been exercised for many years by the Church in this country, "after the manner of the best Reformed Churches, as far as the nature and constitution of this country will allow," invited any who desired it to offer overtures, to be formed into acts by the Synod, "for the better carrying on in the matter of our government and discipline." But in 1722, evidently upon mature deliberation, the protesting members consented to withdraw their protest. They submitted a paper, containing four articles, in which they grant "the full executive power of church government in Presbyteries and Synods," using "authoritatively in the name of Christ the keys of church discipline;" admit that the circumstantials of church discipline, "as the time, place, and mode of carrying on in the government of the Church," belonged to ecclesiastical judicatories to determine conformably to the general rules in the word of God, and that if these were called *acts*—the term which the protest was directly aimed at —no offence would be taken, provided they were not to be imposed upon those who conscientiously dissented from them. They allow also the right of appeal from inferior to superior judicatories, and the composing of directories by Synods respecting all parts of discipline, provided that subordinate judicatories might decline from them when they thought conscientiously that they had just reason to do so.

These views, while guarding against a rigid and tyrannic ecclesiasticism, allowed all the freedom which Dickinson and the brethren who joined him in the protest required; and it is to the honor of the Synod that they were "so universally pleased with the abovesaid composure of their difference," allowing the withdrawal both of the protest and its answer, "that they unanimously joined together in a thanksgiving prayer, and joyful singing the one hundred and thirty-third Psalm."

Upon the basis thus offered by Dickinson the Synod harmonized. With a clear understanding of his position and sympathies, the Synod proposed measures which, if successful in their results, would introduce into it large numbers of others whose views were substantially those of the protestants; yet not a word of objection was uttered. The liberal spirit of American Presbyterianism was attested by the unanimity of the Synod.

In 1724, the Synod had so increased, and it had become so difficult to secure a full and regular attendance, that the question was raised in regard to some measure of relief. It was finally decided in favor of delegation. The Presbyteries of New Castle and Philadelphia were to delegate half their members yearly to the Synod, and the Presbytery of Long Island was to send two of their number. Every third year, however, there was to be a full meeting of Synod. At this meeting all the members were to be present. The commission was also authorized to call such a full meeting whenever the emergency might require. Members, whether delegated or not, were left at liberty to attend as formerly "if they see cause."

In 1726, the attention of the Synod was called to difficulties which had occurred in the church at Newark, of which Webb was pastor. At his own request, a commission was appointed with a view to compose them; but the result did not answer his expectation. With Hubbell, Jones, and Evans, he joined in a protest against the measures which had been taken; and it was several years before a full reconciliation took place between the protestants and the Synod.

CHAPTER IV.

THE ADOPTING ACT, A.D. 1729.

The year 1729 has been rendered memorable by the celebrated Adopting Act of the Synod. It is difficult at this day to say with whom the measure originated, although the practice which prevailed in the New Castle Presbytery—composed largely of Irish members—of requiring subscription to the Confession of

Faith from the ministers admitted to their body, renders it not improbable that it was first urged by them. It was a new measure. No sufficient evidence has yet been adduced in proof of subscription, or the adoption of a specific constitution, by the members of the original Presbytery. Indeed, such a thing was altogether unknown to them. In 1698, Andrews went to Philadelphia; Makemie had already been in the country for several years; and yet it was not till 1698 that the Irish Synod enacted, in conformity with the law of the Established Church of Scotland, that no young man should be licensed to preach the gospel unless "he subscribe the Confession of Faith in all the articles thereof as the confession of his faith."

Up to this period it had been regarded as important, far less as a security against heretical members than as a testimony to the truthful and scriptural position of a body asking toleration of the civil magistrate. But shortly after this, developments took place which gave it a new importance in the eyes of the Synod.[1] Thomas Emlyn, of Dublin, avowed himself an Arian, and published a defence of his doctrinal positions. Lax views had begun soon after this to gain ground among the Dissenting ministers of London. To vindicate their own character from the suspicions of government, rather than from any suspicion of the orthodoxy of their own members, the Irish Synod in 1705 re-enacted the law requiring subscription to the Westminster Confession of Faith of all persons licensed or ordained. Anxious to secure the repeal of the obnoxious sacramental test, legal protection for their worship and government, and a restoration and increase of the royal bounty, the Irish Church felt it incumbent upon them to vindicate their doctrinal soundness from all possible

---

[1] Reid's History of the Irish Presbyterian Church.

question. But, acknowledging as they did the right of the state to ascertain the belief of religious bodies applying for protection, they felt it necessary to declare their views. Their choice lay between the Thirty-Nine Articles of the Church of England as subscribed by their Dissenting brethren across the Channel, and the Westminster Confession of Faith as adopted by the Church of Scotland. The latter was preferred in 1709, and again in 1714, upon the accession of George I.

But by 1714 a change had taken place in the views of some of the ministers in and near Dublin. They had been educated among the English Dissenters, and preferred a summary of doctrine more concise than either the Thirty-Nine Articles or the Westminster Confession. But even yet they professed to adhere to the doctrines of the Confession; and in the Synod of 1716 it was decided, with only a single dissenting voice, to adhere to it as declaring the faith of the Church. Only in case of objection on the part of government was the formula which had been drawn up to be presented as a substitute.

It was while these discussions were going forward that the seeds of future danger to the Church were sown. In 1703, John Abernethy was settled at Antrim. By his exertions an association of ministers was formed for mutual improvement in theological knowledge. It drew into it some of the most promising and able men of the Church, and was known as the Belfast Society. Discussions arose on the subjects of religious liberty, subscription to confessions, the nature and extent of church power, and opinions were advanced and maintained which tended to an extreme liberalism, not to say radicalism.[1]

It was not long before other ministers of the Church

[1] Reid's History of the Presbyterian Church of Ireland.

took the alarm. The danger was aggravated in their estimate by reports from abroad. The Presbyterian churches of Switzerland had extensively fallen away from the vital doctrines of the gospel. The writings of Whiston, Clarke, and Hoadly, in England, followed by the debates and publications of the Dissenters at Salter's Hall, showed that in London all was not sound even among those who bore the honored names of a Puritan ancestry. In Scotland, moreover, the seeds of unsound doctrine had been widely sown. In 1714–16, Professor Simpson, who occupied the divinity-chair in the University of Glasgow, and under whom not a few of the Irish as well as Scottish ministers had been trained, had been tried by the General Assembly for teaching Arminian and Pelagian errors; and the leniency of the sentence declared the extent to which he was shielded by the sympathy of the Assembly's members. Abernethy himself, and another prominent member of the Belfast Society, had been Simpson's fellow-students, while others had been his theological pupils. With the Belfast Society, moreover, the Dublin ministers, who were in all essential points Independents, were in strong sympathy.

In these circumstances, while there was real danger to the Church, it is not strange that it should have been vastly magnified by the fears and apprehensions of those who had taken the alarm. "There is a perfect Hoadly mania among our young ministers in the North," wrote Francis—afterward Professor—Hutchison from Armagh, in 1718, to a friend in Scotland. He ascribed this antipathy to confessions to "other grounds than a new spirit of charity." It was his conviction that Dr. Clarke's book had shaken, if not changed, the views of several.

It was in 1720 that Abernethy ventured to publish a sermon on "Religious obedience founded on personal persuasion." It was objectionable on several grounds; but its most fatal error was that all doctrines were non-essential on which "human reason and Christian sincerity permitted men to differ." This was opening a wide door for error. It set aside at once not only the subscription that had been required, but all checks upon the admission of unconverted men to the Church and ministry. The practice of some of the Presbyteries was correspondingly lax. It was justly feared that the fruits of the seed already sown would be a harvest of errors more objectionable than any thing which had yet appeared. A war of pamphlets followed. It was impossible to guard the purity or peace of the Church if the principles of the Belfast Society were to be generally adopted. The Dissenters of London were many of them already fast verging toward Arianism. The Dublin ministers did not come far behind them, and the principles of Abernethy and his friends were such that they might claim to be left unmolested even if they chose to take the same position.

In these circumstances, the Synod felt called upon to act. They compromised with the Belfast brethren to preserve unity, but only divided their own councils. It was a great mistake, and they found it so at last. Instead of a simple enforcement through legitimate authority of the discipline of the Church, they sacrificed that discipline to prevent the threatened danger. Peace was not secured. The breach between the subscribers and non-subscribers was only widened. Yet the moderate portion of the party who favored subscription did their best to prevent any division. The sermon before the Synod of 1720 by Robert Craighead, the last moderator, was entitled "A Plea for Peace, or the nature, causes, mischiefs, and remedy of church divisions." But it failed to secure the object designed. At length the reproach of departing from her own standards was publicly brought against the Irish Church. It was loudly echoed by the Episcopalians. It was obvious that something must be done. To remove the scandal, and at the same time to obviate the scruples of the non-subscribers, it was resolved that the members of the Synod be *permitted* to subscribe the Confession. But to this, also, the non-subscribers objected. They were called at length in 1726 to propose their own terms. They were such as it would have been suicidal in the Synod to accept. The subscribers, therefore, who were in the decided majority, introduced an overture declaring their rejection of the new terms of peace, and that the adherence of the non-subscribers to their principles "put it out of their power to maintain ministerial communion with them in church judicatories as formerly, consistent with the discharge of our ministerial office and the peace of our own consciences." The overture was passed by a great majority, and the separation, which had become inevitable, immediately followed.

The conflict had been a fierce one, and disastrous to the interests of the Church. But it was rendered necessary by the dangerous and latitudinarian principles as well as errors of the non-subscribers. Yet the party that opposed them had been moderate and forbearing. They erred rather on the side of leniency than of harshness.

Of this conflict the American Presbyterian Church could not remain a disinterested spectator. During the whole period of it, the Irish emigration to this country was large, and it was steadily increasing. It was scarcely to be doubted that some of the non-subscribers, whose principles were not altogether popular in the Irish Church, would soon be directing their course also to the Western world. They would naturally seek a connection with the Presbyterian Church in this country, and such a connection would only renew among the weak churches scattered through the colonies the agitations that had done such mischiefs in Ireland.

The character of the Church in this country was, moreover, at stake. It needed the sympathy of the foreign Churches that were yet sound in the faith, and still it would be sure to forfeit that sympathy if it showed an indisposition to exclude error. The Presbytery of New Castle was undoubtedly most deeply sensible of this. Thomas Craighead was one of its leading members, and he would naturally share the views of his brother, the moderator of the Irish Synod. It is not surprising that their sagacity should have led them to take precautions against the threatened evil. These precautions were first used in the Presbytery of New Castle, and afterward commended themselves to the good sense of the Synod.

Yet the thing was not done in haste. The separation of the Irish Synod took place in 1726. Three years passed before the Adopting Act of the American Synod, and this act was framed in the very spirit of the sermon of Robert Craighead's "Plea for Peace" before the Irish Synod. It showed nothing of the rigor of a fierce orthodoxy, but a sound attachment to acknowledged standards.

At first, indeed, the proposal of it threatened division. In 1727, the year following the action of the Irish Synod which led to the separation of the Belfast party, an overture looking toward the adoption of such a measure was presented to the Synod by John Thomson, of Lewes, Delaware. It was then opposed, especially by the New England members. Even Andrews objected to it as impolitic and tending to division; while Dickinson, of Elizabethtown, sound indeed in the doctrines of the Confession, was, strangely enough, altogether opposed to creeds or confessions of faith drawn up by uninspired men.

For two years the overture was not acted upon. It was opposed in 1727, and "staved off" by those who hoped "they should have heard no more of it."[1] But as the facts came to be better known, and the object of the overture to be better understood, the measure gained favor among its opponents. Unable to go with the Scotch and Irish "in all their disciplinary and legislative notions," the party composed of those from New England, England, and Wales had at first strong suspicion of the tendency and design of the overture. Almost to a man they regarded it with aversion. The proposal that all ministers or intrants should sign it, or else be disowned as members, was especially obnoxious. It threatened the introduction of a system of church discipline and church legislation such as in the days of Cromwell had lost England to the Presbyterian Church, and gave occasion for Milton's celebrated saying that "*presbyter* was only *priest* writ large."

In 1728, the subject was again introduced. A delegated Synod met this year, and the Irish and Scotch members were in the proportion, to the others, of two to one. They could, if resolutely bent upon carrying their measure at all hazards, have forced it through. But "the Synod, judging this to be a very important affair, unanimously concluded to defer the consideration of it till the next Synod," which it was agreed should be a full one. The adoption of this course showed a conciliatory spirit, and gave Dickinson, Andrews, Pierson, Pumroy, and Morgan, an opportunity to consult and determine how far it was best to go.

In 1729, the committee to whom the subject was referred was judiciously chosen. It consisted of An-

---

[1] Andrews's Letter to Colman.

drews, Dickinson, and Pierson, on one side, and Thomson, the author of the overture, Craighead, and Anderson, on the other. Craighead was unquestionably moderate in his views, and Conn, who was also on the committee, was scarcely to be reckoned on either side. The result was a compromise, honorable to both parties, and evidently betraying the strong influence of the New England, English, and Welsh members. After long discussion, it was presented, in the following words:—

"Although the Synod do not claim or pretend to any authority of imposing our faith upon other men's consciences, but do profess our just dissatisfaction with, and abhorrence of, such impositions, and do utterly disclaim all legislative power and authority in the Church, being willing to receive one another as Christ has received us to the glory of God, and admit to fellowship in sacred ordinances all such as we have ground to believe Christ will at last admit to the Kingdom of Heaven; yet we are undoubtedly obliged to take care that the faith once delivered to the saints be kept pure and uncorrupt among us and so handed down to our posterity. And do, therefore, agree that all the ministers of this Synod, or that shall hereafter be admitted into this Synod, shall declare their agreement in, and approbation of, the Confession of Faith, with the Larger and Shorter Catechisms of the Assembly of Divines at Westminster, as being in all the essential and necessary articles good forms of sound words and systems of Christian doctrine, and do also adopt the said Confession and Catechisms as the Confession of our faith. And we do also agree that all the Presbyteries within our bounds shall always take care not to admit any candidate of the ministry into the exercise of the sacred functions, but what declares his agreement in opinion with all the essential and necessary articles of said Confession, either by subscribing the said Confession of Faith and Catechism, or by a verbal declaration of their assent thereto, as such minister or candidate shall think best. And in case any minister of this Synod, or any candidate for the ministry, shall have any scruple with respect to any article or articles of said Confession or Catechisms, he shall, at the time of his making said declaration, declare his sentiments to the Presbytery or Synod, who shall, notwithstanding, admit him to the exercise of the ministry within our bounds, and to ministerial communion, if the Synod or Presbytery shall judge his scruple or mistake to be only about articles not essential and necessary in doctrine, worship, or government. But if the Synod or Presbytery shall judge such ministers or candidates erroneous in essential and necessary articles of faith, the Synod or Presbytery shall declare them uncapable of communion with them. And the Synod do solemnly agree that none of us will traduce or use any opprobrious terms of those that differ from us in these extra-essential and not-necessary points of doctrine, but treat them with the same friendship, kindness, and brotherly love, as if they had not differed from us in such sentiments."

The ministers of the Synod then present, with the exception of Mr. Elmer, who declared himself not prepared, after proposing all the scruples that any of them had against any articles and expressions in the Confession and Catechisms, unanimously agreed in the solution of those scruples, and in declaring the Confession and Catechisms to be their confession of faith. The only exception made was to those articles of the Form of Government which related to the duties of the civil magistrate. In view of the unanimity, peace, and unity which appeared in these consultations and deliberations of the Synod, they "unanimously agreed in giving thanks to God in solemn prayer and praises."[1]

No change was subsequently made in the language of the Adopting Act. Some of those who were more strict on subjects of ecclesiastical order, and who felt that they had reason to complain of their brethren on account of its violation, insisted upon a more literal and rigid interpretation of the agreement which had been made obligatory. But the history of the period shows that this arose not from any superior attachment to sound doctrine, but mainly from the conviction that the rules of order were not observed with sufficient care and fidelity.

The attempt was indeed made, in 1736, to put a construction upon the Adopting Act which it would not bear. The Irish and Scotch immigration of the period had been unusually large, and in this year the foreign members of the Synod composed the large majority.

---

[1] There are many facts which put the character of the Adopting Act, as a compromise measure, entirely beyond question. Dr. Green was right in his judgment of it. It does present those features which could afford him occasion to say that it gave and took, bound and loosed, in the same breath. In the mention made in Dr. Alexander's Life of a Mr. Hoge, a very aged man who could remember the period of the Adopting Act, we find it very correctly spoken of as the Act "which indulged such persons as were scrupulous in regard to certain articles, to express their exceptions before the Presbytery, who were permitted to license and ordain if they judged the matter not to be of essential importance. When the Act was passed, it gave great dissatisfaction, and some, the number of whom cannot be determined, left the Presbyterian Church and joined the Seceders, who were then beginning to raise their standard. Among these was Mr. Hoge."

The explanation of the plan of subscription given by Samuel Davies on his visit to England, and to which reference will be made hereafter, sufficiently establishes the understanding of the Synod as to the significance of the Adopting Act.

Taking occasion from some complaints that had been uttered in regard to the mode in which the Confession had been adopted, they proceed to declare, for the satisfaction of such complaints, "that the Synod have adopted and do still adhere to the Westminster Confession, Catechisms, and Directory, *without the least variation or alteration, and without any regard to said distinctions,*"—these "distinctions" the scruples expressed at the time of the adoption. As a matter of fact, this was not true; as a matter of right, it was a gross injustice to attempt to change the constitutional basis upon which the Synod had deliberately, and with full notice of its intention, placed itself. In spite of this action, the Adopting Act still stood as the fundamental and constitutional basis of the Synod, and no possible *interpretation* could supersede it.

CHAPTER V.

THE SYNOD FROM THE ADOPTING ACT TO THE DIVISION.

From the date of the Adopting Act in 1729 until the division of the Synod in 1741, the number of ministers rapidly increased. Nearly forty names were added to the list of members. Some few of these had been trained up within the bounds of the Church, but, apart from these, nearly one-half were Irish or Scotch immigrants. The accession from New England was only ten. Thus, in the measures of the Synod, the foreign party, had they been united, might have secured a preponderating influence. But they were not united. The division of 1741 originated in their ranks.

Although originally from Ireland, the Tennents were

not to be numbered on what came to be known at the time of the division as the *Old Side.* Of these, besides the father, William Tennent, there were his sons, John, Gilbert, William, and Charles, all of them earnest and zealous preachers. Gilbert was by far the most conspicuous, and in the history of the period under review, no other name is more frequently mentioned. With a nature incapable of fear, a burning zeal in defence of what he deemed to be truth, a commanding person and powerful delivery, he was destined to exercise, wherever he went, a deep and extensive influence. Yet his charity was sometimes overborne by his zeal. His defence of vital truth assumed, unconsciously, a defiant tone. In dealing with his equals he was betrayed into adopting the tone of a superior, and the model which he seemed to favor was far more that which presented to view the sternness of one of the old prophets, than the gentleness of the beloved apostle.

He was independent and decided in his judgments; tenacious of his convictions, he was not easily to be moved or persuaded by others. Yet, unfortunately, he was by no means always discreet. Soon after his licensure, he was called to New Castle. He declared his acceptance, commenced preaching, but soon after abruptly left. The Synod pronounced his conduct hasty and unadvised. A sharp rebuke was administered, which he is said to have taken meekly.

He soon settled at New Brunswick. A letter of the venerable Frelinghuysen, and a severe fit of sickness, combined with the seeming barrenness of a ministry of eighteen months, humbled him under the sense of his unprofitableness. He rose from his sick bed to preach as he never had before, and the fruits of his labors were soon apparent.

In 1734, he overtured the Synod on the subject of a more careful examination of candidates for the ministry, as well as for the Lord's Supper. He insisted that there should be a closer scrutiny as to the evidences of a gracious and genuine religious experience. The overture was favorably received, and Tennent himself could scarcely have penned any admonition more solemn or searching than that adopted by the Synod. Indeed, it may have been substantially his own production.

In 1736, David Cowell was settled at Trenton.[1] He was a native of Massachusetts, and a graduate of Harvard. His examination and installation were conducted by a committee of the Presbytery of Philadelphia, consisting of Andrews, Evans, Wales, and Treat. William Tennent was appointed, but did not meet with them. The examination of the candidate brought out unquestionably his peculiar views, represented by his opponents as making happiness the chief motive of religion. Gilbert Tennent could not endure this. He corresponded with Cowell, but remained still unsatisfied. The discussion was continued for several months, and in 1738 was brought by Tennent to the notice of Synod. A committee was appointed to consider the matter, but their report was deferred from time to time, until in the following year they brought in a report declaring the substantial agreement of the parties, prefacing it with the caustic expression of their conviction that the principal controversy "flows from their not having clear ideas about the subject they so earnestly debate about, and not from any dangerous errors they entertain."

Tennent seemed at the time to acquiesce; but in the reading of the minutes in the following year, he took occasion to declare his dissatisfaction, and asked that the subject be reconsidered. It was refused by a strong majority. This was somewhat exasperating; and he did not hesitate to allude subsequently, in the harshest

---

[1] See Hall's "Church of Trenton," p. 80; also Synod's Minutes.

terms, to the heretical standing of many of the Synod on the points of controversy. His zeal was inflamed by other causes also. He saw with deep anxiety the coldness and irreligion which prevailed around him. Not a few of the ministers were far from exhibiting that fidelity and devotion which pertained to their solemn office. The report of revivals in New England had kindled his feelings to enthusiasm. The presence and preaching of Whitefield, who had just crossed the ocean, and whose early failing of judging ungraciously the gracious state of his brethren had not yet been checked, encouraged Tennent in his course.

But previous to this the Synod had taken action which he interpreted as designed to injure his father's school at Neshaminy. Candidates for the ministry were to be examined by the Synod's committee, and of course to this examination the Presbyteries, as well as candidates, must submit. This was a sore grievance, and was one of the disturbing influences that contributed to the division of the Synod.

The leading opponent of Tennent and his fellow-protesters in the Synod was Robert Cross, originally from Ireland. He had succeeded Macnish at Jamaica in 1723, and in 1737 joined the Philadelphia Presbytery and was settled as a colleague of Andrews. He was highly respected and esteemed both for character and ability. At Jamaica, "his people almost adored him, and impoverished themselves to equal the sum offered him in the city." But on his removal to Philadelphia he became a leading man in the Synod; and his views of the revival which had begun to prevail in several quarters were very different from those of Tennent. Whitefield was by no means his favorite. When he preached in Philadelphia, he came under Cross's definition of an itinerant; and for two or three years the Synod had been growing more decided in its aversion to intrusions not warranted by the permission of Presbytery. Cross was obnoxious to many for his well-known views on the subject. He did not preach —it was said—so as to alarm the conscience. He had "preached most of his people away from him," said Whitefield, in 1740. "He lashed me most bravely the Sunday before I came away." And yet, subsequently, when the snow rendered it impracticable to use the roofless "Great House," he offered his meeting-house to Whitefield; and it was accepted. Such was the man who was destined to take the leadership of the *Old Side* in the protest which brought about the division.

Of those who sympathized most deeply with Tennent, Samuel Blair deserves prominent mention. He was a native of Ireland, but came to this country in his childhood. From his early years his life had been most exemplary. "He grew in stature and in grace." He had studied at the Log College,[1] and became eminent for his attainments. In 1733, he was licensed by the Philadelphia Presbytery, and, after preaching for some years at Middletown and Shrewsbury, became pastor at Fagg's Manor in 1740. The place had been settled by Irish emigrants ten years previously, and Blair, with the exception of "some hopefully pious people," found religion ready to expire. Under his labors a powerful revival commenced.

One who assisted him, and whose sympathies likewise were on the side of Tennent, was Alexander Craighead of Middle Octorara. He was probably a son of Thomas Craighead already mentioned, and commenced his ministry in 1735. None were more zealous in promoting the revival. In company with Whitefield, Tennent, and Blair, he traversed Chester county, and "they made the woods ring, as they rode,

---

[1] See Alexander's "Log College."

with their songs of praise." He preached, without regard to the wishes of his brethren, and against the rule of the Synod, wherever opportunity offered. He claimed that ministers should not be confined within the bounds of a single congregation, and in harsh terms he inveighed against the judicial blindness and hardness of "Pharisee preachers." His zeal soon carried him away; and, though dividing with Tennent and Blair, he soon disowned them, because they would not come into his views for adopting the Solemn League and Covenant.

In John Cross, another friend of "the Revival," Tennent was equally unfortunate. He was a "Scottish worthy," and his place of settlement was "the mountains back of Newark."[1] In 1734–35, there was a powerful revival in his congregation. He accompanied Whitefield and Tennent on their preaching-tours, and was remarkably distinguished for his fervor and success. "He is a dear soul," said Whitefield, "and one that the Lord delights to honor." At a later period, grave charges were substantiated against him. "His dreadful scandals came to light in the midst of the revival." This, however, was not till after the division.

Eleazar Wales was from New England, a graduate of Yale, in 1727, and settled at Allentown, N.J., in 1730. He afterwards removed to Crosswicks, and finally to Millstone, in 1735, where he became, with Tennent, a member of New Brunswick Presbytery.

Richard Treat was likewise from New England, and a graduate of Yale. He settled at Abington in 1731, and for several years acted with the majority of the Synod. But in 1739, on hearing Whitefield, he aban-

---

[1] He was settled at Baskingridge, according to Hoyt's Church of Orange.

doned his former hope, and from that period preached with new fervor.

Besides these men, who firmly adhered to Gilbert Tennent at the time of the division, were his father and his two brothers William and Charles. William was a powerful preacher, and his sermons, though unpolished in diction, were remarkably impressive. As a revivalist he was scarce inferior to his brother Gilbert, while he seems to have been more discreet and far more disposed to peace. Charles was settled at White Clay and Christiana Village in 1737.

The great majority of the Irish members of the Synod, except Blair and the Tennents, sided with Cross, of Philadelphia, in signing the Protest which caused the division. Andrews, of whom he was the colleague, was evidently swayed by his influence, yet did not join in the Protest. Cathcart, at Brandywine; John Thomson, the originator of the overture which resulted in the Adopting Act; Francis Alison, now at New London, but the most thorough scholar which the Old Side could boast; Richard Sanckey, of Hanover, a plagiarist, if not worse; Elder, of Paxton; Craig, of Tinkling Spring, Va., where he preached to the oldest congregation in the State; Cavin, of Falling Spring, a man of whom his people complained that he never asked about the state of their souls; Thomson, of Pennsborough; Boyd, of Octorara; Martin, of Lewes, Del.; and Jamison, at Zion's Hill, in the same State, joined with Cross in the signing of the Protest.

Besides these two parties, which from the period of the Adopting Act began to be more distinctly marked, there was a third, occupying an intermediate position, and who might, if they had acted in time, have prevented the division. These were, principally, Dickinson, of Elizabethtown; Pemberton, of New York; Pierson, of Woodbridge; Horton, of Connecticut Farms;

Burr, of Newark; Pumroy, of Newtown; Hubbell, of Morristown; and Gillespie and Hutcheson, of New Castle Presbytery. Several of these were as warm friends of the revival as the Tennents, and, had they been present at the critical moment, might easily have turned the scale.

The seeds of the division, however, had long been sown. From the time of the Adopting Act, in 1729, the discordant elements of which the Synod was composed began to betray themselves. The question was not in regard to the Adopting Act itself. In this, all parties seemed readily enough to acquiesce. The members who were absent when it was passed expressed their approval of it in the following year. The several Presbyteries reported the uniform acceptance of the Confession by those whom they licensed and ordained. The only complaint anywhere to be heard on the subject was the laxness rather than the severity of the rule; and this complaint came only from a few over-anxious, with fears transmitted from the experience of the Irish Synod.

In spite of the apprehensions expressed by the friends of vital religion at the sad decline which it had experienced, the Church was still extending its bounds. Help was given from the fund to several needy churches, and new congregations were continually forming and applying for ministers. At Wall Kill, Goshen, Crosswater, Trenton, and in Delaware and Virginia, there were urgent demands for the institutions of the gospel,—demands which the Synod exerted itself to meet. In 1732, the Donegal Presbytery was erected, of which Anderson, who had removed from New York, Thomson, Boyd, Orr, and Bertram, were the original members. In the following year, the Presbytery of Philadelphia was divided, and a portion of it set off to constitute the Presbytery of East Jersey, which in 1738 was in conjunction with the Presbytery of Long Island, thenceforth known as the Presbytery of New York. At nearly the same time, the Presbytery of New Brunswick was erected, the members of which were Gilbert and William Tennent, Samuel Blair, Eleazar Wales, and John Cross.

There was, beyond doubt, a sad decline of vital piety among the churches. Some of the ministers whom Tennent rebuked, and into whose congregations he intruded, were unquestionably "Pharisee preachers." Among them, too, were bitter opponents of the revival, if not of Evangelical religion. But the majority of the Synod were by no means men of this stamp. Some of their measures were unwise and characterized by party zeal; but in an impartial judgment they by no means deserve the odium heaped upon them by their opponents.

The Irish members plausibly contended that there was danger to the Church from intrants from Ireland. The tide of immigration had within a few years rapidly increased. It was not at all improbable that, unless vigilance was exercised, the churches would be cursed by unworthy men. Indeed, the Synod had already been called to deal with one who might serve as a specimen. Samuel Hemphill, with ample credentials to the Synod from the Presbytery of Strabane, was received as a member on his easy subscription to the Confession of Faith. He preached at New London with much acceptance, and without exciting any suspicion of his deistical sentiments. Adverse reports from Ireland led to an investigation; but the ministers of New Castle Presbytery declared themselves satisfied with his teachings. He imposed himself on Andrews, and preached all winter at Philadelphia. Franklin liked his preaching, which soon ran into downright Deism. Andrews was at length forced to bring charges against him. They were sustained by evidence; and Hemphill was suspended. This was in 1735. His trial was by the Synod's commission; and, when the case came before the body at its next session, Hemphill sent them an insulting letter, and closed by saying that he thought "they would do him a deal of honor if they would entirely excommunicate him."

If such conduct was felt to be exasperating, the danger which it indicated was seen to be imminent. It led the Synod to take decisive measures for the security of both ministers and churches. "Wolves in sheep's clothing" were "invading the flock of Christ." "Devouring monsters" were "numerous abroad in the world." "The late bold assault that hath been made upon us" "should put us to our arms, and excite us with care and diligence to put ourselves in a posture of defence against all future attempts."

The overture, accordingly, adds, "Seeing we are likely to have the most of our supply of ministers, to fill our vacancies, from the North of Ireland," and, in view of the "great danger of being imposed upon by ministers and preachers from thence," it is proposed to the reverend Synod to order a more careful inspection of credentials of those who come from abroad, no one to be called till he have preached six months within the Synod's bounds, and no student to be received to enter upon his trials, till he have given most of the ministers of the Presbytery opportunity to take a view of his parts and behavior.

To these measures, taken by themselves, there could be no reasonable objection. But the attempt was made—which, in fact, if valid, would have destroyed the Adopting Act—to require every minister to receive the Confession and Form of Government, not in the systematic way prescribed in the Adopting Act, but on the *ipsissima verba* principle. This was the beginning of one of the difficulties which led to the division of the Church. And three years later, in 1738, a proposal was made by the Presbytery of Lewes, which was regarded by the Tennents as especially obnoxious. Premising the great importance of a learned ministry, and the lack of any institution for collegiate education within the bounds of the Church, which obviated the "grievous disadvantage," or furnished "a degree," it urged the appointment of a committee of Synod by whom the candidates were to be examined, and whose certificate might serve instead of a diploma.

The approval of this measure by a great majority was especially obnoxious to the Tennents and to New Brunswick Presbytery. In connection with the acts of the previous year, it was thought to bear especially against them. In 1737, it was ordered that no probationer or minister of one Presbytery be allowed to preach in the bounds of another, without the permission of the latter, and, upon being informed that it would be considered objectionable, he was to desist. If this measure interfered with the itinerating evangelism of John Cross and the Tennents, the other seemed to intimate not the highest esteem of William Tennent's school at Neshaminy, where quite a number of young men had been educated for the ministry. Most of the ministers of the Synod had enjoyed the advantages of a collegiate course,—the Irish and Scotch members at Glasgow, and the New England members at Yale or Harvard. It was natural for them to imagine that no private institution could answer the demand for an educated ministry. But in this matter they scarcely did justice to William Tennent's "Log College." This institution gave to the Church some of her best men,—men eminent alike for piety and learning. The elder Tennent himself was an honor to the Church of his adoption. In 1718 he abandoned the Episcopal communion, scrupling at her government, discipline, and the encouragement, or at least toleration, which she extended to Arminian error and unchristian practice. With a wise forecast, he perceived that the demand of the Presbyterian Church for more ministers must ultimately be met within herself. He set about the work of supplying the want, and under him the two Blairs, Finley, Rowland, and his own sons, were educated for the ministry.

Not long after his settlement at Neshaminy, in 1726, he erected, within a few steps of his own dwelling, the humble edifice which was to acquire such an enviable notoriety. The spirit in which it was established augured well for its future. In Ireland and Scotland the signs of prevalent worldliness, foreshadowing a sad apostasy, were already apparent. In this country the primitive zeal of Makemie's compeers was already on the decline. "Revivals of religion were nowhere heard of, and an orthodox creed and a decent external conduct were the only points on which inquiry was made when persons were admitted to the communion of the Church." Vital piety had almost deserted the Church. The substance of preaching was a "dead orthodoxy," in which little emphasis was laid upon regeneration, a change of heart, or the terrors of the law against sin. With such a state of things Tennent had no sympathy. His warm evangelical spirit led him to strive with all his energies to effect a change. The young men who came under his influence, in their course of education, were inspirited to become his efficient allies. When Whitefield visited Tennent, in 1739, he found much to admire in what had already been accomplished. "*Our* ministers," he says, "are glorious *without*. From *this* despised place, seven or eight worthy ministers of Jesus have lately been sent forth, more are almost ready to be sent, and the foundation is now laying for the instruction of many others."

Tennent's relation to the Synod, according to Whitefield, was much like that of Erskine, of Scotland, to the "judicatories of Edinburgh." He was "secretly despised." A prejudice existed against him and his institution. It was only increased when Tennent invited Whitefield to Neshaminy and gave him a cordial encouragement in his work. His own people were not altogether united in him. The difficulty originated in the fact that he had never been formally installed; and when a hearing of the case had been had before the Synod of Philadelphia, it was declared that the disaffection was due to ignorance and prejudice. The people were recommended to lay aside their groundless dissatisfactions and return to their duty, otherwise they would be treated by the Synod as disorderly. The minute stating the result of the Synod's deliberations was unanimously adopted.

This was in 1737. Two years later, it is doubtful whether the vote would have been so decisive. Tennent fraternized with Whitefield, and the students whom he had trained were the ones who intruded their itinerant evangelism upon other congregations, in violation of the rules adopted by Synod. In their view, those rules were tyrannic and unwarranted. They claimed that no "Pharisee preacher" could be authorized to exclude them from publicly addressing those of other congregations who desired it.

The act of 1738, in regard to the examination of candidates by a committee of the Synod, was especially grievous to the friends of the Log College, as that in regard to intrusion into other congregations was to the friends of the revival. The New Brunswick Presbytery objected to it, and their objections were stated in the Synod of 1739. The subject therefore was reconsidered, and it was ordered that the candidates should be examined, not by the committee that had been appointed, but by the whole Synod or its commission. The principle of the previous year was virtually reaffirmed, and it was scarcely less objectionable in shape. Gilbert Tennent cried out that it was to prevent his father's school from training gracious men for the ministry. He protested against it, and his father, his two brothers, Samuel Blair, and Eleazar Wales, his co-Presbyters, and several elders, joined with him in the protest.

The difficulty was aggravated by the fact that the New Brunswick Presbytery had, during the past year, not only licensed John Rowland, without regard to the Synod's rule, but sent him to supply a vacancy within the bounds of Philadelphia Presbytery. The Synod pronounced their action disorderly, and refused to admit Rowland as a preacher till he submitted to the Synod's examination. At this juncture the conclusion arrived at in the case of the controversy between Tennent and Cowell gave the former, although he did not object publicly at the time, a new occasion of offence.

To make matters still worse, the Synod of the same year took steps for erecting a school or seminary of learning,—appointing Pemberton, Dickinson, Anderson, and Cross, of Philadelphia, to prosecute the affair. The first two were from New England, the third from Scotland, and the last from Ireland; for pecuniary aid was to be sought from all quarters. The step was a wise one; but it altogether ignored Tennent's school, which was entitled to honorable mention. It showed, moreover, that the Synod had no thought of any separation as yet which would exclude Pemberton, Dickinson, or any of the New England men.

Before the meeting of the Synod in 1740, some important events occurred. Whitefield made his first visit within the bounds of the Presbyterian Church, and the warm and fervent spirit of Gilbert Tennent drew him to his views and party. A strong popular feeling was enlisted in his favor. The attraction of his fame and eloquence drew crowds to hear him, and his awakening and convincing discourses produced a general concern. In New York and Philadelphia thousands thronged around him, and large numbers were brought under conviction. Treat, of Abington, who had, to this time, acted with the majority of the Synod, and Campbell, of Tehicken, gave up their hopes and mourned as self-deceivers and soul-murderers.

In the course of a few months, through Whitefield's influence, a great change was wrought. He preached in New York for Pemberton, at Elizabethtown for Dickinson, at Wilmington twice to five thousand, at New Castle to two thousand five hundred, at Christiana Bridge to three thousand, on Sabbath at White Clay to eight thousand; and his farewell sermon at Philadelphia was attended by ten thousand.

These numbers may be somewhat exaggerated; but the fact that in Philadelphia there was religious service every day, and three services on the Sabbath, for a year after, indicates the powerful hold which he had taken of the popular mind. The members of the Old side for the most part disliked him, and refused him their pulpits. Pemberton and Dickinson, by welcoming him, had become more closely drawn to sympathize with Tennent, with whom Whitefield was in strong sympathy.

Here, then, on a grand scale, the rules of the Synod in regard to intrusion had been violated, and those implicated with Whitefield were more than the New Brunswick Presbytery, who during the year had aggravated their original offence by taking Finley on trial, licensing Robinson and McCrea, and ordaining Rowland.

Yet, with the great good effected, there were some mischiefs; and these mischiefs were nearly the entire result which the prejudices of the Old side permitted them to perceive. Their peace had been disturbed. Some of their congregations had been divided or greatly reduced in numbers. The people, many of them, did not hesitate, with the sanction of Whitefield and Tennent, to pronounce their ministers unconverted; and in some cases at least they were not far from the truth.

In these circumstances the Synod of 1740 met. The subjects of the Synod's rule for the trial of candidates, and the preaching of ministers within the bounds of other Presbyteries, were the first introduced for discussion. Tennent wished a revision of the conclusion reached in regard to his controversy with Cowell, but was met by an overwhelming negative. The rule for the trial of candidates was then considered. Any member of the Synod was allowed to propose any expedient to secure peace. All were agreed that the Synod were proper judges of the qualification of their own members; but the protesting brethren objected to the insertion in the minutes of the agreement of the previous year, as unnecessary.

There was "an uncomfortable debate" on the subject, but on the final vote it was decided to abide by the agreement for the present, or till some other expedient could be found to answer its design. The majority was not large in its favor, for of fifty-nine members of the Synod, the protestants of the previous year, joined by fifteen others present at the Synod, formed a powerful minority. Dickinson, Wilmot, Burr, Pierson, Nutman, and Horton must have voted with the majority, or they would have turned the scale in favor of the protesting party.

In regard to the other rule of the Synod bearing upon the intrusion of ministers and licentiates within the bounds of other Presbyteries, the Synod was forced to retrace its steps. Whitefield had "rode over" it triumphantly, if not defiantly; and the New York brethren, as well as the New Brunswick Presbytery, had lent him to some extent their countenance and sanction. Popular feeling, moreover,—and that, too, in the city where the Synod was assembled,—would have resented with indignation any such restriction as would be required by a strict interpretation of the rule of the previous year. It was, therefore, declared that the object of the rule was to prevent "divisions in our congregations," and not to hinder "itinerant preaching." And in regard to those who might have been licensed to preach without the Synodical examination required, the Synod declared that they did not deny such to be "truly gospel ministers," but only that they could not be admitted as members of the Synod till they had complied with its rules.[1]

Here at least, from whatever cause, was manifested a disposition to compromise differences. This was equally obvious when Gilbert Tennent asked for an *interloquitur*,—a secret session for mutual conference. It was late in the closing session, and he was directed to proceed with what he had to offer. The house was crowded with spectators, nearly all of them in sympathy with him. The intervals of Synod had been spent by the New side in preaching. There were two sermons at least, and sometimes more, every day,—sometimes on Society Hill, sometimes at the Baptist church. Dickinson was not sound enough on revivals to be allowed to preach. Rowland and Davenport were more popular, and their course and views were regarded with extensive, if not general, approval. The crowd that had listened to them was now assembled in the house where the Synod was convened.

---

[1] Such is the substance of the overture introduced. It is doubtful whether it was adopted.

Tennent arose, and read a terrible representation on the state of the ministry. The picture which he drew —largely from his own fancy and fears—was appalling. If his statements were to be accepted, his first duty would have been to table charges against a majority of the Synod, or withdraw at once from all connection with it. No sooner had Tennent finished than Blair arose and read a paper drawn up in the same strain. Both were allowed to proceed without interruption. When they had closed, they were exhorted to spare no man in the Synod, but to point out the guilty, that they might at least be distinguished from the innocent. This they were not prepared to do. They would prove the matters charged against particular members; but they admitted that they had not spoken with the persons aimed at, or sifted carefully the reports which they had credited.

With the calmness of dignity and self-respect, yet with a courteous regard to the statements of Tennent and Blair, the Synod declared, in view of their representations, that they "do, therefore, solemnly admonish all the ministers in our bounds, seriously to consider the weight of their charge, and, as they will answer it at the great day of Christ, to take care to approve themselves to God in the instances complained of. And the Presbyteries are recommended to take care of their members in these particulars."

Before adjourning, the Synod readily granted the request of Newtown and Tinicum to be placed under the care of New Brunswick Presbytery. This body in many quarters now enjoyed a high degree of popularity, while in others its name was a synonym for mischief and enthusiasm. Notwithstanding the rules and the authority of Synod, the obnoxious Presbytery continued in its former course. It licensed Finley without regard to the Synod's rule of examination, and sent him to preach at Rising Sun to a party who were erecting a building just across the highway from the old church. Tennent himself went forth to evangelize in West Jersey, Pennsylvania, and Maryland.

From this field he directed his steps to New England. Whitefield had just visited Boston at the request of the ministers, and had preached there, and all along the road to New Haven, as the meeting-houses were thrown open to him. Tennent was urged to water the seed that had been sown. His labors were manifold, and his popularity was second only to Whitefield's.

The Synod of 1741 met; but the division which resulted was already foreshadowed in what had taken place within the bounds of the Church. Everywhere there were divisions and alienations. New Castle Presbytery was divided with Evans, Cathcart, and Alison on the Old side, and Charles Tennent and Blair on the other, while Gillespie and Hutcheson were dissatisfied with both. In Donegal Presbytery, Craighead at New London, and Alexander at Brandywine Manor, countenanced the itinerations of Finley and sympathized with the Tennents. They complained that candidates were licensed without proper examination in regard to heart-religion. They did not hesitate to make open objections to Black, Elder, Sanckey, Thomson, and Cavin, and, in the case of some of them, only on too solid grounds.

Yet the language and conduct of the New side were on many occasions utterly inexcusable. In January preceding the meeting of Synod, Finley preached a sermon entitled "Christ reigning and Satan raging." It was extremely harsh, bitter, and denunciatory. In a printed letter he spoke scornfully of "the babbling ignorant priests that would seem such friends to holiness." "Are not these," he asks, "the devil's advocates?" Thomson's doctrine in his sermon on Conviction and Assurance was condemned as "Moravian, Muggletonian, and detestable."[1]

It was impossible, while such proceedings were sanctioned by the New Brunswick party, and were producing a most exasperated state of feeling in its opponents, that the Synod should meet in harmony. It did not so meet. The members on the side of the protestants were too bold and confident; nor can we altogether defend their course as orderly. To add to the difficulty, the entire New York Presbytery, who might have acted as mediators, were absent. Standing aloof in great measure from the strife, they, with Gillespie, Hutcheson, and other moderate men, might at least have deferred the rupture. Disapproving of many things which had been endorsed by Whitefield and Tennent, they were yet the firm friends of sound doctrine, of good order, and of vital religion.

In their absence, the opposing parties in the Synod came face to face. The first thing was to listen to objections against certain persons sitting in Synod. The individual most obnoxious was A. Craighead, who belonged to the Tennent party and who had been arraigned before the Donegal Presbytery. He had contemned their authority, and had been suspended for contumacy. While his case was pending, the members of the Old side brought in their protest against the right of the protestants of the previous year to sit in the Synod. They charged to their "unwearied, unscriptural, anti-Presbyterial, uncharitable, division practices," for the past year, "the dreadful distractions and convulsions which all of a sudden have seized this infant Church; . . . that she is in danger of expiring outright." Against such disorderly

---

[1] See Webster's History.

feelings they felt it their "duty to bear testimony." With such conviction, they protested that it was "the indispensable duty of the Synod to maintain and stand by the principles of doctrine, worship, and government" summed up in the acknowledged standards of the Church; that no one who had not adopted or subscribed these standards "according to our last explication of the Adopting Act," no one holding doctrines opposed to them, or persisting in practices "contrary to any of the known rights of Presbytery" or "orders agreed to by the Synod," should be allowed to sit and vote till he repented of his wrong; that the protesting brethren of the previous year had forfeited their rights as members, for many reasons afterwards specified; that if, notwithstanding their present protestations, the others should continue, as during the past year, in their anti-Presbyterial practices, they should be looked upon as guilty of schism, and not members of "the true Presbyterian Church in this province."

It will be observed that "the last explication of" the Adopting Act was that of 1736. The majority of the Synod, therefore, demanded as a condition of membership a principle fundamentally different from that of the Adopting Act. They demanded, in short, an *ipsissima verba* subscription. And because of the refusal to yield to this demand, among others, they proceeded to what was a virtual excision, and what they did not hesitate to characterize as such in their subsequent documents. This view is strengthened by the fact that they refer in the protest to the manner in which their Presbyteries adopt the Confession. But it can be shown by existing documents that the Presbyteries of New Castle and Donegal had adopted an *ipsissima verba* subscription,—one contrary to the principle of the Adopting Act. The *systematic* in contradistinction from the *ipsissima verba* subscription, was re-established at the reunion in 1758.

The members of the Old side then proceeded to give their reasons for their protest. These were found in the conduct of the favorers of the New Brunswick party, which embraced some in each of the Presbyteries of New Castle and Donegal, denying the authority of Presbyteries and Synods to go any further in judging of appeals and references than to give their best advice; their protest and action against the Synod's rule for the examination of candidates; their "irregular irruptions upon congregations to which they have no immediate relation, sowing the seeds of division among people," and alienating their minds with unjust prejudices against pastors; their "rash judging and condemning all who do not fall in with their measures, as carnal, graceless, and enemies of the work of God, as instanced in Tennent's Nottingham sermon, and his and Blair's papers read before the last Synod; their disorderly itinerations through other congregations, which through them had become shattered and divided; their strange notions as to what constituted a call to the ministry;" their "preaching the terrors of the law in such a manner and dialect as has no precedent in the word of God, but rather appears to be borrowed from a worse dialect;" their "working on the passions and affections of weak minds, making persons cry out in a hideous manner, or fall in convulsion fits;" their maintaining that all true converts could be absolutely certain of their gracious state, and able to narrate the time and manner of their conversion, and that the people were under no tie to their own pastors, but might leave them when they pleased, and ought to go where they could get most good.

For these reasons, they pronounced union with the obnoxious brethren "monstrously absurd,"—one party owning, and the other disowning, the judicial determinations of the whole; one party desiring to join with another party which they condemned "wholesale," meeting with them once in the year, but working against them at all other times, disregarding the authority of the common standards, yet arrogating authority to palm and obtrude members upon the Synod contrary to its judgment.

Such were declared to be but a part of the reasons why the Old side protested against those who sustained the action and cause of the New Brunswick Presbytery. They did not maintain that they themselves were guiltless, but justified the "Divine proceedings against" them, and avowed the duty and necessity of a reformation of the evils whereby God had been provoked.

The protest was read and laid upon the table. Several, who had not seen it before, signed their names. There was great confusion. Andrews, who was moderator, had no previous knowledge of the measure, and left the chair. As the elders signed their names, some cried out that they were subscribing what they had not heard or considered. Others declared that it was a protesting of lies before Almighty God. Each party was too excited to deliberate. The friends of the New Brunswick Presbytery wished to speak in their own defence. Blair and others, too confident of their strength, insisted that the protesters ought to withdraw, for they were not a majority of the body. The sympathy of the spectators was on the side of Blair and Tennent. The galleries rang with cries to cast the protesters out.

No pacific measures, no offers of compromise, were presented. The New Brunswick party were firm in the conviction that they were in the majority, and canvassed whether they or their opponents were to be regarded as the Synod. The latter maintained that, on which side soever the majority might be, the New Brunswick party had no right to sit in the Synod.

The roll was called. Andrews, who had to act on the spur of the occasion,—for he had not been let into the secret of the protest, which must have been long contemplated, as it was carefully drawn,—decided at once that he could not join with the New Brunswick brethren. The moderate members were unwilling to act with them, and some who would have sustained them had left. Gillespie and McHenry did not appear. Hutcheson hesitated. Elmer and his elder had gone home. The New Brunswick party were clearly in the minority. They withdrew, followed by a great crowd.

The division was accomplished. Treat and Wales were the only New England ministers who withdrew with the excluded party. The others grieved, in common with the more moderate members present at the Synod, over what had taken place. There had been a struggle for the ascendency between two rival parties, each aspiring to control the Church, and each combining with its conscientious convictions no small measure of human passion. The New Brunswick party were zealous for what they regarded as vital evangelical truth, and believed it to be a part of their mission to unmask the hypocrisy, worldliness, and sin of the Church, and, in the over-earnestness of their purpose, forgot charity and discretion. The others, indignant under the sense of wrong, were forced to appeal to the authority of the common standards and the rules of the Synod, which their brethren had too much disregarded.

Thus one party appealed to the word of God, the other to the Confession of Faith. One, zealous for truth, fell the victim of its theories; the other, resolute for order, could see only the letter of the constitution, which they yet violated by the operation which they gave to a protest which was virtually an exscinding act. Their extraordinary zeal for the Confession was less from any superior attachment to its doctrines, than from the fact that they endeavored to appeal to the standards and authority of the Synod as the means of self-defence.

CHAPTER VI.

THE PERIOD OF THE DIVISION.

At the time of the division of the Synod, the prospect of the New Brunswick party was not the most encouraging. They were not only a minority in numbers as the Synod was then constituted, but there was danger lest they should become the victims of their divisive principles, since the New York Presbytery, friendly to order, could not approve their course, and still adhered to the Old side. This, however, was not because they endorsed the action of the latter party, or approved the protest by which the New Brunswick members were excluded. In 1742, Dickinson was chosen moderator, and the first business brought before Synod was, on his suggestion, for a conference with the rejected brethren, "in order to accommodate the difference and make up that unhappy breach."

A committee was appointed to consider what could be done. It consisted of seven; and Dickinson, Pemberton, and Pierson were members of it. The ejected ministers were invited to confer with the Synod. They did so; but the conference reached no satisfactory result. The parties could not agree as to who should be judges in the case. The New Brunswick party would submit the business to the consideration of none who had signed the protest of the previous year. They were met by the latter with the not very soothing declaration that they, the protestants, with the members that adhered to them after ejecting the others, were the Synod, and had acted as such in the ejection, and in so doing only cast out such members as they deemed unworthy of membership, because they maintained and practised things subversive of the constitution. They could not, therefore, be called to account by absent members, "or by any judicature on earth." They were willing, however, to give the reasons of their conduct to the absent brethren, and to the public, for their consideration or review.

The New York members—Dickinson, Pemberton, Pierson, Elmer,[1] and the two Hortons—were not satisfied with this. They entered their protest against the exclusion of the New Brunswick Presbytery by a protest and without giving them a previous trial, as "an illegal and unprecedented procedure, contrary to the rules of the gospel, and subversive of our excellent constitution." They protested also against the refusal of the present Synod to try the legality of the protest of the previous year. They maintained that the members excluded by the protest were still members, and were to be owned and esteemed such until they were pronounced excluded after a regular and impartial process against them. As to the seeming condemnation by the protestants of the previous year, of the revival, and the language that had been employed in pamphlets sanctioned, if not issued, by the Old side, they pro-

---

1 Elmer, though reckoned with the "New York members," belonged to the Presbytery of Philadelphia (printed minutes of Synod, p. 141); he was from New England, and settled first at West Brookfield (Mass.), then at Cohansey, or Fairfield, N.J. Noyes Parris was probably his predecessor at Cohansey.

tested against all passages in them which seemed to reflect "upon the work of Divine power and grace, which" had "been carrying on in so wonderful a manner in many" of the congregations. At the same time, to clear themselves from all responsibility for the indiscretions and faults of the New Brunswick party, they said, in conclusion, "We protest and declare against all divisive and irregular methods and practices, by which the peace and good order of our churches have been broken in upon."

The protest was recorded. The only attempt to reply to it in the minutes of Synod is the statement that the protest on the first point was opposed to the facts of the case, and that the excluded members were excluded by vote of the Synod if they refused to give satisfaction for the points complained of, and that upon this they withdrew. Francis Alison alone insisted on its being inserted in the minutes of Synod, that he judged it an open infringement on the rights of society, and of the members of Synod as Presbyterians, that the body should be called to account and the legality of its acts judged by absent members.

In the following year (1743), the Presbytery of New York brought up the subject again by overture to the Synod. They proposed that the excluding protest should be withdrawn, and the excluded members resume their seats in Synod; that candidates for the ministry should submit to the former agreement of the Synod in regard to examination, or procure a diploma from a New England college; that the pulpits of ministers should be open to their brethren when regularly applied for, and, unless the reasons for a refusal should be approved by the Presbytery or Synod, such refusal should be regarded as unbrotherly and tending to division or separation; that if any minister should imagine he had cause to complain of any of his brethren, he should first seek a private conference, and, if that failed, cite him on specific charges for trial before the Presbytery. Former matters of difference and debate in Synod were to be buried in oblivion, and in case this plan of accommodation, or others that might be proposed, should fail, the Synod should unitedly agree that another Synod be erected by the name of the Synod of New York, and liberty be left to members to unite with either as they saw fit,—the two Synods sending yearly each two correspondents to the other.

The overture was rejected by the Synod, and Dickinson, Pemberton, Pierson, and Burr, while complaining "of no unfriendly or unbrotherly treatment" from the Synod with relation to themselves, gave in a paper in which they declared that they regarded the New Brunswick Presbytery and its adherents as fully as themselves entitled to sit as members of the Synod, and in consequence that they could not, while that Presbytery was excluded, see their way clear to sit and act as though they, with the members present, were the Synod of Philadelphia.

Burr sent at the same time to the New Brunswick brethren a proposal of terms for their admission to the Synod, which were read and approved. These terms required subjection to the agreements or censures of Synod,—the desisting from licensure and ordination of men who had not complied with the Synod's rules of examination, or the alternative proposed in the Conference of the previous year,—the refraining from itinerant intrusion, or the setting up new separate societies within the bounds of the Presbyteries, or fixed pastoral charges,—the renunciation of the obnoxious positions taken by Gilbert Tennent in his Nottingham sermon, which took "all government out of the hands of a Synod or Presbytery, and gave it to any person of ignorance and impudence enough to bring God's house into confusion,"—an acknowledgment of their guilt in these respects, and "the dreadful tendency" of their practices to promote division and confusion among the churches.

If the excluded brethren had any thing to complain of with regard to the members of the Synod, they were to be welcome to table charges against them in a proper judicatory, whether the terms proposed were acceptable or not, and, in case of their acceptance, the excluded members should be heartily received.

To this the ministers of the conjunct Presbyteries of New Brunswick and New Castle[1] replied, by declaring that there could be no regular steps taken towards a union till the illegal protest was withdrawn, while the paper of proposals contained "sundry misrepresentations and unreasonable demands."

It was already in contemplation to erect another Synod. Although no action was taken in reference to it by the Synod of Philadelphia, their views were expressed by a paper inserted in their minutes. In this they say that they "cannot approve and confirm schism by Synodical authority;" yet "if our New York brethren see cause, contrary to our judgment and inclination, to divide themselves from us, and to erect themselves into a new separate body, while it is not in our power to hinder them, though we cannot in conscience approve of their so doing, yet we hope by the grace of God we shall sincerely and conscientiously endeavor to cherish and cultivate a truly Christian and charitable disposition towards them."

No further steps to promote a reunion were taken

---

[1] The old New Castle Presbytery was divided so as to form two, each bearing the same name,—one the Old side, the other the New. The latter, of course, was the one in sympathy with the New Brunswick Presbytery.

till 1745. Of the New York Presbytery, Dickinson, Pemberton, and Pierson were present in Synod. They bore with them a Presbyterial commission, desiring the Synod to appoint a committee of conference with them for the removal of grounds of dissatisfaction and difference. The committee was appointed, but the plan which they drew up was one which the New York brethren declared that they would not accept. They could not regard it as a proper basis of union. It forbade any member to preach in another's congregation without being invited by him or judicially appointed to it; while it declared that all erections within the bounds of regular congregations, which had been set up by "itinerant preaching and divisive practices," should be deemed contrary to the peace and good order of the Church, and not to be maintained.

The plan was quite inadmissible, and in the circumstances of the times was especially obnoxious to the New side. The question on which it took issue was not one which concerned the excluded brethren alone.

The extended revival of religion at this period—associated in many minds with the names of Whitefield and Tennent, but connected also with the labors of such men as Edwards and Bellamy—had produced a division in the Church throughout the land. Some favored it and some opposed it, while a large body of the more moderate and discreet, but not less devoted, ministers were free to admit the irregularities which it occasioned, while they stood ready to vindicate the good which it had accomplished. The verdict of impartial history must pronounce it, with some qualifications, a powerful movement for good. If it sometimes burnt the standing corn, it consumed an immense mass of stubble. Vital religion all over the land was strengthened by it. Hundreds and even thousands of souls were converted. The pulpit was armed with a new power. A dead orthodoxy was quickened to life, and a genuine reformation was in many cases the result.

But neither the movement nor the opposition to it was confined to the limits of the Presbyterian Church. They extended alike to New England. Some of the Boston ministers opposed the revival. They preached and published against it. The Legislature of Connecticut, in 1742, at the instigation of certain ministers, enacted that any clergyman who should preach in any parish not under his immediate charge, without invitation from the settled minister or a majority of the congregation, should forfeit his salary and be bound to *peaceable* and *good behavior* in the full sum of one hundred pounds lawful money until the next court. Non-residents, not licensed by an association, were liable to arrest by any magistrate as *common vagrants*, to be sent out of the colony.[1] Nor was the law suffered to remain a dead letter. Davenport and Dr. Finley (President of Princeton College at a later date) were banished under this act, and Pomeroy (of Hebron) and others deprived of their salaries. In 1743, all the pulpits of New Haven county were closed against the ministers of New Brunswick Presbytery. To have accepted or endorsed the plan of the Old side, would have been regarded as a guilty acquiescence in the injustice.

There was therefore now no longer any hope of reconciling the two parties. It only remained to proceed to the erection of a new Synod. The New York brethren could not remain in a connection from which their New Brunswick brethren were illegally debarred. This was distinctly understood, and, in view of it, the Synod of Philadelphia declared, "it particularly affects us, that some of our New York brethren do not

---

[1] Trumbull's History, ii. 163.

at present see their way clear to continue in Synodical communion with us." Yet, in view of their proposed erection of a new Synod, they desired to declare, "in the most friendly way possible," that if the project was carried out, they should "endeavor to maintain charitable and Christian affections towards them, and show the same upon all occasions by such correspondence and fellowship" as they should "think duty and consistent with a good conscience." Accordingly, in September, 1745, the New Brunswick party and the members of the New York Presbytery met at Elizabethtown, N.J., and formed themselves into the Synod of New York. For the New York members no other course was left open. They could not approve the exclusion of the New Brunswick Presbytery by an illegal protest, yet their continued adherence to the Synod of Philadelphia would seem to endorse it. Nor was it a light matter, in their esteem, that the latter body by its public declarations and in the popular judgment had set itself in opposition to the revival, by opposing its methods and speaking of it in their public acts in a tone of depreciation. However they might disapprove the course of the New Brunswick party on some points, they were in strong sympathy with them in regard to their estimate of the revival itself as a wonderful exhibition of the power and grace of God.

Yet, in uniting with them to form the Synod, they were careful to guard against those causes of division and offence which had occasioned in great part the division of 1741. The principles upon which they consented to unite distinctly condemned insubordination to the rules and agreements of Synod. If any one felt himself aggrieved by these, and could not in conscience submit to them, he was peaceably to withdraw, without raising dispute or contention upon the debated point, or unjust alienation of affection among the members. Supposed errors in doctrine or in conduct were not to be a subject for scandal, but discipline. "Factious separating practices or principles" were by no means to be encouraged; yet all who were of competent knowledge, orthodox in doctrine, regular in life, and diligent in promoting vital godliness, should be cheerfully admitted to their communion. To avoid divisive methods and to strengthen the discipline of Christ in the churches, a correspondence was to be maintained with the Synod of Philadelphia, by appointing two members who were "to concert with them such measures as may best promote the precious interests of Christ's kingdom in these parts." The basis of the new body was the agreement that the Westminster Confession of Faith, with the Catechisms, "be the public confession of their faith in such manner as was agreed unto by the Synod of Philadelphia in 1729." The Directory of the Westminster Assembly was approved as "the general plan of worship and discipline."

In the Synod as thus constituted, three Presbyteries —New York, New Brunswick, and New Castle—were represented. From the first, there were Dickinson, Pierson, Pemberton, Burr, the two Hortons, Timothy Johnes, Eliab Byram, and Robert Sturgeon. Of New Brunswick, besides Gilbert and William Tennent, there were Robert Treat, Joseph Lamb, James McCrea, William Robinson, David Youngs, Charles Beatty, and Charles McKnight. Of New Castle, there were the two Blairs,—Samuel and John,—Charles Tennent, and Samuel Finley. Johnes was of Welsh descent, but a native of Southampton, L.I. He was a graduate of Yale, and in 1742 commenced at Morristown a ministry of many years, and one which was remarkably blessed. Byram was a Massachusetts man, a warm friend of Brainerd, and was setttled at Mendham in 1743. Sturgeon was probably at Bedford, in West Chester county,

N.Y., where, although from Scotland, he had gone as a licentiate of a New England council. Lamb, for many years at Mattituck, L.I., had been called to Baskingridge, and joined the New Brunswick Presbytery in 1744. McCrea and Robinson had been educated at the Log College,—the first now settled at Lamington, where he had gathered a church, and the latter just in full career as a pioneer missionary of Presbyterianism in Virginia and the Carolinas.[1] Finley, Youngs, and McKnight were all ordained by the New Brunswick Presbytery in 1742. Finley was at Nottingham (Maryland), where his school, until he was called to succeed Davies in the presidency at Princeton, was highly celebrated. Youngs, a native of Southold, and a classmate at Yale of Buell and Brainerd, was settled at Setauket in 1742. McKnight was settled at Cranberry and Allentown.

The name of Beatty is associated with that of the founder of the Log College, whom he succeeded at Neshaminy. Although a native of Ireland, and yet but a boy when he reached this country, he had received a classical education; and it is not altogether improbable that during his stay in New England, where he remained for two years, or at Goshen and Wall Kill, N.Y., to which places the family removed, he may have prosecuted his studies, under pastoral supervision, with renewed diligence.

As he grew up to manhood, he engaged in trade. As the manner of the day often was, he travelled with his goods. On foot, or with his pack-horse, he went forth to display his "auld-warld gear" to the people in their own homes.[2] In the course of his wanderings, he reached Neshaminy. At the Log College, Tennent and his pupils were surprised by a pedlar proffering his

---

[1] Afterward settled at St. George's, Del. [2] Sprague's Annals.

merchandise to them in Latin. Tennent replied; and the conversation was carried on in the Latin tongue, with such evidence of scholarship, religious knowledge, and fervent piety on the part of the pedlar, that Tennent commanded him to sell what he had and prepare for the ministry. Beatty was disposed to comply. He studied at Neshaminy, was licensed in 1742, and in less than a year was called to take the place of Tennent himself.

Thus, within the four years that had intervened from the separation to the formation of the New York Synod, the New Brunswick Presbytery had gathered around it a noble band of young men, animated with the spirit of the revival and eager to go forth to their work. As the Synod was formed, the field to be occupied was greatly extended. Applications for ministers and missionaries came from afar,—from Virginia and the Carolinas. Extraordinary efforts were made to meet the demand. A large number of the ministers, especially the younger portion of them, were sent out repeatedly on missionary tours.

The Old side had also received some accessions. In 1742, John Guild, Samuel Evans, and Alexander McDowell were ordained. The first was a native of Massachusetts, a graduate of Harvard, and was settled at Hopewell; Evans was the son of the Evans of the Welsh Tract. McDowell, who afterward took charge of the Synod's school, is said to have come from Virginia, and to have settled at Nottingham in 1743–44.[1]

Bell, Hindman, and Griffith were ordained in 1743, by the Old side. Neither proved to be of much service. Bell had been educated at the Log College. He

[1] This is questionable, however. Dr. Finley settled at Nottingham in 1744, and remained there seven years. See Allen's Biographical Dictionary.

adhered to the Old side, but, in little more than a twelvemonth after his ordination, renounced all connection with Presbytery. Hindman labored for a short time as a missionary in Virginia. Griffith succeeded Thomas Evans at Pencader.[1] He died some time after 1751, when he was a missionary in Virginia.

In the following year, John Steel and James Scougal were the only accessions received. Both were from Ireland: the first, from Londonderry Presbytery, settled at New London, and the other, from the Presbytery of Paisley, took charge of the Old-side congregation of Snow Hill.

Thus, in the four years that had elapsed since the division, the New Brunswick party had gained vastly upon the Old side. Long Island Presbytery, some portions of which strongly sympathized with the Tennents, had furnished it several candidates. Davenport, with all his extravagances, had "a zeal for God and the conversion of men that was scarce to be paralleled;" and he and those who were under his influence did much to strengthen the popularity of the New side. The New York Presbytery would have decidedly turned the scales in its favor, if they had been even before.

In the thirteen years that followed, from the erection of the Synod of New York in 1745 to the reunion of the Synods in 1758, the preponderance was increasingly in favor of the New side. Samuel Davies, the great pulpit orator, and President of Princeton College, who commenced his ministry in 1747, was in himself a host. John Brainerd (1748) was the worthy brother of the great missionary to the Indians; and his name would have done honor to any Church.[2] Samuel Blair, senior,

---

[1] So stated by Webster, p. 483.

[2] Settled in Deerfield, West Jersey, and missionary to the Indians.

at Fagg's Manor, had commenced his school, and had begun to send out men well qualified for the work of the ministry. John Rodgers, afterward the associate of Davies, and pastor at New York, was one of his pupils.[1] He studied theology with Gilbert Tennent, and in 1749 commenced his labors on the early field of Presbyterian effort in this country, the Eastern Shore of Maryland.[2] Elihu Spencer, one of the ablest men whose names adorn the Presbyterian annals, was missionary to the Oneidas in 1748, and succeeded Dickinson, at Elizabethtown, in 1750, and Rodgers, at St. George's, in 1766.[3]

Samuel Buell, whom the New Haven Association classed with Brainerd among "strolling preachers that were most disorderly," had settled at East Hampton in 1746, and in the following year helped to form the Suffolk Presbytery. He was a man of powerful and pungent address, and nearly one hundred were added to his church at a single communion season. In 1751, Naphtali Daggett, afterward President of Yale College, was settled at Smithtown, L.I. John Todd, who was called to wear the mantle of Davies on his departure for England, and again on his removal to Princeton, entered upon his Virginia field and was installed by Hanover Presbytery in 1751.

In the same year, Robert Smith, under whom so many of the ministers of the Presbyterian Church subsequently received their theological education, was installed at Pequa, and the earlier years of his ministry

---

[1] Others were Alexander Cummings, President Davies, James Finley, and Hugh Henry.

[2] Life of Rodgers, p. 54. Subsequently he was at St. George's, and Middletown, Del.

[3] Webster, 588. Spencer performed much missionary labor in the Southern States.

were signally blessed. In 1756, George Duffield, who had been educated at Nassau Hall, and had served as tutor there for two years, commenced his ministerial career. Besides these, at the time of the reunion, the Synod of New York had upon its list of members the names of Whitaker; Kettletas, of Jamaica; Thane, of Connecticut Farms; Richards, of Rahway; Smith, of Orange; Lewis, of Hopewell and Maidenhead, afterward of Mendham; Kennedy, of Baskingridge; Hait, of Amwell; Chesnut, of Charlestown and New Providence; Martin, of Newtown and Salisbury; Lawrence, of the Forks of the Delaware, afterward of Cape May; Arthur, who succeeded Tennent at New Brunswick, when the latter removed in 1744 to the Second Church in Philadelphia; Hunter, of Greenwich and Deerfield; Jacob Green, of Hanover, N.J.; Greenman, of Pilesgrove; Ramsey, of Fairfield; Roan, associated with Robinson and Blair in the missionary work in Virginia, where his zeal seems to have exceeded his discretion and to have drawn reproach upon his party; Tuttle, of Kent county, Del.; Harris, of Indian River, near Lewis; Prime, long settled at Huntingdon, L.I., but not till 1747 a member of Presbytery; Brown, of Bridgehampton; Sylvanus White, of Southampton, and son of the venerable Ebenezer White; Talmadge, of Brookhaven; Reeve, of Moriches, father of the celebrated Tapping Reeve, at the head of the Law School at Litchfield; Ball, of Bedford; Smith, of Rye and White Plains; Sackett, of Peekskill, or Cortland Manor; Ayres, of Blooming Grove, a pupil of Bellamy, and first on the roll of the alumni of Nassau Hall; Graham, of Poughkeepsie; Moffat, of Wall Kill; Elmer, of New Providence,[1] N.J.; Hugh Knox, a pupil probably of President A. Burr, and, singularly enough, the teacher of

[1] Webster, 609.

Alexander Hamilton; Maltby, for some time tutor at Nassau Hall, and afterward pastor of a church in Bermuda; Reed, of Bound Brook, the first member of Nassau Hall who became a member of Synod; Worts, of the High-Dutch Congregation of Rockaway; Henry, of Rehoboth, Wicomoco, and Monokin, a graduate of Nassau Hall, and a pupil of Samuel Blair; Campbell, of Tehicken, afterward of South Carolina; Bay, of Round Hill, and Marsh Creek, Pa.; John Hoge, of Cedar Creek, one of the pioneer laborers in Virginia; Sterling, of Upper Octorara; McAden, one of the pioneer laborers in the Carolinas; Robert Henry, of Cub Creek, Prince Edward county, Virginia; and John Martin, of Albemarle, a pupil of Davies, afterward a missionary to the Cherokees, and finally settling in South Carolina.

A mere list of the names and places of settlement of these men shows the rapid extension of the Presbyterian Church, as represented by the New side, both at the North and South. In Orange and Dutchess counties, N.Y., on Long Island, within the very bounds of the Old side in New Jersey and Pennsylvania, in Virginia and the Carolinas, there was a rapid increase of the New-side ministers. Indeed, the Synod of New York had great advantages, in securing supplies, over the Synod of Philadelphia. Nearly, if not full, one-half of the ministers added to it, during the period previous to the reunion, were from New England; and Nassau Hall was already established and sending out graduates, who were justifying the fond anticipations of its founders.

On the other hand, the Old side had great difficulties to encounter. Their opposition to revivals seems to have wellnigh paralyzed the spiritual vigor both of pastors and churches. Their own candidates for the ministry were few in number, and the tide from Ireland had already begun to ebb. The sympathies of the foreign churches were by no means altogether on their side, especially after the mission of Tennent and Davies to England and Scotland in behalf of Nassau Hall. They wrote to Scotland for ministers, but few came. They corresponded with President Clap, of New Haven, and entertained him with their complaints of the New side, and their condemnation of the proceedings which issued in ordaining Brainerd, on his expulsion from Yale, for the mission work among the Indians. To Dickinson and the founders of Nassau Hall, such correspondence, uniting the sympathies of the Old side and the opponents of revivals at New Haven, was only a new argument in favor of prosecuting the task of establishing a college at Princeton.

But the Old side derived little real advantage from it. President Clap might sanction their devotion to the cause of order, but he could not send them the men who could cope in zeal with Brainerd, McKnight, Buell, Spencer, Graham, Daggett, Youngs, Bostwick, Arthur, and Davenport,—all of them graduates of Yale, and carrying with them to the New side the fervor and active zeal of Whitefield and the Tennents, from whose lips some of them had caught the flame.

Yet the Old side put forth honorable efforts in the cause of learning and ministerial education. It would have been inconsistent with their professions not to have done so. They commenced a Synodical school under Alison, the best scholar on their side, and continued it for several years. Some of their best men were trained in it.

But the list of accessions which they received before the reunion was small, compared with that of the New side. In 1745–6, they received on Synodical examination, Thorn, afterward settled at Chesnut Level; John Dick, who took charge of Drawyers and Appoquinimy; Hamilton, of Rehoboth and Monokin; and Hector Alison, who succeeded Dick at Drawyers and Appoquinimy, and afterward settled at Williamsburg, South Carolina. From 1748 to 1754, the only new members added to the Synod, who remained for any length of time in its connection, were Joseph Tate, of Silver Spring, Marsh Creek, and Donegal; Sampson Smith, succeeding Thorn in 1752 at Chesnut Level; Robert McMordie, of Upper Marsh Creek, and Round Hill; Evander Morrison, of Middle Octorara; and John Miller, of Duck Creek.[1] The only other members who united with the Old side, previous to the reunion, that deserve mention, were John Kinkead, of Chester and Montgomery counties, Pa.;[2] Alexander Miller, who settled in the Great Valley, Va.,—neither of whom reflects honor upon the party to which both belonged;—and William McKennan and Matthew Wilson, the first settled at Wilmington and Red Clay, and the latter at Lewes and Cold Spring, Del.

Of all the members who united with both Synods, from 1745 to 1758, only twelve are known to have been from Scotland, nine from Ireland, three from England, nine from New York and the Middle States, while nearly thirty were from New England and Long Island. Of the twenty others, of whom passing men-

---

[1] Dover, St. Jones, and "People of Kent," are all the same congregation,—*Dover*. This congregation is on the Records in 1714, and Mr. Anderson, of New Castle, is ordered to supply them: then Henry Hook, in 1723. The first pastor was Archibald Cook, installed June 7, 1727; died September 7, 1729. Mr. Hook was ordered to supply Kent in 1725 and 1726, and also to preach at Duck Creek (Smyrna, Del.) occasionally in 1726. This is the origin of Duck Creek Church.

[2] In the minutes of Synod for 1753, p. 210, we read, "A member of the congregation of Norrington applied to the Synod, supplicating the ordination of Mr. Kinkead, as fast as the stated rules and methods used in our Presbyteries will permit."

tion is made, some remained but a short time in this country, while the place of the others' nativity is for the most part unknown.

The increase of membership of the New side from these various sources—mainly from New England and Scotland—was to that of the Old side nearly as eight to one. They secured the sympathy of all the friends of the revival, and manifested great energy in the supply of the destitute and missionary fields within the bounds of the Church.

The prospects of the Old side were rendered more discouraging from the sudden check given to Irish emigration. With all the sympathy of President Clap, they secured but one or two ministers from New England, not more than two or three from Scotland, while most of the number added were their own licentiates.

In these circumstances they became continually less indisposed to a reunion. Especially was this the case after the erection of the Synod of New York; the constitution of which embodied some of the most important principles for which the Old side had contended, and to which the New Brunswick party, on mature deliberation, chose to submit. Indeed, in Burr's proposal for union, laid before the Synod of Philadelphia in 1745, and which embodies the principles adopted a few months afterward in the constitution of the New York Synod, he said, "We think that a subscription of these Articles (the agreements of the Synod) will be a renouncing disorder and divisive practice, and, when obtained, will lay a foundation for maintaining peace, truth, and good order, which was what was desired in the protest by which the Brunswick brethren stand excluded."

The grounds of division were thus much narrowed. They were, in fact, reduced to the mode of subscription and the protest itself. The New York Synod distinctly required, that if any member objected to the life or doctrine of another, he should not spread abroad popular rumors to his prejudice, but table charges before the proper judicatory. If one could not conscientiously submit to the agreements of Synod, he should peaceably withdraw. Factious, separating principles or practices were to be discouraged, and no one was to intermeddle with parties separating from Presbyterian or Congregational churches within their bounds.

In accepting these terms of communion, the New Brunswick brethren virtually renounced all the obnoxious positions which they had hitherto maintained. The way was thus opened for proposals of union from both parties. They came in the first instance from the Synod of New York. This body wished to secure from the united Synod a declaration in favor of the revival as a "work of God's glorious grace,"—one something like that which they had made themselves at their first meeting at Elizabethtown. To this the Synod of Philadelphia objected, and the Synod of New York did not insist absolutely upon this point. In 1745–49, and nearly every successive year afterward, proposals were made, or communications interchanged. A commission was appointed, composed of members of both Synods, who met at Trenton in 1749. The three points of difference were the protest, the paragraph about essentials, and the constituting of the Presbyteries on the union of the Synods. These points were discussed from year to year. In regard to the protest, the New York Synod insisted that "by some authentic and formal act of the Synod of Philadelphia" it should "be made null and void." This the Synod of Philadelphia refused; and the matter was finally settled by their declaring that the protest was the act of the individual members who signed it, for which they were alone responsible: it was not, and should not be considered the act of the Synod. In this view of the subject, the Synod of New York had nothing further to object.

The "paragraph about essentials" was one to which the Old side attached much importance. It had doubtless been much insisted upon by the Presbyteries, who were instructed by the Synod to consider the terms of union, and give in what they thought necessary to the Old-side members of the commission that was to meet at Trenton. The difficulty was not with subscription to the terms of the Adopting Act of 1729, but subscription "according to our last (1736) explication of the Adopting Act, without the least variation or alteration." This point was one adhered to, not so much from tenacity for orthodox doctrine as from zeal for orderly practice. In the protest of 1741, it is the violation of the thirty-first article (on Synods and Councils) of which the protestants complain. It was this which they said the New Brunswick brethren "*pretend* to adopt." But, in their zeal for order and subjection to the authority of Synod, they went too far. They would have violated the spirit of the Adopting Act by a rigid interpretation of their "last explication." In establishing the principles of authority, they would have made every line and letter of the Confession infallible as the Scriptures themselves, instead of the whole the embodiment of the system of Scripture truth.

This, therefore, was a point on which the Synod of New York could not yield to the Old side. With regard to order and authority they had taken the same ground already with them; but, with a broader view of "the paragraph about essentials," they distinctly said (1753), "Difference in judgment should not oblige a dissenting member to withdraw from our communion, unless the matter were judged by the body to be essential in doctrine or discipline. And this we must own is an important article with us, which we cannot any way dispense with. And it appears to us to be strictly Christian and scriptural, as well as Presbyterian, otherwise we must make every thing that appears plain duty to us a term of communion, which we apprehend the Scripture prohibits. And it appears plain to us, that there may be many opinions relating to the great truths of religion that are not great themselves, nor of sufficient importance to be made terms of communion. Nor can these sentiments 'open a door to an unjustifiable latitude in principles *and practices*,' any more than the apostolic prohibition of receiving those that are weak to doubtful disputations. What is plain sin and plain duty in one's account is not so in another's; and the Synod has still in their power to judge what is essential and what is not. In order to prevent an unjustifiable latitude, we must not make terms of communion which Christ has not made; and we are convinced that he hath not made every truth and every duty a term."

These were the noble sentiments, fearlessly avowed and eloquently advocated, of the New side. These they could not consent to yield. Union or no union, they could not purchase the desired result by a compromise which bound them to a rigid interpretation of the last explication of the Adopting Act, and which placed the letter above the spirit of the Confession and on the same level of authority with the letter of the divine word.

In regard to Presbyteries, the New side insisted that they should remain constituted as they were at present till the way was open for a change for the better,—till "a favorable opportunity of advantageous alteration." The Old side were not disposed to yield this point. They were anxious to have "indemnity for the past" as well as security for the future, either by the disbanding of separate congregations, or their union under the pastor of the Old side.

This was indeed a difficult matter to settle; and it was evident that no Synodical arrangements would at once secure harmony or remove old differences. These, time and charity alone could heal. Yet the Synod of Philadelphia proposed (1751) that "all names of distinction should be forever abolished, and that Presbyteries be made up everywhere of ministers contiguous to each other," so that there should be no more "such party names as *old* and *new* Presbyteries, *old* and *new* congregations."

This was all well enough in theory; but the Synod of New York justly replied, that it seemed a "jarring discord to force people" into a union "faster than they had clearness to go." The "favorable opportunity" they did not apprehend would occur immediately upon the union of the Synods.

Thus, on the last point the two parties were not agreed. Instead of sending a reply, the Synod of Philadelphia (1754), noting "a very pacific temper in the members of both Synods," proposed a conference. This resulted in the approval, by the Synod of Philadelphia, of a plan of union of the two Synods as (now "two distinct judicatures") "two contiguous bodies of Christians, agreed in principle, as though they had never been concerned with one another before, nor had any differences, which is the truth as to great part of both Synods, and should now join the Synods and Presbyteries upon such scriptural and rational terms as may secure peace and good order, tend to heal our broken churches, and advance religion hereafter."

Thus, in 1755, every thing seemed in a fair way to union. In the following year, although the Synod of New York had not obtained full satisfaction in regard to the protest, they acceded to the request of the Synod of Philadelphia to appoint a Committee of Conference. Both the Tennents,—Gilbert and William,—Samuel Finley, Treat, and John Blair, were among the members appointed. This alone served to show the strong disposition in favor of union; for some of these had been the chief and original offenders.

At this conference the subject of the protest was satisfactorily disposed of, and the report given in to each Synod was favorably received. The arrangement was therefore made that the two Synods should have their next meeting at the same time and place, and, if matters should appear ripe for it, the union should be perfected.

Accordingly, the Synod of New York met in Philadelphia, May 25, 1758. The Synod of Philadelphia was already in session. The plan of union, as finally matured by the joint commissions of the two Synods who met on the 22d for conference, was laid before both bodies and unanimously approved. This approval was notified by each to the other, and on May 29 the two bodies were united as one, under the name of the Synod of New York and Philadelphia. The relative strength of the two bodies, thus united in one, was far different from what it was at the time of the protest. In 1742, the Synod of Philadelphia numbered, exclusive of New York Presbytery, twenty-six ministers; with them, thirty-eight. At the time of the union they were reduced to twenty-two. More had been lost by death and removal than had been gained by additions.

On the other hand, the Synod of New York had a list of seventy ministers, thus outnumbering the Old side in the proportion of more than three to one. Numbering at first but eight or ten, even with their licentiates included, the New side was nearly doubled by the accession of New York Presbytery in 1745; and from that period they had rapidly increased.

Thus, on the formation of the united Synod it numbered ninety-four ministers,—of whom forty-two were present and fifty-two absent. There were also fourteen elders who took their seats in the united Synod. It thus composed at its first session an assembly of fifty-six members; and among them were many whose names are worthy of lasting remembrance. Gilbert Tennent, now removed to the pastorate of a church in Philadelphia, was moderator. Bostwick, who had succeeded Pemberton at New York,—Rodgers, who was afterward to be transferred to the same field,—Richards, at Rahway,—the Finleys, Duffield, and Samuel Davies, were among the members present. Dickinson did not survive to witness the result for which his soul ardently longed. He had been cut off by death in 1747, in the very meridian of his years and usefulness.

A far different scene was now presented in Philadelphia from that which was witnessed upon the formation of the first Presbytery, a little more than half a century before. The Church was then struggling for existence. It was persecuted both in Virginia and New York, and had scarcely a foothold in either province. A few feeble churches on the Eastern Shore of Maryland, one or two in Delaware, one in Philadelphia, and one or two in New Jersey, composed its entire strength. Now it numbered nearly one hundred ministers, and more than as many churches. The field of its operations had been vastly extended. Virginia, the Carolinas, the destitute but rapidly settling portions of Pennsylvania and New Jersey, as well as the river counties of New York, were calling upon it for aid. It was inviting laborers from abroad,—from New England, Scotland, and Ireland,—and training them up at home. Princeton College had gone into successful operation.

Alison was at the head of the College of Pennsylvania; and quite a number of the ministers were engaged at once in pastoral duty, and in training pious young men to meet the demands of the churches.

CHAPTER VII.

PRESBYTERIANISM IN VIRGINIA.

SCARCELY had Makemie gone to his rest, when another portion of Virginia, far distant from that which had been the scene of his labors, opened an inviting field for Presbyterian missionary effort. The Virginia government encouraged immigration along its frontier settlements, where the hardy pioneers might serve as a defence against the incursions of the Indian tribes. There was no question now raised in regard to their faith and order. If they could carry a rifle, or plant along the western forest a line of protection against savage inroads, they were sufficiently orthodox. Their distance, moreover, from the settlements on the Eastern Shore, prevented any umbrage being taken at a dissent which did not attract notice or give offence. Thus, in obscurity and neglect, Presbyterianism, in spite of Virginia laws, planted itself unmolested west of the Blue Ridge. Germans, Quakers, and Irish Presbyterians, from Pennsylvania, took possession of the county of Frederick. A great part of this region was of the most inviting kind. Between the North Mountain and the Shenandoah extended at that time a spacious prairie, barren of timber, but clothed with the richest herbage. It was traversed by herds of buffalo, elk, and deer, and furnished the Indians a favorite hunting-ground.

Into this region there poured a mixed population, leavened by a Presbyterian element; while still beyond it, more to the southwest, the county of Augusta was almost exclusively occupied by a Scotch-Irish population. Among the names of the early settlers we find not a few which have since become eminent in the history of the Church. It is enough to mention those of McDowell, Alexander, Lyle, Stuart, Matthews, Crawford, Campbell, Moore, Brown, Wallace, Patton, Wilson, Caruthers, Cummins, and McKee.

These "Presbyterians of the valley" were a bold, hardy, perhaps austere, but religiously disposed population. More fortunate than their brethren east of the mountains, they were left unmolested in the exercise of their religious freedom. As early as 1719, "the people of Potomoke," near the present town of Martinsburg, were supplied, at their request, with preaching, by the Synod of Philadelphia. Rev. Daniel Magill was appointed to visit them, but, although not settled among them as pastor, he organized a church and labored in the region for several months. In 1732, Joist Hite, with sixteen families from Pennsylvania, fixed his residence at Opeckon, a few miles south of the present site of Winchester. Other families were scattered on Cedar Creek and Crooked Run. In 1734, Michael Woods, from Ireland, with a large family, settled near Wood's Gap in Albemarle, and his descendants were the founders of the Mountain Plain congregation. From this period the tide of immigration flowed in, in a steady stream. Settlements were soon formed, mostly by Presbyterians, in Jefferson county, on Cub Creek in Charlotte, on Buffalo Creek in Prince Edward, at Concord and Hat Creek in Campbell, and at Rockfish in Nelson. Congregations were gathered at Opeckon,

Timber Ridge, Back Creek in Berkeley, Forks of James in Rockbridge, and Triple Forks of the Shenandoah.

In 1738, the congregations had become so numerous, and the necessity of ministers so urgent, that application was made to the Synod of Philadelphia for aid. In response to the appeal, John Craig was sent to labor with the joint congregations of Tinkling Spring and Augusta, and for twenty-five years this pioneer laborer occupied his post. But already he had been preceded by those who had transiently visited this region in the character of missionaries. James Gelston had been sent out in 1737 by the Presbytery of Donegal, and had labored at Opeckon. James Anderson, despatched by the Synod to confer with Governor Gooch on the subject of liberty for Dissenters, had visited several settlements, preaching as he went. This was in 1738.[1] In the next year he was followed by Dunlap, a probationer of New York Presbytery, who spent nearly three months in the neighborhood of Staunton. In the same year, John Thompson, of Donegal Presbytery, itinerated through the settlements of the whole region, and by his influence, upon his return, Craig was sent to occupy the post at Augusta and Tinkling Spring.

---

[1] Anderson's mission was quite successful. In 1739, he reported to Synod that he had waited on the Governor of Virginia with the Synod's address, and received a favorable answer. The substance of this is contained in a letter from the Governor to the moderator of Synod. In this letter he says, "As I have always been inclined to favor the people who have lately removed from other provinces to settle on the western side of our great mountains, so you may be assured that no interruption shall be given to any minister of your profession who shall come among them, so as they conform themselves to the rules prescribed by the Act of Toleration in England, by taking the oaths enjoined thereby and registering the places of their meeting, and behave themselves peaceably towards the Government. This you may please to communicate to the Synod as an answer of theirs."—*Minutes of Synod*, 147.

Scarcely was he settled, when the division of the Synod occurred (1741). He, in common with most of the Presbyterians west of the Blue Ridge, espoused the cause of the Old side. In some respects this was unfortunate for them. The Old side were weak, and unable to occupy the missionary fields which opened before them. They had few ministers or licentiates. For several years the only one whom they could send to Virginia, as a fellow-laborer with Craig, was Alexander Miller,[1]—a man who had already been put on trial for drunkenness, lying, sedition, and "opposing the work of God, then in progress in neighboring congregations." Yet for him—though we must hope that he was a better man after his trial—the congregations of North and South Mountain, in Virginia, made application in 1745.

From this time the visits of Presbyterian clergymen were more frequent. The celebrated John Blair itinerated among the congregations of the Valley in 1745 and 1746. William Robinson and John Roan, although their attention was mainly directed to the region east of the Ridge, did not altogether neglect them. But by the middle of the century the population of the Valley had increased so rapidly as to have far outstripped the supply of the means of grace. Their destitution was a subject of anxiety to both the Synods. That of Philadelphia, unable to afford supplies, made application for aid to the General Assembly of the Church of Scotland. That of New York applied for assistance to the Eastern Association of Fairfield, in Connecticut. The sympathies of the two bodies are manifest in their respective applications.

Yet they were not themselves idle. The Synod of Philadelphia sent out, among others, to the vacant congregations, Francis Alison and John Craig,—the last

---

[1] Webster, 618; and Foote's Sketches.

already mentioned as settled as a pastor at Tinkling Spring and Augusta. In 1753, John Brown, of the New side, took charge of the united congregations of New Providence and Timber Ridge. The Presbyterians of the Valley were thus divided between the two Synods; but the superior activity and numbers of the New side were giving them a decided advantage when the reunion of the two parties took place in 1758.

From this period, the growth of Presbyterianism in Virginia was more rapid. Hanover Presbytery was formed in 1755, comprising in it all the ministers of Virginia, except John Hoge, of Opeckon, and one or two others, west of the mountains. Amid difficulty and discouragement it prosecuted its work. The intolerant laws of the province were a sore grievance. As an Episcopal church was built in each county town, it was but natural that the Presbyterians should locate their houses of worship elsewhere. Till after the commencement of the Revolution, there was not in the Valley a single village which had a Presbyterian church-edifice.[1] The oldest congregations were all in the country, amid a sparse population; and near by, in quiet solitude, was the enclosed grave-yard.

The first houses of worship which were erected were rude wooden structures; but they were sanctified by hallowed associations, and were endeared to the worshippers by attractions beyond those of mere architecture. When, at a later period, they were replaced by more commodious and commanding structures, the new erection was a monument to the pious zeal and self-denial of the builders. The difficulties to be overcome, where the heavy timbers had to be dragged, sometimes without the aid of wheels, for a distance, and the sand for plastering had to be brought in sacks

---

[1] Captives of Abb's Valley, p. 14.

on horseback for several miles, may be better imagined than described.

But these were not the only hardships which the settlers had to meet. On the frontiers of civilization, they stood in constant dread of the savage foe. Warlike tribes, revisiting their old hunting-grounds, exulted to take vengeance upon the white man for his intrusion upon what they still considered their own domain. British agents incited them during the war to assault the feeble settlements. Amid the quiet loveliness of nature, and within the sheltering scenes of the Valley, horrid tragedies of barbarous ferocity were enacted. The solitary settler knew not when the terrible blow would fall that was to desolate his dwelling and perhaps doom himself or his household to captivity or death. There was not a little to remind him of the hardships of his ancestry in times when Londonderry and Enniskillen were household words. We cannot doubt that the impending terror and the stern tuition of his frontier life gave a peculiar tinge to his devotion, and we know that amid the scenes of the Valley were trained some of the noblest pioneers of Presbyterianism in the new regions of Kentucky and Tennessee.

The rise of Presbyterianism in Hanover is inseparably connected with what is known by tradition as *Morris's Reading-House.* This was the first of several buildings in that region, erected to accommodate those who were dissatisfied with the preaching of the parish incumbents, and anxious to enjoy the privilege of listening on the Sabbath to the reading of instructive and devotional works on religion. The origin of this movement was somewhat singular. The people had, for the most part, never heard or seen a Presbyterian minister. But reports had reached them of revivals in Pennsylvania, New Jersey, and New England. A few leaves of Boston's *Fourfold State*, in the possession of a Scotchwoman, fell into the hands of a gentleman, who was so affected by their perusal that he sent to England by the next ship to procure the entire work. The result of its perusal was his conversion. Another obtained possession of *Luther on Galatians;* he, in like manner, was deeply affected, and ceased not to read and pray till he found peace in Christ.

These persons, with two or three others,—all heads of families,—without previous consultation or conference, absented themselves at the same time from the worship of the parish church. They were convinced that the gospel was not preached by the parish minister, and they deemed it inconsistent with their duty to attend upon his ministrations. Four of them were summoned on the same day, and at the same place, to answer to the proper officers for their delinquency. For the first time they here learned their common views. Confirmed in them by this unexpected coincidence, they thenceforth chose to subject themselves to the payment of the fines imposed by law rather than attend church where they felt that they could not be profited.

They agreed at first to meet every Sabbath alternately at each other's houses, to read and pray. Soon their numbers increased. Curiosity attracted some, and religious anxiety others. The Scriptures, and Luther on Galatians, were first read. Afterward a volume of Whitefield's sermons fell into their hands (1743). "My dwelling-house," says Mr. Morris, "was at length too small to contain the people. We determined to build a meeting-house merely for reading." The result was that several were awakened and gave proof of genuine conversion. Mr. Morris was invited to several places, some of them at a considerable distance, to read the sermons which had been so effective in his own neighborhood. Thus the interest that had been awakened spread abroad.

The dignitaries of the Established Church saw the parish churches deserted, and took the alarm. They urged that indulgence encouraged the evil, and hence invoked the strong arm of the law to restrain it. The leaders in the movement were no longer regarded as individual delinquents, but a malignant cabal, and, instead of being arraigned merely before the magistrates, they were cited to appear before the Governor and Council.

Startled by the criminal accusation which was now directed against them, and of the nature, extent, and penalties of which they had indistinct conceptions, they had not even the name of a religious denomination under which to shelter their dissent. At length, recollecting that Luther, whose work occupied so much space in their public religious readings, was a noted reformer, they declared themselves Lutherans.

But it so happened that, on the way to Williamsburg to appear before the Governor, one of the company, detained by a violent storm at a house on the road, fell in with an old volume on a dust-covered shelf, which he read to while away the time. Amazed to find in it the expression of his own religious sentiments, so far as they had been definitely formed, he offered to purchase the book; but the owner gave it to him. At Williamsburg, he with his friends more carefully examined the work, and all were agreed that it expressed their own views. When they appeared before the Governor, therefore, they presented this old volume as their creed. The Governor, Gooch, himself of Scotch origin and education, looked at the volume, and found it to be the Confession of Faith of the Presbyterian Church of Scotland. He consequently denominated the men arraigned before him Presbyterians, and dismissed them with the gentle caution not to excite disturbance. One of the party firmly believed that this leniency on the part of the Governor and the Council was due, in part, to the impression made by a violent thunder-storm then shaking the house in which they were assembled, and wrapping every thing around them alternately in darkness and in sheeted flame.

The first Presbyterian minister who visited this region was William Robinson. In the winter of 1742–3, he was sent as an evangelist, by the Presbytery of New Castle, to visit the Presbyterian settlements in the Valley of the Shenandoah, and those on the south side of James River, as well as those on the plain in North Carolina. The Hanover Dissenters heard of him, and sent a deputation to invite him to come and preach. First satisfying themselves of the soundness of his principles, and being informed of the awakening character of his preaching, they were anxious to hear him. On July 6, 1743, they listened to the first sermon ever preached by a Presbyterian minister in Hanover county, Va. The congregation was large the first day, but it was vastly increased on the three following days. Many were awakened, and some converted, while scarce an individual of the large assembly remained unaffected. The four days of Mr. Robinson's stay were long remembered. The people wished to express their gratitude to him by presenting him a considerable sum of money. He refused to receive it. They urged it upon him, but he still refused. They then procured the secret conveyance of it into his saddle-bags, the evening before he was to leave. The increased weight of his baggage excited his suspicion. Discovering the benevolent artifice, he no longer declined receiving the money, but informed his kind friends that he would appropriate it to the use of a young man of his acquaintance who was studying for the ministry, but embarrassed in his circumstances. "As soon as he is licensed," he added, "we will send him to visit you: it may be that you may now, by your liberality, be educating a minister for yourselves."

This possibility was soon to become a reality; although Robinson did not live to see his prophecy fulfilled. That young man was Samuel Davies, and four years later (1747) he found his way to Hanover.

Meanwhile, the people were visited by Rev. John Blair, a younger brother of Rev. Samuel Blair, like him an alumnus of the Log College and a pupil of the elder William Tennent. He was ordained by the Presbytery of New Castle, a few months before Mr. Robinson's visit to Virginia, and from his parish in Cumberland county, Pa., made two missionary tours to the regions visited by Mr. Robinson. He preached with great power in various places, and organized several new congregations. Among the other regions visited by him in 1746, was the county of Hanover. The most remarkable effects followed his short stay. "His hearers, agitated beyond control, poured forth tears and sighs, and often broke out into loud crying." Opposers were roused to devise means to arrest the work. Absences from the parish church were more carefully noted, and the law was invoked to prevent apostasy from the ceremonies of the Church of England.

These efforts were put forth with more vigor in consequence of the visit of Rev. John Roan to this region. Less discreet than either Robinson or Blair, his bold, earnest, stirring appeals, commingled with rebukes of the clergy of the Established Church for neglect of their official duties, provoked animadversion. The result was the prosecution of Roan, and an order forbidding any meetings of "Moravians, Muggletonians, and New Lights." The prosecution, on the flight of the principal mover of it, was dropped, and, on the address of the Synods to the Governor, the order was rescinded. Gilbert Tennent and Samuel Finley, deputed by the Presbytery to visit Virginia as missionaries, were kindly received by the Governor, who gave them permission to preach in Hanover. Their visit was a season of refreshing. "Several careless sinners were awakened," and quite a number "who had trusted in their moral conduct and religious duties" were aroused from their security.

After the return of Tennent and Finley, the people of Hanover were visited by Whitefield. He came and preached four or five days, and his labors were favorably received and largely blessed. But after his departure these Presbyterians were not only destitute of a pastor, but were grievously harassed by the pains and penalties of the law. "Upon a Lord's day," says Mr. Morris, "a proclamation was set up at our meeting-house, strictly requiring all magistrates to suppress and prohibit, as far as they lawfully could, all itinerant preachers." For that day they were constrained "to forbear reading." But before the next Sabbath their fears were relieved. They received the glad intelligence that Mr. Davies was coming to preach among them,—that he had qualified himself according to law, and had obtained the licensing of four meeting-houses, —a thing "which had never been done before."

From this period a brighter prospect opened before them. The name of Hanover county was thenceforth to be ever associated with that of a man whom after-ages will delight to honor. Samuel Davies was born of Welsh ancestry, in New Castle county, Del., in 1723. His mother, in the judgment of filial reverence and affection, was "one of the most eminent saints he ever knew upon earth." His very name—Samuel—was given him in the spirit of Hannah of old. This early dedication to God had a powerful effect upon his own mind. In his childish years, habits of secret prayer were formed, and "he was more ardent in his supplications for being introduced into the gospel ministry than for any thing else." At the age of twelve years, he received impressions of a religious nature, that were abiding. In his fifteenth year he made a public profession of religion, and united with the Church. His classical course was commenced under the tuition of a Welsh minister by the name of Morgan.[1] When Rev. Samuel Blair opened his famous school at Fagg's Manor, young Davies was put under his charge.[2] The standard of classical attainment was high, and the acquisition of theological knowledge was sedulously encouraged. From the commencement of the course, Davies applied himself to his studies with zeal and energy. Aided by the means extended to him through Mr. Robinson by the people of Hanover, he felt strongly drawn toward them, and, when licensed by New Castle Presbytery, July 30, 1746, his first thoughts were turned in that direction. In little more than six months from the date of his licensure, he was ordained an evangelist for the purpose of visiting the congregations in Virginia, especially those in Hanover county. After some hesitation on the part of the Council, although the Governor favored his application, he received the license of the Government "to officiate in and about Hanover at four meeting-houses."[3]

Davies proceeded to Hanover, and "was received with an outburst of joy." His coming with his license was "like a visit from the angel of mercy." For several months he labored throughout the region with unremitted energy. His weak frame was prostrated

1 Sprague's Annals, iii. 40; Webster, 374, 549.

2 Life of Davies: Preface to his sermons. 3 Foote's Sketches.

under this burden of effort. He was forced at the close of the summer to return to Delaware, with greatly reduced health, and with strong indications that he was the subject of a confirmed consumption. Still, in spite of his weakness, he continued his labors on the Eastern Shore of Maryland—preaching during the day, even while he was so ill at night as to need persons to sit up with him.

In the spring of 1748, his health was somewhat improved, and there were slight prospects of his recovery. His services were instantly in demand. But the application from Hanover presented to his mind claims superior to any other. Accompanied by his intimate friend Mr.—afterward the celebrated Dr.—John Rodgers,[1] for whom he in vain endeavored to procure, of the Government, a license to preach, he directed his course to Hanover, and recommenced his labors. The field before him was a broad one, embracing not only the region about Hanover, but most of Virginia, and portions of North Carolina. But in many places the civil authorities placed obstacles in the way of Dissenting worship. Davies argued for freedom with characteristic boldness and vigor. He claimed, in controversy with Peyton Randolph, the king's attorney-general, that the English Act of Toleration for the relief of Protestant Dissenters extended to Virginia. On one occasion he appeared in person before the General Court, and replied to Randolph in a strain of eloquence that is reported to have won the admiration of the most earnest of his opponents, who said that in him "a good lawyer had been spoiled." He persevered in his efforts in the cause of toleration, till, crossing the ocean, he had the opportunity to bring the

[1] Rodgers was banished from the colony, and returned and settled in St. George's, Del.

matter before the king in council, and received a declaration, under authority, that the Act of Toleration did extend to the colony of Virginia.

Davies went to Hanover with the feeling that he was a dying man. He hoped that he "might live to prepare the way for some more useful successor." But, with a hallowed ambition, he desired, before his lips were closed in death, to win some few more, at least, as the seals of his ministry. "He longed to carry with him to the heavens some gems for the eternal crown." Lifted above all earthly considerations, all fear of consequences, and standing, as he believed, almost face to face with eternity, he prepared to deliver his solemn message.

A blessing followed his labors. The desire to hear the young Dissenter whom a large part of the Council had wished to keep out of Virginia, and whose license they would have revoked but for the influence of the Governor, spread in every direction. People rode from great distances to attend upon his ministry. To avoid collision with the public authorities, resolutely bent on executing the laws in favor of the Established Church, petitions from different neighborhoods for an increased number of authorized houses of worship were laid before the General Court. The petitions were granted, and three new places of preaching were added to the four already occupied by Davies. The seven were located, three in Hanover, one in Henrico, one in Goochland, one in Louisa, and one in Carolina. The nearest were twelve or fifteen miles from each other, and "some of the people have thirty or forty miles to the nearest." The extreme points of Davies's parish were eighty or ninety miles apart.

The county court of New Kent gave license, upon the petition of a number of inhabitants, for Davies to preach in St. Peter's parish, but the General Court annulled the proceeding, and the license was revoked.

In spite of opposition, however, the influence and fame of Davies were spreading far and wide. The meeting-house near his own residence (twelve miles from Richmond, and near *Morris's Reading-House*) was quite too small for the multitudes which assembled in pleasant weather. "The thick woods were then resorted to; and the opposers of the Dissenters were exasperated at the sight of crowds listening to the gospel in the deep shades of the forest." All classes were alike interested. Even the negroes, of whom Mr. Davies baptized forty during the first three years, crowded to listen. "Sometimes," said he, "I see a hundred and more among my hearers."[1]

The report of this state of things went abroad, and gladdened the hearts of Christians of New England. "I heard lately," writes Jonathan Edwards (May 23, 1749), "a credible account of a remarkable work of conviction and conversion among whites and negroes, at Hanover, Va., under the ministry of Mr. Davies, who is lately settled there, and has the character of a very ingenious and pious young man." To many others, the intelligence was not less cheering than to the great preacher of Northampton. Here, then (1750), a little more than a hundred years ago, is the picture of Presbyterianism in Virginia. Among the Scotch-Irish emigrants along the frontier counties and in the Valley of the Shenandoah, there were five congregations without a settled pastor and dependent upon such temporary supplies as the Synod could send them. In five counties around and including Hanover, there were seven preaching-stations, supplied by the labors of a single pastor, feeble in health, but zealous, eloquent, and unremitting in his exertions. Even he had to encounter a strong adverse influence and the intolerant

[1] Foote's Sketches.

measures of the Colonial Government. In vain was the earnest appeal addressed to Presbytery and Synod for more laborers. All that could be done was to send itinerants to labor for a few weeks, or possibly months, among the destitute and frontier settlements.

Thus Davies was left alone. "In the whole 'Ancient Dominion' he had no fellow-laborer with whom his heart might rejoice. West of the Blue Ridge there were Miller[1] and Craig, and on its eastern base, at the head of Rockfish, Mr. Black; but these were members of the Synod of Philadelphia, and for some years had no communication with Mr. Davies." The task devolved upon him was overwhelming. He felt the demand to be one which was imperative, and he did his best to meet it. He preached not only on the Sabbath, but on week-days, to "laboring people, of whom the Dissenters were mostly composed." He exerted himself to procure other laborers to enter the field. Rodgers, who had accompanied him, and in whom he had hoped to find an efficient ally and a sympathizing brother, had been denied a license by the Government Council. The needs of the field were repeatedly laid before the Synod. In 1749, it met at Maidenhead, and, upon representation of the circumstances of Virginia, "Mr. Davenport is appointed, if he recover a good state of health, to go and supply." The next year the Synod recommended to the Presbytery of New Brunswick "to endeavor to prevail with Mr. John Todd, upon his being licensed, to take a journey thither, as also to the Presbytery of New York to urge the same upon Messrs. Syms and Greenman. Mr. Davenport is appointed to go into Virginia to assist in supplying the numerous vacant and destitute congregations there. The same is also recommended to Mr. Byram."

---

[1] Alexander Miller was not installed until August 1, 1757.

The visit of Davenport was a profitable one. "Blessed be God," writes Davies to Dr. Bellamy, "he did not labor in vain." Todd became (November 12, 1752) the assistant of Davies, and, after his acceptance of the presidency at Princeton, the leading man in the Hanover Presbytery east of the Blue Ridge. Byram, who had accompanied Brainerd in his first journey to the Susquehanna, and who is mentioned by him with much affection as a kindred spirit, visited Virginia, but did not remain long. The petition of Todd to be qualified to officiate in Hanover county was procured with great difficulty, and the Council absolutely refused to license any more meeting-houses. In spite, however, of all restrictions, the missionary tours of Davies in the surrounding counties were frequent and extensive. He preached at the places where he lodged, and "many neighborhoods have traditions of his usefulness. Every visit enlarged his circuit, and increased the number of places that asked for Presbyterian preaching."

In 1752, Davies met the Synod of New York in its sessions at Newark. He represented before it the destitution of Virginia, and Mr. Greenman and Mr. Robert Henry were appointed to go there during the course of the year. Greenman was a young man who had been educated at the charge of David Brainerd; and Henry was a recent graduate of New Jersey College.

Just at this period a messenger from Virginia to Jonathan Edwards, at Stockbridge, invited him—with a handsome subscription for his encouragement and support—to settle in Virginia, in the neighborhood of Davies. But he was installed at Stockbridge before the messenger came. This was the main obstacle to his removal. Speaking with reference to a connection with the Presbyterian Church, he said (July 5, 1750), "As to my subscribing to the substance of the Westminster Confession, there would be no difficulty; and as to the Presbyterian government, I have long been perfectly out of conceit of our unsettled, independent, confused way of church government in this land, and the Presbyterian way has ever appeared to me most agreeable to the word of God and the reason and nature of things."

We will not pause to dwell upon the results that might have followed the transfer of Edwards to Virginia. In conjunction with Davies, his influence would unquestionably have been widely felt. But, failing to secure his services for the people whom he had encouraged, doubtless, to make the application, Davies set himself to work to supply, as far as he was able, the lack of ministerial service in other ways. He multiplied his own preaching excursions, extending them to the eastern base of the Blue Ridge; he sought to enlist the interest of members of Northern Presbyteries in the Virginia field, and, beside all, to raise up preachers of the gospel in Virginia. He promoted classical schools wherever their establishment promised usefulness, and encouraged and assisted pious youths in their preparatory course. Among those largely indebted to him, who afterward attained to usefulness and distinction, were John Wright, Patillo, of Carolina memory, John Martin, the first licentiate of Hanover Presbytery, William Richardson, the celebrated James Waddel, and James Hunt.

Thus devoted, unwearied, sagacious, and energetic in his efforts, Davies multiplied himself into a host. Everywhere he proved himself equal to his position, ready for the emergency. "He seems," as one said of him on seeing him pass through a court-yard, "as an ambassador of some mighty king." He was at once the champion of freedom, the friend of learning, the founder of churches, and, next to Whitefield, the most eloquent preacher of his age.

CHAPTER VIII.

THE SYNODS AND THEIR SCHOOLS.

FROM the period of the division in 1741, each branch of the Church was intent upon making provision to train up young men for the ministry. The importance of prompt and efficient measures for this object was especially felt by the members of the Synod of New York. The destitution around them called aloud for laborers, and after Brainerd's expulsion from Yale College, and the refusal of the corporation to grant him his degree, notwithstanding his humble confession of his error, it was felt that circumstances demanded that another institution should be established; to be located within the bounds of the Presbyterian Church.

The prominent mover in the enterprise was Jonathan Dickinson, of Elizabethtown, N.J. He settled at this place in 1708, although he did not join the Philadelphia Presbytery until 1717.[1] For many years he had been accustomed to receive young men for instruction in the different branches preparatory to their entering upon the study of some one of the liberal professions. He was, consequently, fully aware of the importance and necessity of a thorough education He had, moreover, before the division, been the acknowledged leader of the old Synod, and he was no less the leader of the Synod of New York after the separation. His commanding influence, large experience, and intellectual

[1] Sprague's Annals, iii. 14.

superiority marked him out as the individual fittest to preside in so important an undertaking. Under his counsels a charter was procured for a college from Governor Hamilton, and the infant institution went into operation at Elizabethtown, with Dickinson at its head. Continuing still the discharge of his pastoral duties, he took charge also of the instruction and discipline of the students. It was, however, only for a brief twelvemonth that he was permitted to occupy this important post. The charter was given in October, 1746, and his death occurred October 7, 1747.

This, at the outset, was a great loss. Dickinson was no common man. Those who have read his writings need no other proof of it. Dr. John Erskine, of Edinburgh, said that the British Isles had produced no such writers on Divinity in the eighteenth century as Dickinson and Edwards. Bellamy, who knew him well, spoke of him as "the great Mr. Dickinson."

A successor for him was found, however, in Aaron Burr, pastor at Newark.[1] Burr had been called to New Haven as a colleague of Noyes, but declined the call. For nearly ten years he had been settled in his present charge, and had given proof of his ability and fitness for the vacant post. He had under his charge already a large Latin school, when Dickinson's students were removed from Elizabethtown and put under his charge. A new charter was procured for the college, and Burr was appointed President under it in November, 1748. On the same day he conferred the Bachelor's degree upon a class who were prepared to receive it. The corporation record states that he delivered upon the occasion, as his Inaugural, "a handsome and elegant Latin oration."

Until the autumn of 1755, the college was located

---

[1] Sprague's Annals, iii. 68; Webster, 448.

at Newark,[1] and Burr continued to discharge the double duty of pastor of the church and President of the institution. But in the course of the following year, buildings having been erected at Princeton for the accommodation of the students, and Burr having been dismissed from his pastoral charge, the college went into operation under his presidency, in the place where it has since been permanently located.[2]

---

[1] The first entry in the minutes of the College of New Jersey is a copy of the charter granted by Governor Belcher. The next states that "on Thursday, October 13, 1748, convened at New Brunswick, James Hude, Andrew Johnston, Thomas Leonard, Esqs., Mr. William P. Smith, and Rev. Messrs. John Pierson, Ebenezer Pemberton, Joseph Lamb, William Tennent, Richard Treat, David Cowell? Aaron Burr, Timothy Johnes, and Thomas Arthur, thirteen of them nominated in the charter to be trustees of the college; who, having accepted the charter, were qualified and incorporated according to the directions thereof." November 9, Governor Belcher, Messrs. Peter Van Brugh Livingston, Samuel Hazard, and Rev. Messrs. Samuel Blair and Jacob Green, were qualified as additional trustees. Burr was chosen President, and the first commencement was held the same day. There were six graduates.

For several years the students were scattered in private families in Newark, the public academical exercises being generally performed in the county court-house. Governor Belcher at length urged the erection of the college edifice, although the funds were so scanty that but for his advice and aid the enterprise would have been deemed impracticable. At a meeting at Newark, September 27, 1752, he advised the trustees to proceed immediately to determine upon a location for the college. The people of New Brunswick not having complied with the terms proposed to them for fixing the college in that place, it was voted that it should be established in Princeton, upon condition that the inhabitants of said place secure to the trustees two hundred acres of woodland, ten acres of cleared land, and £1000 of *proclamation* money, all which is to be complied with in three months. On January 24, 1753, it was announced that the conditions were fulfilled.—*Am. Quar. Reg.* Aug. 1834.

[2] The college building was for some years the largest college

But the means for effecting this change of location, and placing the institution upon a solid basis, were procured with some difficulty. The Synod, in 1752,[1] ordered collections in the churches on its behalf, and besought Pemberton, of New York, to cross the ocean and advocate its claims in Scotland and England. He declined the mission, and the Synod then selected Gilbert Tennent and Samuel Davies in his place.[2] A better choice could scarcely have been made, although Virginia was exceedingly reluctant to relinquish the services of her favorite preacher. The deputation was kindly received abroad. Davies especially was greeted with welcome, and his reputation as a pulpit orator was established as securely in England as in Virginia. Funds were collected from Presbyterian and other Dissenters in England, and from the churches in Scotland, and the college was placed on a secure basis.[3]

But already it began to be known by its fruits. It promised to realize the fond anticipations of its founders. Although hitherto without a fixed location, without permanent funds, library, apparatus, faculty, or building, it had a noble President, and had been sending out graduates. When Davies and Tennent set out for England (1753), it numbered already fifty graduates, twenty-six of whom entered the ministry. Of these, five went to Virginia, and one became a pioneer missionary in North Carolina.

A notice of the mission of Davies and Tennent to England is important as illustrating the mutual relations of the Presbyterian Church in this country and of the churches of Great Britain. They embarked on

---

structure in the United States. It was first named Belcher Hall, but the Governor declined the honor, and suggested instead of it Nassau Hall. It accommodated nearly one hundred and fifty students.

[1] Minutes of Synod, 248. [2] Ibid. 252. [3] Foote's Sketches.

their voyage for England, November 18, 1753, and in just one month anchored in the Downs.[1] Eighty pounds had been handed them by the treasurer of the college to bear their expenses. It is illustrative of the character of Davies, as well as the feeble resources of the American churches, to read in his diary, just before receiving the money,—"Was uneasy to find that the trustees seem to expect that I should furnish myself with clothes in this embassy. With what pleasure would I do it were it in my power! but, alas! it is not; and therefore, notwithstanding all the pliableness of my nature, I *must* insist upon their providing for me in *this* respect, as one condition of my undertaking the voyage." It may be that the sum advanced was raised to eighty pounds to meet this necessity.

Before Davies embarked, he was surprised at a clause in a letter which was shown him from Dr. Berdt, of London, to Colonel Grant, of Philadelphia, to the effect "that the principles inculcated in the College of New Jersey are generally looked upon as antiquated and unfashionable by the Dissenters in England." It gave him premonition of a kind of difficulty he would have to encounter, which until then he had not anticipated. But upon reaching England, he found the statement of Dr. Berdt only too true. His severest trials were from the degeneracy of the children of the Puritans.

His first saddening intelligence was from his correspondent, Mr. Gibbons, "who informed us of the general apostasy of the Dissenters from the principles of the Reformation." "The Presbyterians, particularly," says Davies, "being generally Arminians or Socinians, seem shy of us." A more welcome reception awaited the deputation "at the Amsterdam Coffee-House, where

---

[1] For a full account of the mission, see Foote's Sketches; also, life of Davies, in the American Quarterly Register, 1837.

the Congregationalist and Baptist ministers met on Tuesdays."

The difficulties to be encountered were by no means of a trifling nature. Several, upon whom they had depended, told them that they could do nothing for them. Objection was made to the college as "a party design; that though the charter was catholic, yet so many of the trustees were Presbyterians, that they would manage matters with arbitrary partiality; that the trustees in New York City complained that there were not more trustees of other denominations." Mr. Jackson was "afraid our college would fall into Episcopal hands." Tennent, moreover, was confronted with his Nottingham sermon, which "the inveterate malignity of the Synod of Philadelphia," as Davies phrases it, had forwarded, with accompanying accusations against its author, to obstruct the success of the undertaking.

Tennent promptly disavowed the divisive principles of his sermon, and confessed his errors. Davies was perplexed and mortified at these unexpected embarrassments. But, with prudence and sagacity, he was enabled in great measure to overcome them.

Still, among those upon whom they had counted as friends of their enterprise, there were not a few who disapproved of all subscriptions or tests of orthodoxy. Among these was one whose name was of great importance,—Mr. Chandler. He even objected to the Adopting Act. He was at last won over to give his name and contribution to the cause. Others very reluctantly endorsed it. "Dr. Benson talked in a sneering manner of the account of conversions in Northampton," published in England by Drs. Watts and Guise. When he subscribed, it was "with this sneer, that he was no friend to subscriptions." Mr. Bradbury, whom Whitefield had once reproved for singing a song in a tavern, was "a man of a singular turn, which would be offensive to the greatest number of serious people." With Mr. Thompson, Jr., who, though educated a strict Calvinist, had imbibed "the modern latitudinarian principles," Davies had an amicable dispute about the lawfulness and expediency of subscribing tests of orthodoxy beside the Scripture. Mr. Bowles told him he had heard that Davies's sermon, preached for Mr. Chandler, had been complained of as "too rigidly orthodox." The estimate formed by the Calvinistic clergy, of the Salter's Hall divines, may be judged of by the pun of one of them when requested to print his sermon on the text, "Salt is good," etc. He replied that "he believed he would, and dedicate it to the preachers at Salter's Hall, for they wanted seasoning." Mr. Prior told Davies, "with the appearance of great uneasiness," that he had heard "we would admit none into the ministry without subscribing the Westminster Confession, and that this report would hinder all our success among the friends of liberty." Davies's reply shows with what propriety the fathers of American Presbyterianism have been represented as *ipsissima verba* men. "I replied," he says, "that we allowed the candidate to mention his objections against any article in the Confession, and the judicature judged whether the articles objected against were essential to Christianity; and if they judged they were not, they would admit the candidate, notwithstanding his objections." "Alas," exclaims Davies, "for the laxness that prevails here among the Presbyterians!"

Indeed, English Presbyterians no longer deserved the name. The Presbyterian standards had been thrown aside. All tests of orthodoxy were universally rejected. Candidates at ordination were only required to declare their belief of the Scriptures. Presbyterian order and discipline had fallen into total neglect. Calvinistic preachers chose rather to consort with the Independents and Baptists at Amsterdam Coffee-House, than with their brethren of the same name. Indeed, there was nothing like government exercised jointly by either body of Dissenters. The only associations of the Independents were their meetings at the Coffee-House, where they assembled "for friendly conversation. The Presbyterians have no other Presbyteries. The English Presbyterians have no elders nor judicatories of any kind." It may easily be perceived that the title by which they were known was a misnomer. Grave errors had crept in among them; but the presence of these errors was favored, not by Presbyterian discipline, but by its utter absence.

Repeatedly the members of the deputation were overwhelmed by discouragement. Tennent's trial, however, was peculiar. His Nottingham sermon preceded and embarrassed him wherever he went. Once and again he wished himself back in Philadelphia. After a month's stay in London, Davies writes, "From the present view of things, I think if we can but clear our expenses we shall be well off."

But light had begun to break in at last. Davies was cheered by the interest which English Dissenters took in the hardships of their brethren in Virginia, and the prospect of that relief to obtain which had been a main consideration in inducing him to accept the appointment of the trustees. Friends to the college were found, moreover, in unlooked-for quarters. In spite of Mr. Cross's letters, the representations emanating from the hostility of the Philadelphia Synod, and the prejudice excited by the Nottingham sermon, the friends of the enterprise increased every day. The Presbyterians were not very hearty in the cause, but they generally subscribed. At "the Amsterdam Coffee-House, among the Baptist and Independent ministers," Davies enjoyed most satisfaction. At "Hamlin's, among the Presbyterians," he says, "they are generally very shy and unsociable to me." But his tact, prudence, and perseverance overcame great difficulties. "A larger account of the college" was drawn up and circulated for the satisfaction of contributors. By April 7, 1754, twelve hundred pounds were already secured. This was an unexpected success. Davies, upon his arrival, had felt that "we could not raise our hopes above three hundred pounds." Yet before he and Tennent had set out for Scotland, the amount had risen to seventeen hundred pounds.

Scotland did not at first appear a very inviting field for effort. There was reason to apprehend the influence of the representations of the Synod of Philadelphia upon the minds of the members of the Assembly. *Moderatism*, moreover, was triumphant throughout the Church. "Alas!" exclaims Davies, "there appears but little of the spirit of serious Christianity among the young clergy." Yet it was exceedingly important to secure the Assembly's approval of the design of the college. "It will be attended," says Davies, "with many happy consequences; particularly it will recommend our college to the world, and wipe off the odium from the Synod of New York as a parcel of schismatics."

Although "there was hardly ever a greater appearance of opposition," the measure in favor of the college passed the Assembly unanimously. There was not even the show of objection. The cause was advocated by Lumisden, Divinity professor at Aberdeen. He urged the importance of a learned ministry, the necessity of the College of New Jersey to this end, and the duty of the Assembly to promote such institutions, especially among the Presbyterians of the colonies, "who are," said he, "a part of ourselves, having adopted the same standard of doctrine, worship, and government with this Church." A national collection was ordered in the Scottish Church, and Tennent crossed the Channel to present the cause in Ireland at the General Synod.

Davies now retraced his steps to England, in order to visit the principal towns. Before he set out, however, he read with admiration a piece, newly published, under the title of "*Ecclesiastical Characteristics*," ascribed "to one Mr. Weatherspoon, a young minister." He describes it as "a burlesque upon the high-flyers, under the ironical name of *moderate men;* and I think," says he, "the humor is nothing inferior to Dean Swift." That young minister was to be Davies's worthy successor in the presidency of the college.

Borne down by an almost constant depression of spirits, Davies was yet incessantly active. At nearly every place at which he stopped, he was invited to preach, and was listened to by admiring crowds. Yet his own estimate of his efforts is very humble. Many passages which had been most effective among his Virginia congregations, he was compelled to omit. His flagging spirit would not allow him to deliver what rose above the measure of his own present spiritual condition. At Glasgow he preached six times in ten days. Here, as well as at Edinburgh and London, he was urgently solicited to publish a collection of his sermons.

Returning to England, Davies again found friends where least expected. The Bishop of Durham gave him five guineas. He was cheered by intelligence from Tennent that the General Synod would take up collections within their bounds. The observations, however, which he made upon the condition of the Dissenters saddened him. At Hull he says, "The word *orthodox* is a subject of ridicule with many here." The Presbyterians had "gone off from the good old doctrines of the Reformation." At Leeds he found that the Dissenting ministers had "so generally imbibed

Arminian or Socinian sentiments, that it was hard to unite prudence and faithfulness in conversation with them." Admitting their learning, candor, good sense, and morality, their entertaining and instructive companionship, as well as friendship "to the liberty of mankind," he adds, "they deny the proper divinity and satisfaction of Jesus Christ, on which my hopes are founded. The greatest part of the Presbyterian ministers in England," so far as he had observed, had fallen into this fundamental and fatal error. In consequence, they regarded his cause generally with lukewarmness, if not with coldness. "The new-fangled notions," and apostasy from "the old-fashioned faith," seriously obstructed his success. Sometimes, indeed, the difficulty was from another quarter. At Nottingham, "some of the rigid Calvinists," he says, were "not pleased with my sermon, because not explicit on original sin. How impossible," he adds, "to please men!" Yet he collected at Nottingham over sixty pounds.

By the 5th of October, 1754, Tennent had executed his mission to Ireland, and succeeded in collecting about five hundred pounds. He joined Davies in London, and on the 13th of November embarked for Philadelphia. Davies, who wished to go at once to Virginia, waited a few days longer for a vessel, and on the 18th—just twelve months from his embarkation from America—set out on his return voyage. The mission had been eminently successful. The collections must have risen to between four and five thousand pounds. It was far above what either member of the deputation had dared to hope. It placed the College of New Jersey upon a sure basis, and cheered the hearts of all friendly to the interests of ministerial or liberal education and the Presbyterian Church.

It was not long after Davies's return from England

before he was called to make another sacrifice, not inferior to the one which he had already made as member of the deputation to England, and in the same cause. President Burr died suddenly, in the vigor of his years, in 1757, and his father-in-law, the great Jonathan Edwards, was chosen as his successor. The latter was inaugurated February 16, 1758, but died on the 22d of the following March. James Lockwood, pastor at Wethersfield, Conn., was chosen to fill the place, but want of unanimity, and other circumstances, prevented his acceptance. All eyes were now turned toward Mr. Davies as the man for the vacant post. He submitted the application to Presbytery, and the decision was against his removal from Virginia. The trustees now applied to the Synod, and urged their interference. By them, after solemn deliberation, Mr. Davies was dismissed from his people to assume the presidency of Nassau Hall.

He accepted the post with great reluctance. It was hard for him to part from a people with whom it was in his heart to live and die. But duty called, and he could not hesitate. Yet his public career was short. He preached his farewell to his people in Hanover, June 1, 1759, was inaugurated July 26, 1759, and on February 4, 1761, he took his farewell of earth. Yet he lived to see the success of the most important enterprise in which the Presbyterian Church had yet engaged, fully assured.

While the Synod of New York was thus engaged in laying the foundations of the College of Nassau Hall, the Synod of Philadelphia was not idle. In 1739, John Thompson, a leading man of the Old side, proposed to the Presbytery of Donegal the erection of a school, to be placed under the care of the Synod. The design was approved by the latter body in May of the same year. Pemberton, Dickinson, Cross, and Anderson were nominated to prosecute the design, and secure subscriptions in New England and in Europe. The co-operation of the Boston clergy was assured through Dr. Coleman, but the breaking out of the Spanish war in the following year prevented the prosecution of the design.

In 1743, two years after the division, the business was resumed. The next year the Synod approved the design and took the school at New London, Pa., under its care. It was to be supported by annual contributions from the congregations, and "all persons who please, may send their children and have them instructed *gratis* in languages, philosophy, and divinity." Francis Alison, the finest scholar in the two Synods, was appointed master, and authorized to appoint his own usher. He was to be allowed by the Synod twenty pounds per annum, and his assistant fifteen pounds. Several ministers and gentlemen contributed books to begin a library,—in this respect imitating the example of the founders of Yale.

In 1749, the plan of the school was modified. Mr. Alison's salary was increased, and tuition was allowed. In 1752, he removed to Philadelphia to take charge of the academy there. The school received a check by his removal, although it continued in operation under the care of Alexander McDowell, to whom, in 1754, Matthew Wilson was added as assistant. The latter was to teach the languages, while McDowell continued, "from a sense of the public good," to teach logic, mathematics, natural and moral philosophy, &c.

In the following year it was ordered by Synod that application be made to the trustees of the German schools to procure a sum of money to encourage the Synod's school. In consideration of this aid, it was stipulated that "some Dutch children" should be taught the English tongue, and three or four, if they offered themselves, Latin and Greek. As soon as this favor could be obtained, Rev. Sampson Smith was to open a school at Chesnut Level.

A donation of books had been sent from Dublin; and these were to be "the foundation of a public library, under the care of the Synod." None of them were to be lent "beyond Potomac River." The application to the trustees of the German schools was favorably entertained, and twenty-five pounds were granted for the year to the Synod's school. This was in 1757.

The union of the Synods in the following year opened Princeton College to the Old as well as the New side. It did not, however, supersede the educational labors of ministers who were members of the Synod. Several of these had—after the manner of William Tennent at Neshaminy—schools of their own. Some of these were continued, and accomplished much good. Samuel Finley's school at Nottingham was highly celebrated. It sent out a large number of eminent men. Among them were Governor Martin, of North Carolina, Dr. Benjamin Rush, Colonel John Bayard, Governor Henry, of Maryland, Rev. Dr. McWhorter, the celebrated James Waddel, and Rev. William M. Tennent, of Abington. Finley was an accomplished scholar and a skilful teacher, and to such eminence had he attained, that on the death of Davies he was called to succeed him in the presidency at Princeton.

At Fagg's Manor, Samuel Blair established a classical school, which became scarcely less distinguished. He had been educated at the Log College, and must have been one of the first pupils of the institution. Among those who received from him the substantial parts of their education were Samuel Davies, Alexander Cummings, John Rodgers, James Finley, and Hugh Henry, all of them useful and some of them distinguished in the ministry.

Besides these, it is probable[1] that Andrews had a school in Philadelphia. Dickinson had one at Elizabethtown, the germ of Nassau Hall. Thomas Evans had one at Pencader. Davies devoted a part of his time to the training of young men. The Old side endeavored to give their institution at New London, under Alison, a higher rank than those established by individual enterprise. They corresponded with President Clap, of Yale College, to secure for their students a diploma on easy terms. In their reply to Clap's inquiries, they speak in no very respectful tone of Tennent's school at Neshaminy. They aimed at something higher, but they failed to secure what they desired. The New side were foremost—in spite of the reproach cast on the Tennents—in the cause of education.

CHAPTER IX.

THE SYNOD OF NEW YORK AND PHILADELPHIA, 1758–1775.

The basis upon which the Synod of New York and Philadelphia was erected was one upon which the two Synods could consistently unite.[2] The first article of the "plan" was to this effect:—"Both Synods having always approved and received the Westminster Confession of Faith and Larger and Shorter Catechisms as an orthodox and excellent system of Christian doctrine, founded on the word of God, we do still receive the same as the Confession of our Faith, and also adhere to the plan of worship, government, and discipline con-

---

[1] Webster, 124. The grounds of probability are not stated.

[2] Minutes of Synod, p. 286.

tained in the Westminster Directory, strictly enjoining it upon all our members and probationers for the ministry, that they preach and teach according to the form of sound words in said Confession and Catechisms, and avoid and oppose all errors contrary thereto."

In case of a decision by the majority of a Presbytery or Synod, the minority were actively to concur, or passively submit, or, if this could not be done, the individual, after sufficient liberty of remonstrance, was peaceably to withdraw. Protest was allowable and entitled to record, provided always that the protest was not to be against members, or introduce facts and accusations without proof, till fair trial had been refused. The protest of 1741, *as a Synodical act*, was fully disavowed, and declared invalid as an objection to the union. No accusation affecting ministerial standing was to be brought otherwise than by private brotherly admonition, or by regular process. No Presbytery might make appointments within the bounds of another without their consent, nor one member officiate in another's congregation without his permission; although when the privilege was asked it was to be accounted unbrotherly to refuse. Candidates for licensure or ordination were to give satisfaction as to their learning, Christian experience, and skill in divinity, declaring their acceptance of the Confession of Faith, and promising subjection to the Presbyterian plan of government. The several Presbyteries were to continue in their present form where an alteration did not appear for edification; and divided congregations, each supplied with a pastor, were to be allowed to continue such if they preferred. Yet, to promote a complete union as soon as possible, the united Synod might model the several Presbyteries as might seem most expedient.

In regard to the revival, the members of the New

York Synod were left free to declare, and did declare upon the record, their adherence to their former sentiments in its favor, and that a blessed work of God's Holy Spirit in the conversion of numbers had been carried on; that, where certain features of conviction and Christian experience were present, exceptionable circumstances did not warrant the rejection of it, or its denial as "a gracious work of God." In regard to particular facts, the judgment of members of the present Synod might differ; but in their sentiments concerning the nature of a work of grace they were agreed. In conclusion, all under the care of the Synod were recommended to beware of a contentious disposition, to study peace and mutual edification, and it was agreed that "all former differences and disputes are laid aside and buried."

If much evil had resulted from the division, there were some lessons which it taught of no slight value, and the tide of excited and conflicting feeling at least left behind it, in the basis on which the united Synod was erected, something better than ordinary drift-wood. The principles of the Church were more clearly defined. The liberal and tolerant spirit of compromise which conceded to both parties equal orthodoxy, although one was strenuous for some things accounted by the other non-essential, was especially manifest. The essential features of a work of grace, and of Christian experience, were admitted and acknowledged by both parties; and they came together with lessons of forbearance and mutual concession that were of the highest importance.

Few changes were made by the Synod in the modelling of the several Presbyteries. That of New Brunswick remained as before, except that Cowell, of Trenton, and Guild, of Hopewell, were added to it.[1] New York

[1] Minutes of Synod, 288.

and Suffolk were continued without any change. The Presbytery of Philadelphia was to consist of Cross, Gilbert Tennent, Alison, Treat, Chesnut, Martin, Beatty, Greenman, Hunter, Ramsey, Lawrence, and Kinkead, —nearly equally from the Old and New sides. Lewes Presbytery was to consist of John Miller, Tuttle, Harris, Henry, and Wilson; while the First and Second Presbyteries of New Castle and Donegal, each of them divided in 1741 by the protest, were left for the present without change.

At the same time, also, the Presbytery of Hanover in Virginia was constituted. It embraced Davies, Todd, Henry, Wright, Brown, Martin, and Craighead, of the New side; and Black, Craig, and Alexander Miller, of the Old side,—the last three laboring in the Great Valley, and the former, with the exception of Craighead in North Carolina, east of the mountains, in the neighborhood of Hanover.

A committee of correspondence with the churches in Britain and Ireland was appointed, and one of the subjects of their correspondence with England was to be the aid from trustees in London for the fund raised for German emigrants, with a view to securing aid for educating youths for the ministry.[1]

The Synod closed its session by the appointment of a day of fasting and prayer. It was the day already appointed by the government; and, in view of the calamities of war, the danger from unchristian foes, and the sins of ingratitude, religious decay, vice, and immorality, the Synod was led to recommend its observance with a view to "deprecate the wrath of God, to pray for a blessing on His Majesty's armaments by land and sea, in order to procure a lasting and honorable peace," for "the overthrow of unchristian errors,

---

[1] Minutes of Synod, 290.

superstition, and tyranny, and the universal spread of pure and undefiled religion."

Through the period extending from the union of the Synods to the commencement of the Revolutionary War, the growth of the Church was rapid and almost uninterrupted. The troubles of the division were still felt, however, within the bounds of Donegal,[1] New Castle, and Philadelphia Presbyteries. Donegal petitioned (1765), against the remonstrance of a strong minority, for a division into two Presbyteries;[2] or, in case this was refused, that the members added to them when the Presbyteries were remodelled might be ordered to return to their former judicatures. Declining the request, the Synod formed, of the ministers west of the Susquehanna, the new Presbytery of Carlisle, and annexed the others to the Presbytery of New Castle, thenceforth to be known by the name of Lancaster. The old members of Donegal Presbytery felt themselves greatly aggrieved by this arrangement, and it was brought before Synod again in the following year. Several expedients were proposed for relieving the difficulties which existed, but it was finally resolved to revive and restore the Presbyteries of Donegal and New Castle. This, however, was far from satisfactory. The Old-side members of Donegal, seven in number, refused to unite with that Presbytery. They met by themselves, assuming the old name for the Presbytery which they claimed to constitute, and wrote to the Synod, declaring themselves "laid under the disagreeable necessity of entering a declination from its juris-

---

[1] In 1759 the First and Second Presbyteries of New Castle were united, and Messrs. Sampson Smith, Robert Smith, John Roan, and John Hogge, were added to Donegal Presbytery.—*Minutes*, 292. In the course of the six years which followed, dissatisfactions arose.—*Ibid.* 350.

[2] Minutes, 348–9.

diction."[1] Nothing was left for the Synod but to pronounce them no longer members of the body. In 1768, they applied to be received and acknowledged, but their request was refused, except on the condition that they should unite with the Presbytery of Donegal properly constituted. If this condition were complied with, the Synod declared itself not indisposed to remodel the Presbyteries in such a manner as to give the best satisfaction which the circumstances of the case allowed. The proposal was then made to allow the dissatisfied members to unite as they were willing with the Presbyteries of Donegal, New Castle, and Philadelphia Second, and this proposal was accepted,—four members of the Presbytery of Donegal, Duffield, Cooper, Slemmons, and Roan, entering their dissent.[2]

The Second Presbytery of Philadelphia was thus strengthened by the accession of several of the Old-side members of Donegal, viz.: Steel, Elder, Tate, and McMordie. This Presbytery had been formed mainly of the Old-side members of the Presbytery of Philadelphia, in 1762.[3] It consisted originally of Robert Cross, Francis Alison, John Ewing, John Simonton, and James Latta. Cross had been the leader, and Alison the scholar, of the Old side. Ewing, pastor of the First Presbyterian Church of Philadelphia,—and thus associated with Cross,—and Latta, settled the previous year as pastor at Deep Run, were both pupils of Alison, and had been for some years tutors of the college over which he presided. The Presbytery was thus formed on the *elective affinity* principle, and, much to the dissatisfaction of many of the Synod, professed to be conscientiously opposed to the practice of examining candidates for the ministry as to their experimental acquaintance with religion. So strong, indeed, was their

---

[1] Minutes, 366. [2] Ibid. 383, 384. [3] Ibid. 321.

feeling, that they declared that, sooner than belong to a Presbytery which adopted the practice, they would break off from all connection with the Synod.

The attempt was made, but in vain, in 1766, to reunite the First and Second Presbyteries of Philadelphia. The decision of the Synod was in favor of the continued separate existence of a body which, in the judgment of many, only served to perpetuate old party lines, and seemed "to indicate a temper of schismatical tendency."[1] It was maintained that the Synod involved itself in a self-contradiction in erecting a Presbytery which refused to examine candidates for the ministry in regard to the subject of personal religious experience. The precedent, moreover, was declared to be a bad one, and injurious in its tendency to perpetuate division. In spite, however, of all objections, the Second Presbytery was still continued; and, although the attendance of its members at meetings of Synod was quite irregular, it received an accession of members who strongly sympathized with it.

Of these, Patrick Allison was the first to join it. A pupil of his namesake, Dr. Alison, at the institution in which the latter was Vice-Provost, he was ordained by the Second Presbytery, and took charge, in 1765, of the first church gathered at Baltimore. In 1768, Elder, Steel, and McMordie were transferred to it from the Presbytery of Donegal. Two years later, Samuel Eakin, who gave the Synod no little trouble by his conduct, was received, and in 1772 Hugh McGill, from Ireland, who proved scarcely less obnoxious. In 1773 they ordained Robert Davidson. Their licentiates during the period were James Long, Thomas Read, afterward of Delaware, John King, and John McLean, who went to the Carolinas.

---

[1] Minutes, 355.

In 1772, George Duffield was called to the Pine Street Church of Philadelphia; and, although dismissed from and recommended by the Presbytery of Donegal, the Second Presbytery of Philadelphia refused to receive him.[1] On the question of his settlement, the feelings of animosity between the Old and New side were revived, and the attempt was made to exclude him from the church. Both parties applied to the Synod,—Mr. Duffield by complaint of the proceedings of the Presbytery, and the incorporated committee of the Market and Pine Street churches by petition and remonstrance. The Synod pronounced that Mr. Duffield had just cause of complaint, declared him minister of the Third Presbyterian congregation of Philadelphia, and ordered that he be put upon the list of the Second Presbytery.

Except within the bounds of the Presbyteries of Donegal and Philadelphia Second, the disastrous influence of the division soon disappeared. In the Presbytery of Hanover, the Old-side members of the Valley, and the New-side east of the mountains, were not in entire sympathy; and the former—on the ground, however, of their distance from their brethren—asked to be formed into a separate Presbytery. The petition was not approved by the Synod, but assurance was given that, when a sufficient number to warrant the erection of a new Presbytery should be secured, the request should be granted.[2]

Meanwhile (1763), an application was presented to Synod from a Presbytery in New York on the east of the Hudson, desiring to be incorporated with the Synod and to be strengthened by members set off from the Presbyteries of New York and Suffolk. The application was favorably received, and John Smith and

[1] Minutes, 433 [2] Ib. 292.

Chauncey Graham, of New York Presbytery, and Eliphalet Ball and Samuel Sackett, of Suffolk Presbytery, were united with them to constitute the Dutchess county Presbytery.[1]

In 1766, the Presbytery was represented in Synod, and, besides, the members set off from Suffolk and New York, it consisted (1768) of Wheeler Case, Ichabod[2] Lewis, Elisha Kent, Solomon Mead, Joseph Peck,[3] and Samuel Dunlop. The churches which first came under the care of Presbytery had been organized for several years,—some of them by the Fairfield and Litchfield Associations of Connecticut, and others by the Presbytery of New York.

It was in October (27th), 1762, that three ministers, Solomon Mead, of South Salem, and Joseph Peck and Elisha Kent, pastors of churches in Philips Precinct, between Fishkill and South Salem, met to consult about forming a Presbytery.[4] Their conclusions were

---

[1] In 1765 (Minutes, p. 39), we read, "There is no account from Dutchess county Presbytery, whether they have regularly formed themselves according to the order of the Synod."

[2] *Thomas* Lewis in the Minutes,—which is probably a mistake.

[3] The name is repeatedly written *James* in the Minutes,—sometimes, perhaps, abbreviated for Joseph. Dr. Hodge incorrectly writes it *John*.

[4] A letter from Dr. Johnston, of Newburgh, on the files of the church of Poughkeepsie, is the authority for the statement in the text. A manuscript letter from Darius Peck, Esq., of Hudson, enables me to trace the Presbyterianism of Dutchess county to a Milford origin. The Presbyterian church at Milford was organized by a secession from the Congregational church in 1741. It was at the very crisis of the agitation between the Old and New side in the Synod. One of the first members of the Milford church was Joseph Peck, a descendant, doubtless, of one of the early settlers of the town who bore the same name. For a time a Rev. Mr. Kent supplied the pulpit.—(Lambert's History of New Haven Colony.) This was unquestionably Elisha Kent who, twelve years before, was graduated at Yale, and for several years was pastor of Newtown, Conn. He is

in favor of the measure, and they proceeded, by prayer and the adoption of the Confession and Catechisms, to form themselves into a Presbytery. In the following spring they applied to the Synod to be received. Their request was granted, as has been stated: the two members from New York Presbytery, and the two from Suffolk, were added to their number. In 1765 their number had been increased by the accession of William Hanna, settled at Albany, Samuel Dunlop, pastor of the Scotch-Irish congregation at Cherry Valley, and Wheeler Case, a licentiate of Suffolk Presbytery, who succeeded Mr. Graham as pastor at Poughkeepsie, in connection with which he ministered to the church in Charlotte Precinct, but better known subsequently, and at the present time, as the church of Pleasant Valley. Previous to 1770, the Presbytery ordained Samuel Mills and Ichabod Lewis, who became permanent members of the body, and in 1772 they received Benjamin Strong from Fairfield Association.

Of these early members of the Presbytery, Elisha Kent was settled over a church in Philips Precinct, not far from Fishkill, in the place early known as Kent's Parish. He was a graduate of Yale College in 1729, and for several years afterward was settled at

---

the only minister of the name of Kent discoverable at this period. In 1748, he had been for some time settled at Philippi, or Phillipstown, below Fishkill. Joseph Peck, associated with him in labors in the same region,—Philips Precinct,—was not a graduate of Yale or Princeton, and must have studied with some minister. In the circumstances, it seems probable that he was a son of the Joseph Peck of Milford, that he studied with Mr. Kent, and that the two removed at nearly the same time to settle upon the Hudson in neighboring churches. Solomon Mead, of the class of 1748 at Yale, soon after came into the same region, settling at South Salem. The three churches, South Salem, and the two of Philips Precinct, —now probably Kent and Phillipstown, or Cold Spring,—were within a few miles of each other.

Newtown, Conn. After his removal from this place, he supplied for a time the (New-side) church at Milford, and probably about the year 1742 removed to Putnam county, N.Y., taking charge of the first church gathered in all this region. There is reason to believe that this was largely composed of families who had removed at about the same time from the vicinity of Newtown and Milford, Conn., to whom he was known, and by whom he was invited to become their minister. The first notice we have of him in this new field is as Bellamy's correspondent, in 1749.

"Kent's Parish" embraced undoubtedly a large field, including not only Kent,—the town which commemorates the family to which Chancellor Kent belonged,[1]—but the town of South-East, where a settlement had been effected as early as 1730.[2] In 1737, "South-East-town" was formed as a precinct, and by this time quite a large number of families had located within the circuit of a few miles. The pastorate of Mr. Kent continued till some time after the commencement of the war; and Fredericksburg, where Samuel Mills was subsequently settled, is probably the same with South-East and "Kent's Parish." The other church within the limits of Philips Precinct was that under the care of Joseph Peck, located in Philipstown,—the Philippi of 1789,—where several families had settled as early as 1730.[3] His pastorate continued till about 1770;[4] and during the war, Ichabod Lewis, who had been forced to leave his own field, probably supplied this place.

---

[1] Chancellor Kent was the grandson of Rev. Elisha Kent.

[2] New York Gazetteer. The statement there made that Mr. Kent began to preach at South-East in 1730 is probably incorrect. He graduated in 1729, and labored for several years at Newtown and Milford.

[3] A Mr. Davenport is said to have built the first house at Cold Spring, in 1715.

[4] Probably settled at New Fairfield in 1774.

The church of which Solomon Mead was pastor was gathered about the year 1750, or very soon after the settlement of the town. The first notice of the church occurs May 19, 1752, "when a convention of ministers assembled at Salem, upon the desire of the people,"[1] to install Solomon Mead as pastor of the church. A graduate of Yale College in 1748, Mr. Mead was probably from the town of Greenwich, where families of that name had early settled; and it is to be presumed that the convention of ministers was an ecclesiastical council composed of Connecticut pastors settled on the western border of the State. The pastorate of Mr. Mead continued till 1800, although his life was protracted till 1812, and to the ripe age of eighty-six years he continued the patriarch of the Presbytery, venerated far and near for his piety and his worth.

Chauncey Graham—till his transfer by the Synod, a member of New York Presbytery—was the son of John Graham, for many years pastor of Southbury, Conn.[2] Rumbout, near Fishkill, was organized as a church, July 3, 1748, and Poughkeepsie was "gathered" in July, 1750, by a committee of the Presbytery of New York. Of these two churches, Graham, who had been graduated at Yale College but a little more than two years previous, was ordained pastor, January 29, 1749–50, by an ecclesiastical council, consisting of Messrs. Stoddard, Case, Judson,[3] and their "messengers." Mills and Bellamy were invited, but did not attend. In the following year, Graham, whose father was a native of Scotland, united with the Presbytery of New York, and was present at the meeting of the Synod at Newark

---

1 Bolton's West Chester County, i. 268. 2 Webster.

3 Anthony Stoddard, of Woodbury; Benajah Case, of New Fairfield; and David Judson, of Newtown. The Mr. Mills invited was Jedediah Mills, of Huntington.

in 1751. For several years after the Presbytery was formed in 1763, he was its stated clerk. He left Poughkeepsie in 1752, after which it was dependent on stated supplies till the settlement of Wheeler Case, in 1765, over Pleasant Valley and Poughkeepsie. Mr. Graham was dismissed in 1773, and died in 1784.

John Smith—settled at Rye and White Plains, having been ordained by the Fairfield Association (probably May 15, 1729)[1]—was the son of Thomas Smith, of New York, one of the leading men who seceded from Anderson's congregation and invited Jonathan Edwards to preach to them. He was an intimate friend of Edwards, and yet did not unite with the Presbytery of New York until 1752. His ministry continued till his death in 1771, although, at his request, Ichabod Lewis was settled as his colleague for several of the closing years of his life.[2]

Samuel Sackett commenced his labors[3] at Crumpond[4] and Cortland Manor (now Yorktown and Peekskill) as early as 1742. In 1743, he was installed at Bedford, and directed to visit the Highlands. His labors were extended to Crumpond, Salem, and Cortland Manor,—although only occasionally, except at Crumpond, which he supplied half the time from 1747 to 1749. In 1753, his adoption of the views of Edwards and Bellamy on the subject of baptism led to alienation of feeling on the part of his people, and his resignation of his office. In 1761, after having labored for several years at Hanover, in Cortland Manor, he was installed at Crumpond.

Eliphalet Ball succeeded Sackett at Bedford, and,

---

[1] Webster, 652.

[2] Probably in 1766–67, as Mr. Lewis was a graduate of Yale in 1765.

[3] Webster, 546.

[4] Ibid. A congregation was formed at Crumpond in 1738–39. The land for the meeting-house was given January 2, 1739.

along with him, was a member of the Suffolk Presbytery until transferred to the Dutchess county Presbytery. His pastorate continued, with the exception of four years (1768–1772), till 1784. In 1788, he removed with a part of his Bedford congregation to the place which from him received the name which it still retains,—Ball's-town (Ballston).

William Hanna, of Albany, was another of the early members of the Presbytery. He was a native of Litchfield county, and a licentiate of the Litchfield Association. In spite of Bellamy's dissuasives, he was ordained in 1761, by a council of Connecticut ministers, consisting of Graham, of Southbury, Lee, of Salisbury, and Gold and Smith, of Sharon. The church placed itself under the care of the Presbytery, and he was received as a member in 1763.

Still another of the early members of the body was Samuel Dunlop, of Cherry Valley. In 1741, he had commenced his labors on this outpost of civilization, among a people whom he had induced to follow him into the wilderness. A native of the north of Ireland, he applied himself with success to his countrymen settled in Londonderry, N.H., and quite a number of Presbyterian families were induced to cast in their lot with his. The result was the formation of the church of Cherry Valley, which came under the charge of the Presbytery soon after the latter was erected.[1]

Wheeler Case, a licentiate of Suffolk Presbytery, was the first pastor of Pleasant Valley, where he commenced his labors in November, 1765.[2] Poughkeepsie for some years formed a portion of his charge, but during the war it became so enfeebled as to be virtually extinct.[3] Mr. Case continued in the pastorate of Plea-

---

[1] History of Londonderry. Campbell's Tryon County.

[2] N.Y. Gazetteer.

[3] Mr. Ludlow's Historical Sermon.

sant Valley for more than twenty years, and was a member of the Presbytery from the date of his settlement.

In 1769, Samuel Mills, a graduate of Yale College in 1765, was settled at Bedford, and became a member of the Presbytery. For seventeen years his pastorate continued; and he was repeatedly appointed a delegate to the convention of Congregational and Presbyterian ministers that met annually previous to the war.

Ichabod Lewis, a classmate of Mills at Yale College, was called as colleague of John Smith at Rye and White Plains, at about the same time that Mills was settled at Bedford. The burning of the church-edifice and the insecurity of the whole region forced him, in 1776, to withdraw northward, where—residing at Salem—he supplied for several years the church at Philippi, his friend Mills also having removed to take charge of the adjoining parish of Fredericksburg.

In 1770, Benjamin Strong, who for many years had been settled at North Stanwich, on the western border of Connecticut, became a member of the body. He did not, however, remain many years in the connection.

In 1766, John Close was licensed, and, in 1775, David Close was ordained by the Presbytery. The last labored for a time within its bounds; the other found a destitute and inviting field on the west of the Hudson.

On the west side of the Hudson, Presbyterian churches were organized at an early period. Smith, in his history of New York, speaks of the large number of Scotch-Irish who settled in Orange and Ulster counties. The very names of these are significant of the nationality of the first immigrants. The church at Goshen was organized previous to 1721, when John Bradner became its first pastor. Here he remained for eleven years, and was succeeded by John Tudor and

Silas Leonard,—the last, pastor from 1738 to 1764. In 1766, Nathan Kèr commenced his pastorate of the church, which continued down to 1804.[1]

As early as 1729, an application to the Synod of Philadelphia for supplies of preaching among them was made by the people of Wall Kill, through their commissioner, John McNeal. In the course of the following year, they were supplied in part by Gelston, who had previously been a member of Suffolk Presbytery, but in 1735 was reported as laboring in the Highlands, where rumors against his character led to his trial and suspension from the ministry. He was followed by Isaac Chalker, whose pastorate closed in 1743, and subsequently by John Moffat and John Blair, the last of whom left in 1771. He was followed by Andrew King, whose pastorate extended from 1776 to 1815.

The church at Bethlehem had a house of worship as early as 1730. Isaac Chalker was the first pastor. He was succeeded by Enos Ayers, who took charge of this church conjointly with that of Blooming Grove, where a church-edifice was erected in 1759. At Bethlehem he was succeeded by Francis Peppard, who had charge also of the church organized at New Windsor in 1766, and by Abner Reeve in the church at Blooming Grove. John Close, recently ordained by Dutchess county Presbytery, took charge of the two churches of Bethlehem and New Windsor from 1773 to 1799. In both places he was succeeded by Jonathan Freeman, whose pastorate continued until 1805.

The church at Blooming Grove was supplied, after Abner Reeve left it, in his zeal for Independency (1764–1770), by Amaziah Lewis, Benoni Bradner (1786–1802), and Luther Halsey.

---

[1] Eager's Orange County.

Before the close of the century the Scotchtown church was organized (1798), and Methuselah Baldwin became its pastor. Here he remained for nearly forty years. The church at Crawford was of still older date, and Jonathan Freeman was pastor of it—in conjunction with New Windsor—for several years. Meanwhile a congregation was gathered at Newburgh; but no church seems to have been organized till about 1796–98. Relinquishing his labors at Crawford, Jonathan Freeman supplied Newburgh in its stead, in conjunction with New Windsor. This was in accordance with the course of his predecessor at the latter place, John Close, who had divided his time between the church at New Windsor and the congregation at Newburgh for several years (1785–1796). Freeman was succeeded at Newburgh by Eleazer Burnet and John Johnston,—the pastorate of the latter extending from 1807 to 1857. The church at Albany was formed before 1761. Previous to this, the feeble congregation had been endeavoring to secure the means of erecting a house of worship, and application was afterward repeatedly made to Synod to secure aid. Their case was recommended to the attention and charity of friends of the cause, and, through great embarrassments, the house of worship was at length erected and a pastor secured. The church of Schenectady was organized a few years later, and for some years formed a joint charge with Currie's Bush, now Princetown.[1]

In 1770, a letter was received from the Presbytery of South Carolina, requesting to know the terms on which a union with the Synod might be obtained. This was a body, composed in part of New England and in part of Scotch elements, which had existed in the low country of the Carolinas as far back probably

[1] For fuller accounts of congregations, see chap. xviii.

as 1729, and it may have been in existence even some years earlier. It continued[1] under the same name down to the period of the Revolutionary War, when its meetings were interrupted and its members scattered. The Presbytery of Charleston, formed after the close of the conflict, claimed to occupy the same ground and to be substantially the same body. The Synod answered their letter, but no reply was received.

The Presbytery of Hanover had already increased so that, in the view of a number of its members, a division was desirable. In 1770, a petition to this effect was laid before Synod, and the ministers south of Virginia and within the bounds of North Carolina were formed into the Presbytery of Orange. Upon its erection it consisted of six members, Hugh McAden, Henry Patillo, James Cresswell, Joseph Alexander, Hezekiah James Balch, and Hezekiah Balch. Thus at the close of the period under review, the Synod was composed of ten Presbyteries,—Dutchess, Suffolk, New York, New Brunswick, Donegal, Lewistown, New Castle, the First and Second of Philadelphia, Hanover, and Orange. Nearly as many ministers had been received or ordained as were in connection with the

---

[1] In 1695, a church was formed in Dorchester, Mass., "with a design to remove to Carolina to encourage the settlement of churches and the promotion of religion in the southern plantations." The church embarked, with its pastor, Rev. Joseph Lord, in December. "On February 2, 1696, the Lord's Supper was administered for the first time in that colony." This colony settled at Dorchester, eighteen miles from Charleston. In 1698, Rev. John Cotton, son of the Boston minister, was dismissed from Plymouth, and gathered a church in Charleston. He died in 1699. In 1705, the "Dissenters" had three churches in Charleston and one in the country (Dorchester). In 1754, Mr. Osgood, pastor of Dorchester, with a colony from that church, organized the church in Midway, Ga. (Holmes's Annals, i. 461, 469, 492.) A colony from Midway formed the Presbyterian church in Burke county, Ga. F.

Synod at the time of its erection in 1758. Most of these had been trained within the bounds of the Presbyteries, and by these more than seventy had been ordained. Among the accessions from abroad were the celebrated Dr. Witherspoon, from the Presbytery of Paisley in Scotland, Alexander McLean, James Gourly, and perhaps one or two others from North Britain. McGill, Rhea, Huey, and two or three others were all that came from Ireland. James Sproat, Jonathan Murdock, and A. Lewis, were from the Congregational Association of New Haven; and Dutchess county Presbytery received Benjamin Strong from Fairfield West. Several others were from New England, but they were for the most part educated or ordained within the bounds of the Presbyterian Church.[1]

---

[1] The members received and for the most part ordained by the Presbyteries during this period were as follows. New Brunswick Presbytery ordained Alexander McWhorter, William Kirkpatrick (1760), James Hunt, James Caldwell, John Hanna, John Clark (1761), Samuel Parkhurst, Joseph Treat, William Mills (1762), William Tennent, Jr., Enoch Green (1763), Amos Thompson, Thomas Smith, Jacob Ker, Nathan Ker (1764), James Lyon, John Roxborough (1765), David Caldwell (1766), Jeremiah Halsey (1768), William Schenk, Jacob Vanarsdalen (1772). New York ordained Azel Roe (1762), Francis Peppard (1765), Jedediah Chapman (1767), James Tuttle (1769), William Woodhull (1770), Alexander Miller, Jonathan Murdock, Oliver Deming (1771), Amzi Lewis (1772), Matthias Burnet, Joseph Grover (1775). New Castle ordained John Strain, John Carmichael (1761), Samuel Blair (1766), John McCreary, William Foster, Joseph Smith (1769), John Woodhull, Josiah Lewis (1771), Thomas Read, James Wilson, James Anderson (1772), Thomas Smith (1774). Lewes Presbytery ordained Joseph Montgomery (1762), Alexander Huston (1765), Thomas McCraken (1768), John Brown (1769). Hanover Presbytery ordained Henry Patillo (1758), James Waddel (1763), David Rice (1765), Thomas Jackson, Samuel Leak (1769). Suffolk Presbytery ordained Benjamin Goldsmith (1765), David Rose (1766), Elam Patten, John Close (1767), Joshua Hart (1772), John Davenport (1775). The

The growth of the Church was thus from its own natural increase, and the missionary efforts that were put forth. These efforts, though unequal to the demand, were strenuous and unremitted. The applications addressed to the Synod, both from the North and South, were urgent and repeated. Virginia and the Carolinas presented inviting fields for missionary effort; but the laborers were few. From the Great Valley west of the mountains, from the region in and around Prince Edward, from the Presbytery of Orange, embracing a large part of North Carolina and extending into South Carolina and Georgia, the applications for aid were

---

First Presbytery of Philadelphia ordained John Murray (1766), Alexander Mitchel (1769), James Boyd, James Watt (1770), William Hollingshead (1774), Nathaniel Irwin, Daniel McCalla (1775). The ministers ordained by the Second Presbytery of Philadelphia were Patrick Allison (1763), Samuel Eakin (1770), Robert Davidson (1774). Donegal ordained John Craighead (1768), Hezekiah J. Balch (1770), Hugh Vance (1772), William Thom (1773), Thomas McFarren (1775). Dutchess county Presbytery ordained David Close (1773), Blackleach Burritt (1774). The Presbytery of Orange ordained Thomas Reese, John Simpson (1774); and the Presbytery of Lancaster, during its brief existence, ordained Samuel Blair (1766).

The members received from other bodies by the Presbyteries during this period were few in number. Suffolk received Thomas Payne in 1764; New Brunswick, Jonathan Leavitt, from New England, in 1765, John Witherspoon, from Scotland, in 1769, and James Gourly, from Scotland, in 1775. The First Presbytery of Philadelphia received James Sproat, successor of Tennent in Philadelphia, in 1769. Dr. Sproat had been converted under Tennent's preaching, and had been settled at Guilford, Conn., for nearly twenty-five years. (Sprague's Annals, iii. 125.) New Castle received Daniel McClealand, in 1769. Donegal, Joseph Rhea, from Ireland, in 1771, Robert Hughes, also from Ireland, in 1773, and Daniel McClure and Levi Frisbie, missionaries from New England, in the same year. The last two, however, were not received by the Synod. In 1775, Colin McFarquhar was also received from Scotland. Orange Presbytery received James Campbell and James Edmonds, from South Carolina, in 1774; and Dutchess county, Benjamin Strong, in 1772.

renewed, sometimes with each successive year. The Synod sent among them all whom it could spare. Licentiates, and ministers recently ordained, were directed to labor in these destitute regions from a few weeks to several months. Some of the ablest members of the Synod, as Duffield, McWhorter, Spencer, and Treat, were employed from time to time to itinerate through the region and organize churches.[1] By such methods the Synod attained a large acquaintance with the Southern field, and their interest and sympathies were excited in its behalf.

This was also the case with the frontier settlements of Pennsylvania and the northern settlements of New York. Duffield and Rodgers were active in visiting them and encouraging the feeble churches, or organizing them where they were not yet established.

The incessant demand for ministers led to measures for securing a larger number of candidates and making provision for their education. The project of appointing a Professor of Divinity at Princeton College was agitated as early as 1760, only two years after the union of the two Synods. No adequate provision, however, could be made at the time for his support, and the matter was for the time deferred. Yet the Synod (1761) declared that "the Church suffers greatly for want of an opportunity to instruct students in the knowledge of divinity;" and it was therefore agreed that every student, after taking his first degree in college, should "read carefully and closely on this subject at least one year, under the care of some minister of an approved character for his skill in theology," under his direction discussing "difficult points in divinity, forming sermons, lectures, and such other useful exercises as he may be directed to, in the course of

[1] See Minutes for successive years of this period.

his studies." Practice in public speaking was recommended, and probationers were "to forbear *reading* their sermons from the pulpit, if they could conveniently."[1]

But these provisions came far short of meeting the emergency. The college at Princeton, a few years later (1768), secured the services of the celebrated Dr. Witherspoon, of Scotland, who was invited to the presidency of the college on the death of Dr. Finley. A new and energetic effort was now made throughout the bounds of the Church to secure a larger endowment for the institution. It was prosecuted with much vigor and a good degree of success. Dr. Witherspoon, in addition to his other duties, gave lectures on divinity, and instructed the students who desired it, in the Hebrew language. This, in the circumstances, was the best provision that could be made. The Synod, encouraged by the prospect, engaged to add fifty pounds a year to his salary.

The first difficulty, the securing of a Divinity Professor, was thus met. Another remained. The necessities of those engaged in a course of preparation for the ministry were often urgent, and for lack of means they were sometimes compelled to abandon their purpose. The Synod endeavored (1771) to meet this difficulty by "a scheme for supporting young men of piety and parts at learning for the work of the ministry, so that our numerous vacancies may be supplied with preachers of the gospel." By this scheme, it was the aim of the Synod to throw the burden upon those who were most interested in the success of the project. Each vacant congregation asking Presbytery for supplies was to pay annually two pounds into a common fund. Every minister a member of the Presbytery

---

[1] Minutes, 309, 310.

was to pay one pound, and any who were willing to contribute were to have the opportunity of annual subscription. Individuals who applied for aid were to be examined and approved by the Presbytery, and were to preach one year after licensure in the vacancies within its bounds. In case any persons thus educated should withdraw from their purpose of laboring in the ministry, they were to give bonds for the repayment of what they had thus received.[1]

Here, then, was the model of a Presbyterian Education society. It was probably the first of any kind that had yet been devised in this country. The plan had originated with the Presbytery of New Castle, and was overtured to the Synod, who approved it and earnestly recommended it, or a like scheme, to the several Presbyteries.

In 1773, the subject was again brought to the notice of Synod.[2] It was found that the Presbyteries of New York and New Brunswick, and the Second Presbytery of Philadelphia, had "complied fully" with the recommendations of the Synod, and had succeeded so far in "raising money for poor pious youths" as to have "several young men at education." Some of the other Presbyteries had done something, but had not answered the design of the Synod. They were now ordered "to prosecute this important plan as speedily as possible." But the approaching scenes and troubles of the Revolutionary conflict defeated any successful or general prosecution of the project.

The subject of missionary labors among the Indians was not overlooked. David Brainerd had labored with devoted zeal among the tribes along the Delaware, and had made Crossweeksung, Kaunaumeek, and the Forks of the Delaware, classic in the literature of Christian

---

[1] Minutes, 419, 420. [2] Ibid. 438.

missions. His brother John, not unworthy of such a kindred, had longed to tread in his steps; but the French War, and trouble among the tribes, had deranged his plans. He settled, therefore, as pastor of the congregation at Newark, waiting for a more favorable opportunity. In 1760, he laid his case before Synod, then in session at Philadelphia. He asked advice, whether he should leave his present comfortable position at Newark and resume his mission to the Indians. The Synod dared not repress his zeal. Though "tenderly affected with the case of Newark congregation, yet, in consideration of the great importance of the Indian mission, they unanimously advise Mr. Brainerd to resume it." The interest of the Indian fund was given him for the year, in order to "his more comfortable subsistence." It was subsequently renewed, and the congregations throughout the Church were urged to take up collections for his support and in order to sustain an Indian school.[1]

But the attention of the Synod had already been called to the Oneida tribe.[2] At first they could not see their way clear to make any effort to sustain a mission among them; but when, in 1763, the faithful Occam had already entered the field, and derived but a scanty support from "the Society in Britain," the Synod generously resolved to place at his disposal for the year the sum of sixty-five pounds; and, in order to secure it, collections were ordered in the several congregations. At this time Sergeant had joined the Indian mission under the care of Brainerd.

In 1768, "the Synod, taking under consideration the deplorable condition of the Indian tribes, the natives of this land, who sit in heathenish darkness and are perishing for lack of knowledge," appointed a com-

---

[1] Minutes, 311, 316, 324.

[2] Ibid. 324.

mittee "to draw up and concert a general plan to be laid before the next Synod, to be by them approved, in order to prepare the way to propagate the gospel among those benighted people." The committee consisted of some of the ablest members of the body. Allison, Read, Treat, Ewing, William Tennent, McWhorter, Caldwell, Williamson, Thomson, and Blair, composed it, and were to meet in October, at Elizabethtown, to devise the plan.

But the troubled state of the frontier,—such that Cooper and Brainerd, who had intended to visit the Indians on the Muskingum, were forced to abandon their project,—the intrigues of the French, and the near approach of the war, effectually prevented the success of any enterprise which the Synod might have chosen to prosecute. It was thirty years before the ground which was thus lost could be regained, or the attention and sympathies of the Presbyterian churches be effectually drawn to the religious claims of the aboriginal tribes. Yet it was the full intention of the Synod to prosecute the matter on a well-devised system. A part of this was developed in the overture from the New York Presbytery, on the subject of a missionary collection in all the churches of each Presbytery,—a plan which was adopted by the Synod in 1767. This was with a view not only to secure missionary labor for the Indians, but to relieve "the unhappy lot of many in various parts of our land who are brought up in ignorance," whose "families were perishing for lack of knowledge," and "who, on account of their poverty and scattered habitations, are unable, without some assistance, to support the gospel ministry among them." It was publicly acknowledged and declared to be the "duty" of the churches "to send missionaries to the frontier settlements, who may preach to the dispersed families there, and form them into societies for the public worship of God."

Here were the germs both of Home and Foreign Missions, thirty years before the great missionary movement at the beginning of the present century commenced. But for the war, it is possible that Brainerd might have had the honor reserved for Carey, and the American Church—like the child teaching the parent to read—have set England the lesson that by many years should have antedated the formation of her missionary societies.

The correspondence of the Synod with other churches was not overlooked. In 1759, Davies, Cross, and Tennent were on a large committee to propose to the Presbyterian churches abroad to settle some plan by which this object could be secured. In successive years, committees of correspondence were appointed or continued; but they had been unable to meet, and for seven years no digested plan was laid before Synod. In 1766, Alison, Blair, Beatty, and P. V. Livingston were appointed a committee to prepare and bring in a plan "as soon as possible." They reported in favor of a correspondence with the churches of Holland, Geneva, Switzerland, the General Assembly of Scotland, the seceding Synods, the ministers in and about London, the Irish Synod, the ministers of Dublin and of New England, and the churches in South Carolina. For four or five years, the correspondence which was thus recommended was more or less maintained; but the last notice of it appears in 1771.

The regular correspondence with the consociated churches of Connecticut bears date also from 1766. Already the Synod had given evidence of regarding them in a different light from that of "individual ministers, convened as a temporary judicatory for the single purpose of licensing or ordaining a candidate." While declaring (1764) that "every Christian society should maintain communion with others as far as they can with a good conscience," yet "no society was bound to adopt or imitate the irregularities of another," in order thereto, "contrary to its own established and approved rules of procedure." Hence the candidates of the New-Light party in Ireland, of Congregational Councils in New England, and others, were not to be received by the Presbyteries without examination.

But in regard to the associated churches of Connecticut a different feeling prevailed, and, at the same time that the correspondence with foreign churches was reduced to system, a plan for closer intimacy with those of Connecticut was devised. Arrangements were made, in concert with the General Association of Connecticut, for a convention of Congregational and Presbyterian ministers, to be held annually, in order to promote objects of common interest to both denominations. The convention was to meet alternately in Connecticut and within the bounds of the Presbyterian Church, but was to exercise no authority over the ministers or churches. Its general design was "to gain information of" their "united cause and interest; to collect accounts relating thereto; to unite their endeavors and counsels for spreading the gospel and preserving the religious LIBERTIES of the churches; to diffuse harmony and to keep up a correspondence throughout this united body, and with friends abroad," and to vindicate the loyalty and reputation of the churches thus represented.[1]

---

[1] This is a very *covert* and *delicate* statement, concealing the *real* object. The phrase "*preserving religious liberty*" is very significant. "*To vindicate the loyalty and reputation of the churches*" reveals the design. Episcopacy, combined with hyper-Presbyterianism (Scotch) in New England, which desired a Presbyterian Establishment on the basis of the *Solemn League and Covenant*, remonstrated with the

The convention met at Elizabethtown, in 1766. It drew up a plan of union between the Congregational, Consociated, and Presbyterian Churches, which was reported to the Synod the following year. It was amended by them, and finally adopted by both parties. From this period the conventions were held annually until 1776. The disturbance occasioned by the war led to its neglect, and no effort was made to revive it till 1792.

The object of this convention was simply Christian and patriotic. There were common dangers which threatened alike the Presbyterian churches of the Middle States, and the Congregational churches of New England. It was well known that, while civil liberty was threatened by stamp acts, a project for the sacrifice of religious freedom to Episcopal ascendency in the colonies was cautiously but resolutely cherished in England. It was believed, on what was regarded as good authority, that nothing less was contemplated than the extension to these shores of the English Establishment, for which Dissenters here would be taxed as they were in England.

To present a united front of resistance to such a pro-

English Parliament against the holding of Synods in New England. Under the 16th of Richard II., the power to convoke conventions was vested in the Crown, and continued to be exercised even by Cromwell. New York and Virginia had already Episcopal Establishments, and the effort was made to put the entire country under diocesan bishops, as in England. The object of the convention of Presbyterians and Congregationalists was to prevent this; and by their extensive correspondence they aimed to prevent such a result. The opponents of the Dissenters were also enemies of the existing colonial governments. Through influence from this source, the Congregationalists lost their Synods, and the convention was formed to resist *silently* the attempt to subject them to Royalty and Episcopacy. (Holmes's Annals, i. 536. Printed Minutes of the convention. These last were printed in pamphlet form a few years since.) F.

ject; to make common cause with all Dissenters subject to disabilities in any of the colonies,—as in Maryland and Carolina; to diffuse among the people facts and information which should enable them to determine intelligently in regard to the great questions looming up in the distance; to secure careful estimates of the number of Episcopalians and non-Episcopalians in the different colonies,—these were the objects which the convention kept ever in view. It is evident, from a perusal of its minutes, that the men who composed it were not disturbed by the apprehension of merely imaginary dangers. They perceived the identity of interest between the cause of civil and that of religious liberty; and we cannot doubt that the influence of their deliberations powerfully contributed to the successful issue of the great conflict which some already felt was near at hand.

Soon after the arrival of Dr. Witherspoon in this country, an effort was made to secure a union of the "seceding" ministers with the Synod. At the request of the ministers themselves, a committee was appointed to converse with them (1769). That committee failed to meet, and another was appointed in the following year. Their conference proved barren of results; and in 1774 the Associate Presbytery in Pennsylvania, "for reasons which appeared to them valid," declined any further measures with a view to union.

The necessities of missionary labor had called the attention of members of the Synod to the wisdom of making provision for the circulation, especially in frontier settlements, of religious books. In 1772, the charity of the public was asked for the promotion of this object. The books which were specified as those most desirable for circulation were Bibles, the Westminster Confession, Assembly's and Vincent's Catechisms, Doddridge's "Rise and Progress," Alleine's

"Alarm," Watts's Songs for Children, and "A Compassionate Address to the Christian World." These books were designed to be given to the poor; and, in 1773, committees were appointed in Philadelphia and New York to see to their procurement, and each was authorized to draw upon the treasurer of Synod for an amount not exceeding twenty pounds. The germ of the Publication cause, as well as those of Home and Foreign Missions, was thus manifest at a period anterior to the Revolutionary conflict.

The subject of Psalmody was one which occasioned in some quarters no little disquiet. Many were indisposed to give up the old version of the Psalms, and some of the Scotch were especially tenacious of it. The church at New York had been sorely rent by troubles which had originated from this source. In 1763, the question was introduced into Synod, "As sundry members and congregations within the bounds of our Synod judge it most for edification to sing Dr. Watts's *Imitation of David's Psalms*, do the Synod so far approve said imitation as to allow such ministers and congregations the liberty of using it?" The reply was, that, as many of the Synod had not examined the book, they were not prepared to answer, but, inasmuch as it was approved by many members of the body, no objection would be made to its use till the subject of Psalmody was further considered. Members were recommended to examine the matter and be prepared to present their views the next year. But in 1764 the matter was postponed, and in 1765 it was referred to Dr. Finley and Mr. McDowell. Upon their report it was decided that the Synod "look upon the inspired Psalms in Scripture to be proper matter to be sung in Divine worship, according to their original design and the practice of the Christian churches, yet will not forbid those to use the Imitation of them whose judgment and inclination lead them to do so." For a time this decision seems to have been acquiesced in; but in 1773 trouble arose in the Second Presbyterian Church of Philadelphia. Of this church, James Sproat—converted while in Yale College under the preaching of his predecessor, on his tour through New England—was pastor. Watts's version had been introduced among the congregation, to the great annoyance of certain members. The Session favored the measure, and the Presbytery confirmed the judgment of the Session. An appeal was had to Synod, and, after discussion, a committee was appointed to confer with the original parties. Upon their report, it was decided to be unwise to affirm or disapprove the several distinct propositions laid down by the Presbytery in their judgment, and, as the Synod had not then time to "consider fully the different versions of the Psalms in question," and it had already been declared that each congregation might determine the matter for themselves, the Synod contented itself with recommending to both parties peace and harmony, forbearing all harsh sentiments and expressions, and especially all intimation that either version was "unfit to be sung in Christian worship." It was more than fifteen years later that Dr. Latta, of the Second Presbytery of Philadelphia, issued his pamphlet against Anderson, of the Associate Church, contending that the principal subjects of Psalmody should be taken from the gospel. The pamphlet was widely scattered, and, although great agitation had been produced on the subject, even beyond the mountains in the feeble churches of Kentucky, it went through four editions, and was never answered. Thus a leading member of the Old-side Second Presbytery of Philadelphia became the champion of the dreaded innovation.

For some time the authority of the Synod's *Commission* had been called in question. It was argued that the Synod had no right to delegate its full authority to a portion of its members. There were serious doubts, moreover, as to the utility as well as powers of Commission, and in 1774 the Synod found it necessary to vindicate its course in the annual appointment which had been made with undeviating uniformity from the date of its erection. Provision, however, was made to guard against any abuse of its powers from deficient attendance, and its decisions, like those of the Synod itself, were declared to be without appeal. Its proceedings and judgments, however, might be reviewed, and in this review the Commission might be present and assist.

It was at this period (1774) that Rev. Dr. Ezra Stiles and Rev. Samuel Hopkins called the attention of the Synod to the claims of the African race. They were agitating the plan of sending two natives of Africa on a mission to propagate Christianity in their native country, and they asked the Synod to approve and countenance the undertaking. The request was favorably received. The Synod declared itself "very happy to have an opportunity to express their readiness to concur with and assist in a mission to the African tribes, especially where so many circumstances concur, as in the present case, to intimate that it is the will of God, and to encourage us to hope for success." They gave assurance that they were ready to do all that was proper for them in their station, for the encouragement and assistance of those who had originated the movement.

With the cause of civil and religious liberty the American Presbyterian Church has been identified from its earliest period. From the time when Lord Cornbury imprisoned Francis Makemie for preaching in New York, the voice of the Church which boasts him as its founder has ever been on the side of freedom and against all intolerance. Throughout her entire history, and in all her records, there is not an act on this great subject which has received her sanction, for which she needs to offer an apology. On the other hand, the cause of civil and religious freedom has never found a more earnest and steadfast champion. This is abundantly illustrated in the history of our Revolutionary conflict.

The Synod of 1775 met at Philadelphia, May 17, 1775. It was a time of great popular excitement. Just four weeks to a day before they assembled, the first blood shed in the Revolutionary conflict flowed at Lexington. Just one week before, the General Congress had assembled, and was now sitting but a short distance off in the same city. Outside the place where the Synod was convened, in the streets of Philadelphia, and indeed throughout the land, nothing but the scenes and interests of the opening conflict was talked of. Yet this body calmly attended to its own proper business, and, when the fitting time had arrived, gave appropriate expression to its patriotic sympathies and its religious convictions on the subject of colonial rights. Rarely, on any occasion, has there been a parallel utterance more significant or effective; and it came at the opportune moment, when political zeal needed to be tempered and sustained by religious sanctions.

The members present in the Synod were less in number than was usual upon similar occasions; but this is easily accounted for. The Presbyteries of Suffolk, Lewes, Philadelphia Second, Hanover, and Orange, were without a single representative; Dutchess county Presbytery had but three,—Wheeler Case, Samuel Mills, and Ichabod Lewis; New Castle and Donegal had each but one, and Philadelphia First but two. In all there were only twenty-four ministers and five elders. But their very presence upon the occasion indicated their character, and the smallness of their numbers was compensated by the vigor of their spirit.

Foremost among them was the venerable Dr. Witherspoon, Scotch in accent and in strength of conviction, but American in feeling to his heart's core, and destined for six years to represent his adopted State in the General Congress, and draw up many of the most important state papers of the day. With a clear intellect, a calm judgment, indomitable strength of purpose, and a resolute and unflinching courage, he combined that conscientious integrity and religious feeling which made him among his associates in the Church what Washington was in the field, and secured for him the respect and veneration of all. But, if a host in himself, there were others present worthy to be his allies. There was Robert Cooper, for a time chaplain in the army, and who was near being taken a prisoner at Princeton; Dr. John Rodgers, of New York, chaplain during the war, first of Heath's brigade, then of the Convention of the State and of the Council of Safety; McWhorter, who shared the councils of Washington on the memorable 26th of December, 1776, when the American troops crossed the Delaware, and who was afterward chaplain of Knox's brigade; James Caldwell, inheriting with his Huguenot blood a feeling of opposition to tyranny and tyrants, a member of the Jersey regiment under his parishioner, Colonel Dayton, with a price set upon his head by the enemy, his church burned, his wife shot by a refugee, and himself at length (1781) by a drunken soldier; Jedediah Chapman, the fearless missionary pioneer, and the father of Presbyterianism in Central New York,—and others beside, well worthy to stand in the foremost rank of American and Christian patriots.

These were the men who fearlessly committed themselves on the side of freedom. In the alarming posture of public affairs they judged it their duty to appoint a day of "solemn fasting, humiliation, and prayer," to be "carefully and religiously observed" by all the congregations under their care. Anticipating a similar appointment by "the Continental Congress, now sitting," they directed that if not more than four weeks distant from it, it should supersede their own.

The measure—then unusual—of a pastoral letter, was adopted. Witherspoon, Rodgers, and Caldwell were the leading members of the committee appointed to draw it up. It bore throughout the stamp of their deep feeling and patriotic as well as religious zeal. It noticed the threatening aspect of public affairs and the apprehended horrors of a civil war, and, in view of these things, recognized the Synod's duty of addressing the numerous congregations under its care "at this important crisis." In a tone that must have sounded in strange contrast with the echoes of war, it pressed home upon the attention of all, the great truths of God's sovereignty and providence, and personal duty in relation to the claims of gospel repentance, faith, and obedience.

The letter then proceeds to express the views of the Synod, which they declare they "do not wish to conceal, as men and citizens." It urges loyalty to the king, but union on the part of the colonies: mutual charity and esteem among members of different religious denominations: vigilance in regard to social government and morals: reformation of manners: religious discipline: the careful securing of the rights of conscience by the magistrates; personal honesty and integrity; humanity and mercy, especially among such as should be called to the field. "That man will fight most bravely," they say, "who never fights till it is necessary, and who ceases to fight as soon as the necessity is over."

Such was the spirit of this noble letter. Five hundred copies of it were to be printed and circulated at the Synod's expense. Thus they were scattered abroad throughout all the congregations, contributing in no small measure to kindle and sustain the patriotic zeal of the country. The Presbyterian Church, by the act of its highest judicatory, thus took its stand at Philadelphia by the side of the American Congress then in session, and its influence was felt in a most decisive manner throughout the bounds of the Church.

CHAPTER X.

THE REVOLUTIONARY WAR AND THE REORGANIZATION OF THE CHURCH. 1775–1788.

THERE were some very obvious reasons why the Presbyterian Church in this country should take the noble stand it did, at the critical moment when the people were called to choose between resistance and submission to arbitrary power. The same reasons also were valid when the question of national independence was to be met.

The history, traditions, and sympathies of the Church, —the principles upon which its very existence was based, —the nature of its system, combining liberty with law, —the aims which it stood pledged to cherish, as well as the dangers which it had to fear in case an arbitrary system was to triumph and be established by the power of the sword,—contributed to unite the members and friends of the Church, almost as one man, in the patriotic cause. Its constituent elements, it is true, had been drawn from sources widely diverse; yet each brought with it traditionary memories, cherished with sacred fondness, which were singularly harmonious in their nature and bearing. Within its fold were men whose ancestors had resisted the Spanish tyrant, even to the death, on the dikes of Holland,—some who had listened in childhood to the story of what their ancestors, driven into exile by the revocation of the Edict of Nantes, had suffered less than a century previous,—some whose parents had wandered houseless in Scottish glens, or who had indignantly witnessed the despotic attempt to impose Episcopacy on Scotland,—not a few who must have seen and heard the heroes of Londonderry or Enniskillen,—and hundreds, if not thousands, who might proudly boast that in their veins flowed the blood of the Pilgrim Fathers of New England. Each had some treasured memory of the past, some ancestral association, which he cherished as a pledge of unswerving fidelity to the cause of civil and religious freedom.

The date of the foundation of the Church in this country, moreover, was significant. It seemed born just in time to inherit the legacy of the noblest spirits, the persecuted heroes of England, Scotland, Ireland, and the Continent. When Makemie first landed on these shores, a majority, possibly, of the two thousand Non-Conformists of 1662 still survived. Baxter had just been fined nearly two hundred pounds for preaching within five miles of a corporation, and was now writing his New Testament Paraphrase, for which the vengeance of Jeffries was soon to sentence him to a two-years imprisonment. Owen, sinking under his gigantic labors, was feeling even yet the bitterness of the intolerance that sought to identify him with the conspirators of the Rye-House Plot. Manton, silenced in the pulpit, was calmly waiting the summons to a higher service. Bates, who might have had "any bishopric in the kingdom" if he would but conform, was in a green old age, busy with his elegant pen. Calamy, of London,—whose father for preaching had been sent to Newgate, and whose son, now a boy of twelve years, was to be the historian of the heroes of Non-Conformity,—was looking eagerly toward the New World, to learn what welcome the exiled for conscience' sake found upon its shores; and to him, with his friends in the great metropolis, Makemie himself was to turn for sympathy and aid in his arduous task. Indeed, in the early history of the Presbyterian Church, every vessel that passed from the Old World to the New might have borne with it some story of persecuted faith, some illustration of religious intolerance, to make the voluntary exile for conscience' sake pledge himself anew to the cause for which he, as well as his fathers, had suffered. Then came the grievous hardships to which for successive generations "Dissenters" had been subjected in Virginia, the establishment of the Episcopal Church in the Carolinas, the fines and imprisonment of Makemie in New York, and the bigoted jealousy which up to the very moment of the Declaration of Independence denied the Presbyterians of that city a charter of incorporation, to confirm, even by the exasperations of wrong, the fidelity of the Church to the principles upon which, by New Testament authority, it had been established.

And yet—in spite of temporary grievances, now fast passing away—Presbyterians loved, and had good reason to love, this land of their nativity or adoption. Here were no cumbrous hierarchies, no prescriptive rights of nobility or primogeniture, no courts of Star Chamber and High Commission, no obtrusive and impertinent interferences, save in a few instances, with freedom of worship, or the enjoyment of civil and religious rights. Here were institutions which, if left undisturbed, came nearer than any others on the globe to realizing the ideal of a free and liberal government. Here the citizen might hope to enjoy for himself, and transmit to his children, the blessings of equal laws and constitutional freedom. Here was a treasure, therefore, worthy to be esteemed above all price,—a treasure not to be surrendered to the arrogant claims and encroachments of the British ministry, or to be yielded to the terror even of invading armies. Nor did it need any remarkable sagacity to perceive that the mischief to be dreaded was involved in the very principle on which encroachment was based. Let that principle be yielded, and no limit could be set to the arrogance that demanded the first concession. One right after another might be wrenched away, and religious liberty would not long survive the loss of civil privilege.

With the Presbyterian and Congregational Churches of the land, this consideration had great weight. They knew that there were among them many whose work was to spy out their liberties and send back sinister reports across the ocean. They were well aware that upon them were the eyes of men to whom the trappings and forms of Episcopacy were as delicious as the leeks and onions of Egypt to the Israelites in the desert. They knew that with thousands on both sides of the ocean it was a favorite project to cement the unity of the empire by the introduction and establishment in this country of diocesan bishops. Not that they envied "the Episcopal churches the privileges of a bishop, for the purposes of ordination, confirmation, and inspecting the morals of the clergy;"[1] not that they would deny to others the rights or privileges which

[1] Language employed in reference to the subject,—Minutes of the convention of delegates from the Synod and Connecticut Association, p. 13.

they claimed themselves; but they wanted no bishops with powers such as were "annexed to the office by the common law of England." "Our forefathers," said they, "and even some of ourselves, have seen and felt the tyranny of bishops' courts. Many of the first inhabitants of these colonies were obliged to seek an asylum among savages in this wilderness, in order to escape the ecclesiastical tyranny of Archbishop Land and others of his stamp. Such tyranny, if now exercised in America, would either drive us to seek new habitations among the heathen, where England could not claim a jurisdiction, or excite riots, rebellion, and wild disorder. We dread the consequences, as often as we think of this danger."

Nor was the danger merely imaginary. The Episcopacy which our fathers dreaded was the Episcopacy which they had known in England, commingling the exercise of civil with that of ecclesiastical prerogative. It was the Episcopacy which turned out the Non-Conformists, and which forced Scotland almost into open revolt. It was the Episcopacy which, grafted on the old Virginia intolerance, would exterminate "dissent," impose tithes and church-rates, and set up ecclesiastical courts sure to encroach on the rights of conscience. Disavowing the desire to introduce it with its more obnoxious features, the clergy of New York and New Jersey yet petitioned for the Episcopate, pleading that nearly a million of the inhabitants desired it. Americans in England were openly told that bishops should be "settled in America, in spite of all the Presbyterian opposition." The matter was no secret.

As early as 1748, in the times of Archbishop Secker, —perhaps earlier,—it had been proposed to introduce Episcopacy into New England by elevating some of the most distinguished of the clergy to an episcopal preeminence over their brethren. But the bribe held out was promptly and nobly spurned. Whitefield, on one of his last visits to this country, had communicated information,[1] which he had derived from an official source, of the project entertained in England of making in this country the Episcopal the Established Church. Enough was known to excite jealousy and suspicion, and unite all non-Episcopal denominations in resistance to the project. In the *Political Register* of 1769 is a picture entitled "An attempt to land a bishop in America." The name to be read on the vessel's side is that of Hillsborough, the then Colonial Secretary. The vessel has touched the wharf, but a crowd of earnest people with long poles are pushing her from her moorings. One of the multitude has a book entitled "*Sidney on Government*," another has a volume of "*Locke's Essays*," a third, in Quaker garb, has "*Barclay's Apology*" open before him, while from the lips of a fourth issues a scroll inscribed, "No lords, spiritual or temporal, in New England." Half-way up the shrouds of the vessel is a bishop in his robes, his mitre falling, and a volume of Calvin's works, hurled by one on shore, is about to strike his head. From the bishop's lips issues a scroll, on which is inscribed the *nunc dimittis* of aged Simeon, while in the foreground is a paper with the words, "Shall they be obliged to maintain a bishop who cannot maintain themselves?" At the same time, a monkey near by is throwing a stone at the bishop. The picture is significant as expressing the popular feeling in opposition to Episcopal projects.

This feeling found prompt and decided expression in the papers of the day. It was at just this period (1766) that a voluntary Episcopal convention of the clergy of New York and New Jersey was held; and by them the petition for bishops, already referred to, was drawn

---

[1] Gordon's America, vol. i.

up to be forwarded to England. Dr. B. Chandler, of Elizabethtown, was requested to write and publish an appeal to the public in favor of the project. The appeal was published in 1767, but was soon ably answered by Dr. Charles Chauncey, of Boston.

The paper controversy had now commenced: by the close of the following year, articles had been published sufficient in number and length to be comprised in two volumes, which were published at New York in 1768. The convention of Congregational, Consociated, and Presbyterian Churches, which began its annual meetings in 1766, had its attention called to the subject. Indeed, the convention itself originated in the general apprehension of the common danger. The opposition was not to bishops vested only with spiritual powers, but to the governmental sanction of an episcopate whose temporal ambition would be thereby inflamed, and which would not be disposed to rest till it enjoyed the prestige and emoluments of an Establishment.

There was, therefore, grave reason for apprehension. The projects of the British ministry were scarcely even disguised. But the Presbyterian Church was not disposed to meet them with tame submission. The spirit of Makemie still lived in the hearts of those upon whom his mantle had fallen. The cause of civil was with them also the cause of religious freedom. They wanted no Establishment, no Episcopal arrogance, no lords spiritual, on this side of the Atlantic. The mere knowledge of the threatened danger tended strongly to unite them almost to a man in opposition.

Equally significant was the attitude of the Episcopal Church. For the most part it was ultra-loyal. It numbered only here and there a clergyman who manifested the least sympathy for the cause of liberty. They "leaned, with very few exceptions, throughout the colonies, to the side of the crown, and in the Middle and Northern provinces their flocks were chiefly of the same way of thinking."[1] This fact was not without its influence. It reacted upon the minds of the Presbyterians, and made them still more earnest in their efforts and apprehensive in their fears.

Thus was a religious element mingled in the strife. It was not merely a protest against stamped paper and a tax on tea, but it was the cause of civil rights, of conscience, and of religious freedom. It required no little strength of conviction to sustain the patriotism of the country through a seven-years conflict; but what was required was found to exist. The Revolution came, and it found no more steadfast friends and adherents than in the ranks of the Presbyterian Church.

The influence of the war upon the condition and prospects of the Presbyterian Church, throughout the country, was most disastrous. Its members were almost all decided patriots, and its ministers, almost to a man, were accounted arch-rebels. Their well-known views and sympathies made them specially obnoxious to the enemy, and to be known as a Presbyterian was to incur all the odium of a "Whig." It is not strange, therefore, that they should have been the marked victims of hostility, or that they should have been, in many cases, mercilessly molested in property and person.

In initiating the Revolution, and in sustaining the patriotic resistance of their countrymen to illegal tyranny, the ministers of the Presbyterian Church bore a conspicuous and even foremost part. Throughout that most trying and disastrous period through which the Church and country had as yet been called to pass, they proved themselves alike faithful to both. Their conduct fully justified the noble utterance of the Synod of 1775, a few weeks after the first blood was

[1] Hildreth, iii. 56.

shed at Lexington. They preached the duty of resisting tyrants. They cheered their people in the dreary periods of the conflict by inspiring lofty trust in the God of nations. Some of them were engaged personally in the army. Some occupied a place in the civil councils. Others were personal sufferers from the vengeance of an exasperated foe, and others, still, sealed their devotion to their country by their blood.[1]

Among those who advocated the cause of the colonies, and who from the pulpit endeavored to strengthen patriotic zeal by Christian principle, it would be almost invidious to name any; for nearly all were alike guilty in this respect. Dr. Witherspoon, Patrick Allison in Baltimore, William Tennent in Charleston, George Duffield in Philadelphia, John Miller at Dover, James Waddel and John Blair Smith in Virginia, led the way in vindicating from the pulpit the cause of American freedom.

On the fast-day (May 17, 1776) Dr. Witherspoon preached a sermon,—afterward published and dedicated to John Hancock,—in which he entered fully into the great political questions of the day. It manifested his loyal zeal in behalf of his adopted country, and his ability to vindicate her cause. Republished, with notes, in Glasgow, it subjected its author to the odium of a rebel and a traitor. A member of the Provincial Congress of New Jersey, he was elected by that body to the Continental Congress, and took part in defending the project of the Declaration of Independence. During the debate on its adoption, he is reported to have said, "That noble instrument on your table, which secures immortality to its author, should be subscribed this very morning by every pen in this

---

[1] The facts that follow have been derived from very various sources, although most of them are from Sprague's Annals.

house. He who will not respond to its accents, and strain every nerve to carry into effect its provisions, is unworthy the name of a freeman. Although these gray hairs must descend into the sepulchre, I would infinitely rather they should descend thither by the hand of the public executioner than desert at this crisis the sacred cause of my country."

John Carmichael preached, at their request, to the militia of the city of Lancaster. The discourse of Miller, of Dover, who was bold in the expression of his patriotic ardor, was especially remarkable. Several days before the Declaration of Independence, he so far anticipated the spirit of that decisive measure as to address his people from that significant text, indicative enough of his own views,—"We have no part in David, nor any inheritance in the son of Jesse: to your tents, O Israel!" Robert Davidson, pastor of the First Presbyterian Church of Philadelphia, at the commencement of the war, preached before several military companies from the text, "For there fell down many slain, because the war was of God." A fortnight after, it was repeated before the troops at Burlington. Sermons of this stamp were by no means infrequent. Many of the soldiers were Presbyterians, and in the camp sought the privilege of hearing their own pastors, who sometimes, in their anxiety for their spiritual welfare, followed them to the field.

Of John Craighead, pastor of Rocky Spring Church, Pa., it is said that "he fought and preached alternately." At the commencement of the war he raised a company from the members of his charge, and joined Washington's army in New Jersey. His friend Dr. Cooper, of Middle Spring Church, is also said to have been the captain of a company.[1] He preached "before

[1] Mr. Craighead was a humorist, and many good jokes are told of him. One day, it is said, going into battle, a cannon-ball

Colonel Montgomery's battalion under arms," near Shippensburg, Pa., August 31, 1775, a sermon entitled "Courage in a Good Cause."[1] Dr. King, of Conococheague (Mercersburg), was eminent for his patriotic zeal. He not only volunteered his services, and went as chaplain to the battalion which marched from his region, but many were the addresses which he delivered to inspirit the hearts of the people in their devotion to the cause of the country.

From one of these, something may be gathered of the tone of pulpit utterance in that trying period. "Subjection," he said, "is demanded of us, but it is not the constitutional subjection which we are bound to pay; it is not a legal subjection to the king they would bring us to. *That* we already acknowledge. But it is a subjection to the British Parliament, or to the people of Great Britain. This we deny, and, I hope, will always deny. They are not our lords and masters; they are no more than our brethren and our fellow-subjects. They call themselves, and it has been usual to call them, the *mother-country*. But this is only a name, and, if there was any thing in it, one would think that it should lead them to treat us like children, with parental affection. But is it fatherly or motherly to strip us of every thing, to rob us of every right and privilege, and then to whip and dragoon us with fleets and armies till we are pleased? No! as the name does not belong to them, so their conduct shows they have no right to claim it. We are on an equal footing with them in all respects;

---

struck a tree near him, a splinter of which nearly knocked him down. "God bless me!" exclaimed Mr. Cooper, "you were nearly knocked to staves." "Oh, yes," was his reply; "and, though you are a *cooper*, you could not have set me up."—*Nevin's Churches of the Valley*, 211.

[1] This sermon is in possession of the Presbyterian Historical Society.

with respect to government and privileges; and, therefore, their usurpation ought to be opposed. Nay, when the king uses the executive branch of government which is in his hand, to enable one part of his subjects to lord it over and oppress another, it is a sufficient ground of our applying to the laws of nature for our defence.

"But this is the case with us. We have no other refuge from slavery but those powers which God has given us and allowed us to use in defence of our dearest rights; and I hope he will bless our endeavors and give success to this oppressed people, and that the wicked instruments of all these distractions shall meet their due reward. I earnestly wish that in such troublous times, while we plead for liberty, a proper guard may be kept against any turbulent or mobbish outbreak, and that unanimity may be universal both in counsel and action, and that we may still have an eye to the great God, who has some important reasons for such severe corrections. Let us look to the rod and Him that hath appointed it; let us humble ourselves before him daily for our sins, and depend upon him for success. If he be against us, in vain do we struggle; if the Lord be for us, though an host should encamp against us, we need not be afraid."

In one of the darkest hours of the strife,—after the repulse in Canada,—he said, in a funeral discourse on the death of Montgomery, "Surely we have still reason for the exercise of faith and confidence in God, that he will not give a people up to the unlimited will and power of others, who have done all they could to avert the calamity, and have so strenuously adhered to the cause of reason and humanity,—a people who have been attacked with unprovoked violence, and driven with the greatest reluctance to take up arms for their defence,—a people whom he himself, by a series of gracious actings, hath gradually led on to this condition. . . . Therefore, when these are our circumstances, we may rationally judge that God is not an unconcerned spectator, but that he sees and will reward the persecutors. Many things, indeed, seem to be against us; a very great and powerful enemy, who have been long trained to victory; their numerous and savage allies, who, having lost their liberty, would have others in the same condition; our weakness and inexperience in war, internal enemies, the loss of many of our friends, and a beloved and able general. But let not these destroy our hopes or damp our spirits. To put too much confidence in man is the way to provoke God to deprive us of them. This may, perhaps, be the darkness which precedes the glorious day. . . . It is agreeable to God's method to bring low before he exalteth, to humble before he raises up. Let us trust in him and do our duty, and commit the event to *his* determination, who can make these things to be for us which, by a judgment of sense, we are ready to say are *against* us."

In a similar strain did he exhort the soldiers marching to the field, or address the people who remained behind. "Be thou faithful unto death," was the text of one of his discourses. "There is no soldier," he said, "so truly courageous as a pious man. There is no army so formidable as those who are superior to the fear of death. Consequently, no one qualification is more necessary in a soldier than true religion." These words were accompanied by the tender counsels of a pastor whose affections followed his men to the scenes of danger and death. With the greatest earnestness he urged them to watch over their own souls, and not to bring dishonor on the cause to which they were attached.

While several of the Presbyterian ministers performed service and led companies to the field, a large number were engaged as chaplains in the army. Alexander McWhorter—afterward Dr. McWhorter, of Newark, —was chaplain of Knox's brigade while it lay at White Plains, and often had General Washington among his hearers. James F. Armstrong—afterward of Elizabethtown—joined a volunteer company before his licensure, and, soon after he was ordained, was appointed by Congress "chaplain of the second brigade of the Maryland forces." Adam Boyd was chaplain of the North Carolina brigade. Daniel McCalla was sent to Canada as chaplain with General Thompson's forces at the commencement of hostilities. Dr. John Rodgers was chaplain of Heath's brigade. George Duffield, in connection with Mr. (afterward Bishop) White, was employed as chaplain of the Colonial Congress.

It was not infrequently that the minister of peace felt called upon to engage in active service in the armies of his country; and not a few of the young men who had won distinction in the use of carnal weapons became afterward still more eminent in the service of the gospel. When an unusual number of his people had been drafted to serve in the militia, James Latta, of Chesnut Level, with a view to encourage them, took his blanket, shouldered his knapsack, and accompanied them on their campaign. James Caldwell, chaplain of the Jersey brigade, accompanied his own parishioners to the camp, and, with a price set upon his head, it is not surprising that when he preached at "the Old Red Store" he was first seen to disengage himself of his pistols. Samuel Eakin, of Penn's Neck, was a strong Whig, and the idol of the soldiers. Gifted with extraordinary eloquence, and accounted scarcely inferior to Whitefield, he was ever on the alert to kindle the patriotic zeal of his countrymen. When there were military trainings, or the soldiers were ordered to march, he was present to address them and thrill them by his eloquence.[1] John Blair Smith, teacher, and afterward President, of Hampden-Sidney College, was chosen captain of a company of students, and, after the battle of Cowpens, hurried to join the retreating army, and was only dissuaded by the remonstrances of the commanding officer, who represented to him that his patriotic speeches at home would be far more valuable than his services in the camp. James Hall, of North Carolina, subsequently the pioneer missionary in the Valley of the Mississippi, was selected as leader and accepted the command of a company formed mainly from his own congregation, whom his fervid and pathetic appeals had inspired to arm against Cornwallis. Such was his reputation that he was offered the commission of brigadier-general.

When Tarleton and his British dragoons spread consternation throughout the surrounding Valley of Virginia, William Graham, John Brown, and Archibald Scott exhorted the stripling youths of their congregations—their elder brethren were already with Washington—to rise, join their neighbors, and dispute the passage of the invader and his legion at Rockfish Gap, on the Blue Ridge. Graham was the master-spirit; but he was heartily supported by his co-Presbyters. On one occasion, when there was backwardness to enlist, he had his own name enrolled. The effect was such that the company was immediately filled, and he was unanimously chosen captain. It is worthy of mention that Dr. Ashbel Green, many years before he aspired to be an ecclesiastical leader, had attained the distinction of orderly sergeant in the militia of the Revolutionary period, and had risked his life in the cause of his country. Dr. Moses Hoge served for a time, previous to

---

[1] Barber's New Jersey, 430.

entering the ministry, in the army of the Revolution. Dr. John Brown, President of Georgia University, had at the early age of sixteen exchanged the groves of the Academy for the noise and bustle of the camp, and fought with intrepid spirit, by the side of Sumter, his country's battles. Dr. Asa Hillyer, of Orange, N.J., while a youth, assisted his father, a surgeon in the Revolutionary army. Joseph Badger was in the battle of Bunker Hill, and served as soldier, baker, nurse, &c., in Arnold's expedition to Canada. James White Stephenson, of South Carolina,—teacher of Andrew Jackson,—served throughout the war, and on one occasion had his gun shivered in his hand by the enemy's shot, which glanced and killed the man who stood by his side. Lewis Feuilleteau Wilson, who studied medicine before his attention was directed to theology, served for several years as surgeon in the Continental army. Simpson, of Fishing Creek, S.C., encouraged his people to deeds of heroism or patient endurance, and was himself found bearing arms, and was in several engagements; and Joseph Alexander, of the same State, was often a fugitive from his own home, while he offered his dwelling at all times as a hospital for sick or wounded soldiers.[1] Jonas Coe, one of the early members of the Albany Presbytery, joined the army, along with his father and four brothers, while yet a youth of sixteen. Robert Marshall, afterward an eloquent minister in Kentucky, was in six general engagements, one of which was the hard-fought battle of Monmouth. James Turner, the eloquent Virginian preacher, could boast that at the early age of seventeen he had seen service in the Revolutionary army.

These are but a few of that large band identified with the interests of the Presbyterian Church, and

---

[1] Dr. Howe's Historical Discourse.

then, or at a later period, serving at her altar, who freely risked their lives in the service of their country. Whether in the bosom of their own congregations, or serving in the camp, they were animated by the same devotion to the cause of God and their native land. Their message everywhere was welcome. The soldier was inspired to bolder courage by the look and words of his own pastor, or the pulpit exhortations of those who shared his hardships and his perils. The camp betrayed the presence of a conservative influence which checked the vices which are wont to be indigenous to it, while many who never listened to the gospel before were privileged to hear it at a crisis when at every hour they stood in peril of their lives.

To the privations, hardships, and cruelties of the war the Presbyterians were pre-eminently exposed. In them the very essence of rebellion was supposed to be concentrated, and by the wanton plunderings and excesses of the marauding parties they suffered severely. Their Presbyterianism was *prima facie* evidence of guilt. A house that had a large Bible and David's Psalms in metre in it was supposed, as a matter of course, to be tenanted by rebels. To sing "Old Rouse" was almost as criminal as to have levelled a loaded musket at a British grenadier.

To the Presbyterian clergy the enemy felt an especial antipathy. They were accounted the ringleaders of rebellion. For them there was often not so much safety in their own dwellings as in the camp. When their people were scattered, or it was no longer safe to reside among them, the only alternative was to flee or join the army, and this alternative was often presented. Not unfrequently the duty of the chaplain or the pastor exposed him to dangers as great as those which the common soldier was called to meet. There was risk of person, sometimes capture, and sometimes loss of life. Some ministers fled for safety. Dr. Rodgers was forced to absent himself from New York till the close of the war; McKnight, of Shrewsbury, N.J., was carried off a captive; Richards, of Rahway, N.J., took warning and fled. Dr. Buell, of East Hampton, L.I., who remained at his post, repeatedly ran imminent risks even from the men whom his wit and urbanity finally disarmed. Duffield was saved from capture at Trenton only by the timely warning of a friendly Quaker. At one time, while the enemy were on Staten Island, he preached to the soldiers in an orchard on the opposite side of the bay. The forks of a tree served him for a pulpit; but the noise of the singing attracted the notice of the enemy, and soon the voice of praise was interrupted by the whistling of balls. But the preacher, undismayed by the danger, bade his hearers retire behind a hillock, and there finished his sermon. Daniel McCalla was confined for several months in a loathsome prison-ship near Quebec. Nehemiah Greenman, of Pittsgrove, N.J., fled to the wilderness to escape the indignities so largely dealt out by the enemy to the Presbyterian ministers. Azel Roe, of Woodbridge, N.J., taken prisoner by the enemy, was for some time confined in the Old Sugar-House. He came near having a fall in a small stream which the company had to ford on the way. The commanding officer politely offered to carry Mr. Roe over on his back. The offer was accepted, and the suggestion of Mr. Roe to the officer that he was priest-ridden now, if never before, so convulsed him with laughter that he was like to have dropped his load. Less merciful was the experience of John Rosbrugh, of Allentown, N.J., first a private soldier and afterward chaplain of a military company formed in his neighborhood, and who was shot down in cold blood by a body of Hessians to whom he had surrendered himself a prisoner.

There was a strange commingling of carnal and spiritual weapons in the experience of the camp. Joseph Patterson, one of the fathers of the Presbytery of Redstone, had just knelt to pray under a shed, when a board, in a line with his head, was shivered by the discharge of a rifle. Stephen B. Balch preached a sermon on subjection to the higher powers, while General Williams, to the annoyance of royalists who were present, protected him with loaded pistols in his belt. The ministers on the frontiers, exposed to the attacks of the Indians, were compelled to go constantly armed. Thaddeus Dod, with his people, exchanged his church for the fort that had been built on the Monongahela. Samuel Doak, of the Holston settlements, paused in his sermon at the alarm of an attack, seized his rifle that stood by his side, and led his male hearers in pursuit of the foe.

Not a few of the ministers of the Presbyterian Church were called into the civil service of their country. Dr. Witherspoon was for several years a member of the Continental Congress; his sagacity and discretion were highly esteemed, and his pen was in frequent requisition. Many of the most important state papers of the day, in relation to such intricate subjects of political economy as the emission of paper money and the mode of supplying the army by commission, were written by him; and in calls for the observance of days of fasting and prayer, his pen was usually employed. Jacob Green, the father of Dr. Ashbel Green, was a zealous patriot, and was elected, though contrary to his expressed wishes, a member of the Provincial Congress of New Jersey. He was chairman of the committee that drafted the Constitution of the State. Henry Patillo was a member of the Provincial Congress of North Carolina. J. J. Zubly was a delegate from Georgia to the Continental Congress.[1] William Tennent, of the Circular Church, Charleston, was a member of the Provincial Congress of South Carolina, and amid the fearful emergencies of the period, and at different hours of the same day, he was occasionally heard, in his church and in the State-House, addressing different audiences, with equal animation, on their temporal and spiritual interests. And, not content with this, in company with William H. Drayton, he made the circuit of the middle and up country of the State, to stimulate the people to resistance.[2] David Caldwell was a member of the convention that formed the State Constitution of North Carolina; Kettletas, of Jamaica, was chosen a delegate to the New York Convention; and Duffield, Rodgers, McWhorter, and others, were often consulted by civil and military officers in the trying crises of the Revolutionary period, and they were always prompt to render their services. Like Thomas Read, of Delaware, roused from his bed at midnight to describe the region which the army was to traverse and in which he might act as a guide, they were never wanting when their country required their counsel or their aid.

It is not strange that their course was regarded as specially obnoxious by the British troops. Their houses were plundered, their churches often burned, and their books and manuscripts committed to the flames. The church of Midway, in Georgia,—then Congregational,—rendered itself obnoxious to the foe by its patriotic zeal. In November, 1778, a special detachment from Florida attacked the settlement, burned the church-edifice, almost every dwelling-house, the crops of rice,

---

[1] He did not, however, approve the Declaration of Independence, and was subsequently banished from Georgia.

[2] Dr. Howe's Historical Discourse.

then in stack, drove off the negroes and horses, carried away the plate belonging to the planters, and outraged even the graves of the dead. Some of the members of the congregation were seized and imprisoned. Dr. McWhorter had removed to Carolina while the enemy, under Cornwallis, threatened the Southern country. Under the apprehension of danger, he fled with his family, and on his return found that his library, furniture, and nearly all that he possessed had been sacrificed. Not less unfortunate were Elihu Spencer, at Trenton, and David Caldwell and Hugh McAden, of North Carolina. On many occasions the soldiers studiously destroyed all that they could not carry away, and the Presbyterian clergy were generally the special objects of vengeance.

As might be expected, religion suffered greatly throughout the entire period of the war. The church-edifices were often taken possession of by an insolent soldiery and turned into hospitals or prisons, or perverted to still baser uses as stables or riding-schools. The church at Newtown had its steeple sawed off, and was used as a prison and guard-house till it was torn down and its siding used for the soldiers' huts. The church at Crumpond was burned to save it from being occupied by the enemy. That of Mount Holly was burned by accident or design. The one at Princeton was taken possession of by the Hessian soldiers, and stripped of its pews and gallery for fuel. A fireplace was built in it, and a chimney carried up through its roof. Supposing it would be defended against him, Washington planted his cannon a short distance off and commenced firing into it. It was subsequently occupied by the American soldiers, and the close of the war found it dilapidated and open to the weather, while its interior was quite defaced and destroyed. The church of Westfield was injured by the enemy and its bell carried off to New York. The church of Babylon, Long Island, was torn down by the enemy for military purposes. That of New Windsor was used as a hospital. This was the case also with the one at Morristown; and repeatedly in the morning the dead were found lying in the pews. The one at Elizabethtown was made a hospital for the sick and disabled soldiers of the American army. Its bell sounded the note of alarm at the approach of the foe, while its floor was often the bed of the weary soldier, and the seats of its pews served as the table from which he ate his scanty meal. At length it was fired by the torch of the refugee, in vengeance for the uses to which it had been devoted. The churches at New York were taken possession of by the enemy. Prisoners were confined in them, or they were used by the British officers for stabling their horses. Ethan Allen describes the filth that had accumulated in the one with which he was acquainted, as altogether intolerable.[1] The loathsome victims of disease, foul with their own excrements, lay stretched upon the floor. And throughout the country the church-edifices, unless some selfish motive prevented, were treated with but little more respect. More than fifty places of worship throughout the land were utterly destroyed by the enemy during the period of the war.[2] The larger number of these were burned, others were levelled to the ground, while others still were so defaced or injured as to be utterly unfit for use. This was the case in several of the principal cities, at Philadelphia and Charleston, as well as New York.[3]

Even where the church-edifice was left unmolested, the congregation was often scattered. At Albany, for

[1] Life of Ethan Allen. [2] Life of Dr. Rodgers.

[3] Other denominations sometimes suffered as well as the Presbyterians. The Quaker-meeting house at Birmingham, Pa., was used as a hospital after the battle of Chadd's Ford.

the most part beyond the reach of the enemy, the ordinances of religion almost altogether ceased, and with the return of peace the church had to be organized anew. This was no infrequent experience. Pastors, in many cases, were not allowed to continue their ministry, or like Rodgers, of New York, Richards, of Rahway, Prime, of Huntington, or Duffield, of Philadelphia, were forced to flee for their lives.

But all did not escape. Caldwell, of Elizabethtown, was shot by a sentinel who was said to have been bribed by the British, or the Tories, to whom he was especially obnoxious. Moses Allen, a classmate of President Madison at Princeton, pastor of the Midway church, Georgia, and chaplain of a regiment, was drowned near Savannah, February 8, 1779, in attempting to swim ashore from a prison-ship, the barbarous captain of which refused his friends boards for his coffin. And not a few others incurred hardships which in all probability shortened their days. It is certainly remarkable, considering their exposure, and the almost venomous hatred with which they were regarded by the enemy, that among the Presbyterian ministers the direct victims of the war were so few.

There was too much else to engage public attention to allow much regard to be given to the claims of religion. The clash of arms drowned the voice of the preacher, save when it was heard in camp during the intervals of fight. Even there it was sometimes disturbed by the cannon's roar and the rolling drum. Academies and colleges were almost entirely deserted. The young men, many of them, hurried away from the scenes of study to aid their country on the field of battle; and sometimes the teacher, like Daggett, at New Haven, or Smith, at Hampden-Sidney, headed his pupils in resistance to the invader. At Yale but a small number of students were left within the college walls, and for a time these were removed to other towns of the State. James Latta's school at Chesnut Level was closed, for the usher and the older scholars had joined the army. The operations of the College of New Jersey were suspended, the class of 1778 numbering but five students. The classical school in Culpepper county, Va., where Moses Hoge was pursuing his studies, was altogether broken up. Hampden-Sidney had scarcely a name to live. James White Stephenson gave up his classical school near the old Waxhaw church, dismissed his pupils,[1] and knew no other life than that of a soldier until the return of peace.

In these circumstances, it is not surprising that the course of the Presbyterian Church should be retrograde rather than on the advance. The camp, with all the safeguards that could be thrown around it, and with all the counteracting influence which the chaplains could exert, was a school of immorality, profanity, and vice. Many places, especially in Virginia, were sadly cursed by the disbanded soldiery. Civil order was established as yet on very insecure foundations. Religious institutions were paralyzed in their influence, even where they were still sustained. Sabbath desecration prevailed to an alarming extent. Infidelity, in many quarters, soon acquired a foothold. The *civil* character of the war, especially in the Southern States, gave it a peculiar ferocity, and produced a licentiousness of morals of which there is scarce a parallel at the present day. Municipal laws could not be enforced. Civil government was frustrated, and society was well-nigh resolved into its original elements.

Thus at the close of the war religion was, on every side, in an exceedingly decayed state. The churches presented to view a wide scene of desolation. That

---

[1] See Sprague, i. 550.

of Newtown numbered but five members at the close of the war; and scores of others were in an equally lamentable condition. The stated ordinances of the gospel had been discontinued, and the young men who should have been prepared to enter the ministry had been constrained to abandon their purpose.

The meetings of the Synod during the period of the war were gloomy and disheartening. There was but a small attendance, and the reports which were brought by the few who came, were discouraging in the extreme. Little could be undertaken, and less accomplished. At the opening sessions of 1776 there were but eighteen ministers and three elders present; in the following year, only twenty-six ministers. In 1778, the enemy had taken possession of Philadelphia, and the Synod was opened at Bedminster with eleven ministers and three elders. In the following year there were twenty ministers and seven elders, and in 1780 only fifteen ministers and four elders, at the opening sessions. Nearly all that could be done was the annual appointment, continued through the war, of a day of humiliation, fasting, and prayer. Applications for aid were received, but it was beyond the power of Synod to supply the demand. They came from the North, the South, and the West, but the most urgent and importunate were from Virginia, where the Hanover Presbytery found the popular sympathy turning strongly in favor of Presbyterianism, and where the opposition to English tyranny created a prejudice with many against the Episcopal Church as lukewarm in a cause in which it must be necessarily divided against itself.

With the return of peace, the Presbyterian Church began to revive. The meetings of Synod assumed somewhat of their former aspect. In 1780, it had commenced its sessions with only fifteen ministers and four elders present, and in 1781, with only twenty-one ministers and four elders. In 1783, there were forty-three ministers present at the opening session; in 1784, thirty; in 1785, thirty; in 1786, thirty-eight; and in 1787, under the urgent call to consider the subject of a new organization of the highest judicature of the Church, there were fifty-two.

The period of the war had been one of peculiar hardship to the ministers of the Church. Their salaries, paid, if at all, in depreciated currency, proved quite insufficient, and in 1782 their condition claimed the attention of Synod. In 1783, on the report of a committee appointed the previous year, a pastoral letter was drawn up and printed, addressed to the congregations, on the subject of ministerial support. The interests of religion were pronounced to be "in danger of suffering greatly, at the present, from the many discouragements under which the ministers of the gospel labor, from the want of a sufficient support and liberal maintenance from the congregations they serve."

The restoration of peace brought with it the same difficulty which had been before experienced from the immigration of foreign ministers and candidates. Although no longer so numerous as to form a party in the Church, some of them were regarded with well-grounded suspicion. Applications to Synod to receive or ordain men of this class were becoming frequent, and in 1784 the members of the several Presbyteries were enjoined "to be particularly careful" in view of "imminent danger from ministers and licensed candidates of unsound principles coming among us." In the following year the question of relaxing the terms of literary qualification in candidates for the ministry was brought up. By a great majority it was carried in the negative. It was also proposed that the term of studying divinity should hereafter be two years instead of one; but action upon it was deferred to the next meeting, when, in the press of other matters, it was crowded out.

The subject of procuring Bibles for distribution among the poor, especially on the frontiers, by means of collections in the churches, was brought up in 1783. The Synod recommended that collections should be made; but the recommendation was complied with in only a few instances, and was renewed again in 1785. The neglect was due in part to the exhausted and impoverished condition of the country at large, and in part to the absence of members and even of whole Presbyteries. To such an extent had this latter evil grown, that a letter was addressed to the Presbyteries of Hanover, Orange, Dutchess, and Suffolk, urging attention to the subject, and kindly remonstrating with them for a neglect which might tend to "the great injury, if not the entire mouldering away, of the body."

The purport of the letter seems to have been misapprehended by the Suffolk Presbytery. Several of its ministers were originally Congregationalists, and quite a large proportion of the people were descendants of New England settlers. They seem also to have been disturbed by the proposal, already agitated, for a new form of government and discipline. Not a member of the body appeared in Synod the following year; but in 1787 a letter was received from them, addressed to the moderator of the Synod, praying that their union with the body might be dissolved. Dr. McWhorter was directed to prepare a reply. It was kindly worded, and was intended to meet their objections of "local situation," non-concurrence "with the draught of the form of government," and non-compliance of the churches within their limits. As to the first of these, it had always been the same. In regard to the second, the "draught was submitted for overture and amendment;" while the indisposition of the churches to comply might be the result of groundless prejudices, hastily imbibed,—prejudices "which, by taking some pains and by giving a proper explanation of the matter, might be readily removed."

To enforce the arguments for a reconsideration of its resolution by the Presbytery, Drs. McWhorter and Rodgers, and Messrs. Roe, Woodhull, and Davenport, were appointed a committee to meet and converse with them. The result of the conference was that the Presbytery withdrew their petition, and were prepared in the following year to enter with the other Presbyteries as constituent elements of the newly-organized Assembly.

The spirit of this proceeding is indicative of the tolerant temper of the Church. This temper had not changed. The annual convention of Congregationalists and Presbyterians had been dropped from necessity at the commencement of the Revolutionary conflict, but the spirit in which it had originated still survived.

Nor was the Synod neglectful of its position as the advocate of civil and religious freedom. Scarcely had the war closed, when rumors were afloat in some quarters which seemed to intimate the purpose of the Presbyterian Church to seek an alliance with the state. It occupied, indeed, a highly respectable position. Its ministers had been chaplains in the army. Its leading man, Dr. Witherspoon, had been a leader in the General Congress. It was, in fact, the only denomination which, from position and influence, could be considered in the light of a candidate for the special favors of the state. But any charge of seeking such favor on its part was utterly ungrounded. The Synod scarcely deemed it necessary to make a disavowal of it; but some of its members insisted on the necessity of such a disavowal. In consequence, a minute was adopted by the Synod of 1781, which the next Synod ordered to be expunged. But in 1783, on the principle that no minute in any instance should be expunged, it was ordered to be restored. It was to the effect that it had been represented to Synod that the Presbyterian Church suffers greatly in the opinion of other denominations, from an apprehension that they hold intolerant principles; and in view of this "the Synod do solemnly and publicly declare that they ever have, and still do, renounce and abhor the principles of intolerance, and we do believe that every peaceable member of civil society ought to be protected in the full and free exercise of their religion."

Nor did the Synod overlook the subject of civil freedom, at least in its moral aspect. Upon a review of the Minutes in 1780, it appeared that "an affair respecting the enslaving of negroes" had been before the Synod of 1774. By succeeding Synods it had, "by some means, been passed over." It was now discussed, but without definite action. In 1787, however, it was declared that "the Synod of New York and Philadelphia do highly approve of the general principles in favor of universal liberty that prevail in America, and of the interest which many of the States have taken in promoting the abolition of slavery; yet, inasmuch as men, introduced from a servile state to a participation of all the privileges of civil society, without a proper education, and without previous habits of industry, may be, in some respects, dangerous to the community; therefore they earnestly recommend it to all the members belonging to their communion to give those persons, who are at present held in servitude, such good education as may prepare them for the better enjoyment of freedom. And they moreover recommend that masters, whenever they find servants disposed to make a proper improvement of the privilege, would give them some share of property to begin with, or grant them sufficient time and sufficient means of procuring, by industry, their own liberty, at a moderate rate, that they may thereby be brought into society with those habits of industry that may render them useful citizens; and, finally, they recommend it to all the people under their care, to use the most prudent measures consistent with the interest and the state of civil society in the parts where they live, to procure eventually *the final abolition of slavery in America.*"

So important did this utterance afterward appear, that by the Assembly of 1793 it was ordered to be republished in the extracts from the Minutes, thus receiving the authoritative re-endorsement of the Presbyterian Church.

The plan of union between the Synod and the Associate Presbyterian Church had proved a failure. The letter of 1769 put an end to any hopes of it which might before have been entertained. But, in 1784, a plan of correspondence between the Synod and the two Synods of the Reformed Dutch and Associate Presbyterian Churches was discussed, and measures taken for rendering it effective. The desire was expressed by members of those bodies in favor of "a friendly intercourse between the three Synods, or laying a plan for some kind of union among them, whereby they might be enabled to unite their interests and combine their efforts;" and by these members some such measure was pronounced to be practicable. A committee, therefore, was appointed to meet with corresponding committees from the other Synods, to consider what plan could be devised. The convention met at New York in 1785, and gave to the subject their deliberate attention. There seemed to be on the part of the committees from the other Synods a jealousy in regard to the soundness and rigid discipline of the Synod of New York and Philadelphia. The question was raised in regard to its standards and the manner in which they were to be regarded and adopted. Although the convention assumed only the powers of counsel and advice, suggestions were made and measures adopted to secure mutual harmony between the different bodies. In the following year the committee asked of the Synod more definite instructions in regard to some points on which they had been unable to give entire satisfaction. In view of the meditated change in the constitution of the form of government, it was decided that "the mutual assurances mentioned in the Minutes of the last convention may be made with much more propriety after the intended system is finished than at present." The conventions continued to be held annually for several years, and committees were appointed for the purpose at each meeting of Synod.

The rapid extension of the Presbyterian Church after the paralyzing effect of the Revolutionary conflict had begun to pass away, directed attention toward measures for perfecting its organization, as well as putting forth a full declaration of its principles. The separation of the colonies from the mother-country required a corresponding change in that part of the Confession which referred to civil government. It was evident that the future policy of the Church must now be initiated; and the project was entertained of a division of the Synod and the formation of a General Assembly. Unless some such measure should be speedily adopted, it was feared that the body which hitherto had been the supreme judicature of the Church would become too large and unwieldy to perform its duties with efficiency and vigor, or that "the attendance of members would fall into neglect."

As early as the annual meeting of the Synod in May, 1785, a committee was appointed to prepare the form of a Constitution for the Church, to be submitted to the Synod of the following year. Their report was duly made in 1786, and referred to another committee to meet in the autumn of that year, with powers to digest a Constitution for the Presbyterian Church, to print it, and send copies of it to each of the Presbyteries. These again were to report their judgment of the same, in writing, at the Synod of 1787. These reports were made, and the Synod, after reading and considering the draught of the preceding year, and availing itself of the written suggestions of the Presbyteries, issued another pamphlet, more complete than that of the committee, and ordered a thousand copies to be distributed to the several Presbyteries. The system thus presented formed the basis of the deliberations of the Synod of 1788, which issued in the formation and publication of the Constitution of the Church. The full title of the volume issued is, "The Constitution of the Presbyterian Church in the United States of America: containing the Confession of Faith, the Catechisms, the Government and Discipline, and the Directory for the Worship of God, ratified and adopted by the Synod of New York and Philadelphia, May the 16th, 1788, and continued by adjournment until the twenty-eighth of the same month. Philadelphia. Printed by Thomas Bradford. MD.CCLXXXIX."[1]

In the discussions which preceded the final adoption of the Constitution, the question was raised, "Shall the Supreme Judicatory be denominated a General Council or a General Assembly?" The question was, indeed, one only of name; for in either case the body would be possessed of the same powers. But the very fact that it was agitated, and that Dr. Witherspoon

[1] I transcribe the title-page of the only copy of the work which I have met, now in my possession.

himself voted in favor of "Council," shows that the body did not feel themselves bound to any rigid adoption of the Scottish model.

In the Confession of Faith no alteration was made, except in the part treating of civil government and the civil magistrate. Instead of giving the latter, as in Scotland, the power to call and supervise Synods, it declared it the duty of civil magistrates "to protect the Church of our common Lord, without giving preference to one denomination of Christians above the rest, in such a manner that all ecclesiastical persons whatever shall enjoy the full, free, and unquestioned liberty of discharging every part of their sacred functions, without violence or danger."

Some minor changes were made, but all of a similar import.

The vote on the adoption of the Catechisms of the Church excited no debate. They do not appear to have been even read over, with a view to adoption *seriatim*. No alteration had been proposed in relation to them, until, just at the moment when the vote was to be taken, Rev. Jacob Ker, of Delaware, arrested the proceedings by calling attention to a clause of the Larger Catechism in answer to the question, "Which are the sins forbidden in the second commandment?" He stated that the Catechism, as it then stood, specified, among the sins forbidden, "tolerating a false religion;" and he made a motion that the clause be stricken out. The motion was carried without debate, and the Catechisms of the Church were then adopted without further alteration.

In the adoption of the Directory for Worship, the forms of prayer therein introduced were stricken out, and the subjects were presented in a doctrinal form. When this had been done, the Constitution of the Church stood forth complete. For three years it had been under consideration. Repeated draughts of it had been made, and the widest publicity had been given them. The object was twofold,—to perfect the instrument and to obviate future objection. Even yet entire cordiality of sentiment was not effected. There was at least "a small minority" whose leanings were toward a more liberal and less rigid system. One clergyman, a member of both the committees for preparing the draughts, but kept at home by indisposition, addressed a letter to the adopting Synod, strongly objecting against a high-toned Presbyterian system: yet the vote on the Adopting Act was nearly, if not quite, unanimous.

Although the Scottish Confession had been adopted by so strong and decisive a vote, it was not in the spirit of a rigid ecclesiasticism.[1] The highest judicature was an "Assembly," and not a "Council;" but it began its existence by acts which indicated that none of the exclusiveness of the Scotch National Church had been allowed a triumph in the selection of a name. Dr. Witherspoon opened the Assembly of 1790, by appointment, and Dr. John Rodgers—on whose motion a few years later the delegates of the Connecticut and other General Associations were allowed to vote as well as speak in the Assembly—was chosen the first moderator. In the very next year, on motion of Dr. Ashbel Green, arrangements were made for a plan of

---

[1] Quite a number of the leading ministers of the Church might be mentioned who had decided leanings toward a liberal construction of Presbyterian formulas. For instance, Henry Patillo, the patriarch of the Church in North Carolina, says, at this very time, "I have often thought that the popular congregational government of the Independents, joined to the Presbyterial judicatures as a final resort, would form the most perfect model of church government that the state of things will admit of."—*Patillo's Sermons*, Wilmington, N.C., 1788.

intercourse between the Assembly and the New England churches. "I am responsible," says Dr. Green, in his autobiography, "for the correspondence between them and us."

CHAPTER XI.

THE ASSOCIATED PRESBYTERIES, 1779-1818.

Just ten years before the meeting of the first General Assembly, a secession took place from the Presbytery of New York, which deserves at least a passing notice in the history of the Church. It was based mainly on the principle of the independency of the local church; although conjoined with this was the assumption that the power of ordination was vested not in the church, but in the Presbytery.[1]

The originator of the movement was Jacob Green,[2] from 1746 to 1790 the pastor of the Presbyterian church of Hanover, New Jersey. He was a native of Malden, Mass., and a graduate of Harvard College in 1744. Although he had cherished a Christian hope, he was led to abandon it on listening to the sermons of Whitefield (September, 1740), and especially to a powerful one by Gilbert Tennent in January, 1741. His mental exercises were of a most humbling nature. He was bowed to the dust under the deep sense of

---

1 This account is largely derived from a manuscript "History of the Secession from the Synod of New York and Philadelphia in 1780, which assumed the name of 'The Associated Presbytery of Morris County.'" By Rev. Dr. N. S. Prime.

2 Father of Rev. Dr. Ashbel Green.

his unworthiness, and extracts from his diary show how thorough must have been the work of his conviction.

After teaching for about a year, subsequent to his leaving college, he met again with Whitefield, who engaged him to go to Georgia to take charge of the Orphan-House. On reaching New Jersey, he learned from him that he had just received information which rendered it impracticable to assure Mr. Green of permanent employment. He offered, however, to employ him for six months, or refund to him the expense that he had already incurred. By the advice of Dickinson and Burr, he chose the latter alternative, with a view to labor as a minister within the bounds of the Presbytery. In September, 1745, he was licensed by the Presbytery of New York, and almost immediately was invited to preach at Hanover, where, in November of the following year, he was regularly ordained and installed pastor.

After more than thirty years' experience of the Presbyterian system, he deliberately resolved to withdraw from his connection with it. He did not object to its doctrines.[1] He made no complaint of his brethren in the Presbytery, for whom generally he expressed his high esteem as "worthy and excellent ministers of the gospel." His exceptions were directed against the

[1] Although this was the case, yet his views of the Abrahamic covenant, baptism, and kindred subjects were such as, through his published discourses, to bring him into controversy with some of the New England ministers. Shortly after the re-union (1758), he avowed himself, in his published work on Baptism, an *Edwardian*,—representing Stoddard and Edwards as the leading exponents of conflicting views. It is altogether probable that his strong New-side sympathies led him to regard the union with the Old side as quite objectionable, and strengthened his purpose to withdraw from Synod. He is the first minister in this country—so far as I am aware—who publicly declared himself an "Edwardian."

exercise of power by the Synod, according to "the Directory of Church Government authorized by the General Assembly of the Church of Scotland." "They assumed," he said, "the authoritative enacting style in their Minutes, appointing and requiring, instead of recommending and desiring." They moreover assumed a "legislative power," "appointed ministers and candidates to travel to distant parts, supply vacancies, &c.,"—had "*ordered*—not *desired*—contributions,"—had claimed a power to liberate ministers from their people, against the will of the latter,—as, for instance, "several presidents for the college." They had required candidates to study a year after taking their degree,—had ordered licentiates to write their notes at large and show them to some minister,—had *enjoined* the keeping of registers of births, baptisms, marriages, and burials,—had also *enjoined* ministers not to use notes in preaching; and, in the union of the two Synods, the Westminster Confession, "without any liberty for explanation in any article, was *enjoined* upon all their ministers, who were to teach and preach accordingly."

Some of these orders and injunctions were undoubtedly regarded by Mr. Green in the light of personal grievances. He was licensed without the year of study required after graduation. After the New England manner, he doubtless preferred the use of "notes." Collections in his congregation he would rather have "desired" than "ordered;" and his liberal sympathies revolted at the rigidity of the "Scotch system." But he greatly mistook, either through prejudice or inadvertence, when he assumed that the "Scotch system" was in force; and quite a large amount of his repugnance might have been overcome if he had known or remembered that provision had been made for the "scruples" of the candidate, and that he was to be admitted by the Synod or Presbytery, unless his scruple or mistake concerned some "essential and necessary" doctrine. In justice to himself, moreover, he should have stated that the injunction not to use notes was materially qualified by the clause which left it to the "convenience" of the minister.

But he had taken his position, and, in spite of the kind remonstrances of the Presbytery, he was not disposed to recede from it. He insisted upon his right quietly and peaceably to withdraw, cherishing the kindest feelings toward his ministerial associates, and uniting with them still in ministerial communion, or sitting, if desired, as a corresponding member of the Presbytery. Of his two congregations, one (Hanover Neck) chose still to remain under the care of the Presbytery, retaining him as their pastor; and to this the Presbytery made no objection.

At the same time (October, 1779) that Mr. Green thus requested the privilege of quietly withdrawing from Presbyterial connection, Joseph Grover,[1] reported in 1774 as a licensed candidate from New England, and who since that time had been settled at Parsippany, sent in to the Presbytery a paper declaratory of his "quiet withdrawal." He had been surprised to find, after his settlement, that he was viewed as a member of Synod, and when "lately admonished by the Synod for not attending Synodical meetings," he appears to have felt that his ecclesiastical freedom was infringed upon, and, consequently, chose to seek release from a body with which he did not suppose himself to have entered into connection.

At the May meeting of the Presbytery, Amzi Lewis, pastor (from 1772) of the churches of Florida and Warwick, N.Y., "entered a declinature" which, at his

---

[1] Erroneously said to have been a graduate of Yale College.

request, was returned to him, when he declared "that he peaceably withdrew from the Presbytery, and chose no longer to be considered as a member of the same." At the same time, Ebenezer Bradford, a graduate of Princeton in 1773, and from July 14, 1775, pastor of the church of South Hanover,[1] "gave in a declinature, whereby he withdrew from the Synod and this (New York) Presbytery." Efforts were made to induce the seceding brethren to retrace their steps, but they proved futile. The churches were regarded still as under the care of the Presbytery, and measures were taken to bring before them the question of their future ecclesiastical connection. Hanover Neck and South Hanover seem alone to have been disposed to remain in their former ecclesiastical relations.

This was the entire extent of the original secession.[2] Of the four ministers who withdrew, all but Mr. Green were young men, with brief experience in the ministry, and all of them, with the single exception of Mr. Bradford, were from New England, while Mr. Bradford was the son-in-law of Mr. Green. They withdrew, to the regret of the Presbytery, by whom they were esteemed and respected, and that esteem and respect were largely reciprocated. To the last appeal of the Presbytery, the seceding brethren returned a kind reply, in which they stated that they had formed themselves into a Presbytery, and had "no inclination to dissolve the voluntary connection into which they had

---

1 Subsequently known as Bottle Hill, now Madison.

2 So it would appear from Dr. N. S. Prime's manuscript "History of the Associated Presbyteries." But several years previous to the organization of the Morris County Presbytery, at least in 1769 or 1770, Abner Reeve, of Blooming Grove, N.Y., Moses Tuttle, of New York Presbytery, and Mr. Dorbe, of Parsippany, declared in favor of Independency, and withdrew from Synod and Presbytery.—*Webster*, 668-9.

entered, or cease to be a distinct Presbytery." A small body like their own they considered better adapted to transact business "with ease and advantage," and more likely to prove harmonious. Nor was this all. "We think you have," said they, "such notions of Presbyterial power and church government, as are not agreeable to our free sentiments."

The "distinct Presbytery" whose existence was thus announced was formed at Hanover, May 3, 1780. The four seceding ministers united themselves in "a voluntary society for promoting the interests of religion," and, as they considered themselves "Presbyterians, in a scriptural sense," they agreed to call themselves, and to be known by the name of, "The Presbytery of Morris county." To this, at a subsequent date, they saw fit to prefix the term "Associated;" and with this qualification of the title they were subsequently known.

Their platform was Presbyterian in form, but Congregational in fact. The ministers were to meet as a Presbytery ordinarily twice a year; each church was authorized to send two elders or lay delegates; all jurisdiction over the churches was disclaimed, except so far as they should apply for advice or assistance; and no "rules" should be made "authoritative," while all agreements should be alterable, as circumstances should require.

In 1781, the Presbytery published a duodecimo of seventy pages, presenting "A View of a Christian Church and Church Government," with an appendix, representing the case and circumstances of the Associated Presbytery. The preface discusses the question, whether Christ has instituted or appointed any particular form or mode of church government. The six sections of the body of the work are devoted to discountenancing the idea of a "provincial" Church; presenting a sound definition of the "particular" or local

Church; vindicating ministers and elders, whose offices are regarded as identical, together with deacons and evangelists, as permanent officers of the Church; claiming that admonition and excommunication are the only censures of the Church, from which in no case is there to be any appeal; rejecting all ecclesiastical authority of Presbyteries and Synods, and giving the preference to *pro re nata* councils. Certain questions of casuistry, raised by the discussion of their peculiar principles, are taken up and decided in the closing section.

In the appendix is found a reply to the proposal of the Presbytery of New York, that the seceding members should reconsider their declinature and become again members of the Synod. This they are willing to do on three conditions, that they remain a distinct body, which is their choice,—that they meet in Synod as a voluntary society, to consult and promote the interests of religion,—and that they shall have "an unrestrained liberty to license and ordain for the gospel ministry any persons whom they shall think proper."

The last of these conditions was, for the Associated Presbytery, a vital one.[1] But the liberty it claimed had been exercised more than forty years before, in a manner which no Presbytery or Synod at this juncture would be disposed to endorse. The reply of the se-

---

[1] Webster states that Mr. Green, previous to his withdrawing from the Presbytery, had grown "dissatisfied with the hindrances in the way of supplying our vacancies: 'first we make them gentlemen, and then ministers.' He proposed to Bellamy to establish two schools, one in New Jersey and one in Connecticut, for educating men up to a certain point in languages and philosophy, and then licensing them. He wished to imitate the Baptist way, that our growing country might not be left unblessed with sound doctrine and firm discipline." He is said to have disliked the Congregationalism of New England as much as the Scotch type of Presbyterianism.—*Webster*, 528–9.

ceders was, therefore, equivalent to a final refusal to return. It was soon manifest that, so far from this, they anticipated an increase which would distance competition on the part of those from whom they had withdrawn. They proceeded immediately to the prosecution of their favorite scheme, introducing into the ministry a number of men of limited qualifications. Yet they were far from denying the importance of proper education, and, in order to secure for their candidates some special privileges for instruction, instituted a society, and by contributions, bequests, &c., collected a fund, for the management of which they obtained from the New Jersey Legislature, May 30, 1787, an act of incorporation. The style of the corporation was, "The Trustees of the Society in Morris county, instituted for the promotion of learning and religion;" and among the names of the trustees, along with those of laymen and those of the seceding ministers, was that of Jedediah Chapman, of Orange, a member of New York Presbytery,[1] although a native of Connecticut.

In the course of ten or twelve years, the new Presbytery had become greatly enlarged. Its most considerable growth was, as might have been expected, in a region where it was assured of Congregational sympathy. The counties of Dutchess and Westchester, N.Y., lying along the New England line, afforded the most inviting field for its efforts. Here were already several churches, which, by local proximity and ecclesiastical sympathy, were predisposed to favor such a system as that of the Associated Presbytery. Here, also, after the close of the war, new and feeble congre-

---

[1] The fact *may* be taken either as an indication of the individual sympathies of Mr. Chapman, or of the mutual kind feeling between New York Presbytery and the Seceders.

gations were in the process of being gathered, and the licentiates of the Presbytery would naturally seek in this field places of labor. In this quarter, therefore, the new organization received the largest accessions. Indeed, there is no evidence that a single church united with them west of the Hudson and north of the New Jersey line.

At a meeting of the Associated Presbytery in October, 1791, it was deemed expedient that a new association should be formed, to embrace the churches of Westchester county and vicinity. Accordingly, in January, 1792, a meeting was held, at which a body was organized under the name of "The Associated Presbytery of Westchester." The individuals originally composing it were Amzi Lewis,—who in 1787 removed from Florida to North Salem, taking charge of the Academy and at the same time acting as pastor of the Presbyterian church,—John Cornwell, Silas Constant, pastor of Crumpond, John Townley, of Greenburg,—all of whom were from the original Presbytery,—together with Abner Benedict, soon after settled at North Salem, Daniel Marsh, of Poughkeepsie, and Medad Rogers. At a subsequent period, among the members of the body were Andrews, of Pound Ridge, Abraham Purdy and Abner Brundige, of Somers, Bradford, Knight, Blair, Osborn, St. John, Jones, Austin, Bouton, Hosea Ball, McKnight, Frey, and others. The churches brought into this connection were those of Sing Sing, Greenburg, Peekskill, Yorktown, Red Mills, Gilead, Somers, North Salem, Southeast, and Pound Ridge, together with those of North Stamford, Cornwall, and New Fairfield, in the State of Connecticut. The Presbytery continued its meetings till about the year 1820, when it was formally dissolved, and the members connected themselves with other ecclesiastical bodies, some with the New York Presbyteries, and others with those of Bedford and North River.

Meanwhile the numbers had increased in the more northern portion of the region bounded by the Hudson and the New England line. It was, therefore, proposed to form another Presbytery in this region. The project was unanimously favored by the parent Presbytery, Westchester Presbytery, and Berkshire Association, of Massachusetts, who were consulted in reference to it. Accordingly, Messrs. John Camp, John Stevens, Beriah Hotchkin, Robert Campbell, David Porter, and Luther Gleson, ministers in the State of New York, convened at New Canaan, November 12, 1793, and after a mutual interchange of views formed themselves into an Associated Presbytery, based on the same principles with those of Westchester and Morris county, and assumed the name of "The Northern Associated Presbytery in the State of New York."

The distinct organizations having been thus multiplied, some method of intercommunication, which should serve as a bond of sympathy and union, remained to be devised. Committees from the different Presbyteries were appointed to consider the subject. They met at Poughkeepsie, April 10, 1794, and agreed to recommend to the several Presbyteries the appointment of two or more correspondents, whose business it should be to communicate, by letter or otherwise, such information of the doings or prospects of their respective bodies as might be thought useful or necessary to co-operative effort. These correspondents, moreover, were to meet annually as a Convention of Correspondence, to consider generally the wants of the entire field, and make such recommendations to the several Presbyteries as they should deem adapted to promote the cause of Christ.

The proposal was approved by the Presbyteries, and

the annual convention was held. At its meeting in 1795, it adopted, and subsequently (1796) published, a small bound volume of one hundred and two pages, entitled "A brief account of the Associated Presbyteries, and a general view of their sentiments concerning religion and ecclesiastical order." It contained a history of the several organizations, and their sentiments on the subjects of Christian doctrine and church order. "We are at present," they say, "united in a general scheme of doctrine, which may be denominated Calvinistic, Edwardian, or Hopkinsian, and we consider those systems which in our day and country are generally distinguished by those terms, as essentially orthodox. Yet we call no man *Father*. Nor do we know of any public system or Confession of Faith, consisting of many particulars, which we can unitedly adopt without exception or explanation, and with this liberty we know of none which we cannot adopt."

Their own Confession of Faith consisted of eighteen articles, mainly accordant with the Westminster Confession, and their exposition of their ecclesiastical sentiments was what might be expected from the principles of their organization.

A Fourth Presbytery, with the consent of the Northern Associated Presbytery, was organized at Milton, February 3, 1807. It took the name of the Saratoga Associated Presbytery. Its constituent members were Elias Gilbert, Daniel Marsh, Charles McCabe, Elisha Yale, and Lebbeus Armstrong. The churches were Greenfield, Moreau, Bennington, Vt., Kingsborough, Malta, and Milton. The last, if no other, had been taken under the care of the Presbytery of Albany as early as January 10, 1792, and remained in that connection till January 21, 1800, when at a church-meeting, presided over by Mr. Gilbert, of Greenfield, it was voted to adopt the system of doctrine and order of the Associated Presbyteries.

Members who subsequently united with this Presbytery were Sylvanus Haight, Reuben Armstrong, Cyrus Comstock, Silas Parsons, and Joseph Farrar. The only church which joined it was one organized by Messrs. Comstock, and Lebbeus and Reuben Armstrong, in Luzerne and Hadley. After continuing its meetings till September, 1818, the several members of the Presbytery requested and obtained letters of dismission to unite with other ecclesiastical bodies, and the "Saratoga Associated Presbytery" adjourned *sine die.*[1]

It was doubtless at about the same time that the Westchester Associated Presbytery disbanded. In 1819, some of its churches had come under the care of Presbyteries connected with the General Assembly; and previous to 1825 there were but two or three which were not connected with the Presbytery of North River or the Presbytery of New York.

Thus the most rapid growth of this secession was within the first twenty years of its existence. It embraced, at the time of the formation of the Annual Convention, quite a large number of churches, spread over a large extent of country. But with the single exception of the transient organization of the Saratoga Associated Presbytery, numbering at the most but seven or eight churches, it made no further advance. One church after another relinquished connection with it, until at last nearly all were absorbed by the surrounding organizations, either Congregational or Presbyterian; and in thirty years afterward all the memorials of it that remained were to be found in the fast-vanishing records of its churches and extinct Presbyteries.

---

[1] The records of the body were left in the hands of Rev. Elisha Yale, of Kingsborough.

CHAPTER XII.

THE CAROLINAS—RISE AND PROGRESS OF THE CHURCH.

THE final and successful attempt to colonize "Carolina" was due to a project formed by certain courtiers of Charles II. for their own profit and aggrandizement. Their selfish scheme was veiled with the pretext of "a generous desire of propagating the blessings of religion and civility in a barbarous land." A project couched in these terms was presented to the king by eight persons whose fidelity had cheered his exile, or whose treachery had regained for him his throne. Among them were Clarendon, Monk, and Shaftesbury. They claimed to be "excited by a laudable and pious zeal for the propagation of the gospel," and they "begged a certain country in the parts of America not yet cultivated and planted, and only inhabited by some barbarous people, who had no knowledge of God."

Their request was readily granted. The charter was doubtless drawn by their own hands, and secured them every thing "saving the sovereign allegiance due to the crown." They immediately took liberal measures to procure a settlement. A few colonists were already on the ground, and to them, on taking the oath of allegiance and submitting to the proprietary government, their lands were assured and their rights conceded. Arrangements were made for a popular government, limited only by the laws of England and the veto of the proprietaries. To all, the most perfect freedom of religion was assured.

A singular spectacle is this,—a body of men whose

names were indissolubly associated with the legislation that harassed English Dissenters, and surrendered justice to High-Church bigotry, yet adopting—when left to look simply at their own pecuniary interests—a policy as liberal as the most fanatic of Cromwell's Independents could have desired. The same hands which framed the intolerant Act of Conformity in England shaped a satire on their own folly in the constitution which they gave to Carolina. While with relentless severity they silenced such men as John Owen, and filled English prisons with men like Baxter, Bunyan, and Alleine, they allowed the colonists the most perfect and entire freedom of opinion. The New England settler, the English Dissenter, the Scotch Presbyterian, were alike welcome, and alike invited to a refuge from oppression. It may even excite a doubt, whether persecution in England was not made more virulent by a policy which demanded exiles to people the colonies.

The early settlers were from diverse localities,—New England,[1] Virginia, Barbadoes, and at length in increasing numbers from Ireland and Scotland. For many years it is doubtful, however, whether the province was visited by a single clergyman. Its growth was for a long period very slow, and among the scattered and far from homogeneous population no effort seems to have been made to establish religious institutions of any kind. More than half a century passed away (1663–1715) before the Presbyterian Church could be said to exist within the northern portion of the colony.

---

[1] In 1658, a small company of emigrants from Massachusetts, carrying their religious institutions with them, settled around Cape Fear. For many years their condition was one of poverty and hardships. In 1667, the Bay Legislature recommended them to their former fellow-colonists as objects worthy of charitable relief. Contributions were made for them, and a vessel was sent them laden with supplies.—*Felt's New England*, ii. 232, 307, 417.

The original Presbyterianism of the Carolinas was mainly of the Scotch type. As early as 1729, Scotch emigrants settled on Cape Fear River, Cumberland county, N.C. In 1736, we trace the arrival of others. In the winter of 1739, Whitefield preached, "not without effect," at Newton, on Cape Fear River, where among the congregation were many settlers who had recently arrived from Scotland.[1] The rebellion of 1745 sent large numbers of Highlanders over to this region. Many who had taken up arms for the Pretender preferred exile to death or subjugation in their native land. Ship-load after ship-load landed at Wilmington in 1746 and 1747. In the course of a few years more they were joined by large companies of their countrymen, who wished to improve their condition and become owners of the soil upon which they lived and labored. For the most part, they were a moral and religious people, noted for their industry, economy, thrift, and perseverance.[2]

No minister of religion came out with the first settlers. It was nearly ten years after the emigration of 1747 before they secured the services of a Presbyterian minister. The first one who labored among them was James Campbell, who from 1730 had been settled over a church of Scotch emigrants in Pennsylvania.[3] Despondent in regard to his own spiritual con-

---

[1] Webster, p. 531.

[2] The materials for the early history of Presbyterianism in Virginia and Carolina have been largely drawn from Foote's Sketches.

[3] Webster makes Campbell a native of Argyleshire, Scotland, emigrant to this country in 1730, licensed by New Castle Presbytery in 1735, and "well received" by Philadelphia Presbytery, May 22, 1739. After preaching for four years, part of the time at Tehicken, he became convinced that he was still unconverted, and ceased to preach. After conference with Whitefield and Tennent, he resumed his labors. After his ordination in 1742, he divided his

dition, he had ceased to preach, but at an interview with Whitefield, whom he met as he traversed the country, his doubts were overcome and his difficulties removed. He resumed his ministry, and at length took up his residence on the left bank of Cape Fear River, a few miles above Fayetteville. Here and in the surrounding region he labored with untiring zeal for nearly a quarter of a century. His labors had no bounds but his strength. He had three regular congregations, one at "Roger's Meeting-House," one at "Barbacue Church," and one at McKay's, now known as Long Street.

Here were the pioneer churches of the region. As emigration continued and population increased, new neighborhoods were formed, and new congregations gathered. One after another the numerous churches in Cumberland, Robeson, Moore, Richmond, and Bladen counties were organized, and new laborers were demanded. In 1770, Rev. John McLeod came from Scotland, accompanied by a large number of Highland families, to cheer the heart and strengthen the hands of the pioneer missionary.

More worthy of special mention for his labors in this field is Hugh McAden, a graduate of Nassau Hall and a theological pupil of John Blair. He was licensed in 1755 by New Castle Presbytery, and was immediately sent out as a missionary to the Carolinas. On a portion of his route he had been preceded by that "burning and shining light," William Robinson, whose success in Carolina was far less than in Virginia. By him Duplin and New Hanover, and the scattered settlements of that region, were visited. But his journey was attended by much exposure and many hardships.

---

time between Greenwich and the Forks of the Delaware. On the division, he adhered to the New side, and was sent to preach to the vacant churches.—*Webster*, 530.

McAden fared but little better. His journal[1] still exists, and attests his indefatigable zeal and devoted purpose. He passed through Virginia, and extended his labors into the northern part of South Carolina. At various places on his route he was warmly welcomed, and at some was invited to remain. He found the people greatly scattered, but anxious generally to hear preaching.

In 1759, he was dismissed from New Castle to Hanover Presbytery, which then included the greater part of Virginia, and, extending indefinitely south, covered his destined field of labor. This embraced the congregations of Duplin and New Hanover, the largest at that period within the bounds of the State. Here he remained for ten years. After this he took charge of the churches of Hico, Dan River, and County Line Creek, with which he labored till his death in 1781.

At the time when he commenced his labors in North Carolina, there were some Presbyterian churches built, and many worshipping assemblies, yet few, if any, organized churches, and no settled minister. McAden himself belonged to the New side. He was in sympathy with Hanover Presbytery, and was a man of kindred spirit with Robinson and Davies.

Among the members set off by the Synod to form the Presbytery of Hanover, in 1755, occurs the name of Alexander Craighead. He was licensed by Donegal Presbytery in 1734, became afterward a warm friend of Whitefield, and was an earnest and awakening preacher. His zeal for the "Solemn League and Covenant" carried him away, and for some years his name disappears from the Synodical records. He had associated himself with the Cameronians; but in 1749 he

---

[1] Foote, in his Sketches of North Carolina, gives this journal in full.

had found his way to the western frontiers of Virginia. Here he labored for several years, in a situation much exposed to the hostile inroads of the Indians; and when Braddock's defeat sent terror through the whole valley and large numbers of the population fled to the South, he followed them to North Carolina.[1] Crossing the Blue Ridge, he found a location among the settlements along the Catawba and its smaller tributaries. In January, 1758, he was directed to preach at Rocky River, and visit other vacancies till the spring meeting of the Presbytery. At this meeting a call from Rocky River was presented for his services, and here he was installed during the course of the year. Thus Rocky River was the oldest church in the upper country, and Sugar Creek was within its bounds.

Here Mr. Craighead passed his closing days. Unmolested by Virginia intolerance, which he could ill brook; far removed from interference from his own ecclesiastical brethren who might be disposed to criticize his revival movements, he poured forth, among a people prepared to receive them, his really noble and manly principles of civil and religious freedom, which bore fruit in the Mecklenburg Convention and the bold stand of his adopted State in favor of national independence.

Into this region there had already begun to pour a strong tide of immigration. It was mainly from Ireland; but it reached this Mesopotamia of North Carolina by different routes. Part came by the port of Charleston, and part by Philadelphia and the Delaware. The two streams met and commingled, producing a class of population worthy of the highest honor. They carried their principles with them into the wilderness. They built churches, and earnestly sought ministers or

---

[1] Webster, 437.

missionaries from the Synod; and in the Revolutionary conflict the strength of their principles was tested by their devotion to the cause of liberty of person and conscience.

Almost contemporaneously with the settlement of Mr. Craighead at Rocky River, the congregations of Hopewell, Steel Creek, New Providence, Poplar Tent, Rocky River, Centre, and Thyatira, were gathered. Their applications to Synod for aid in procuring preaching were frequent and earnest. Nor were they altogether unheeded. Year after year, missionaries were appointed to visit the destitute settlements of Virginia and Carolina. In 1764, McWhorter and Spencer were sent to North Carolina, and by them quite a number of the churches in the neighborhood of Mecklenburg were organized.

In 1765, a call was presented to Hanover Presbytery, for Henry Patillo, from the congregations of Hawfields, Eno, and Little River. Patillo had been a student under Davies, and had been licensed by Hanover Presbytery in 1757. As a patriarch of the Presbyterian Church in North Carolina, his name is worthy of more than merely a passing mention.[1] Of large frame and somewhat coarse features, but honest and candid to a proverb, his genial spirit and freedom from all assumption bound the hearts of others to him, and made them forget the plainness of his countenance and homeliness of his manner, in the integrity of his heart and the fervent simplicity of his purpose. He was above the influence of all merely earthly considerations. He confessed no attachment to any thing of a perishable nature, except books. He was always poor, and never envied wealth. He sustained himself in his preparation for the ministry by teaching the children of his neighbors. His

[1] Sprague, iii. 196.

dwelling—for he was married at the time—was a "house sixteen feet by twelve and an outside chimney, with an eight-feet shed, a little chimney to it." Yet even thus he was well content.

But Mr. Davies, who fell in with him upon a preaching-excursion to the Roanoke, and encouraged him to study for the ministry, did not need to blush for his pupil. Patillo proved himself "possessed of an originality of genius, and endowed by nature with powers of mind superior to the common lot of men." But, above all, he was most devoted to his work. He lived for Christ. All the ardor of his nature, all the genial warmth of his friendship, was enlisted in the duties of his sacred calling. Sustained by an unwavering faith, he was always cheerful, always active. It was rarely that his sky was clouded or his spirit disheartened. For thirty-six years—the last twenty-one at Nutbush and Grassy Creek—he was zealous and indefatigable in the service of Christ; and the Church in North Carolina may well be proud to name him among her founders. Of the first Provincial Congress of the State (1775) he was elected a member, and was unanimously elected chairman of the committee of the whole, on the subject of a National Confederation.

Early in 1765, a call was presented to the New Brunswick Presbytery, by the congregations in Buffalo and Alamance settlements, for the services of David Caldwell.[1] He was a native of Lancaster county, Pennsylvania, the son of a plain farmer, and was twenty-five years of age before he was converted. He at once commenced his preparations for the ministry, under Robert Smith, of Pequa, was graduated at Nassau Hall in 1761, and in 1763 was licensed to preach.

His first labors were in the region where he was

---

[1] Sprague, iii. 259.

afterward settled. He visited North Carolina as a missionary of the Synod, and labored there somewhat over a year. On his return in 1765, he entered upon his parochial duties. It may give some idea of the feeble condition of his united congregations, that both of them gave him in all but a salary of two hundred dollars. It was, therefore, a matter of necessity for him to make other provision for his support. He accordingly purchased a small farm, and at nearly the same time commenced a classical school in his own house. His usefulness as a teacher was scarcely inferior to his usefulness in the pulpit. Some of the most eminent men in Church and State were trained under his instructions. His scholars ranged generally in number from fifty to sixty.

Mr. Caldwell's congregations needed a man of his discretion to preserve their harmony. The church at Buffalo was composed of *Old-side* members; that at Alamance of *New-side*, or followers of Whitefield. In him, however, they were united; and they had good reason to be.

Tradition says that the first sacramental occasion observed by Presbyterians in Granville was in 1763. William Tennent, Jr.,[1] recently ordained by New Brunswick Presbytery for a Southern mission, officiated. For six months he labored in this region, under the direction of the Presbytery of Hanover. The congregations were regularly organized by James Cresswell, licentiate of Hanover Presbytery, who supplied them for some years.

The interests of the Presbyterian Church in North Carolina were not neglected by the Synod of New York and Philadelphia. Repeatedly that body sent some of its best men as missionaries into the field,

---

[1] Subsequently of Charleston.

to gather congregations and organize churches. Among the names of those who were thus commissioned, we meet with those of William Tennent, Jr., Nathan Ker, George Duffield, William Ramsey, James Latta, Elihu Spencer, and Alexander McWhorter. In 1770, Hezekiah Balch, whose life is identified with the history of the Presbyterian Church in East Tennessee, was ordained as an evangelist by the Presbytery of New Castle, and entered on his labors as a missionary of the Presbytery of Hanover in North Carolina.

As the number of ministers and churches in this region increased, the need was felt of another Presbytery, the membership of which should consist of ministers south of the Virginia line. At a meeting, therefore, of Hanover Presbytery (1770), a petition was prepared for Synod, asking for a Presbytery for Carolina and the South. The petition was granted, and Hugh McAden, Henry Patillo, David Caldwell, James Criswell, Hezekiah Balch, Hezekiah James Balch, and Joseph Alexander, were constituted a Presbytery, by the name of Orange. From time to time the Presbytery was strengthened by the accession of new members, most of them originally from the North, but at an early age residents of North Carolina. Thomas Reese, a native of Pennsylvania, had removed when quite young, with his father's family, to Mecklenburg county, N.C., where he prosecuted his studies at an academy under charge of Rev. Joseph Alexander, the successor of Alexander Craighead, as pastor of Buffalo and Sugar Creek, in 1768. Mr. Alexander was a fine scholar, a graduate of Princeton and a licentiate of the Presbytery of New Castle. In connection with a Mr. Benedict, he taught a classical school of high excellence and usefulness. When the Presbyterians subsequently proposed to secure of the king a charter for a college, he was named as the first professor.

Under his care young Reese pursued his preparatory course. In 1768, at the age of twenty-six, he was graduated at Princeton. Returning to Carolina, he devoted some time to the study of theology, and was the first minister ordained by the new Presbytery of Orange in 1773. Soon after this he entered upon his labors in the pastorate of Salem Church, Sumter District, S.C. In 1792 or 1793, he removed to Pendleton District, S.C., where he labored for several years. A distinguished scholar, and eminently devoted to his work, he exerted a wide and healthful influence. Anxious only for the salvation of souls, "his success in his ministerial labors evinced the presence and power of the Holy Spirit."

In 1776, the Presbytery of Orange licensed the celebrated James Hall,—a man with whose life the history of the Presbyterian Church throughout the Southwest is largely interwoven. He was of Scotch-Irish descent, a native of Carlisle, Pa. At an early age he removed with his parents to Iredell county, N.C., and within the bounds of the congregation of which he afterward became pastor. From early childhood his mind was religiously impressed. At the age of twenty he made a public profession of religion, and at about the same time he resolved to devote himself to the work of the ministry. In 1774, at the ripe age of thirty-one, he was graduated at Princeton, and such were his mathematical attainments that President Witherspoon expressed a desire that he should be retained as a teacher in the college. But the consciousness of his sacred purpose to devote himself to the work of the ministry forbade his acceptance of the offered position.

His theological course was pursued under Dr. Witherspoon. Upon its completion he returned to North Carolina. On every side the broad field of spiritual destitution invited laborers. Various congregations pressed

Mr. Hall to become their pastor. These applications he felt it necessary to decline, and finally settled—where his early years were spent—over the united congregations of Fourth Creek, Concord, and Bethany. In 1790, he secured a release from the first two, retaining only his connection with Bethany, that he might have more time to devote to the cause of domestic missions.

In this cause he was a pioneer and veteran laborer. Over a vast region of country his excursions were extended and his influence felt. In his own congregations his labors were eminently blessed. As the fruit of revivals, eighty were received to the communion at one time, and sixty at another. Few men have left behind them a more enviable memory. Devotedly pious, unwearied in his endeavors, sagacious in his plans, and self-denying in the work which he loved above every thing else, his ministry for forty years "was one glowing scene of untiring activity and earnest zeal to win souls to Christ." Precious memorials of him, as a warm and active friend of revivals, still survive among the churches of the region in which he labored. His solemn, pungent appeals in the pulpit, his grave, impressive manner, his long and toilsome missionary tours, and the constancy of a consecration to his work which improved for usefulness every opportunity that offered, have invested his name with peculiar interest.

A worthy compeer and co-Presbyter of Hall was Samuel Eusebius McCorkle, who, like him, a native of Pennsylvania, early removed to North Carolina. In 1766, he commenced his preparatory course of study at Dr. Caldwell's school in Guilford county, and in 1772 was graduated at Princeton in the same class with Dr. McMillan and Aaron Burr. In 1774, he was licensed by the Presbytery of New York, and by the Synod was commissioned to go southward and labor for at least a year under the direction of the Presbyteries of Hanover and Orange. After spending two years as a missionary in Virginia, he accepted the call of the church at Thyatira, where his early years had been spent, and where his parents still resided. For thirty-five years his course of usefulness and successful labor was continued in the region where he first settled. For ten or twelve years, he, like many of his brethren in the ministry, took charge of a classical school, which bore the significant name of *Zion Parnassus*. He was a thorough scholar and a devoted minister, less of a missionary than a student, and so intensely devoted to theological investigations that his temporal interests were sometimes too much neglected. He wrote his discourses, but used no manuscript in the pulpit. His tall and manly form, his grave and solemn countenance, and his impressive and thrilling tones, made his discourses most effective in riveting the attention and arousing the conscience. In the revivals of 1801 and 1802, his influence, like that of Hall, was deeply and widely felt.

Quite a number of churches had been gathered in the bounds of North Carolina before the Presbytery of Orange numbered any under its care south of the State line. The Presbytery of Charleston stood apart by itself, and occupied but a limited portion of the State. The Williamsburg church was formed as early as 1736, and for many years enjoyed great spiritual prosperity. But for some time previous to the Revolution its prosperity had declined, chiefly, it is said, in consequence of receiving large accessions from the North of Ireland, in which, to say the least, spirituality was not the predominant element. Throughout the war of the Revolution the church was vacant, and its difficulties were only aggravated by the subsequent settlement of a Mr. Kennedy. By a secession the Bethel Church was formed previous to 1790, over which, in connection with that of Indian town, James White Stephenson was settled from 1790 to 1808.[1]

In 1782, Francis Cummins accepted a call from Bethel Church, in the district of York, S.C., where he was ordained toward the close of that year. Like McCorkle, Hall, and Reese, he was a native of Pennsylvania, but had removed with his family, while yet a youth, to Mecklenburg county, N.C. Here he enjoyed and improved the opportunity afforded him for an education superior to any which had hitherto offered. In the neighboring college, then called "Queen's Museum," under the instruction of Rev. Dr. McWhorter, who had recently removed thither from New Jersey, he pursued his studies, and was graduated in 1776. His theological studies were pursued under the direction of Rev. James Hall, and in 1780 he was licensed to preach by the Presbytery of Orange.

His fields of labor were numerous and varied. Indeed, his labors were never confined to a single congregation. There were some twenty churches which considered him as, in some sense, their pastor, during the whole course of his ministry. Twenty-four years were spent in South Carolina, and twenty-five in Georgia. Yet, during this long period, his time was almost always laboriously divided between teaching and preaching. The churches in that region were at this period so generally missionary stations, and the ministers so few in number, that their efforts were spread necessarily over a broad field.

Of this arduous work, Dr. Cummins performed his full share. Indeed, he seemed peculiarly adapted to it. An accurate scholar, an able and well-read theologian,

---

[1] Sprague, iii. 552.

with a physical development in keeping with his large intellectual gifts, and a high, capacious, and intellectual forehead which proclaimed him no ordinary man, his presence in the pulpit was sure to command attention and awaken interest. His deep-toned voice, somewhat authoritative and dictatorial manner, and perfect self-command, conjoined with his mental and spiritual gifts, rendered him eminent as a preacher. He lived to a ripe old age of nearly fourscore, and died in 1831.

These were among the most eminent of the early ministers of Orange Presbytery. But there were others who labored in the region for a longer or a shorter period. In 1760, Rev. Robert Tate came from Ireland to Wilmington, and opened a classical school for his support. Many of the young men of New Hanover, who took an active part in the Revolution, enjoyed his instructions. While residing at Wilmington, where no Presbyterian church was organized until after the war, he was accustomed to make preaching excursions through New Hanover and the adjoining counties, particularly up the Black and South Rivers. During the war, on account of his ardent Whig principles, he found it prudent to leave Wilmington and reside in the Haw-fields, in Orange. Without being settled as a pastor, he performed a large amount of missionary labor. His cultured manners, genial conversation, and winning deportment gave him great influence, especially among the young.

Rev. William Richardson labored for a while at Providence, although his residence was in South Carolina and he was a member of the Charleston Presbytery. He was a licentiate of Hanover Presbytery in 1758.

Rev. John Debow was the second pastor of the congregations of the Eno and the Haw. He commenced his labors as a licentiate of the Presbytery of New Brunswick in 1775, but died eight years afterward.

In 1785, Rev. William Bingham commenced his labors at Wilmington and in the surrounding country. He was a native of Ireland, and an excellent scholar. He sustained himself by conducting a classical school, in the management of which he was exceedingly popular. At a later period he removed to the upper country, and taught with great success in Chatham and Orange.

At about this period, James McGready, whose name figures so largely in connection with the revivals in Kentucky at the commencement of the present century, commenced his labors in North Carolina. His unsparing denunciations of wickedness, and his terrible appeals, which won him the title of "Boanerges," rendered him, while popular with some, greatly obnoxious to others. But his labors were not in vain. Among those who were deeply affected by his influence was the Rev. William Hodge, who is said to have been a native of Hawfields, and who accompanied McGready to Kentucky. While McGready was preaching on Stoney Creek and along the Haw River in 1789, Hodge was one of his constant hearers. In listening to the bold, fearless preacher, he felt his own desire to preach the gospel revived, and, on being licensed by the Presbytery of Orange, he went hand and heart with his teacher in the revival work.

Meanwhile, the Presbytery of Orange was extending toward the West. Eastern Tennessee was included within its bounds. Here were to be found some of its most earnest and devoted members. Among them were Charles Cummings and Hezekiah Balch. These, with Samuel Houston, Samuel Carrick, John Cossan, and James Balch, formed at a subsequent period the Presbytery of Abingdon, in East Tennessee.

The Presbyterian Church in the Carolinas had passed through a trying period. The influence of the war was disastrous to public morals, while many of the churches and congregations were sadly scattered. In some cases the people dared not assemble. A meeting for religious purposes would have been accounted treason, and, while the country was in the hands of the British troops, would but too surely have invited a visit of the dragoons.

The pastors, moreover, were especially obnoxious. From the first they had manifested a warm zeal in the cause of national independence. Some of them had for years before the crisis been inculcating those principles of civil and religious freedom which bore fruit in the results of the Revolutionary conflict. Indeed, they might be said to have given the impulse to the popular mind around them, which resulted in the Declaration of the celebrated Mecklenburg Convention. In the proceedings of this body, the influence of the Presbyterian element which helped to compose it is plainly seen. Nor were they wanting to themselves or to their country when the crisis came. Patillo was a member of the first Provincial Congress in 1775, and its chairman when it sat in committee of the whole. Caldwell was a member of the State Convention in 1776. Craighead had already for more than a score of years been a zealous and uncompromising champion of those principles of civil and religious liberty of which the Mecklenburg Declaration was a practical exposition. As members of the convention, sat several elders of the Presbyterian churches in the Mecklenburg district. There were at least seven of these, four of them of the well-known name of Alexander. The Rev. Hezekiah James Balch was also a member; and among the young men who listened to the doings of the convention were Joseph (afterward General Joseph) Graham, long an elder, and Humphrey Hunter, minister, of the churches of Unity and Goshen. Of this number also was Francis (afterward Rev. Dr.) Cummins, then a student at

"Queen's Museum," in Charlotte, and like the others, in full sympathy with the proceedings of the convention.

Among the sufferers by the war, the Presbyterian clergy held a distinguished rank. By the British and Tories they were singled out for vengeance, and upon the head of one was set a price of two hundred pounds. McAden was fast verging to the grave; but he and his congregation suffered severely; and scarcely had his ashes been laid in the grave, before devastation spread over the scene of his labors. Two weeks after his death, the British encamped in the yard of Red-House Church, where he had preached, searched his dwelling, plundered and destroyed his papers, and carried desolation through the region. James Tate, a staunch Whig, was forced to flee from Wilmington to escape the grasp of British power. Thomas H. McCaule was a zealous patriot, and his field of labor was in the track of the hostile armies: he was by the side of General Davidson when the latter was shot off from his horse. The congregations of Eno, Hawfields, Buffalo, and Alamance, were the scenes of the plunderings of Cornwallis's army. The sufferings and privations which they endured were fearful. The catalogue of outrage would fill a volume. The house of Dr. Caldwell was broken open, his library and valuable papers destroyed, and his property stolen, while he, watched as a felon, spent night after night in the solitudes of the forest. Many an effort was made to draw him from his hiding-place. His house was watched; sudden visits were made to surprise him; but, eluding all the arts of his enemies, he escaped their hands.

Such a state of things could not but be sorely disastrous to the churches. Attention was diverted from religion to the discussion of political questions. The community was rent into embittered parties by civil feuds. The ravages as well as the license of war produced desperation and excited to reprisals; morality was at a low ebb; congregations were scattered, and the seed of that infidelity which at a later period ravaged the land was now, in part, sown.

With the return of peace the prospect brightened: the congregations could assemble again, with none to molest or make afraid; the pastors could and did resume their duties, and once more regularly occupied their pulpits. But, before religion could fairly regain the ground it had lost, there was to be another conflict, but one not waged with carnal weapons. Infidelity was to fall before the bold reproof of a faithful ministry and the wonderful outpouring of the Divine Spirit.

The Presbyterian Church in the Carolinas showed itself from the first a fast friend of education. The pioneer laborers deeply felt the necessity not only of giving an impulse to the general intelligence, but of training up an educated ministry. They perceived clearly the necessity of providing for the enlarged demands of an extensive and still extending missionary field. Hence, wherever a pastor was located, there was in connection with his congregation a classical school. This was the case at Sugar Creek, Poplar Tent, Centre, Bethany, Buffalo, Thyatira, Grove, Wilmington, and the churches served by Patillo in Orange and Granville.

The oldest of these was under the care of Joseph Alexander, at Sugar Creek; and here a large number of ministers received their classical education. The prejudices of George III. denied it a charter, for it was in the hands of Presbyterian Whigs. But "Queen's Museum" flourished without a charter, and the debates preceding the Mecklenburg Declaration were held in its hall. It was but a fitting tribute to its usefulness and promise, when the Legislature of North Carolina, in 1777, chartered the institution, under the name of Liberty Hall Academy. It was entirely under Presbyterian direction, and under the supervision of Orange Presbytery. The Rev. Alexander (afterward Dr.) McWhorter, of Newark, was solicited to take charge of it; but his residence was only temporary, and the pre-eminence of Liberty Hall as supplying the place of a college for the South was transferred to Mount Zion College, Winnsborough, S.C., over which Thomas H. McCaule presided for several years.

Classical schools of a high order, under Presbyterian direction, were more numerous after the Revolutionary War. Dr. Caldwell continued his in Guilford till his death. Dr. McCorkle sustained one in Rowan, and afterward in Salisbury. Dr. Robinson sustained the one at Poplar Tent, with some intermissions, till near the close of his life. Dr. Wilson was very successful at Rocky Hill, and Dr. Hall at Bethany. There was also a flourishing one, under William Bingham, in Chatham, and one in Burke. Providence, Grove, and Fayetteville, enjoyed a succession of classical teachers.

With the establishment of the University of the State, at Chapel Hill, in 1789, the preponderance of classical schools ceased to be so entirely on the side of the Presbyterian Church. Yet at a later period the cause was taken up by them again, with revived energy, and with results that nobly justified the effort.

As we have already seen, the first attempt to colonize South as well as North Carolina resembled in its origin an investment of capital by a company of land-jobbers.[1] The proprietaries furnished the emigrants with means to embark, but sent out with them their

---

[1] Bancroft, ii. 166.

own commercial agent, and undertook the management of all commercial transactions. As might have been expected, the colony was a scene of turbulence, and industry was unproductive, till the old Constitutions were abandoned and the colonists learned to rely on their own energy.

The first band of emigrants to South Carolina set sail in January, 1670. The period, in England, was one of sharp persecution for Dissenters. Eight years before, the terrible Act of Conformity had expelled nearly two thousand ministers from their parishes and pulpits. Cavalier statesmen were unscrupulous enough to take advantage of the fruits of their own bigoted counsels. In the first band, along with the commercial agent, was William Sayle, the proprietary Governor, "probably a Presbyterian," who, more than twenty years before, had attempted to plant an "Eleutheria" in the isles of the Gulf of Florida.

The emigrants had hardly landed before they instituted a polity on a liberal basis. Representative government was established, and continued to be cherished. It was in vain that Locke theorized or Shaftesbury speculated. The Utopia of their dreams was not to be realized. It was not long before Dutch enterprise offered the colonists the luxury of cargoes of slaves. From the banks of the Hudson, lured by stories of the fertility of the soil, came an unlooked-for accession to the population. In little more than a year after the arrival of the first colonists, two ships with Dutch emigrants from New York arrived, and these were soon followed by others with their countrymen from Holland. Even Charles II. provided at his own expense—a munificence the more marked for its isolation, and perhaps designed to manifest his sympathy with Carolina rather than New England—two small vessels, to transport to Carolina a few foreign

Protestants. But the most considerable emigration was from England. The prospect of immunity from the molestation of informers and acts against conventicles and Non-Conformity, tempted Dissenters to a colony where their worship would be tolerated and their rights respected. A company of them from Somersetshire were conducted to Charleston by Joseph Drake, brother of the gallant admiral, and the fortune which the latter had acquired was employed to plant South Carolina with a people who dreaded the evils of oppression and the prospect of a Popish successor to the throne.

The condition of Scotland, likewise, impelled not a few to project a settlement in Carolina. But a comparatively small number, however, under the lead of Lord Cardross, who soon returned, crossed the Atlantic. A colony of Irish under Ferguson received a hearty welcome, and were soon merged among the other colonists. More important, however, for a short period at least, was the accession to the population from the exiled Huguenots. The French king essayed to torment them into conversion, but he only tormented them out of the kingdom; and not a few found their way to the shores of South Carolina. Here were fugitives from Languedoc and Saintonge and Bordeaux, from Northern and Southern France,—Calvinist Protestants seeking the shelter which the worldly policy of High-Church statesmen extended to the adherents of every creed.

At an early period, also, the population of South Carolina received into its bosom a Puritan element from New England. Although by the Charter of the State the Church of England was the only one legally recognized, yet it contained provisions favorable to other creeds. The Colony, though founded by bigoted Churchmen, was governed by "Dissenters." Blake was a Presbyterian, and Archdale a Quaker.[1] There were also in the colony "godly Christians, both prepared for and longing after the edifying ordinances of the gospel."

The first from abroad to respond to their appeal was Joseph Lord, of Charlestown, Mass., who, four years before, had graduated at Harvard, and had since been teaching at Dorchester, and studying theology with the pastor of the church.[2] On the 22d of October, 1695, those who offered to go with him were embodied in a church, over which he was ordained pastor.[3] From the churches of Boston, Milton, Newton, Charlestown, and Roxbury, came pastors and delegates to assist in the services at the gathering of this little flock, and "to encourage the settlement of churches and the promotion of religion in the Southern plantations." In little more than a month the company were ready to embark; and their faith and ardor did not abate at the prospect of separation from old associations. The parting scene was solemnized by the holy services of religion. Their former pastor, Mr. Danforth, preached "a most affectionate and moving valedictory." On the 5th of December, the colony—a whole church—set sail, and for the first time New England sent forth missionaries beyond her bounds. For a time the voyage was bois-

---

[1] Graham's History of North America, ii. 167.

[2] Graham (History of North America, ii. 170) says, "At the close of the seventeenth century, there were only three edifices for divine worship erected within the Southern province, containing respectively an Episcopal, a Presbyterian, and a Quaker congregation, and all of them situated in the town of Charleston. Throughout all the rest of the province there were neither institutions for public worship, nor schools for education."

It is evident that he overlooked his own statement (p. 166) of the settlement which, just before the close of the century, had been made at Dorchester by the New England emigrants.

[3] Am. Quar. Reg., Aug. 1841.

terous and unpleasant, and it was fifteen days before they landed in Carolina. Following the course of the Ashley River, they found on its northeasterly bank, about twenty miles from Charleston, a rich piece of land, whose virgin soil and whose stately woodlands, with their interlacing vines and evergreen misletoe and drapery of moss, were well adapted to their purposes, and which they immediately selected as their future home, giving to it, in memory of their native place, the name of Dorchester. Here, on February 2, 1696, "they raised their grateful Ebenezer," by celebrating, for the first time in Carolina, the sacrament of the Lord's Supper.

Mr. Lord remained with this people for more than twenty years. Hugh Fisher was his successor; and, upon his death, John Osgood, a native of the colony (Dorchester), was ordained (1734–5). In 1754, the church mostly removed, with their pastor, to Midway, Georgia.

At Charleston, also, beside the Huguenot Church, (1686), originating with the expulsion of Protestants from France, by the revocation of the Edict of Nantes, there was, as early as 1690, a meeting-house for a congregation (known, till 1730, indiscriminately as Presbyterian, Congregational, and Independent) of which Benjamin Pierpont (1691–1696–7) was pastor, and whose successors were Mr. Adams,[1] and John Cotton, son of the Boston minister.[2] This at first may have embraced alike settlers from Scotland and from

---

[1] Am. Quar. Reg., Aug. 1841.

[2] Graham (History of North America, ii. 167) says, "In the year 1698, he [Blake] had the satisfaction to see John Cotton, a son of the celebrated minister of Boston, remove from Plymouth, in New England, to Charleston, in South Carolina, where *he gathered* a church and enjoyed a short, but happy and successful, ministry." This must be a mistake. The statement of the American Quarterly

New England. But the two elements were not altogether congenial, and in 1730 the Scotch demanded an organization of their own.[1] Its germ was found in the secession of twelve families from the old Church.

Up to the close of the seventeenth century, all denominations had enjoyed an equal freedom. The law favored none at the expense of others. But in 1703[2] the Governor, Sir Nathaniel Johnson, as if in concert with Lord Cornbury at New York, determined to introduce into the colony the system which Dissenters had learned to regard with well-grounded jealousy. By skilful arrangements, and through elections at which it is said that the most despicable classes of the population were allowed to vote, a legislature was secured favorable to the Governor's design. By a close

---

Register, taken from a Charleston publication, is doubtless more reliable. See, however, Sprague, i. 29.

[1] Dr. Smythe, in his History of the Second Presbyterian Church of Charleston, says, "As early as 1690, the Presbyterians, in conjunction with the Independents, formed a church in Charleston, which continued in this united form for forty years. During this period, two of their ministers, the Rev. Messrs. Stobo and Livingston, were Presbyterians, and connected with the Charleston Presbytery. After the death of the latter, twelve families seceded, and formed a Presbyterian Church on the model of the Church of Scotland. Their building was erected in 1731, on the site of the present, which was completed in 1814."

Dr. Howe, in his Historical Discourse, states—evidently a mistake—that the date of the founding of the First Presbyterian Church of Charleston was 1741. It should have been ten years earlier. That Stobo was the successor of Cotton in charge of the same church, I see no reason to doubt. Cotton died (Sprague, i. 29) Sept. 8, 1699, and Stobo, who brought no colonists or congregation with him, arrived in 1700. What more natural than that under Stobo, himself a Presbyterian, the Independents and Presbyterians should unite?

[2] Hewatt's South Carolina, i. 167, 172.

vote it was enacted that the Episcopal should be the established Church, and that it should be supported by a tax on all classes of citizens alike, including Dissenters, who were likewise deprived of all civil rights.[1] The colony was divided into ten parishes, and arrangements were made to secure the necessary number of missionaries from England.

The measure met with strong opposition. The Presbyterians exclaimed against it, and the Quakers were not silent. John Archdale told the Governor that the Dissenters had not forgotten the hardships to which they had been subjected in England in consequence of acts of conformity. He asserted boldly that, under the Constitution of the colony, freedom of conscience was the birthright of every citizen. Others united with him in his remonstrance. But opposition was vain. Despairing of redress, some of those who complained of what they regarded as a tyrannical measure, and a violation of plighted faith, prepared to leave the colony and remove to Pennsylvania, and a portion of them actually removed;[2] others determined to apply to the proprietaries for redress. The citizens of Colleton county united in a petition, which they sent to England by the hands of one of their number, Joseph Boone. On reaching London, he found the prospect before him far from encouraging. The proprietaries were not disposed to annul the obnoxious measure; but the London merchants united with Boone in urging the petition, and it was carried before the House of Lords. Their action was favorable, and there was a prospect that the prayer of the petitioners for relief would be granted. The queen issued an order declaring the obnoxious laws to be null and void; but her promise to issue a process against the provincial charter was never

---

[1] Simms's South Carolina, 78.

[2] Hewatt, i. 178.

fulfilled. The Episcopal Church was established in the colony. Dissenters were taxed for its support, and at the same time, if they wished to enjoy their own form of worship, were forced by their private contributions to erect churches and sustain ministers

One of the leading opponents of the Governor's project—along with Archdale—was Archibald Stobo, the pastor of the Presbyterian Church in Charleston,—"a survivor of the ministers who accompanied the Scotch emigrants to New Caledonia." He had been a resident of the city since the year 1700,[1] and at the time when the act creating the Establishment was passed, he exerted a powerful and commanding influence. He was possessed of eminent ability,—of "talents which render a minister conspicuous and respected."[2] To a mind well stored with the treasures of learning, and an excellent capacity, he united an uncommon activity and diligence in the discharge of his appropriate duties. Naturally averse to Episcopal jurisdiction, and with an inveterate Scotch antipathy to that prelatic tyranny which had inflicted such persecution on his native land, he was not conciliated by the designs in favor of Episcopal supremacy which he now witnessed in his adopted country. From the first he met the proposed innovation with unqualified opposition; and his influence was powerfully felt. No minister in the colony had engrossed so universally the public favor and esteem, and no one rendered himself more obnoxious to the disfavor of the government. Malignant arts were employed against him, and the Governor resorted to the weapons of slander to break down and to ruin his influence.

The effect of the measure which he so strenuously opposed was disastrous to the Presbyterian churches.

---

[1] Sprague, iii. 251.

[2] Hewatt, i. 178.

The English Society for the Propagation of the Gospel sent twelve Episcopal missionaries to the colony, and their support was largely secured from the public treasury. Spacious churches were built and paid for by taxes, which fell heavily on Dissenters. The state patronage extended to the Episcopal Church soon secured it ascendency also in numbers and strength. The friends of religious liberty in the Assembly were reduced in numbers, and the energy and art of the Governor bore down all opposition. Large numbers of the children of Dissenters were led to abandon the worship of their fathers and connect themselves with the State Church, against which the prejudices of the community were no longer directed.[1]

But Stobo still maintained his ground. By great diligence and ability, he preserved a number of followers; and, in spite of desertions, his congregation was strengthened by the accession of emigrants from Scotland and Ireland. The Presbyterians composed yet "a considerable party in the province," and sustained their own forms and ordinances of worship. At length, encouraged by help from Scotland, Stobo united with two other ministers—Fisher and Witherspoon—in efforts to promote the interests of the Presbyterian Church in the colony. They "associated"[2] themselves for this purpose, and probably united in forming a Presbytery.[3] Churches were gathered,[4] and houses of

---

[1] Hewatt, ii. 51. [2] Hewatt.

[3] The date of this is not given; but it must have been before 1734.

[4] Dr. Smythe, in his History of the Second Presbyterian Church of Charleston, states that the churches belonging to the Presbytery were those of Wiltown, Pon Pon, St. Thomas's, Stoney Creek, Salt-catchers, Black Mingo, the original and first incorporated church of Williamsburg, Charleston, Edisto, and the church of John and Wadmalaw Islands.

worship erected, at Wiltown and "three of the Maritime Islands," and subsequently at Jacksonburg, Indiantown, Pon Pon, or Walterborough, Port Royal, and Williamsburg.[1]

In 1710, a letter from South Carolina, published in London,[2] stated that there were in the colony five churches of British Presbyterians. Some of these may subsequently have become extinct. The church on Edisto Island[3] dates from 1717; that of Pon Pon, or Walterborough, of which Stobo, on leaving Charleston, became pastor, from 1728; those on John's and James's Islands from 1734 or 1735; that of Wiltown was many years anterior; while the Independent Presbyterian Church of Stoney Creek dates from 1743. The five early churches must have been those of Charleston, Dorchester, perhaps Wiltown or Edisto, and one or more on the Maritime Islands.

The pastors were obtained for the most part, if not in every instance, from Scotland. The Presbytery regarded itself as a portion of the Scotch Kirk, and looked to it for a supply for its pulpits. The presence in the colony of "ignorant" and "fanatic" men who assumed the right to preach, but who were regarded by the members of the Presbytery in the light of ranters, made them jealous as to the character of those whom they admitted to their pulpits or to the care of their vacant churches. In full sympathy, as we have reason to believe, with the Moderates of the Church of Scotland, it would not have been strange if

---

1 Williamsburg was founded by a colony of Irish in 1734.—*Simms's South Carolina*, 132.

2 Dr. Howe's Historical Discourse.

3 In 1705, Henry Brown obtained a grant for three hundred acres of land, which in 1717 he conveyed to certain persons "in trust for the benefit of a Presbyterian clergyman in Edisto Island." —*Hodge*, i. 58.

their antipathy to the revivalists of the New side—who may have penetrated into what the former considered their exclusive domain—should have led them to class the intruders with ignorant fanatics.

The successors of Stobo and Livingston,[1] Alexander Hewatt (1763–1776) and George Buist (1793–1808), were, like himself, natives of Scotland, and were there educated and ordained. At the request of the Church, addressed to ministers in that country, the last two, at least, were sent out to supply the pulpit. Hewatt was a man of learning, ability, and no little of kindly feeling. To his congregation he ever remained strongly attached. Among them for twelve years he continued his labors, till the near prospect of war with the mother-country led him, as is supposed, to return to Scotland. In 1779, he published in London his History of South Carolina.

His successor, Buist, was sent out, at the request of the Church, by Principal Robertson and Dr. Blair, of Scotland. They pronounced him from their own acquaintance to be "a good scholar, an instructive preacher, well bred, and of a good natural temper." The recommendation is characteristic of the moderatism of its authors. Nor did he on his arrival in this country belie the assurance given in regard to his

---

[1] Stobo (Dr. Howe's Historical Discourse) was succeeded at Charleston by Livingston; or rather Livingston, I suspect, took charge of the Scotch Church when formed in 1730, and Stobo withdrew from Charleston to one of the country churches. The labors of the latter continued until as late at least as 1740, in which year the slave insurrection took place. When the intelligence of it reached Wiltown, he was preaching at the church, whither the men, according to custom, had come armed. To this fact the prompt and successful suppression of the insurrection was due. How much longer Stobo lived, we have not the means to determine.

Howe and Smythe both speak of Livingston as Stobo's successor; but the fact is probably as stated above.

qualifications. He was a man of original genius, an eminent classical scholar, and an impressive preacher. He took charge of the church in 1793, and in 1805 was appointed Principal of the Charleston College,—a post for which he was eminently fitted. It was during his pastorate (1805), and not improbably at his instance, that the Presbytery with which he was connected petitioned to be received by the General Assembly.[1] They were not disposed, however, to unite themselves with the Synod of the Carolinas. Their sympathies, if fairly represented by men like Hewatt and Buist, whom the *moderates* of the Church of Scotland could commend, were not very strongly in the direction of the revival in which the churches of the Synod had so recently and so largely shared. The petition was one which the Synod, therefore, for very obvious reasons, opposed. They drew up a remonstrance (Oct. 1805) to the Assembly against the reception of a Presbytery which declined to unite itself first with the Synod within whose bounds it properly belonged, and pronounced the proposed measure unconstitutional and reflecting upon the Synod.

Here the matter rested until 1811. In that year the Presbytery renewed its request to be united with the General Assembly. The prayer of the petitioners was

---

[1] The Presbytery of South Carolina received quite a number of members from New England and the Presbyterian Church long before its connection with the Assembly. William Richardson, in 1760, was dismissed from New York Presbytery to South Carolina Presbytery. In 1768, James Latta, from Philadelphia Presbytery, united with the same body. In 1770, John Maltby, of New York Presbytery, also united with it. In 1768, Dr. McWhorter was appointed by the Synod to correspond with the South Carolina Presbytery; and in 1770 the latter body proposed to unite with the Synod. The troubles of the Revolution doubtless interfered with the execution of the project. See Synod's Minutes, 307, 378, 408–9.

granted, but on such conditions that the Synod had no longer any reason to object. These conditions were the adoption, by the members of Presbytery, of the Confession of Faith and Constitution of the Presbyterian Church, and a compromise or union with the Presbytery of Harmony, subject to the review and control of the Synod.

CHAPTER XIII.

"OLD REDSTONE," 1776–1793.

THE treaty of peace between England and France in 1762, opened to colonial enterprise and immigration the vast territory to the west of the Alleghanies, which France had hitherto claimed, and of which Fort Pitt was one of the defences. Almost immediately settlers began to find their way across the mountains, and in the course of a few years a population of thousands had extended the frontiers of civilization to the vicinity of the Ohio. The emigrants came mainly from Eastern Pennsylvania, Virginia, and the North of Ireland.[1] A large proportion of them were Presbyterians, baptized and brought up in the bosom of the Church, and some of them, before their emigration, members of its communion. For the most part, they were a bold and hardy race. Only strong men, physically and morally, would have braved the hardships they freely encountered,—the hardships not only of the pioneer settler, but those of danger from Indian hostilities.

Almost at the same time that the preliminaries of

---

[1] Old Redstone, p. 52.

peace were signed at Fontainebleau,—in fact, only thirteen days afterward,—the "Corporation for poor and distressed Presbyterian ministers" agreed to appoint some of their members to wait on the Synod at its next meeting, and in their name request "that missionaries might be sent to the distressed frontier inhabitants, report their distresses, learn what new congregations were forming," what was necessary to promote the spread of the gospel among them, and discover what opportunities there might be of missionary work among the Indian tribes.[1] Messrs. Charles Beatty and John Brainerd—brother of the missionary—were accordingly appointed, and provision was made for their absence for several months. But the whole design of the mission was frustrated by the breaking out of the Indian War. French hostility, no longer open and avowed, still instigated its former savage allies to the work of vengeance. The whole country west of Shippensburg was ravaged. Houses, barns, corn, hay, and every thing combustible, were burned. The wretched inhabitants, surprised at their labor, at their meals, or in their beds, were massacred with the utmost cruelty and brutality, and those of them who escaped might almost envy the fate of those who had fallen. Overwhelmed by the common calamity, terrified by danger, reduced by want and fatigue to a state of exhaustion, famished, shelterless, without the means of transportation, their tardy flight was delayed by "fainting women and weeping children." "On July 25, 1763, there were at Shippensburg thirteen hundred and eighty-four poor distressed back inhabitants, many of whom were obliged to lie in barns, stables, cellars, and under old leaky sheds, the dwelling-houses being all crowded."[2]

---

[1] Old Redstone, p. 113. [2] Hist. West. Penn.

The defeat of the Indians in the succeeding autumn drove them beyond the Ohio, and for a time the settlers were unmolested. In 1766, Mr. Beatty, in conjunction with Mr. Duffield, performed his Western mission. At Fort Pitt (Pittsburg) he was invited by McLagan, chaplain to the 42d Regiment,[1] to preach to the garrison, while Mr. Duffield preached to the people, who lived "in some kind of a town without the fort." The missionaries on their return reported[2] "that they found on the frontiers numbers of people earnestly desirous of forming themselves into congregations, and declaring their willingness to exert their utmost in order to have the gospel among them;" but their circumstances were "exceedingly distressing and necessitous," in consequence of the calamities inflicted by the war. The westward limit of their journey was among the Indians on the Muskingum, "one hundred and thirty miles beyond Fort Pitt." The prospect of missions among them was reported as encouraging, and steps were taken to secure the services of two other missionaries for the ensuing year. Although difficulties arose to prevent their going, it is significant at once of the poverty of the people and the liberality of the Synod, that the order was made that the missionaries "take no money from the frontier settlements for their ministerial labors among them."

It is impossible to determine how far the measures of the Synod for mission-labor in Western Pennsylvania were carried out with each successive year; but they were regularly made at each annual meeting, and in some cases at least were successful. The war of the Revolution, however, interrupted the further prosecution of the plan; and yet before its close (1781) Redstone Presbytery had been organized on the field.

---

[1] History of Pittsburg.

[2] Minutes of Synod, p. 375.

A very primitive state of society was that which greeted the eye and shaped the experience of the first pastors of the Presbytery. The persons that composed their congregations were by no means dressed in accordance with the fashions of Eastern cities. In nine cases out of ten, a blanket or a coverlet served as a substitute for a great-coat in winter weather, and the worshipper was not ashamed to wear it.[1] Deer-skin was a substitute for cloth for men and boys. Every thing that was not brought from a distance of more than a hundred miles across the mountains, had to be manufactured by patient industry and primitive agencies. The best dwelling of the settler was for many years a log cabin, and its furniture was of the simplest description. Here and there a fort told the story of danger from Indian invasion, and suggested the hazards by day and night to which the inhabitants were exposed.

Until 1790, it is not known that a church edifice or house of worship was erected in the region. Meetings were held in the shady groves, or, for greater security, within the walls of the forts. They were attended sometimes from a distance of twelve to sixteen miles; and he was fortunate whose residence enabled him, by a walk of not more than five or six, to enjoy the regular ordinances of Sabbath worship. In many cases every man came armed. The guns were stacked, and a sentinel was appointed to sound the signal of alarm in case of danger from Indian attack. The

---

[1] The author of "Old Redstone" relates an anecdote to the effect that when the first court of common pleas was held in Catfish, now Washington, a highly respectable citizen, whose presence was required as a magistrate, could not attend without first borrowing a pair of leather breeches from an equally respectable neighbor, who was summoned on grand jury. The latter lent them, and, having no others, had to stay at home.—Page 44.

perils from this source did not cease till Wayne's victory in 1794.

The toils and hardships of the ministers were excessive. They not only shared the lot of their people in respect to food, clothing, and lodging, but in their extended journeyings from place to place to preach, administer the ordinances, and visit their scattered sheep in the wilderness, were exposed to peculiar hazards. Often did they have to travel a distance of from fifteen to fifty miles in order to discharge their parochial duties, so extended were the fields which they were called to occupy. They were indeed bishops in the primitive sense, and each had his diocese. For days together they were absent from their families. In some places there were no roads, or only those of the worst description. "A blind-path, but seldom used, must be followed, when every neighborhood road to a mill or a smith's shop, being much more distinct, would be almost sure to mislead them."[1] Guide-boards there were none. Bridges had not yet been built, and fording-places were not always easy to be discovered. Yet, braving all perils, exposed to heat and cold, plodding through the mud or facing the storm, they discharged their duty,—brave in a heroism not less noble that it was obscure, not less admirable that it was the fruit of Christian faith and pastoral fidelity.

The support of the clergyman was by no means ample; yet two and sometimes three congregations were united to secure it. Even then he might be necessitated to eke out his salary by cultivating a farm, or unite thrift with charity in the work of instruction. There was indeed ample wealth around him,—such as it was; but it was the riches of a fertile soil, and the verdure of hill and valley; it was nature herself with

---

[1] Old Redstone, p. 133.

her mines and acres waiting for the hand of industry to coin them into shape and imprint upon them the image and superscription of civilization and culture.

But a richer soil than that of the hills and valleys was that which the laborer in the Lord's vineyard was called to cultivate. His parishioners were by no means the miscellaneous drift-wood which emigration usually floats off from older communities to new settlements. Among them were men of culture, and a large proportion of them were characterized by stern religious principle. They were men whose energy and vigor were developed by the circumstances of their lot, and who, in grappling with the forest and repelling or guarding against savage attack, were made more sagacious, fearless, and self-reliant. Their outward condition was far from enviable; since for many years they underwent severe hardships, which rendered it any thing but Eden-like. The "howling" wilderness, literally so, around them,—the danger of starvation, no remote one at many times,—the scarcity of salt and iron,—with roads that for the most part were mere bridle-paths,—all these things might seem to indicate a degraded lot; but the wilderness did not reduce them to barbarism. Their food might be—often was—"hog and hominy;" potatoes and pumpkins were a substitute for bread. Bear's oil sometimes took the place of butter. The dress, too, might betray a mixture of an Indian and a civilized wardrobe. The "linsey-woolsey" hunting-shirt, with its large sleeves, rude belt, and bosom which served as a wallet for bread, jirk, or tow for the rifle,—the breeches made of the skins of beasts, or, if unusually fine, of buckskin,—the moccasins stuffed in cold weather with deer's hair or dried leaves, —the rude furniture of the log cabin, little in advance of that of the wigwam,—all might indicate but a slight superiority over the savage, reluctantly yielding to the encroachments of the white man. But beneath this coarse exterior beat hearts as true to the cause of freedom, intelligence, morals, and religion, as any in the world. "A more intelligent, virtuous, and resolute class of men never settled any country than the first settlers of Western Pennsylvania."[1] They had, indeed, their peculiarities. Some brought with them habits and associations which were not always the most commendable. Their prejudices were strong. A portion of them were of the strictest sect of Seceders. They could breathe forth railings against Watts's Imitation, and denounce a departure from Rouse as heresy. But, as a powerful leaven of the constantly increasing immigration, even these were invaluable, and, as a whole, the material of which the churches of Western Pennsylvania were composed was of just that sort which the times and the emergency demanded,—men stern enough not only to retain their own individuality, but to impress it upon the more yielding mass accumulating around them.

The land was inviting, and it was cheap. The State of Virginia, assuming a right to the territory, sold large portions of it at a merely nominal price.[2] "The purchase-money was trifling indeed,—about ten shillings the hundred acres,—and even that was not demanded." The fees for warrants were two shillings and sixpence; and, on these terms, Virginia disposed liberally of Pennsylvania territory,—a proceeding which resulted in trouble afterward, when the claims of the respective States came to be settled, but for the time it invited immigration, and Western Pennsylvania by the close of the Revolutionary War had not far from twenty thousand inhabitants.

The earliest settlements were of course in the vicinity of Pittsburg, and gradually extended northward toward

---

[1] Old Redstone, p. 43. [2] Ibid. 32.

Lake Erie. "In 1765, Pittsburg was, to a small extent, regularly laid out. In 1765 and 1766, settlements were made at Redstone and Turkey-foot. Several of these were made by heads of Presbyterian families.[1]" About 1768, what is now Fayette county was occupied by emigrants from Berkeley county, Va. At nearly the same time, a considerable number of settlers located on the Youghiogheny, the Monongahela, and its tributaries. In 1770–1, many Scotch-Irish from Bedford and York counties, from the Kittatinny Valley, from Virginia, and some directly from the North of Ireland, commenced settlements in Washington county. As the tide of population increased in volume, and extended from the Monongahela to the Ohio, it was swelled by contributions from various sources, yet not sufficient to change its general character.

Until 1774, the settlers were dependent for gospel-ordinances upon the missionaries sent out by the Synod. This provision was interrupted by the difficulties of distance, Indian hostility, and the excitement that heralded the rupture with the mother-country. It was, moreover, inadequate to the necessities of the field. But one after another of the ministers at the East was induced, by the confusion that the war introduced and the appeals presented by the needy condition of the Western settlements, to remove to that region. At length a sufficient number had entered the field to feel warranted in asking for the erection of a Presbytery. Their distance from the Presbyteries with which they were connected, the utter impracticability of meeting with them, and the necessity of the churches to which they ministered, impelled to the request; and at the meeting of the Synod in May (16), 1781, the Rev. Messrs. Joseph Smith, John McMillan, James Power, and Thad-

---

[1] Redstone, p. 30.

deus Dod, were erected, in accordance with their petition, into the Presbytery of Redstone, and their first meeting was appointed to be held at Laurel Hill, on the third Wednesday of September ensuing. The meeting, however, on account of the incursion of the savages, was held, not at Laurel Hill, but at Pigeon Creek.

Within the bounds of "Old Redstone," extending indefinitely over Western Pennsylvania, the Virginia "Pan-handle," and the borders of the Northwestern Territory, James Power was the first settled pastor. He was born in 1746, at Nottingham, Chester county, Pa. His course previous to entering college was probably pursued under John Blair, at the school of Fagg's Manor. In 1766, he was graduated at Princeton, and in 1772 was licensed by New Castle Presbytery.

His earliest labors as a missionary were in Virginia. A call from churches in Botetourt county was extended to him, but declined. In the summer of 1774, he crossed the mountains, and spent the summer in missionary labors in Western Pennsylvania. The settlements embraced in what are now Washington, Alleghany, Westmoreland, and Fayette counties, were the field which he traversed.

Two years were spent at the East before he returned to make this region his permanent home. Toward the close of 1776, he removed with his family to the scene of his future labors. For several years his life was that of an active and energetic itinerant missionary. He visited the new settlements, preaching, among other places, at Mount Pleasant, Unity, Laurel Hill, and Dunlap's Creek. In the spring of 1779, he became the regular pastor of Sewickley and Mount Pleasant congregations. Quiet in manner, neat in dress, courteous and gentlemanly in his whole deportment, with a memory of persons that was almost fabulous, he was, moreover, a graceful speaker and a devoted pastor. He had no enemies. Parents respected him, and the little children loved to see his face. Plain in speech, earnest but not impassioned in address, his sermons were instructive and persuasive rather than vehement or pungent, and his influence was felt throughout the extensive sphere of his labors, exerting a quiet but steady power.

He had been two years in the Western field when he was joined by another laborer, whose character in several respects was directly the reverse of his own. This was Mr. (afterward Dr.) John McMillan, like himself a pupil of John Blair, a graduate of Princeton, and a student of theology under Dr. Robert Smith at Pequa. In 1776, he accepted a call from the united congregations of Chartiers and Pigeon Creek, and entered upon his self-denying and hazardous work. The cabin in which he was to live, he found when he reached the place, had neither roof, chimney, nor floor. The danger was such from the Indians that he dared not take his family with him till 1778. Even then, when he moved into his house, which his people kindly assisted him to prepare, he had neither bedstead, table, chairs, stool, or bucket. Two boxes served for a table, and two kegs for seats. Oftentimes his family had no bread for weeks together; but, content to dispense with luxuries, they felt that it was enough if they had "plenty of pumpkins, potatoes, and all the necessaries of life."

As he set out upon his journey, McMillan was enjoined by Dr. Smith "to look out some pious young men and educate them for the ministry." He respected the wisdom of the injunction, and, until the academy at Canonsburg was opened, devoted a portion of his time to the training of young men for the ministry. Nearly all of these became useful, and some of them eminent among the ministers of the Presbyterian Church. Not a few were afterward his efficient co-Presbyters and coadjutors. Among these were Patterson, Porter, Marquis, and Hughes.

Of a large frame, commanding presence, a look somewhat stern, with decision and resolution traced in every feature, the outward person was no unbefitting type of the inward man. With a perfect scorn for all that was fanciful or *nice*, an enemy alike to luxury, flattery, studied ornament of speech, or studied grace of manner, he was almost a Knox in boldness, energy, and decision. With a voice that no art could have made musical, but of wonderful power; a vehement and intense utterance which carried conviction and forced, rather than won, assent, and with a concise brevity and energy of expression which presented his thoughts in their naked strength, he was the man who could overawe opposition, and with whom any one would beware how he came in conflict. Repeated revivals occurred under his ministry, and, although by two years preceded in his entrance upon the field by Mr. Power, the superior energy of his nature placed him in the first rank as a pioneer missionary of the Presbyterian Church west of the mountains. He was a man of the stamp which the times and the rude wilderness region around him demanded. His nature was cast in a stern mould, but it enabled him to impress others without yielding himself. His theology was of the type of his instructor, Robert Smith, and his sons, Samuel Stanhope Smith and John Blair Smith, successively presidents of Hampden-Sidney,[1] and, subsequently, the first of Princeton and the second of Union College. His own soul was pervaded by its power, and he could not fail to make others feel something of what he felt

---

[1] The author of "Old Redstone" says, his "views on the subject of natural and moral ability are much the same with those of Dr. Lyman Beecher."

himself. Thus revivals were not only favored, but expected and labored for; and some of the most marked demonstrations of the power of divine truth which the history of the Church affords, occurred under his ministry.

McMillan had been in the field but little more than a year when another laborer arrived,—a worthy compeer in the great missionary work in Western Pennsylvania. In the fall of 1777, the whole region was alarmed by an incursion of the Indians. Fort Henry, at the mouth of Wheeling Creek, was attacked, and the whole West for weeks and months afterward was alive with apprehension of savage forays. In this season of anxiety and trembling, a young man of slender form, black hair, keen dark eyes, and sallow complexion, reached Fort Lindley. To some of its occupants he was well known: he had come from the same region with them, and he was now prepared to cast in his lot with theirs. His name was Thaddeus Dod.

His father was a native of Guilford, Conn., and the son was born at Newark, N.J., March 7, 1740. From early childhood he was the subject of deep religious impressions. Not, however, till after he united with the church at Mendham, at the mature age of twenty-four, did the thought of preparing for the ministry enter his mind. Struggling with his straitened circumstances, now teaching, and now studying, he succeeded in securing the necessary preparation to enter, on an advanced standing, at Princeton in 1771. He studied theology with Dr. McWhorter, of Newark, and Timothy Johnes, of Morristown. The Presbytery of New York licensed him to preach, in 1775.

After preaching in parts of Virginia and Maryland, he crossed the mountains to Western Pennsylvania. Here were many who had emigrated years before from his own region of country,—some who had been associated with him in the scenes of the revival of 1764, when he united with the Church. They invited him to settle among them, assuring him of a hearty welcome, and a support for himself and family, if he would consent to become their pastor.

It was not an enviable post; but he did not feel at liberty to decline it. He preached at the fort, at Cook's settlement, and other places. In 1778, he commenced forming congregations. Lower Ten-Mile and Upper Ten-Mile, each about ten miles from Washington, constituted one church, to which he more especially ministered.[1] Lindley, who gave his name to the fort, was one of the elders,—a descendant of the Puritan Francis Lindley, who was associated with Robinson in Holland and crossed the ocean in the Mayflower. Of the others, there were those well worthy to rank with him. In them the missionary found friends and supporters.

It was not long before a revival commenced at the fort. In this most perilous of the frontier posts, while east of the mountains all was dark and discouraging, the Lord smiled upon Zion. More than forty indulged the Christian hope. It was a blessed season, and the harbinger also of many others that were yet to come in better days.

In 1781, a log academy, considerably larger than any dwelling-house in the region, was put up by Mr. Dod's neighbors and parishioners. "They consisted, indeed, of many persons considerably in advance of the Scotch-Irish in point of education. They had

---

[1] A church was organized at Ten-Mile, August 15, 1781, at the house of Jacob Cook, consisting of twenty-five members. The first sacramental season did not take place till the third Sabbath of May, 1783. The ordinance was administered in Daniel Axtell's barn, three miles north of Fort Lindley.—*Wines's Historical Discourse*, pp. 13, 14.

brought their New Jersey and New England tastes with them."[1] Of the academy which they erected, Mr. Dod took charge; and none could have been better fitted for the post. As a mathematician he was almost unrivalled, and his eminence as a teacher was such that in 1789 he was called to take charge of Washington Academy, just incorporated by the Legislature of the State, and which in 1806 was merged into Washington College.

Few men have left behind them a more cherished memory amid the scenes in which they labored than Mr. Dod. Modest, humble, devout in spirit, of prepossessing manners, and of rare natural and acquired gifts, he was a man to be at once respected, reverenced, and loved. In his mental structure, mathematical talent, classical taste, and poetic imagination were alike combined. His calm decision and cheerful self-denial allowed him to shrink from no task or peril to which duty called. For sixteen years he was spared, to lay deep and firm the foundations of the Church in the region which was honored as the scene of his labors.

He had been but a few months in this Western field, when he was cheered by the accession of one, his senior by several years and his equal in devotion, whose name is worthy to be ranked beside his own. Joseph Smith was a graduate of Princeton in 1764, and five years later, at the age of thirty-three, was installed pastor of Lower Brandywine. In this region he labored till 1778. The troubles and confusion of the war led him to think of seeking another field. In 1779, he crossed the mountains to Western Pennsylvania. His short visit led to his receiving a call from the united congregations of Buffalo and Cross Creek.

---

[1] Old Redstone, p. 145.

He accepted it, and for the twelve remaining years of his life continued pastor of these congregations.

A revival commenced soon after his settlement, and it may almost be said to have continued to the close of his pastorate. A more devoted pastor was not to be found in the whole band of those that preceded or followed him. He was a man of prayer and faith. In the pulpit, and out of it, his power was wonderful. His soul was thrown into his utterance. His voice was "now like the thunder, and now like the music of heaven." His manner "had a strange kind of power about it, totally indescribable." He had the peculiarity of Whitefield, a slight look askance of one eye; and the piercing brilliancy of his glance was remarkably impressive. "I never heard a man," said the Rev. Samuel Porter, "who could so completely unbar the gates of hell and make me look so far down into the dark, bottomless abyss, or, like him, could so throw open the gates of heaven and let me glance at the insufferable brightness of the great white throne." "He would often rise to an almost supernatural and unearthly grandeur, completely extinguishing in his hearers all consciousness of time and place."[1] No one could appreciate the man merely from his written discourses. His tones, his emphasis, his holy unction, and the holy vitality of his soul made them indescribably impressive. His mind had been early disciplined by classical studies and collegiate drilling. He was capable, doubtless, of scholarly reasoning, of cautious logic; but in the earnest glow of his eloquence, in the soarings of lofty and hallowed thought, he spurned them as an eagle would a ladder by which to climb.

Yet he was a man who was regarded with affection

---

[1] Old Redstone, p. 67.

as well as awe. Always cheerful, eminently social, there was a charm in his tones and manner that won the hearts of all with whom he had intercourse. His soul was attuned to praise. Amid hardships from want and exposure, and perils from savage foes, he was still calmly resolute. In pastoral duty he was faithful and unwearied, and large and blessed were the results of his fidelity.

Like Dod and McMillan, he did not neglect the cause of ministerial education. Soon after his settlement, as early as 1785, he commenced a school for the training of young men. He had no building for the purpose, and, with his wife's consent, his kitchen was devoted to the service of mental instead of bodily aliment. Here the first Latin school of the region was commenced, and McGready, Patterson, and Porter began their course. Others soon joined them, and these young men—supported by the ladies of the neighboring congregations, who made up for them their summer and winter clothing (coloring linen for summer wear in a dye made from new-mown hay)—largely composed the future missionaries and ministers of Redstone, Ohio, and other Presbyteries.

Thus, in 1781, the Presbytery of Redstone was constituted with these four ministers, Smith, Dod, McMillan, and Power, as its first members. In 1782, James Dunlap, a graduate of Princeton, and a theological pupil of James Finley, joined the Presbytery, and was installed over the congregations of Laurel Hill and Dunlap's Creek. He afterward became a member of Ohio Presbytery, and subsequently President of Jefferson College at Canonsburg. He was soon followed to Western Pennsylvania by his theological instructor, James Finley, who had accepted a call from the two societies in the Forks of Youghiogheny. He was a brother of President Finley of Princeton, and for several years had been settled at East Nottingham. On repeated occasions he had visited this Western region, and when not a few of his neighbors and parishioners, and some of his own children, had carried into action their purpose to emigrate, he resolved to follow. He became "informally, and without the consent of the Presbytery,"[1] pastor of Rehoboth and Round Hill, and so continued without any further action of the Presbytery, of which for four years he continued a corresponding member before he united with it. As Dr. Hill well remarks, "We were not very strict in observing church rules in those days."

Meanwhile, a veteran in the Eastern field had crossed the mountains. John Clark, already over sixty years of age, had been settled successively within the bounds of Philadelphia and New Castle Presbyteries. In 1781 he became the supply, and afterward pastor, of the united congregations of Bethel and Lebanon, under the care of the Presbytery of Redstone. In 1785, Mr. Barr, from New Castle Presbytery, accepted a call from the united congregations of Pittsburg and Pitt township. In 1788, John Brice, James Hughes, James McGready, and Joseph Patterson were licensed by the Presbytery, and entered soon after upon their fields of labor, the first at Three Ridges and Forks of Wheeling, the last far on in the wilderness, at Short Creek and Lower Buffalo, and Patterson at Raccoon and Montour's Run. McGready, afterward so famous in connection with the great revival in Kentucky, was converted under the preaching of Joseph Smith, and was for a while his pupil. He labored but a short time within the bounds of the Presbytery by which he was licensed, returning soon to Carolina, where his parents resided, and where a

[1] Old Redstone, p. 283.

revival quickly commenced under his labors, among the fruits of which was Dr. Anderson, who succeeded Joseph Smith in the pastorate at Upper Buffalo.

In the course of the following years the Presbytery was strengthened by several others who had been trained up upon the field. John McPherrin, Samuel Porter, Robert Marshall, George Hill, William Swan, and Thomas Marquis, were licensed, and became efficient laborers within the rapidly extending bounds of the Presbytery. Jacob Jennings and Thomas Cooley were received by dismission from other bodies: so that at the period of the formation of the Ohio Presbytery, in 1793, the Redstone Presbytery numbered more than twelve ministers and about three times as many churches.

Rarely, if ever, in the history of the Presbyterian Church in this country has any of its missionary fields been occupied by a more able and devoted band of pioneer laborers than that which was covered by the Old Redstone Presbytery. In wise and sagacious forethought and provision for the prospective wants of the Church, as well as in unwearied and faithful cultivation of their own fields, they have been rarely equalled, and never surpassed. Their self-denial, their energy, and their success alike entitle them to the highest honor. In spirit they were the successors to the Blairs, Finleys, and Smiths of the Revival period who during the division adhered to the New side and the cause of vital piety. Many of them were rarely gifted, and would have done honor to the most exalted station; and the influence which they exerted upon the great Western field then opening with inviting promise to Eastern emigration, cannot be estimated. Deterred by no hardships, appalled by no terror, whether from the wilderness or the savage, they stood firm at their posts, contending to the last with their harness on.[1] They had no supernumeraries, and yet, notwithstanding the crying need of missionary labor, declined to license a man whose piety they approved, but with whose qualifications they were dissatisfied. They wanted, and made provision to secure, *strong* men; and all who joined them seemed to be made partakers of their own spirit. It was of immense importance to the Church that its earliest Western outpost should be held by the hands of these men, whom the providence of God had trained and appointed to the task.

CHAPTER XIV.

GENERAL ASSEMBLY, 1789-1800.

THE original motion for the division of the Synod, with a view to the formation of a General Assembly, proposed the constituting of three Synods. This was in 1785; but in the following year the terms of the measure were modified so as to read, "three or more." Accordingly, the Presbyteries were so divided and arranged as to constitute four Synods,—viz.: those of New York and New Jersey, Philadelphia, Virginia, and the Carolinas. The first embraced the Presbyteries of

[1] "In every thing our fathers were trained to endure hardness as good soldiers. Their first temples were the shady grove, and their first pulpits a rude tent made of rough slabs; while the audience sat either upon logs or the green turf. Not even log churches were erected till about the year 1790. Even in winter the meetings were held in the open air. Not one in ten had the luxury of a great-coat. The most were obliged to wear blankets or coverlets instead."—*Dr. Wines's Historical Discourse*, 1859, p. 10.

Suffolk, Dutchess county, New York, and New Brunswick; the second, those of Philadelphia, Lewes, New Castle, Baltimore, and Carlisle; that of Virginia, the Presbyteries of Redstone, Hanover, Lexington, and Transylvania; that of the Carolinas, the Presbyteries of Abingdon, Orange, and South Carolina.

In order to carry out this arrangement for a division, several changes were made in relation to the Presbyteries. The Presbytery of Abingdon, extending over the borders of Western Virginia, Tennessee, and Kentucky, was divided, and that of Transylvania, embracing Kentucky, was formed out of it. Hanover Presbytery was also divided, and the portion of it northwest of the Blue Ridge, embracing the Valley of the Shenandoah, was set off to form the Presbytery of Lexington. The Presbytery of Donegal was also divided, and the Presbytery of Carlisle erected out of it. A new Presbytery was formed, by the name of the Presbytery of Baltimore, and the Old-side Second of Philadelphia, which had not hitherto altogether harmonized with the Synod, was struck from the list, and its members distributed between the three Presbyteries of Carlisle, Philadelphia First, and Baltimore.

The four Synods, embracing sixteen Presbyteries, were now to be united in a General Assembly. From the widely extended bounds of the Church, it had become altogether impracticable to secure a full attendance of the ministers and elders of the more distant churches. For successive years, several Presbyteries had not been represented in Synod by so much as a single member. The number of churches and ministers, moreover, had so multiplied that it was supposed that an Assembly that would embrace them all would be too unwieldy for wise deliberation. It was therefore resolved to adopt the principle of delegation. Every Presbytery of not more than six ministers might send one minister and one elder to the Assembly. If it consisted of more than six and not more than twelve, it was to send two ministers and two elders, and likewise in the same proportion for every six ministers.

The first General Assembly of the Church met in Philadelphia in 1789.[1] By the appointment of the Synod that ratified the constitution of the Church, it was opened with a sermon by Dr. Witherspoon, and Dr. John Rodgers, of New York, was chosen the first moderator. The first Congress of the United States under the present Constitution was then in session in New York: so that the Federal Government of the country and the present constitution of the Presbyterian Church were nearly contemporaneous, and went into operation at the same time.

It is not surprising that, in such circumstances, the Assembly should have felt the appropriateness of the suggestion that a committee should be appointed to draft an address to the President of the United States; and the selection of the committee, of which Dr. Witherspoon was chairman and Drs. Allison and Samuel Stanhope Smith were members, shows the importance which was attached to the proceeding. The Assembly, doubtless, felt it to be a privilege not only to express to Washington himself the respect they felt for his virtues, but to lend the sanction of their approval to his conduct, and encourage him in the discharge of the arduous duties to which he had been called.

The document, as drawn up and adopted by the

---

[1] See Rev. Dr. Ashbel Green's Autobiography. With a few exceptions, Philadelphia was the place where the Assembly convened regularly each year till after the division of 1838. The distance of the Southern and Western portions of the Church led them to ask that it might meet nearer to them. The request was granted a few times, as in 1792 and 1795, when it met at Carlisle, and in 1799 when it met at Winchester, Va. In 1835, it met at Pittsburg.

Assembly, is worthy to stand as a precedent of appropriate address from a Christian Assembly to a Christian ruler, whose character needed no eulogium beyond his own acts. It was respectful, dignified, and manly in its tone. After referring to his past career, it proceeds, "From a retirement more glorious than thrones and sceptres, you have been called to your present elevated station by the advice of a great and a free people, and with an unanimity of suffrage that has few, if any, examples in history. A man more ambitious of fame, or less devoted to his country, would have refused an office in which his honors could not be augmented, and where he might possibly be subject to a reverse. We are happy that God has inclined your heart to give yourself once more to the public. And we derive a favorable presage of the event from the zeal of all classes of the people, and their confidence in your virtues, as well as from the knowledge and dignity with which the federal councils are filled. But we derive a presage even more flattering from the piety of your character. Public virtue is the most certain means of public felicity, and religion is the surest basis of virtue. We therefore esteem it a peculiar happiness to behold in our chief magistrate a steady, uniform, avowed friend of the Christian religion; who has commenced his administration in rational and exalted sentiments of piety, and who in his private conduct adorns the doctrines of the gospel of Christ, and, on the most public and solemn occasions, devoutly acknowledges the government of Divine Providence.

"The example of distinguished characters will ever possess a powerful and extensive influence on the public mind; and when we see in such a conspicuous station the amiable example of piety to God, of benevolence to men, and of a pure and virtuous patriotism, we naturally hope that it will diffuse its influence, and that, eventually, the most happy consequences will result from it. To the force of imitation we will endeavor to add the wholesome instructions of religion. We shall consider ourselves as doing an acceptable service to God, in our profession, when we contribute to render men sober, honest, and industrious citizens and the obedient subjects of a lawful government. In these pious labors we hope to imitate the most worthy of our brethren of other Christian denominations, and to be imitated by them; assured that if we can, by mutual and generous emulation, promote truth and virtue, we shall render a great and important service to the republic, shall receive encouragement from every wise and good citizen, and, above all, meet the approbation of our Divine Master.

"We pray Almighty God to have you always in his holy keeping. May he prolong your valuable life, an ornament and a blessing to your country, and at last bestow on you the glorious reward of a faithful servant."

Such an address testifies to the high estimate entertained by the Assembly of the religious character of the first President of the Republic, while its endorsement of the effort to render men "the obedient subjects of a lawful government" stands as a precedent for later times.

The reply of Washington was modest, and yet properly characterized by self-respect. He would not be elated by the too favorable opinion of the Assembly; yet, conscious of the disinterestedness of his motives, it was not necessary for him to conceal the satisfaction he felt at general approbation of his conduct. "While I reiterate," he says, "the professions of my dependence upon Heaven as the source of all public and private blessings, I will observe, that the general prevalence of piety, philanthropy, honesty, industry, and economy, seems, in the ordinary course of human affairs, particularly necessary for advancing and confirming the happiness of our country. While all men within our territories are protected in worshipping the Deity according to the dictates of their consciences, it is rationally to be expected from them in return that they will all be emulous of evincing the sincerity of their professions by the innocence of their lives and the benevolence of their actions. For no man who is profligate in his morals, or a bad member of the civil community, can possibly be a true Christian, or a credit to his own religious society."

He closes by desiring the Assembly to accept his acknowledgments for their laudable endeavors to render men sober, honest, and good citizens, and "the obedient subjects of a lawful government," as well as for their prayers for the country and himself.

The correspondence does honor alike to the Assembly and "the great man"[1] whom it wished to cheer and encourage in his arduous position. The popular estimate of his Christian character was no doubt reflected in the language of the Assembly. His own modesty forbade him to accept the full measure of their praise; but he reiterated his professions of dependence on Providence, and gratefully acknowledged their prayers in his behalf.

The liberal ecclesiastical spirit of the first General Assembly is sufficiently attested by the reply to an overture bearing directly on the power and authority of Synods and Assemblies. The overture was to this effect:—"Whether the General Assembly, out of their liberality, charity, and candor, will admit to their communion, in the ecclesiastical Assemblies, as far as they

---

[1] This was the term by which Fisher Ames was wont to speak of Washington.

can consistently with the scrupulosity of their consciences, a Presbytery who are totally averse to the doctrine of receiving, hearing, or judging of any appeals from Presbyteries to Synods, and from Synods to General Assemblies, because in their judgment it is inconsistent with Scripture and the practice of the primitive churches?" In reply, the General Assembly declare "that, although they consider the right of appeal from the decision of an inferior judicature to a superior, an important privilege, which no member of their body ought to be deprived of, yet they at the same time declare that they do not desire any member to be active in any case which may be inconsistent with the dictates of his conscience."

As to the source from which this overture originated, we are left to conjecture. It is barely possible that it may have proceeded from the Presbytery of Long Island, which for some years after the organization of the General Assembly was, on account of the Congregational sympathies of the churches, scarcely prepared to go the full length of the friends of a more rigid ecclesiasticism;[1] but it is more probable that it emanated from the Associated Presbytery of Morris county, N.J., or that of Westchester county, N.Y. These bodies, from old associations, chose to retain the Presbyterian name, while they approximated to Congregational usage, but, unable to sustain themselves permanently, became at length

---

[1] In 1790, the Presbytery of Long Island addressed a circular letter to the churches under their care, in which, among other things, they present an argument in favor of "not only the particular but general government of the churches." The letter is given in the "Presbyterian Magazine," July, 1859, p. 326. In the course of it, the Presbytery state that they "are not insensible that prejudices have been implanted, by ill-designing persons, in the minds of many against Presbyterian government." These they endeavor to remove.

disintegrated, and the constituent churches were for the most part absorbed in other Presbyteries under the care of the Assembly. It was indicative of the spirit of the Assembly, that at its first sessions it should adopt measures to preserve "faithful and correct impressions of the Holy Scriptures." Mr. Collins, of New Jersey, proposed to print an edition of the Bible, and to this end sought the countenance and support of all denominations. The General Assembly warmly favored his project, and a committee of one from each of the sixteen Presbyteries of the Church was appointed to bring the subject before their respective bodies, so that in each congregation an individual should be appointed to secure subscriptions. It was also proposed to inquire whether, and on what terms, Ostervald's[1] notes could be printed with it.

The recommendation of 1789 was repeated in the following year, and the effort to secure the printing of the notes—which could be done only for those who especially desired it—was promoted by measures for obtaining subscribers for five hundred copies at 3*s.* 9*d.* each, or one thousand at 2*s.* 6*d.* each.

In 1795, the interest of the Assembly in the cause of learning was evinced by their recommendation of the agents of "Kentucky Academy."[2] Expressing the earnest wish that the cause of learning and religion might be promoted throughout the world, and especially in this country, they certified to the good stand-

---

[1] Ostervald, a Protestant minister, born, 1663, at Neufchâtel, a friend of Turretin and Werenfels, the three in connection repeatedly styled "the triumvirate of Swiss theologians." Ostervald bore the reputation of being "learned, pious, and humane."

[2] Minutes of 1795, p. 105. Transylvania University, founded by Presbyterians, had been wrested from their hands and given over to the influence of infidelity. The effort was now made to secure an institution of which they might have the control.

ing of Rev. Messrs. Rice and Blythe, recommending them and their cause to all to whom they might apply, and inviting liberal donations "for the promotion of the seminary about to be erected" in the new State of Kentucky.

From the earliest period the Presbyterian Church in this country assumed the character of a missionary Church. In 1707, only two years after the formation of the first Presbytery, it was recommended to every minister of the body "to supply neighboring desolate places where a minister is wanted, and opportunity of doing good offers." Soon after, we find appeals made to the churches in Ireland, Scotland, and London, for ministers and means to supply the infant churches, which were rapidly organized.

One of the first acts of the Synod of Philadelphia after its formation was the initiation of a fund "for pious uses." Each minister was to contribute something himself, and use his influence on proper occasions to induce others to contribute. The fund was under the Synod's control, and was devoted to the aid of feeble churches, assistance in building houses of worship, sustaining the ministry, and extending relief to the widows of deceased brethren who had been left in indigent circumstances. Annual collections were enjoined upon the congregations in 1719, and the first recorded disbursement was in behalf of the Presbyterian Church in the city of New York.

But, while the fund thus inaugurated subsequently assumed a systematic form, the principal mode of its application was in sustaining itinerant ministers who visited the new settlements, gathering the people and organizing churches.

After the union of the two Synods in 1758, the missionary operations of the Church were carried on with increased energy. In 1759, Messrs. Kirkpatrick,

McWhorter, Latta, and Lewis were sent to Virginia to act under the direction of the Presbytery of Hanover, and were succeeded in the following year by Messrs. Duffield and Mills. At the same time provision was made for sustaining John, the brother of David Brainerd, in his labors among the Indians. Collections were successively ordered to promote this object.

The annual appointments for itinerant missionary labor still continued to be made; and in 1773, Mr. Occum, missionary of the British Society, was taken under the care of Synod, and sixty-five pounds were appropriated for his support. In the same year the destitute condition of the frontier settlements was brought to the attention of Synod. Messrs. Beatty and Brainerd were appointed to go to the West and report the result of their researches. Arrangements were also made for devising a more systematic plan of missionary operations.

In the following year it was ordered that each member of the Synod should take up a collection in his congregation, to raise a fund for missionary purposes. The amount realized was only one hundred and twelve pounds; and the Synod, with regret that so little had been accomplished, adopted an overture from the Presbytery of New York, providing for an annual collection in each congregation, and appointing a treasurer for each Presbytery, as well as a general treasurer for the Synod.

During the war the missionary policy of the Church was paralyzed, but upon the formation of the General Assembly the subject claimed its earliest and most serious attention. The necessity was urgent of making provision for missionary effort in the new and destitute settlements. From the close of the war there had been a large and continuous emigration from the East to the West; and in the period which had elapsed since the plan for a General Assembly was first agitated, the region west of the Alleghanies had risen into new importance. Settlements had been commenced in Central and even Western New York, and quite extensively in Western Pennsylvania. Even during the war, applications for missionary aid were frequent. They were now more numerous. The Assembly felt the importance of the subject, and Dr. Allison and Dr. Samuel S. Smith were appointed a committee to prepare a minute with reference to sending missionaries to the frontier settlements.[1] Each Synod was directed to name those of its number whom it deemed properly qualified to discharge the duties of missionary labor, and who would be disposed to undertake the work at least for a portion of the year. This was in 1789; but in the following year the duty was more appropriately committed to each Presbytery, which would naturally be better acquainted with the qualifications of its members. The object of this arrangement was to bring before the Assembly the names of those from whom it might select the persons, in its judgment, best fitted to be sent out into the new fields.

The Assembly moreover (1790) took measures for carrying out the plan which had been devised. Two missionaries, Messrs. Hart and Ker,[2] were appointed to visit the extensive field that was already opened to

---

1 The overture, from the Committee on Bills and Overtures, with reference to which the Missionary Committee was appointed, was to the effect "that the state of the frontier settlements should be taken into consideration, and missionaries sent to them to form them into congregations, ordain elders, administer the sacraments, and direct them to the best measures for obtaining the gospel ministry regularly among them."—*Minutes of Assembly for* 1789, p. 10.

2 Probably Nathan Ker, of Goshen, N.Y., and Joshua Hart, of Suffolk Presbytery.

effort within the bounds of New York and Northern Pennsylvania.[1] The route which they were directed to pursue was then regarded as the extreme west of the New Settlements. They visited Middletown, Stillwater, Fort Edward, Fort Miller, New Galloway, Cherry Valley, Fort Schuyler, Whitestown, Cooperstown, Clinton, Chenango, Tioga, Wilkesborough, Hanover, and other places on the route, as well as the Indian tribes. They were treated everywhere with great respect, and were requested in the most affectionate manner "to offer the thanks of the people to the General Assembly for their pious attention in sending missionaries among them." The request was urgently and earnestly made that the favor might be repeated.

To this request the Assembly responded by sending out in the following year, through the same region, James Boyd and Aaron Condict. The latter—a theological pupil of Jedediah Chapman, who was afterward settled at Geneva—had just been licensed by the Presbytery of New York; and so acceptable did he prove himself in his preaching upon his route, that he was called within a few months to the pastoral charge of the church at Stillwater, twenty miles north of Albany.

It soon became evident that, in some portions of the broad field covered by the Church, the local knowledge possessed by the Synods best fitted them to direct the laborers that were sent out. The Synods of Virginia and the Carolinas therefore (1791), at their own request, were allowed to manage the missions within their bounds. This was also the case afterward with other Synods with which the Assembly sometimes co-operated, and from which they expected annual reports.

---

[1] In 1794, the salary of missionaries was fixed by the Assembly at forty dollars per month.

The Assembly, however, did not give the matter exclusively into the hands of the Synods. There was, indeed, more work to be done than all united could properly perform, and the attention of the Assembly was directed to those regions which came most directly under the notice of its missionary committee as needing aid. Appointments were sometimes made with the understanding that the Presbyteries or Synods should unite with the Assembly in the support of missionaries. The fields which were principally regarded by the Assembly were those in Delaware, Western Pennsylvania, and Northern and Central New York. The latter region was never overlooked in the list of the Assembly's appointments.

To give a wider dissemination to its views on missions, the Assembly of 1791 prepared, and inserted in the printed extracts from its minutes, a circular letter to the churches under its care. It urged in a forcible manner the claims of the cause of Christ upon the members of the Church, and held up before them the animating prospect of the results which by proper exertion might be attained.

In order, moreover, to provide the necessary means for the support of the missionaries, who ought not to be left to bear alone the whole burden, annual collections were directed to be taken up in all the congregations, and to be placed in the hands of the General Assembly. The amount realized from this source was inadequate to any extended operations; but it amounted in 1795 and 1796 to $1,226.50, and at least enabled the Assembly to carry out in form, however feeble in immediate results, a policy which was to bind the Church together in healthful and harmonious co-operation. Securing in 1799 a charter of incorporation from the State of Pennsylvania, the Assembly prosecuted its work with enlarged resources. Donors felt greater security in contributing to its funds. Its plan now was to initiate a system that should at once reach the destitutions of the older and frontier settlements, negroes, including slaves, and the Indian tribes.

Yet, as has been noted, the missionary operations of the Church were carried on not only through the Assembly, but through the Synods. Those of Virginia and the Carolinas, and, subsequently, of Pittsburg and Kentucky, were all directly employed in the work, although some of them retained connection with, and received aid from, the Assembly.

But the Synod of Virginia found itself from the first (October, 1789) better prepared than some of the other Synods to prosecute its work. The influence of the remarkable revival which had visited Hampden-Sidney College and Prince Edward county had, through the labors of Graham and his younger coadjutors, been extended in several other counties, even to Augusta. In some neighborhoods the work was very powerful. Quite a large number of the students in the two institutions were converted, and immediately turned their attention to the ministry. Among them were some whose names occupy the highest places of distinction in the history of the Church: Legrand, Lacy, Allen, Hill, Alexander, Lyle, Campbell, and Stuart, were of the number.

The Synod of Virginia, finding at its command such a noble body of young men preparing for or just entering the ministry, some of them of superior gifts, and all panting for active service, did not fail to seize upon and improve the opportunity of enlarging its sphere of effort. At its first session, October 24, 1789, a Committee of Synod for Missions, consisting of four ministers and three elders, was appointed, to whom the general charge of this important subject was committed.

The committee met in the following April, and proceeded at once to business. The Synod was divided into four districts, corresponding to the four Presbyteries. The pay of a missionary was to be sixty pounds per annum, and Nash Legrand, a probationer of Hanover Presbytery, was first commissioned. The funds were supplied by the voluntary contributions of the people, and the missionaries were to report in person at each annual meeting of the Synod.

The plan worked well. The Synod became an efficient missionary body. Its meetings were anticipated by the people with the deepest interest. From the most distant places within the bounds of the Synod there was an eager desire to be present. The occasion was regarded almost as a solemn festival. Old and young, the patriarchs of the Church and its young missionaries fresh from scenes that kindled their zeal and love, met together.[1] The narrative of what they had seen and felt and experienced, kindled the missionary spirit to new fervor. "The tear of sympathy coursed down many a patriarchal cheek," and with it flowed tears of gratitude for what God had accomplished. Ardent and glowing were the petitions that went up to heaven, as the Synod supplicated upon its youthful members, committed to a great work, the blessing of Heaven. The spirit of devotion glowed brightly. The scene was one of the highest social and religious interest. Heart was bound to heart, and all felt themselves to be laborers together in a common work.

The benefits of these meetings, and especially of the missionary tours, the account of which added so much to their attraction, were great. A marked change was effected in the moral and religious condition of the

---

[1] See Foote's Sketches.

people. The demoralizing effects of the war, and the pernicious spread of French infidelity, were arrested. The pulpits that had been vacant, or occupied by superannuated men, were now supplied by those who abandoned other pursuits and lucrative prospects to engage in the self-denying work of the ministry. Churches that seemed about to die were resuscitated, and new congregations were gathered. On all sides the Church was roused to new life and vigor. "The salutary effects" of this work "are still apparent. Many of the now flourishing churches in the lower counties owe their origin to this epoch; while there is scarcely a romantic dell embosomed amid the huge mountain-ranges, however unpromising its religious aspect may formerly have been, whose echoes are not regularly waked by the voice of hallowed praise upon the Sabbath day."[1]

The band of young men consecrated to the Church as the fruits of the revival was large. It numbered from thirty to forty. But the field that opened before them, inviting them to effort, was correspondingly large and extensive. Virginia itself had broad wastes demanding faithful missionary culture. The Carolinas at the South were calling for laborers. Kentucky and Tennessee had just been opened to civilized enterprise, and population was pouring over the Alleghanies in a ceaseless and swelling tide.

In 1793, a memorial, signed by Warner Mifflin, a member of the Society of Friends, was handed, under cover, to the moderator, read, and ordered to lie upon the table. It related to the subject of slavery, and the Assembly, in response, ordered that the minute of the Synod of 1787 on the same subject be reprinted in the annual issue of extracts from the Minutes. In

---

[1] Foote's Sketches, and Life of Alexander.

1795, an overture was brought in by the Assembly's committee to the following effect:—"A serious and conscientious person, a member of a Presbyterian congregation, who views the slavery of the negroes as a moral evil, highly offensive to God and injurious to the interests of the gospel, lives under the ministry of a person, or amongst a society of people, who concur with him in sentiment on the subject upon general principles, yet for particular reasons hold slaves and tolerate the practice in others. Overtured: Ought the former of these persons, under the impressions and circumstances above described, to hold Christian communion with the latter?"

To this the Assembly replied, "that, as the same difference of opinion with respect to slavery takes place in sundry other parts of the Presbyterian Church, notwithstanding which they live in charity and peace according to the doctrine and practice of the apostles, it is hereby recommended to all conscientious persons, and especially to those whom it immediately respects, to do the same. At the same time, the General Assembly assure all the churches under their care that they view with the deepest concern any vestiges of slavery which may exist in our country, and refer the churches to the records of the General Assembly published at different times, but especially to an overture of the late Synod of New York and Philadelphia, published in 1787, and republished among the extracts from the Minutes of the General Assembly of 1793, on that head, with which they trust every conscientious person will be fully satisfied."

At the same time, Mr. Rice, of Kentucky, Dr. Muir, of Virginia, and Robert Patterson, an elder, were appointed a committee to draft a letter to the Presbytery of Transylvania on the subject of the overture. The report of the committee elicited much discussion.

The original draft contained a paragraph which urged the duty of the religious education of slaves. "A neglect of this," it declared, "is inconsistent with the character of a Christian master; but the observance might prevent, in great part, what is really the moral evil attending slavery,—namely, allowing precious souls under the charge of masters to perish for lack of knowledge. Freedom is desirable, but cannot at all times be enjoyed with advantage. A parent, to set his child loose from all authority, would be doing him the most essential injury. * * * A slave let loose upon society ignorant, idle, and headstrong, is in a state to injure others and ruin himself. No Christian master can answer for such conduct to his own mind. The slave must first be in a situation to act properly as a member of civil society before he can be advantageously introduced therein."

The entire paragraph containing these words was stricken out; and the Assembly, while urging the duty of peace and forbearance, contented itself with saying, that they "have taken every step which they deem expedient or wise to encourage emancipation, and to render the state of those who are in slavery as mild and tolerable as possible." The Presbytery is informed that it will be furnished with attested copies of the Assembly's decisions upon the subject.

The original edition of the Confession of Faith and Catechisms, issued by the Synod of New York and New Jersey as "The Constitution of the Presbyterian Church in the United States of America," was published in 1789. In the introduction the Synod lay down "a few of the general principles by which they have hitherto been governed, and which are the groundwork" of their plan. They declare themselves unanimously of opinion that "God alone is Lord of the conscience." They disclaim any desire "to see any religious constitution aided by the civil power, further than may be necessary for protection and security;" and in this case they would have the aid "equal and common to all others." In consistency with such principles, they hold that every Christian Church, or union or association of particular Churches, is entitled to declare the terms of admission to its communion, the qualifications of its ministers and members, and the whole system of its internal government, appointed by Christ for the preaching of the gospel, the administering of the sacraments, the exercise of discipline, and the preservation of truth and duty. Holding, moreover, to "an inseparable connection between faith and practice, truth and duty," they deem it "necessary to make effectual provision that all who are admitted as teachers be sound in the faith," while they profess their belief that there are truths and forms with respect to which good men may differ, and in these "they think it the duty both of private Christians and societies to exercise mutual forbearance towards each other."

Each particular society is entitled also to elect its own officers, while Scripture prescribes their character, qualifications, and authority. All Church power, moreover, is ministerial and delegated merely, since no Church judicatory may make laws to bind the conscience, and all its decisions should be founded on God's revealed will. While Synods and Councils may err, yet "there is much greater danger from the usurped claim of making laws than from the right of judging upon laws already made and common to all who profess the gospel."

Such were the liberal principles which the Synod took care distinctly to enunciate and embody in the first edition of the Confession of Faith. This edition was published without the Scripture proofs usually appended; it was, moreover, soon exhausted; and it had been issued simply by the authority of the

Synod. In 1792, therefore, a committee was appointed by the Assembly to revise and prepare for publication an edition of the Confession, Catechisms, and Form of Government and Discipline. The committee consisted of the venerable Dr. Robert Smith, of Pequa, Rev. Nathan Grier, of Forks of Brandywine, and Rev. Alexander Mitchell, of Upper Octorara. They were instructed to select and arrange the Scripture texts to be adduced in support of the several articles in the Confession, &c. Dr. Smith undertook to adduce proofs for the Larger and Mr. Grier for the Shorter Catechism; while Mr. Mitchell was to do the same for the Confession of Faith and Form of Government. The death of Dr. Smith left his task incomplete; and in 1793 the moderator, James Latta, was substituted in his place. A partial report was made by Mr. Mitchell, but the subject was recommitted for a report to the Assembly of 1794. In that year Dr. Green and Messrs. John B. Smith, James Boyd, William M. Tennent, Nathaniel Irwin, and Andrew Hunter were appointed to examine the report of the committee, revise the whole, prepare it for the press, and supervise the publication and sale of the work. The change subsequently made in the striking out of certain proofs was in part justified on the ground that the work of the committee had never been submitted to the Presbyteries for their approval, and hence could not be regarded as having the proper sanction of the Church as a part of its Constitution.

The relations of the Assembly to other kindred ecclesiastical bodies were now to be defined. The annual convention of Presbyterian and Congregational ministers which existed before the Revolution and was continued down to 1776, had testified the strong sympathy which existed between the two denominations which were represented in it. It manifested, moreover, the liberal and co-operative spirit of the churches represented by the Old Synod. It had accomplished the main object for which it had been instituted; but, in view of other results still to be desired, the question now recurred as to whether it should be revived or some substitute provided.

The subject was carefully considered. While there were other ecclesiastical bodies—the Reformed Dutch and Associate Presbyterian, as well as Congregational—to be taken into account, it was felt that some plan was desirable which should bring the Assembly into correspondence with them all. The consideration of this comprehensive plan was not neglected: still, the former relations of the Presbyterian to the Congregational Churches entitled the latter to the first place in the Assembly's regard. In view of this fact, therefore, the following resolution was unanimously agreed to by the Assembly of 1790:—

"Whereas there existed before the late Revolution an annual convention of the clergy of the Congregational churches in New England and ministers belonging to the Synod of New York and Philadelphia, which was interrupted by the disorders occasioned by the war;—this Assembly, being peculiarly desirous to renew and strengthen every bond of union between brethren so nearly agreed in doctrine and forms of worship as the members of the Congregational and Presbyterian Churches evidently are, and remembering with much satisfaction the mutual pleasure and advantage produced and received by their former intercourse, did *resolve*, that the ministers of the Congregational churches in New England be invited to renew their annual convention with the clergy of the Presbyterian Church; and the Assembly did for this purpose appoint the Rev. Dr. Rodgers, of New York, and the Rev. Dr. McWhorter, of Newark, N.J., to be a committee to take such measures for the obtaining of the proposed object as they may judge to be most effectual, and to report their proceedings to the General Assembly at their next meeting."[1]

In 1791, the committee thus appointed made their report. Three modes of correspondence were proposed for consideration: the first, by letter of committees of the Assembly and the Connecticut Association respectively; the second, by reviving a convention similar to that which existed before the war; and the third, by sending delegates reciprocally from each body.

Action on the several plans offered was deferred till the General Association of Connecticut had been consulted. Drs. Witherspoon, Rodgers, and McWhorter, and Messrs. Chapman, S. S. Smith, Tennent, and Austin, were appointed a committee to confer with that body.

The result of this conference was the adoption of measures of correspondence, based avowedly on "the importance of union and harmony," and "the duty incumbent on all pastors and members of the Christian Church to "assist each other in promoting, as far as possible, the general interest of the Redeemer's kingdom;" and, in consideration of the fact that "Divine Providence appears to be opening the door for pursuing these valuable objects with a happy prospect of success," it was deemed best that the two bodies should have, each, a standing committee of correspondence, besides a committee of three members having the right to sit in each other's meetings but not to vote. Measures were to be taken to prevent injury to the churches by irregular and unauthorized preachers. The Presbytery or Association was to certify to the

---

[1] This movement was made, and the above paper drawn up, by Dr. Ashbel Green, who also penned the Plan of Union of 1801.

character of its members travelling at a distance; and the certificate of a standing committee, to be appointed by the Assembly and General Association respectively, was to secure their reception as authorized preachers of the gospel in the bounds of the body, whether Presbytery or Association, within which they might be employed.

The plan thus proposed by the convention was unanimously and cordially approved by the Assembly of 1792, and the necessary measures were taken for carrying it into effect. It was endorsed by the Association of Connecticut, the only tangible ecclesiastical body in New England with which the Assembly could correspond; and in 1793 Timothy Dwight, Jonathan Edwards (afterward President of Union College), and Matthias Burnet, took their seats in the Assembly as delegates of the General Association.

From this period the intercourse by correspondence between the two bodies was continued without interruption. The delegates of each body were allowed a seat, but not a vote, in the one to which they were sent. There was a change, however, soon made, when full membership was allowed. On motion of Dr. Rodgers, the plan was so amended in 1794 that the delegates from each body respectively were allowed the right not only to sit and deliberate, but also "to vote in all questions which might be determined by either of them." The Association voted a compliance with this proposal of the Assembly, and down to 1827 the delegates of the General Associations of Connecticut, and afterward of Vermont (1809), New Hampshire (1810), and Massachusetts (1811), were allowed full membership in the General Assembly. Massachusetts was not ready to relinquish her claim to the exercise of the right which was thus conceded until 1830, and even then only after repeated representations from the Assembly.[1]

The correspondence proposed between the General Assembly and the Associate Reformed and Reformed Dutch Synods was, after a delay of some years, referred to a convention of delegates from the three bodies which met in New York in 1798. Their report was adopted by the General Assembly, but rejected by the other two bodies. No active measures to revive this or a similar plan were taken for nearly twenty years.

The subject of Psalmody was one which gave no small occasion of anxiety to those who sought the union and harmony of the churches. The Synod of New York and Philadelphia had left the congregations to their own deliberate preferences in regard to the book to be used. Some still adhered to the old version of the Psalms, and some preferred Watts's Imitation. At the first meeting of the Assembly, Adam Rankin asked to be heard on the subject. He had crossed the mountains from Kentucky to disburden his mind of the apprehensions which he felt in regard to "the great and pernicious error" into which the Synod had fallen by "disusing Rouse's Versification of David's Psalms in public worship, and adopting, in place of it, Watts's Imitation." He asked the privilege of being heard upon a subject in regard to which—with all the intensity of his Scotch nature, aggravated by memories of

---

[1] In 1796 the Synod of Philadelphia resolved to submit to the consideration of the next General Assembly the propriety of taking constitutional measures to effect an alteration in the Form of Government, so as to admit Assemblies to meet only once in three years, if they judge it expedient. The reason urged for this was the difficulty of convening even a quorum of the Synod, inasmuch as its meetings seemed almost unnecessary, from the fact that its proper business had been so largely engrossed by the Assembly.—*Minutes*, 1790–1820, p. 110.

a martyred ancestry—he felt deeply. He was heard "at great length," and the Assembly endeavored to relieve him from the difficulty under which he appeared to labor, but to little purpose. His mind was not open to conviction; and it only remained for the Assembly to exhort him to Christian charity and to guard against disturbing the peace of the churches.

Rankin identified the permission given by the Synod (1787) to use Barlow's revision of Watts, with an exclusive endorsement of it. In this he was mistaken; but the importance of uniformity among the churches in the form and order of public worship had already led many to consider the policy of procuring a book which would meet the necessities of the churches under the care of the Assembly. Nothing of importance was done, however, before 1800. Three years previous (1797), President Dwight was requested by the General Association of Connecticut to revise Watts's Imitation so as to accommodate it to the state of the American churches, and to supply the deficiency of those Psalms which Watts had omitted. This measure was adopted in consequence of the ill odor which Barlow's career in connection with French politics had given to his edition of Watts. Its use in Presbyterian as well as Congregational churches had become obnoxious, and the advocates of Rouse found a very opportune argument against the book which had been the rival of their own favorite.

In these circumstances, Dwight undertook the task. He possessed the confidence of both the Presbyterian and Congregational Churches, and had sat and voted as a member of the General Assembly. When his task was wellnigh complete, the Assembly were informed of it, and, with a view to procure a work that should answer the demands of its own churches, appointed a committee (1800) to meet a similar committee of the

General Association, at Stamford, to examine the result of Dwight's labors. The committee consisted of Drs. John Rodgers, Jonathan Edwards, and Asa Hillyer. They reported their approval of what had been done, and President Dwight, at the recommendation of the joint committee, appended to the Psalms a collection of two hundred and sixty-three hymns. The volume in this revised form, with additions, was "cheerfully allowed" by the Assembly to congregations and churches which might find it for edification.

Thus cautious and guarded was the Assembly in its utterances upon the subject. Nor was it without reason. The exclusive advocacy of any form of Psalmody would have rent the Church in sunder. In Kentucky especially, and in other parts of the Church where Rouse had been in familiar use, its advocates regarded it with a strange tenacity of affection. It was as sacred in their view as the Confession itself. The Presbytery of Charleston—succeeding to that which was known as the Presbytery of South Carolina before the Revolution, and which had applied in 1770 to know the terms on which it might be united with the Synod—sent a communication to the Assembly of 1800, desiring to be taken into connection with that body; but they explicitly stipulated, as an indispensable condition on their part, that they must not be disturbed in their edifying enjoyment of Rouse; and it seems not improbable that even the moderate measure of the Assembly in regard to Dwight's book may have led to their deferring any further steps toward the union. It is at least certain that it was not consummated till several years later.

At the Assembly of 1791, several of the Synods sent in reports in regard to their condition and extent.[1]

[1] See Assembly's Minutes.

The Synod of New York and New Jersey consisted of four Presbyteries,—Suffolk, Dutchess, New York, and New Brunswick. The first consisted of twelve, the second of six, the third of twenty-seven, and the fourth of fourteen, ministers. Within their bounds were thirty-five vacancies, about one-half of which were able to support a pastor. In the following year the Presbytery of Albany, with seven ministers and more than twenty congregations, the larger portion of them vacant, was reported in connection with the Synod of New York and New Jersey. The other Presbyteries now numbered fifty-four ministers and sixty-eight congregations.

In the same year (1792), the report of the Synod of Philadelphia showed that it consisted of five Presbyteries, with an aggregate—independent of the Presbytery of Baltimore, from which there was no report—of sixty ministers and ninety-two congregations. The Synod of Virginia, exclusive of the Presbytery of Transylvania, numbered, in the three Presbyteries of Hanover, Redstone, and Lexington, thirty-two ordained ministers, with more than ninety congregations. A large number of these were in the bounds of Redstone Presbytery, which alone numbered twenty-four. The Synod of the Carolinas—exclusive of the Presbytery of Abingdon, which made no report—contained in the Presbyteries of Orange and South Carolina twenty settled ministers, thirteen unsettled, a portion of them licentiates, with over eighty congregations, twenty-nine of which were vacant in the bounds of South Carolina Presbytery alone. The aggregate in all the Synods was not far from two hundred ministers and about four hundred congregations.

There had thus, in the three years which had elapsed since the formation of the General Assembly, been a rapid growth and extension of the Church. Nor were the labors of the ministry denied signal marks of the Divine favor in powerful revivals in different parts of the land. The rekindled missionary spirit—dating from the formation of the New York Missionary Society in 1797—which was first felt on the Atlantic slope, extended westward beyond the Alleghanies, in Virginia, Pennsylvania, Kentucky, and Tennessee. New churches were gathered on the frontier, and new Presbyteries were reported at each successive General Assembly. In 1793, the Presbytery of Ohio, with five members, was set off from the Presbytery of Redstone, which in ten years had multiplied its numbers more than fourfold. In the following year the Presbytery of Huntingdon, with ten members, was set off from that of Carlisle, erected by the old Synod of New York and Philadelphia at the period just previous to its division into the four Synods. In the same year the Presbytery of Winchester, with five members, was set off from that of Lexington. In 1795, the Presbytery of Hudson, with seven members, was formed of ministers and churches taken from the Presbyteries of Dutchess county and New York. In the same year the Presbytery of Orange, in the Carolinas, was divided, and the Presbytery of Concord erected with twelve members. In the following year the Presbytery of Hopewell, with five members, was set off from the Presbytery of South Carolina. In 1797, the Presbytery of Abingdon was divided, and that of Union, with five members, was erected out of it in Eastern Tennessee. In 1799, the Presbytery of Transylvania was divided to form the new Presbyteries of West Lexington and Washington, the three subsequently constituting the Synod of Kentucky. In the same year, also, the Presbytery of South Carolina was divided to form the First and Second Presbyteries of that name.

Thus before the close of the last century the number

of Presbyteries had increased from sixteen, the number at the time of the organization of a General Assembly, to twenty-six, and the strength and numbers of the Church had increased in nearly the same proportion.

This increase was certainly greater than in the circumstances could have been expected. The influences of the War of the Revolution were eminently disastrous to the churches, not only on account of the direct injuries inflicted, and the diversion of thought and energy into new channels, but on account of the sympathy excited in favor of France and French principles. This sympathy prepared the way for French infidelity, and its emissaries, in the proud assumption of superior intelligence, were bold and unblushing in their attempt to spread their errors and undermine the institutions of Christianity. In these efforts they were only too successful. The cause of religion in many parts of the land seemed to be on the decline, and the prospect grew darker and more discouraging with each succeeding year. Good men despaired of the republic, and Christian men trembled for the Ark of God. The evil seems to have reached its crisis in 1798. In that year the Assembly felt called upon to give expression to its apprehensions, and to sound the note of warning. This it did in an earnest and startling tone.

"When formidable innovations and convulsions in Europe"—such was the language of the pastoral letter—"threaten destruction to morals and religion; when scenes of devastation and bloodshed, unexampled in the history of modern nations, have convulsed the world; and when our own country is threatened with similar calamities, insensibility in us would be stupidity, silence would be criminal. . . . We desire to direct your awakened attention toward that bursting storm which threatens to sweep before it the religious principles, institutions, and morals of our people. We are filled with deep concern and awful dread, whilst we announce it as our conviction that the eternal God has a controversy with our nation and is about to visit us in his sore displeasure."

In this "solemn crisis," the Assembly believe that the causes of the calamities felt or feared are traceable to "a general defection from God, and corruption of the public principles and morals." The evidences of the national guilt were seen in "a general dereliction of religious principles and practice amongst our fellow-citizens; a great departure from the faith and simple purity of manners for which our fathers were remarkable; a visible and prevailing impiety and contempt for the laws and institutions of religion; and an abounding infidelity which in many instances tends to atheism itself, which contemptuously rejects God's eternal Son, our Saviour, ridicules the gospel and its most sacred mysteries, denies the providence of God, grieves and insults the Holy Spirit; in a word, which assumes a front of daring impiety, and possesses a mouth filled with blasphemy."

In this alarming state of things, "a dissolution of religious society" seemed to be threatened by "the supineness and inattention of many ministers and professors of Christianity." "Formality and deadness, not to say hypocrisy, a contempt for vital godliness and the spirit of fervent piety, a desertion of the ordinances, or a cold and unprofitable attendance upon them," visibly pervaded every part of the Church; while there were those who denied or attempted to explain away the pure doctrines of the gospel, introducing errors once unnamed, or named with abhorrence, but now "embraced by deluded multitudes." The profanation of the Sabbath, the neglect of family religion and instruction, ingratitude to God for his benefits, "profligacy and corruption of public morals, profaneness, pride, luxury, injustice, intemperance, lewdness, and every species of debauchery and loose indulgence," were sins which greatly abounded. In view of all this, and the provocation it offered to divine justice, there was reason for foreboding. Deep humiliation, sincere repentance for individual as well as national sins, supplication for the outpouring of the Spirit and a revival of God's work,—these were the duties most solemnly and earnestly enjoined; and, to give effect to the exhortations and admonitions of the letter, the Assembly recommended the last Thursday in the next August as a day of solemn humiliation, fasting, and prayer, in all the congregations subject to its care.[1] The letter itself was to be read on that occasion and its truths to be enforced in appropriate discourses.

The statements of the Assembly, grave and startling as they were, were by no means exaggerated. The prospect for religious progress or improvement was almost cheerless. By public men in high station, infidelity was boldly avowed. In some places, society, taking its tone from them, seemed hopelessly surrendered to the tender mercies of the impious and the blasphemer.

But, ere the Assembly met again (in 1799), the signs of a great change, which was largely to affect the very character of the nation, were apparent. The great revivals of Kentucky, of Central and Western New York, and of New England, were heralded here and there by scenes that testified to the unabated power of the gospel when forcibly presented and applied by the

---

[1] A general fast was appointed by the General Conference of the Methodist Church, for the first Friday of March, 1796, for the same reasons, substantially, as those given by the General Assembly.—*Bangs's History of Methodism*, ii. 22.

power of the Spirit. The little cloud, "no bigger than a man's hand," had expanded and given promise of showers that were to refresh and clothe with verdure the desert sands. The Assembly of 1799 could say, that, amid much lukewarmness and formality, they had "heard from different parts glad tidings of the out-pouring of the Spirit, and of times of refreshing from the presence of the Lord." "From the East," they said, "from the West, and from the South, have these glad tidings reached our ears." The report concluded with a stirring appeal to the churches, couched in a style of lofty and sustained eloquence. It was from the pen of the moderator, Samuel Stanhope Smith.

In the following year (1800) the report was still cheering, especially from the West. The success of missionary labors was "greatly on the increase." God was "shaking the valley of dry bones on the frontiers." "A spiritual resurrection" was taking place there. Hundreds in a short time, and among them some who had been avowed infidels and Universalists, had been received into the communion of the Church.

Thus, the century which was just closing, and which had threatened to close with dark and dismal prospects, was destined to leave behind it a brighter record. A new era had dawned upon the Church,—an era of revivals. A larger measure of missionary zeal was manifest. The spiritual lethargy of the nation was shaken by the reports which came from the West and from the new settlements. Infidelity had been attacked in some of its strongholds, and it had fallen before the power of truth. The sad effects of the War of the Revolution upon the churches began to disappear, and, with inspiring intelligence to cheer them, the pastors of the Church and the missionaries on the frontiers responded with alacrity to the Assembly's appeals.[1]

[1] Only an approximate estimate of the strength of the Presby-

CHAPTER XV.

NEW JERSEY AND PENNSYLVANIA, 1789–1800.

At the time of the formation of the General Assembly, the strength of the Church was to be found principally in New Jersey and Pennsylvania. These two States embraced more than half the churches and nearly half the ministers under the care of the Assembly. Within the State of New Jersey was included the greater portion of the two Presbyteries of New York and New Brunswick, which numbered on this field twenty-six ministers and forty-three churches.[1]

At Newark, after a briefly-interrupted pastorate of nearly thirty years, which had been signalized by three powerful and extensive revivals of religion, was the venerable McWhorter, still in the vigor of his years and the meridian of his usefulness. A classical scholar, a popular preacher, a self-denying and devoted patriot, he commanded the respect of the entire community, while his unquestioned piety and practical wisdom inspired a more than usual measure of confidence. There was a noble manliness in his countenance, person, and movements, which would have sufficed, without "his clerical robes and large full wig," to produce an abiding and favorable impression on the beholder. Dignified

---

terian Church at the close of the period here reviewed (1789–1800) can be made, owing to the imperfection of the reports. The number of ministers, however, could not have been much short of two hundred and fifty, while the churches, which in great numbers were vacant, must have been something over four hundred and fifty.

[1] Exclusive of those in the southern part of the State.

in manner, perspicuous in expression, and yet under the prompting of quick, strong sympathies, the plain correctness of his diction sometimes kindled into fervor or was subdued to pathos. Faithful alike in the pulpit, in the discharge of pastoral duty, and in attendance upon the judicatories of the Church, he holds a high rank and an unblemished name among the venerable fathers of the Assembly which he helped to organize, and among the pulpit celebrities of his own day. For sixteen years more he was to be spared to labor at his post, and then bequeath his falling mantle to one well worthy to wear it,—the gifted, eloquent, and lamented Griffin.

At Princeton, serving still, as he had done for more than twenty years, as pastor of the church and President of the college, was Dr. Witherspoon, already verging upon his "threescore and ten,"—the light of one eye already quenched, the vigor of his frame somewhat shaken, but with an intellect as unclouded as ever, and with a *presence* still second only to that of Washington.[1] For five years more he was to be spared, continuing in the discharge of his duties as President and pastor, and surrendering only with his life the post he had so long filled and adorned.[2]

At Orange, in the full exercise of that vigor of mind and that energy of character which ten years later designated him as the fittest missionary pioneer for Central New York, was Jedediah Chapman, a native of Connecticut, a man of ardent piety, urbane in manners, sound in judgment, and, although not an orator, in the full sense of the word, an acceptable and in-

---

[1] Dr. Ashbel Green, in Sprague's Annals, iii. 297.

[2] Samuel Finley Snowden was installed pastor at Princeton November 25, 1794, dismissed April 29, 1801.—*Sprague's Annals*, iii. 341.

structive speaker. The other principal ministers of the State were Samuel Stanhope Smith, the son-in-law of Dr. Witherspoon, now a professor, and soon to succeed to the Presidency, at Princeton; John Woodhull, already for ten years pastor at Freehold, where for thirty-five years longer he was to be spared to labor; James F. Armstrong, the successor of the lamented Spencer, at Trenton, where for sixteen years more, under great infirmities of body, he was to discharge his ministerial duties; Azel Roe, of Revolutionary and somewhat facetious memory, at Woodbridge; Aaron Richards, at Rahway; Jonathan Elmer, at New Providence; John Joline, at Mendham; Israel Reed, at Bound Brook; Thomas Smith, at Cranberry; Joseph Roe, at Pennington; Joseph Clark, at Allentown; William Boyd, at Lamington; Peter Wilson, at Independence and Mansfield; Ira Condict, at Hardwick; Newton, at Shapanack; Dr. Timothy Johnes, at Morristown; Asa Dunham, at Mount Bethel and Oxford; and Walter Monteith, at New Brunswick.

During the ten years that followed, the population of the State increased about fourteen per cent. The churches grew in about the same proportion in strength and numbers. In 1794 there was a powerful revival at Newark, but the state of religion generally was far from prosperous. The views of French infidelity had begun to pervade the country. The voice of admonition and alarm uttered by the Assembly in 1798 was called for by the general declension of religion. The following year, however, brought to view more cheering prospects. The churches of the State shared to some extent in the revival, and the century closed with such signs of progress as had not been witnessed for many years previous. New churches were reported at Woodbridge (Second), Hackettstown and Pleasant Grove, Flemington and Hardwick. The changes in the several pastorates had been few. The noble-hearted and devout Robert Finley had commenced his pastorate at Baskingridge in 1795. The clear-headed and genial Amzi Armstrong[1] had succeeded Joline at Mendham in the following year. Samuel Stanhope Smith had been chosen to the Presidency of Nassau Hall; and in 1798, George S. Woodhull, son of Dr. Woodhull, of Freehold, was settled at Cranberry, where he remained until his transfer to Princeton in 1820.[2]

Besides these, we find several new names, at a date shortly subsequent,[3] on the list of the two Presbyteries of the State. Elias Riggs had succeeded John Young at Connecticut Farms; Eleazar Burnet had taken the place of Richards at Rahway; Aaron Condict commenced in 1796 his thirty-five years' pastorate at Hanover; Henry Cook had charge of Woodbridge Second Church; Israel Ward had succeeded Elmer at New Providence; John Cornwall was settled at Allentown and Nottingham; David Barclay had succeeded Israel Reed at Bound Brook; Joseph Clark was settled at New Brunswick in place of Monteith, who died in 1799 at Albany; William B. Sloan was at Greenwich, Thomas Grant at Amwell and Flemington, David Comfort at Kingston, and Holloway W. Hunt at Bethlehem, Kingswood, and Alexandria.[4]

Within the limits of the State of Pennsylvania, at the time of the formation of the Assembly, there were,

---

1 Father of Rev. William J. Armstrong, late Secretary of the A. B. C. F. M.

2 Gilbert Tennent Snowden was pastor at Cranberry from 1790 to 1797. He was the brother of S. F. Snowden, settled at about the same time at Princeton, and of Nathaniel R. Snowden, of Harrisburg, Pennsylvania.

3 Assembly's Minutes, 1803.

4 The churches in the southern part of the State were ecclesiastically connected with Pennsylvania Presbyteries.

besides a few churches connected with the Presbytery of New Castle, three Presbyteries,—Philadelphia, Carlisle, and Redstone,—embracing an aggregate of forty-seven ministers and more than twice as many churches. In numerous instances, two or more of these were united to constitute a single pastoral charge, while more than forty, most of them too feeble to support a pastor, were vacant.

The leading member of Philadelphia Presbytery—already for thirty years the pastor of the first church in that city, and for ten years at the head of the University of Pennsylvania, as provost of the institution—was Dr. John Ewing, now in the fifty-eighth year of his age, and destined for thirteen years more to occupy the same commanding position. In natural science and classical learning he had scarcely a rival on the continent. In every branch of collegiate study he was thoroughly versed. His Hebrew Bible was constantly at his side, and was used from choice for devotional purposes. At an hour's warning he was ready and fully competent to supply the place of any professor who might chance to be absent. In the pulpit he sacrificed nothing to display; yet with a cultivated audience few preachers were more popular. On his visit to England before the Revolution, he had frequent interviews with Lord North, and, with all the firmness and zeal of an ardent whig, predicted the issue of the approaching contest, warning the prime minister against its prosecution. In conference with Dr. Johnson, he tamed the rudeness, if not insolence, of the intellectual giant, defending in fearless tone the cause of his country. After liberally applying the terms *rebels* and *scoundrels* to the population of the colonies, Johnson turned rudely to Dr. Ewing, demanding, "What do you know in America? You never read; you have no books there." "Pardon me, sir," said Dr.

Ewing: "we have read the *Rambler*." The graceful blending of retort and compliment pacified the savage essayist, and till midnight he sat with Dr. Ewing in amiable and genial conversation.

In charge of the Second Church, after nearly half a century of pastoral labor, was Dr. James Sproat, a native of Massachusetts, and a graduate of Yale College, in a class of which Dr. Buell, of Long Island, Dr. Hopkins, of Newport, and Governor Livingston, of New Jersey, were members. Till 1787 he was sole pastor of the church; but at this time he received for his colleague Ashbel Green, whose protracted period of service has seemed to link together the present century with the past.

At the time of the formation of the General Assembly, Dr. Sproat, though bending under the burden of years, was a venerable-looking man. With a benevolent countenance, gentle and courteous manners, even the wig and the cocked hat which he still retained could scarcely have added to the dignity of his bearing. As a speaker, he was easy and graceful. He "was such a perfect master of the art of persuasion that he triumphed over the passions of the most crowded auditory with all the charms of sacred eloquence." For personal piety he was pre-eminent. Praise was an employment in which he greatly delighted. Unfeigned humility was the habit of his soul. In prayer he was subdued yet fervent, and, while not a finished scholar like Ewing, he was a master in theology. The vital themes of the gospel were those upon which, in his public discourses, he loved to dwell.

To the yellow fever of 1793 he fell a victim,—following first one member after another of his own family to the grave. The pathos of his last letter to his son is deeply affecting. But when the pestilence had passed by, none left a vacant place more fit to challenge tearful memories than the pastor of the Second Church.

The pastor of the Third Church was Dr. George Duffield, a man who seemed formed expressly for the times and lot in which his life was cast. Irish, English, and Huguenot blood was commingled in his veins, and the history of the family was embalmed in the memories of persecutions through which it had been called to pass. At the age of twenty-two he was graduated at Nassau Hall, and, after studying theology and serving as tutor at the college, he was ordained in 1761 pastor of the united churches of Carlisle, Big Spring, and Monaghan.

His place of settlement was on the frontiers of civilization, and, except at Carlisle, his preaching-stations were exposed to the inroads of the Indians. Often did these make hostile demonstrations which required the male members of his church to arm in self-defence. In all these dangers he cheerfully shared, nor was his courage shaken by the dangers of the camp. The church at Monaghan was protected by fortifications thrown up around it, and behind these—while sentinels were stationed to keep guard—the congregation listened to the expositions and appeals of one who scorned the aid of desk or manuscript. The exposure of the sinner was illustrated by the dangers outside the fort, and the refuge offered in the gospel found its emblem in the defence which this afforded. Through the whole region he was deservedly popular, and his fame secured him repeated calls to more inviting fields.

With all the ardor of his nature he threw himself into the cause of his country in her struggle for freedom. He was the earnest, fearless, and powerful advocate of civil and religious liberty. During the sessions of the colonial Congress, after his removal to Philadelphia (1772), John Adams was one of his hearers and admirers, and a communicant of his church. On one occasion preceding the war, his large church, on the corner of Fourth and Pine Streets,—which the First Church claimed to control, in spite of an appointment which had been made for him to preach,—was barred against his entrance. It was opened by the officers of the Third Church to admit the throng assembled to hear him, and his own entrance was effected through a window. Complaint was made to the magistrate, and the king's officer was called upon to quell what was termed a riot. Shortly after the exercises commenced, the magistrate passed through the aisle, and, taking his stand before the pulpit, read the riot act, and called upon the people to disperse. He was ordered to desist by an officer of the congregation, but he continued the reading. After a second demand and a second refusal, the officer seized the magistrate, who was a small man, and, bearing him through the crowd to the door of the church, ordered him to begone and no more disturb the worship of God. The exercises were then continued without further interruption; but the next day Mr. Duffield was arrested and brought before the Mayor's Court, charged with aiding and abetting a riot, and required to give bail. This he promptly refused. He felt assured that he had merely discharged his duty. In vain did the friendly magistrate offer to make the terms easy. In vain did the mayor himself offer to become his security. He would not accept it. He thanked the mayor for his kindness, but was resolved to assert the liberty and rights of a minister of Christ. He was told that he must then, if now released, appear again in court. But the report of his arrest and threatened imprisonment excited a popular ferment. The "Paxton Boys," by whom he was greatly esteemed and beloved, assembled, and resolved to march in a body one hundred miles to Philadelphia to effect his release if he was imprisoned. But he was not again molested.

The religious views and sympathies of Dr. Duffield ranged him upon the side of the "New Lights." The church of which Dr. Ewing was pastor was in connection with the Old side. Hence the attempt to exclude him from the edifice over which the First Church claimed control. But Dr. Duffield was not a man to be overawed. He fearlessly maintained his ground, and he carried with him to the day of his death the sympathies of his Whig and "New Light" congregation. His death occurred within a few months of the convening of the first General Assembly (Feb. 1790), by which he was appointed stated clerk. In the meridian of his strength and usefulness, at the comparatively early age of fifty-seven, he fell at his post. Whatever may have been his lack of cold, calculating prudence, he was "an eminently devoted Christian and an eminently faithful minister."

His successor was John Blair Smith, President of Hampden-Sidney College, and, subsequent to his pastorate in Philadelphia, of Union College. He was the son of Robert Smith, of Pequa, and brother of Samuel Stanhope Smith, President of Nassau Hall, of which he was a graduate in 1773. No other clergyman within the bounds of Virginia Synod was pronounced as a preacher more worthy to wear the mantle of President Davies. Though president of the college from the year 1780, it was not till six or seven years later that his soul seemed fully roused to the duty and solemnity of the preacher's work. From this time his labors were abundant, and were extended far and near. The powerful revival which ensued, extending through the college and over the surrounding region, was largely due to his instrumentality.

In 1791, he was appointed a commissioner to attend

the General Assembly. During its sessions he occupied the vacant pulpit of the Third Church. Such was the impression made, that he was unanimously called as the successor of the lamented Duffield. Accepting the call, he removed to Philadelphia, where he remained for five years, when he was invited to the presidency of Union College. This post he accepted, and occupied for three years, when he was reinstated over the people of his former charge. He had hardly resumed his labors, however, before the city was again visited by the yellow fever, and he was one of the first victims of the terrible pestilence.

In many respects he was a model preacher. His heart was in his work, and his whole soul glowed with evangelical fervor and the love of souls. His preaching was clear, distinct, pungent, and yet tender, subduing opposition or melting it by the pathos of earnest appeal. Immense congregations would hang upon his lips in breathless silence, or a silence interrupted only by the deep-drawn sigh. All tendencies to noisy demonstration were studiously suppressed. His slender frame and feeble constitution seemed overtasked by his arduous and exhausting efforts; but his buoyant spirit and all-absorbing devotion to his work lent to his flagging energies a recuperative power, and repeatedly was he restored to vigor after anxious friends had abandoned hope of his recovery and given him over as a victim of consumption. Few men within the bounds of the Church have labored more zealously or successfully than John Blair Smith, who fell at the early age of forty-three, and who long deserves to be remembered as one of the most gifted and eloquent preachers of his age.

Another member of the Presbytery, worthy of special mention, was Dr. William M. Tennent, settled since 1781 as the pastor of the three congregations of Abington, Norristown, and Providence. He was a grandson of William Tennent, of Neshaminy, and had been settled for nine years at Greenfield, Conn. In 1785 he was elected a trustee of Nassau Hall, and for more than twenty years discharged the duties of the office. He was known among his brethren not only as a man of devoted piety, but as "a man of great sweetness of temper and politeness of manner," and as "given to hospitality." In 1797 he was moderator of the General Assembly.

At Deep Run was settled James Grier, brother of Nathan Grier, of Delaware. A native of the town, it was here, with the exception of the period of his preparatory studies, that he spent his days and closed his life. From 1776 he had discharged the duties of pastor; but at the early age of forty-three, by the rupture of a blood-vessel, his death was hastened. Tinicum, which was vacant in 1790, had for some years been supplied by him, in connection with his charge at Deep Run. One of his congregation, who lived to a great age, said of him that "it was impossible to hear him preach and refrain from tears." In person he was of medium height, exceedingly thin, erect, and graceful in his movements. His voice was deep and sonorous, and in his later years peculiarly solemn in tone. He used little gesture, but was always earnest, and sometimes deeply impassioned. On a certain communion Sabbath he followed up the sacramental service by a sermon from the text, "The door was shut." After reading it, he closed the Bible with an action somewhat energetic, and, lifting up his hands apparently in deepest agony, exclaimed, "My God! and is the door shut?" The impression upon the whole congregation was perfectly overwhelming, and it is said to have been signally blessed in the awakening of the careless. His successor in 1798 was Uriah Dubois, who subsequently (1804) gathered the congregation of Doylestown, to which, in connection with Deep Run, he continued to minister till the close of his life, in 1821.

The other pastors of the Presbytery were John Symonton,[1] at Great Valley, Francis Peppard, at Allentown, James Boyd, at Newton and Bensalem, James Watt, at Cape May, George Faitoute, at Greenwich, Andrew Hunter, at Woodbury, and Nathaniel Irwin, at Neshaminy. The churches of Fairfield, Deerfield, Pittsgrove, Penn's Neck, Timber Creek, and Tinicum were vacant. Previous to 1800, however, John Davenport was settled at Deerfield, Ethan Osborn at Fairfield, Nathaniel Harris at Penn's Neck and Alloways Creek, Thomas Picton at Timber Creek and Woodbury, at the last of which he had succeeded Andrew Hunter, and Buckley Carll at Pittsgrove. Cape May and the Third and Fourth (recently-formed) Churches of Philadelphia were vacant. William Clarkson had succeeded Faitoute at Greenwich, and had charge also of Bridgeton; Robert Russell had commenced his labors at Allentown; William Latta had been settled in place of Symonton at Great Valley, with the charge of Charlestown; while John B. Linn had commenced his brief pastorate of the First Church, and Jacob J. Janeway his more extended co-pastorate of the Second Church, of Philadelphia.

The patriarch of the Presbytery of Carlisle (1789), with its twenty-six ministers and fifty-five churches, was John Elder, of Paxton and Derry. Here he had resided in the discharge of pastoral duty for more than half a century. Born in Ireland and educated at Edinburgh, he came to this country in 1736, and the next year commenced his labors as pastor. At this time the region was but sparsely settled. In 1720, John Harris, from Yorkshire, located himself on the

---

[1] He died Oct. 21, 1791.

Susquehanna, in the vicinity of Harrisburg, to which he bequeathed his name. Two miles east of the city, which at that time was scarcely a settlement, the little church of Paxton was soon built, and in its beautiful graveyard, "the Westminster Abbey of the capital," "the rude forefathers of the hamlet sleep." The place which they selected for their residence was one of the most beautiful on the continent.[1] About seven miles distant—a sheltering wall from the northern blasts—lies the mountain-range, with its blue summits, which bound the view in that direction. The valley itself, underlaid with blue limestone, and covered originally with the richest and noblest forest growth, includes within it the garden of all the Atlantic slope, extending from Easton on the Delaware, by Reading, Lebanon, and Lancaster, by Harrisburg, York, and Carlisle, by Chambersburg, Hagerstown, and Winchester, until it loses itself in the North Carolina hills. The gem of the whole valley, the point of greatest beauty, is where it is cleft by the Susquehanna.

Nine miles below the present site of Harrisburg was the church of Derry, a memorial to the early settlers of its Irish namesake, endeared to every Protestant heart. The pastor of the two churches was John Elder. The early years of his ministry were years of constant exposure to Indian invasion. The members of his congregation generally were trained as "rangers," and he shared with them the hardships and hazards of a frontier life. Many a family in the course of years mourned for its head, shot down by a hidden foe or carried off to a hopeless captivity. Whether at work in the field, or worshipping God in the sanctuary, the men carried their arms with them; and their pastor himself set them an example. His gun stood by his

[1] Presb. Quar. Rev., April, 1860.

side in the pulpit. The congregation was repeatedly threatened with hostile attack, and sometimes the threat was fulfilled. On one occasion two or three were killed. Mr. Elder himself superintended the military discipline of his people, and was known as the captain of the mounted "Paxtony Boys." He subsequently held a colonel's commission in the colonial service, and had the command of the block-houses and stockades from the Susquehanna to Easton.

He was indeed a man for the times. With a robust constitution, large stature (he was six feet high), commanding presence, great courage, and indomitable energy of purpose, "he was one of the true-blue Covenanter sort, like his fellow Scotch-Irishman, General Jackson, always willing to take the responsibility." His people, mostly his fellow-countrymen, could appreciate his qualities; and his influence over them was almost unbounded. It did not detract from this, that he was equally at home with spiritual and temporal weapons, and that traditional sympathies commended to him the Covenanter war-cry of "The sword of the Lord and of Gideon!" In the division he sided with the "Old Lights," and extended little indulgence toward the other party. Jealous of his own rights over his extended parish, he allowed no one, and especially no "New side" preacher, to interfere with him. At a meeting of Presbytery he complained of a Mr. Hogg (Hoge), a "New-Light" minister who had preached on the outskirts of his parish. The complaint was couched in peculiar phraseology: "a *hog*," he said, "had been rooting in his fields." It was some time after Harrisburg was incorporated, before he would allow any preaching there.

The death of Mr. Elder occurred in 1792, when he had reached the age of eighty-six, and after having been a minister for sixty years. His successor, Dr.

Joshua Williams, a graduate of Dickinson College, and a licentiate of Carlisle Presbytery, was ordained and installed October 2, 1799.

Two of the most memorable members of the Presbytery were located at Carlisle,—one, Dr. Charles Nisbet, President of Dickinson College, and the other, Dr. Robert Davidson, a professor in the institution and the pastor of the church. The project of a collegiate institution in this region had been cherished long previous to the close of the Revolutionary War. Carlisle had even been designated as the fittest location. It was situated on the great western route from Philadelphia to Pittsburg, one hundred and twenty miles west of the former, and only eighteen from Harrisburg. It was embosomed in a valley distinguished through its whole extent for healthfulness, fertility, and the picturesque beauty of the mountain-scenery which formed the frame of this almost Eden-picture.

The first meeting of the trustees of the proposed institution—among them his excellency John Dickinson, James Ewing, Dr. Rush, Robert Duncan, Stephen McPherson, and others—was held September 15, 1783. Measures were taken to secure funds, both in Europe and this country. At the second meeting, April 6, 1784, the sum of two thousand eight hundred and thirty-nine pounds was reported to have been collected. Resolving to press with increased energy the matter of subscriptions, and apply to the State for an endowment, the trustees unanimously elected Rev. Charles Nisbet, S.T.D., of Montrose, Scotland, principal, and Mr. James Ross,—favorably known among classical scholars as the author of a valuable Latin grammar,—Professor of the Greek and Latin Languages. The grammar-school by Ross was at once commenced in "the school-house of the borough," a small two-story brick building, which still occupies its place in an alley a little southeast of what is now the public square.[1] On the 30th of September, the students numbered fifteen, and on the 15th of the following June they amounted to thirty-five.

It was at this time that Dr. Nisbet arrived in this country and took the principal charge of the infant institution. The prospect before him was far from cheering. There was as yet no college edifice. There were no books, apparatus, or adequate funds. The Legislature silently passed over the petition for aid, and the first task devolving upon the principal was to collect the means necessary to carry forward the institution. After having undertaken it with uncertain success, his health failed, and for seven months he felt forced to relinquish his connection with the institution. But upon his recovery, a small grant having been secured from the State, he resumed his post, and the first class of nine was graduated in 1787. In the following year there were eleven graduates, and in 1792 the number reached thirty-three,—a higher number than was again attained. The trustees, however, had been unable to secure a college building previous to 1802, and in some of the intervening years there was no graduating class.

Dr. Nisbet might well feel some disappointment at learning, upon his arrival in this country, the real state of the institution over which he was called to preside. But, bating "no jot of heart or hope," he gave himself up without reserve to the duties of his station, and, by a multiform activity and unwearied diligence, endeavored to supply, as far as possible, every other defect.

If any man could be pronounced capable of doing this, Dr. Nisbet might well be. He was in the full and matured vigor of his years, and, having been born in

---

[1] American Quarterly Register, November, 1836, p. 119.

1736, was, consequently, upon his arrival in this country, little short of fifty years of age. The six years that followed his graduation at the University of Edinburgh had been spent in close study at the Divinity Hall, where he supported himself by his contributions to one of the popular periodicals of the day. After serving as stated supply with the church in the Gorbals of Glasgow, he was settled at Montrose; and it was here that he was laboring at the time that he was invited to Carlisle. Such was his reputation some years previous, that Dr. Witherspoon, who at first declined the call to Nassau Hall, suggested him for the vacant post.

There were many things which seemed to justify the selection of Dr. Nisbet for the office to which he was called. He belonged to the Orthodox wing of the Scotch Church, and combined evangelical zeal with soundness in doctrine. His sympathies all through the Revolutionary struggle were on the side of the Americans. Of the cause of civil and religious liberty he was a fearless and zealous advocate. His intellectual endowments were of a rare order. His mind was remarkably sprightly, and at once comprehensive and discriminating. Whatever his position, he was sure to exercise, even in a minority, a commanding influence. His varied talents and acquirements were combined with sterling integrity and worth. In the discharge of his duties he feared not the face of man. On one occasion during our Revolutionary struggle, he preached on a public fast-day a discourse which was quite unacceptable to the members of the Town Council of Montrose, and soon after its commencement, when they had satisfied themselves as to the character of what was probably soon to come, they rose in a body and left the church. Stretching forth his hand to the seat which they had just vacated, he said, with emphasis, as they withdrew, "The wicked flee when no man pursueth."

In the General Assembly of the Scotch Church, Dr. Nisbet was a powerful debater. His speeches in this body must have told with powerful effect. The very grounds on which they are exposed to criticism—an excess perhaps of wit, or withering and crushing sarcasm—must have inspired a healthful respect for his opposition to the laxness and latitudinarianism of *moderate* rule. In social life, his conversational gifts shone with peculiar brilliancy. His wit and humor are said to have been unrivalled. "His memory was not only excellent, but bordered on the prodigious."[1] The libraries to which he had been privileged to have access were large and rich; but he himself was proverbially called "the walking library." At one time he was able to repeat the whole Æneid and Young's Night Thoughts. But, with all his attainments and his exuberance of wit, he was none the less a sincere Christian, a true patriot, and a warm friend to the interests of religion and mankind. Such was the man who for nearly twenty years devoted his energies to the establishment and direction of Dickinson College. With all the difficulties which it had to encounter, and with such rival institutions as the University of Pennsylvania and Nassau Hall College, located respectively at Philadelphia and Princeton, it is scarcely surprising that no more was effected. The comparative failure, however, was due, not to the principal, but to circumstances which all his tact, energy, learning, and application could not control.

Associated with Dr. Nisbet as a professor in the college, and at the same time settled over the church in Carlisle, was a man who, in the cause of sacred and

---

[1] Life of Nisbet, p. 28.

classical learning and of civil and religious freedom, was in full sympathy with him. Robert Davidson was a native of Maryland, and a graduate of the University of Pennsylvania under Dr. Ewing in 1771. Two years later, such was his reputation for learning that he was appointed an instructor in the university, and chosen as an assistant of Dr. Ewing in the First Church. During the war, his political sympathies and his outspoken zeal for his country rendered his residence in Philadelphia unsafe, and he was forced to remove. When Dickinson College was founded, he was invited, through the influence of Dr. Rush, to become one of its officers. "His name," said Dr. Rush, who knew him well, "will be of use to us; for he is a man of learning and of an excellent private character." His sphere in the institution was the Professorship of History and Belles-Lettres. In discharging his duties, collegiate and pastoral, he was indefatigable. By systematic efforts, he steadily enlarged his acquisitions. He made himself master of eight languages, was well versed in theology, and "familiar with the whole circle of science." Astronomy was his favorite pursuit, and he was an amateur and composer of sacred music; but he had self-denial enough to sacrifice his elegant tastes at the shrine of the sterner duties which absorbed his time and energy.

During the Whiskey Insurrection, he was called to preach to the troops on their march to suppress it. He discharged his duties in a fearless yet prudent manner, avoiding the odium which Dr. Nisbet incurred by his more caustic rebukes. Upon the death of the latter, the charge of the institution devolved upon Dr. Davidson; but in 1809 he resigned his post in the college to devote himself more exclusively to his pastoral duties. His death occurred in December, 1812, in the sixty-second year of his age.

Robert Cooper, of Middle Spring, was one of the leading men of the Presbytery by which he had been licensed, and of which he had been a member for twenty-four years, still retaining his first charge. He was a native of Ireland, and was born in 1732. His father's family were in humble circumstances, and he was forced largely to depend upon his own exertions for the means of completing his education. In 1763, he was graduated at Nassau Hall, then under the presidency of Dr. Finley, and his theological studies were conducted in part under the care of Dr. Duffield, at Carlisle. In 1765, he was called to Middle Spring (Shippensburg); and here he remained till disease forced him to seek a dismission, reluctantly granted, in 1797. Low in stature, of a thin, spare habit, with a countenance more indicative of melancholy than mirth, with a delivery that would by no means be considered attractive, and with a diction rather solid than elegant, the real worth of the man was recognized beneath its disguise, while the integrity of his character commanded respect for his Whig principles and his stern doctrinal views. As a theologian he was somewhat eminent; and numbered among his pupils were Drs. J. McKnight, Joshua Williams, and F. Herron. For several years after his dismission, and even to the close of his life, he engaged in missionary labor, supplying vacant pulpits or assisting his brethren of the Presbytery. It was several years after his resignation before the church found a successor to him in Dr. John Moody.

At Lower Marsh Creek and Tom's Creek was John McKnight, a theological pupil of Robert Cooper. His collegiate course was completed at Princeton in 1773; in 1776 he was ordained, and until the close of the war he labored with a new congregation gathered by his instrumentality. In 1773 he accepted the call to Lower Marsh Creek, and here, with a farm of one hundred and fifty acres, and amid a large and devoted congregation, who strove to anticipate his wants, he spent what he ever regarded as the happiest years of his life.

Only a few months elapsed after the meeting of the Assembly, when Dr. McKnight was called to the city of New York as colleague with Dr. Rodgers. For twenty years he was removed from the scenes of his early days, but in his old age returned again to active labor in his native State. His successor at Lower Marsh Creek was William Paxton, whose protracted ministry extended from 1792 to 1841, a period of almost half a century.

At Lower Marsh Creek was John Black, a native of South Carolina, but a graduate of Nassau Hall in 1771. In 1775, he was installed pastor of this church, but in 1794, after a pastorate of nearly twenty years, was released from his charge, at his repeated and urgent request. His last days were spent in the bounds of Redstone Presbytery. He was possessed of a high order of talent, and was especially fond of philosophical disquisitions. An essay on Psalmody, in reply to Dr. John Anderson of the Associate Church, was from his pen.[1]

At Upper West Conococheague (Mercersburg), John King had been settled for twenty years. A strict Calvinist, an elaborate but not brilliant thinker, with a voice too weak and hoarse for oratorical effect, he never enjoyed an extended popularity; but in close and logical processes of thought, in patience of investigation, and in solid attainments, both in science and theology, he had few superiors. His pastorate closed with his life in 1811.

At East Pennsborough and Monaghan, Samuel Waugh, a graduate of Nassau Hall in 1773, commenced his pas-

---

[1] Sprague's Annals, iii. 556.

torate in 1782. A sound divine, a very acceptable preacher, and highly esteemed by his people, his labors in this position ended only with his life, in 1807. The church of West Hanover from 1788 to 1845 was under the care of James Snodgrass,[1] a man whose modesty did not conceal his sound judgment and eminent devotedness to his work.

In 1793, the united churches of York and Hopewell called as their pastor a young man who had but a few years previous emigrated from Ireland. This was Robert Cathcart. The friend of every good cause, diligent and scrupulously conscientious in the discharge of his duties, with an insatiable thirst for knowledge, and a singularly retentive memory, sternly faithful in the utterance of his convictions, and as immovable in his steadfast devotion to truth as the limestone rocks of York Valley, which he trod for nearly half a century almost as his "native heath," he was spared to witness and condemn in downright earnest the injustice of the Exscinding Acts which rent the Church in twain.

Besides these men, the members of Carlisle Presbytery in 1789 were Hugh McGill, at Tuscarora and Cedar Spring, James Martin, at Piney Creek, Robert McMordie, without charge, James Lang, at Falling Spring and East Conococheague, John Craighead, at Rocky Spring, Hugh Vance, at Tuscarora, Va., and Back Creek, Thomas McFarren, at Lower, East, and West Conococheague, Samuel Dougall, at Path Valley, John Linn, at Sherman's Valley, where he was settled in 1777, David Bard, at Bedford, Joseph Henderson, at Great Conewago, Matthew Stephens, at Derry and Wayne, on the Juniata, James Johnston, at Kishacoquillas, John Johnston, at Hart's Log and Shaver's Creek,

[1] Father of Dr. William D. Snodgrass, now of Goshen, N.Y.

Samuel Wilson, at Big Spring, and Hugh Morrison, at Sunbury, Northumberland town, and Buffalo Valley.

The vacant churches of the Presbytery were York (town), soon supplied by Dr. Cathcart, Hagerstown, Shepherdstown, Charlestown, Falling Waters, Cool Spring, Romney, Patterson Creek, Great Cove, Great Aughwick, Standing Stone, Frankstown, Penn's Valley, Chillisquaque, Warrior's Run, Muncy, Lycoming, Mahoning, Fishing Creek, Dick's Gap, Sherman's Creek, and Upper Paxton.

Previous to 1800, some of these vacancies had been supplied. The death of Dr. John Elder left Paxton and Derry vacant, and Nathaniel R. Snowden, his successor in 1793, became the first pastor of the church of Harrisburg, which lay but two miles from Paxton, and thus within the bounds of his parish. To the charge of the old churches, Joshua Williams had succeeded. David Denney was laboring at Path Valley, while Cooper, Lang, King, Linn, Waugh, Snodgrass, Davidson, Stephen, John Johnston, and Morrison remained undisturbed in their pastorates. Frankstown was supplied by David Bard, dismissed from Bedford; but within the old bounds of the Presbytery there were between thirty and forty churches still vacant. The ministers who had been dismissed were Cooper, McPherrin, Craighead, Jones, James Johnston, Dunham, and Black. Hugh Vance died December 31, 1791, and John Elder, July, 1792.

In 1794, the Presbytery of Carlisle was divided to form the new Presbytery of Huntingdon. Previous to the division it consisted of twenty-five ministers, four of whom were without pastoral charge, while there were sixteen vacancies, and in repeated instances two or more churches had but a single pastor. The order of the Assembly divided the two Presbyteries "by a line along the Juniata River, from its mouth up to the

Tuscarora Mountain, to the head of Path Valley, thence westwardly to the eastern boundary of the Presbytery of Redstone, so as to leave the congregation of Bedford to the south. The ministers south of this line—Snodgrass, Waugh, Linn, Nesbit, Davidson, Wilson, Cooper, Craighead, King, Lang, McPherrin, Paxton, Black, Henderson, McMordie, and Jones—were to constitute the Presbytery of Carlisle; the others,—Bard, John and James Johnston, Stephens, McGill, Martin, Bryson, Morrison, and Hoge,—the Presbytery of Huntingdon. In 1800, the Presbytery of Carlisle had eighteen ministers, five without pastoral charge, and twelve vacancies. The Presbytery of Huntingdon had twelve ministers, four without pastoral charge, and more than twenty vacancies.

The region of Western Pennsylvania was covered in 1789 by the Redstone Presbytery, numbering at that time eight ministers, and thirty-one churches, seventeen of which were vacant, and of the fourteen others all but two were unable alone to sustain a pastor. James Finley was at Rehoboth and Round Hill, John Clark at Lebanon and Bethel, Joseph Smith[1] at Buffalo and Cross Creek, John McMillan at Chartiers and Pigeon Creek, James Power at Mount Pleasant and Sewickley, James Dunlap at Redstone and Dunlap Creek, while Thaddeus Dod was at Ten-Mile, and Samuel Barr at Pittsburg.

The vacancies were Fairfield, Donegal, Unity, Salem, Poke Run, Long Run, Montier's Creek, Glades of Sandy Creek, Muddy Creek, Morganstown, George's Creek, Pike Run, Potato Garden, Mill Creek, King's Creek, Short Creek, and Three Ridges.

In 1792, the number of ministers was twelve, but the number of vacant churches, through the rapid increase

---

[1] Died April 14, 1792.

of settlements, amounted to twenty-four. The new members were Joseph Patterson, James Hughes, John Brice, John McPherrin, and Samuel Porter.

In 1793, the Presbytery of Redstone dismissed five of its members, in order to constitute another Presbytery on its western borders, at that time extending over the scattered settlements on the northwest of the Ohio River. The new Presbytery, though mainly within the limits of the State of Pennsylvania, took the name of Ohio, and the five ministers by whom it was constituted were John Clark, John McMillan, Joseph Patterson, James Hughes, and John Brice.

Of the Presbytery thus erected, the Monongahela River, in its windings till it joins the Alleghany at Pittsburg, formed the eastern and northern boundary. Thence the line ran northward to Presque Island, and from this in a westerly direction, including the frontier settlements in Ohio. The field occupied was one into which immigration was soon to pour at flood-tide. The country was rapidly filling up, and the increase of the Presbytery in the course of a few years was almost unprecedented. In 1794, two more members were added to its list, and in 1800, seven years after its formation, it had nineteen ministers, one only without charge, while under its care it had five probationers for the ministry.

Of its original members, some have already been mentioned in connection with Redstone Presbytery. John Clark, since 1781 settled over the Bethel and Lebanon congregations, was far advanced in years and enfeebled by age when he became a member of the Ohio Presbytery, the erection of which he survived only four years. Grave, sedate, venerable in appearance, he was pronounced a solemn and impressive speaker. His successor was William Woods.

Next on the list stood the name of John McMillan,

and in grateful association with it followed the names of others who had been his pupils but were now his co-Presbyters and coadjutors. Others still were soon to be added to the list. Most prominent among these were Joseph Patterson, Thomas Marquis, James Hughes, and John Brice.

Patterson was a native of Ireland.[1] His father, when a lad, was present at the siege of Derry. The son shared in the scenes of our own Revolutionary conflict. In 1788, he was licensed to preach, and in the following year accepted the call of the united churches of Raccoon and Montour's Run, in Washington county, the former eighteen miles from Pittsburg. Like other ministers of the day, he made frequent missionary tours, and his labors were most abundant. "His journal is replete with interesting and surprising incidents, and strikingly illustrates the deep spirituality and glowing zeal of the missionary."

Thomas Marquis was another of this noble band of pioneers of which the Presbytery was constituted. His father's death while he was yet a child left him destitute, and at twelve or thirteen years of age he went to learn the trade of a weaver. In 1775, he left his home in Virginia, and, now at the age of twenty-two, and already married, took up his residence in Washington county. His cabin was erected, amid all the hazards of frontier warfare, in the woods near the spot where the village of Cross Creek now stands. As dangers thickened, he, with others, took refuge in Vance's Fort. There was not a gospel-minister within seventy miles of the place, but within the fort was one pious man. This was Joseph Patterson, whom we have just mentioned. Although not yet licensed, he acted the part of a faithful Christian, and, with a piety that remained

---

[1] Sprague's Annals. Old Redstone.

firm even amidst the storm and terrors of war, endeavored to act the part of a faithful monitor to the often reckless and hardened men that had fled with him to the fort. A revival commenced, and Thomas Marquis and his young wife were numbered among its subjects.

For several years, though often urged to undertake the work of the ministry, the timidity of Marquis led him to refuse all solicitations. At length his duty became so manifest that he could no longer decline it. He prosecuted his studies, first at Buffalo with Dr. Joseph Smith, and afterward at Canonsburg with Dr. McMillan. It was a period for his family, as well as himself, of great self-denial. His excellent wife was sometimes compelled to labor in the field to keep the children supplied with bread. But the result was that Marquis brought to his Master's work, at the ripe age of forty, such gifts of energy, humility, and perseverance as are rarely combined. In 1793, he was licensed to preach by the Presbytery of Redstone, and in the following year accepted a call from the congregations of Black Lick and Cross Creek. In the first four years of his pastorate, one hundred and twenty-three were added to the communion of the churches under his care. In 1796, he was appointed a member of the first missionary board west of the mountains. His missionary labors were abundant, and his tours frequent and sometimes quite extended. In 1801, he declined a call from Chillicothe, but soon after made an extensive journey "northwest of the Ohio and Alleghany Rivers, seeking the wandering sheep, and gathering them into little companies, for mutual encouragement and as nuclei of other churches." Kind, courteous, frank, but gifted with quick intellect and strong emotion, he was genial in social life, and almost "irresistible in the pulpit." Almost to the last, even when bowed under the weight of more than threescore and ten years, he continued his labors and gave full proof of his ministry.

Another honored member of this Presbytery was Rev. (afterward Dr.) Samuel Ralston. He was a native of Ireland, and his early home was "a nursery of gospel truth, where religion with its Bible and catechisms, instead of politics with its newspapers, early imbued his vigorous mind." He was born in 1756, and migrated to this country, after completing his studies at the University of Glasgow, in the spring of 1794. In 1796, he accepted the call of the united congregations of Mingo Creek and Williamsport (now Monongahela City), where for thirty-five years he continued to labor. Remarkable for mental energy, erudition, and a piety that never wearied in its work, he was gifted with some of the lighter graces of urbanity and wit, and for keenness of satire his "curry-comb" might "well rank with the 'characteristics' of Witherspoon." It defended the revivals of the period—1800–1805—from the charges brought against them on account of the extravagances with which they were connected.

Still another of this little band was James Hughes, brother of Thomas Edgar Hughes, born in York county, Pa., about 1765. He was a graduate of New Jersey College, and studied theology under Dr. McMillan.[1] From 1790 to 1814, he was pastor of Short Creek and Lower Buffalo Churches. Like his brethren, he performed a large amount of missionary labor. None of his excursions were more profitable than the one which he made to Ligonier, Westmoreland county, in 1792. Among his hearers was one destined to become a most efficient co-laborer in the same field. This was Elisha Macurdy, then a young man of twenty-eight years. The sermon induced him to purchase a Bible, to learn

[1] This is somewhat uncertain.

whether the statements and warnings of the preacher were sustained by it. A great and permanent change was the result. A good old lady expressed her confidence in his piety by saying, "If Mr. Macurdy has no religion, God help the world." Yet at this time he was not, in his after-judgment, truly converted. A sermon by John McPherrin brought him to clearer views of the truth, and was blessed in leading him to a genuine Christian experience.

From this moment his course was decided. He sold his farm to defray the expense of his education, and became a member of the Academy at Canonsburg. Here he completed his theological as well as literary course (1798). In connection with the Presbytery, he abounded in missionary service. He was one of the leading spirits of the Western Missionary Society, and had an important agency in connection with the great revival in Western Pennsylvania in 1801–2. For nearly forty years he continued his career of "most self-denying and unremitting labor,—for thirty-five years at Cross Roads and Three Springs (1800–1835)."

Among his teachers in 1796, at Canonsburg, was John Watson. At nine years of age the latter was left a friendless orphan. A neighbor of his father took him into his family; and here young Watson found a large collection of books, especially of novels. These he devoured with a strange eagerness, contriving means to procure them even after they had been carefully locked up. At every leisure moment his beloved books occupied his attention. Addison's Spectator fell into his hands, and was read with great delight. But the Latin sentences, prefixed as mottoes to each number, puzzled him. He was mortified at his ignorance, and resolved to learn Latin. By the aid of a copy of Horace, and an old broken dictionary, without even a grammar, he commenced his task. While thus engaged,

Alexander Addison, President of the Court of Common Pleas in the Western District of Pennsylvania, lodged at the house where Watson lived. Here he found the young bar-keeper, after the family had retired to rest, reading Horace by firelight. To his surprise, he learned the remarkable progress that the youth had already made. With expressions of regret that he had no better advantages, the jurist promised to bring him, on his return at the next session of court, some more suitable books. It was the first encouraging word in regard to his studies which the orphan-boy had heard since his father's death. In due time the jurist returned with the books. "Never," said Watson, relating the incident, "did I experience a more joyful moment. My heart was so full I could not utter a word."

Besides classical works, he was furnished with others on History, Belles-Lettres, Philosophy, &c. These were eagerly devoured. The teacher of the village grammar-school gave him valuable aid. At the age of nineteen, his attainments and worth became widely known, and through the influence of Dr. McMillan he was appointed assistant teacher in the Academy of Canonsburg. This was in 1792. After a service of eighteen months, his venerable patron procured for him a scholarship at Princeton. Returning thence on the completion of his studies, he was immediately chosen principal of the Academy, and soon after, by an able and powerful appeal to the Legislature, he obtained the charter of Jefferson College.

In 1798, he was licensed to preach, and for four years had the pastoral charge of a small congregation three miles from Canonsburg. But his career was short. His labors were arduous, and his health, injured seriously already by severe application to study, was fast giving way. He died in 1802; and over him might have been pronounced, with equal appropriateness, the beau-

tiful lines in which Byron has commemorated the genius and the untimely fate of Henry Kirke White. Yet his memory and influence were not lost. Several distinguished ministers were trained in part under his care, and his name occupies an honorable place on the records of that pioneer Presbytery,—the Presbytery of Ohio.

About the commencement of the present century, another laborer, of kindred spirit and of eminent gifts, had joined the little band. This was Mr. (afterward Dr.) John Anderson, who had received his entire classical and theological education at the Academy of the Rev. David Caldwell, pastor at Buffalo and Alamance in North Carolina. He was remarkable for his ardent and self-denying zeal. In missionary labor he had, even in that age, scarce a rival. He was licensed by the Presbytery of Orange, N.C., in 1791, and for two years labored in the vicinity of the borders of this and the adjoining State of South Carolina. From 1793 to 1798, he itinerated through the States of Tennessee and Kentucky, sometimes crossing the Ohio and preaching to the extreme frontier settlements. Unaided by any missionary association, and often subjected to great dangers and privations, he exhibited just those qualities which were most necessary in the broad field which spread around him. The Ohio Presbytery found in him a most efficient co-laborer, and desired him to take up a permanent residence among them. For nearly a third of a century he was pastor of the Upper Buffalo Church of Washington county.

In the autumn of 1793, Thomas Moore was settled as pastor of Ten-Mile, as successor of the pioneer Thaddeus Dod, who had died a few months previous. He was a native of New England, and was received from the Bristol Association of Massachusetts. With a voice clear and sonorous, a delivery warm and animated, a vigorous intellect, high culture, ardent temperament, and active zeal, he proved a valuable accession to the Presbytery.[1] His Eastern associations made him the principal channel through which reports of the progress of the gospel and revivals among the churches were communicated to the journals in the older States. His own labors, both at Ten-Mile, and subsequently at Salem, were largely blessed. In his ten years' ministry at the former place, about two hundred persons were received to the Church on profession of their faith. The log meeting-house built in 1785 at Lower Ten-Mile proved too small for the congregation, and during Mr. Moore's ministry another was erected at Upper Ten-Mile.

Mr. Moore is said to have been "a terrible scourge of Arminianism." In theology he was a Hopkinsian, and his Calvinism was of an ultra type. Tradition reports—although unwarrantably—that he preached the doctrine of infant-damnation. The report originated, no doubt, in the severe exposition which he was wont to give of orthodox doctrine. He dwelt much, in his preaching, on the terrors of the law. He was bold and uncompromising in his denunciations of sin in all its forms, but especially when it assumed the shape of formalism and hypocrisy in the Church.

Other laborers in the field at this early period were Messrs. John Brice, William Wood, William Wick, G. Scott, Joseph Anderson, A. Gwinn, John McClean, and J. Snodgrass. By these men an extensive field was occupied, and a remarkable amount of missionary labor performed. Five of the nineteen ministers were settled "over the Ohio River,"—one, William Wick, thirty-eight miles west of the river, within eight miles of Youngstown, where he preached a third part of the time as a temporary supply. From the month of

---

[1] Wines's Historical Discourse, pp. 16, 17.

August, 1799, to November, 1800, the Presbytery ordained ten ministers of the gospel, of whom nine were installed, and one dismissed to go and itinerate in the State of Tennessee, while one was received from the Presbytery of Brunswick, thus in the space of little more than a year more than doubling the number of the members of the body.

Meanwhile, three candidates for licensure were on trial, and several more were expecting soon to offer themselves. The churches were chiefly supplied from McMillan's school, "a little academy in Canonsburg, with no resources, supported entirely, till of late, by the Presbyterian clergy and their people." There was an urgent necessity, notwithstanding all that had been done, for more laborers. "In this quarter," writes Rev. Thomas Moore (January, 1801), "the field is wide and extensive, the harvest truly great, but the laborers comparatively few." A most grateful welcome did the missionaries of the Connecticut Missionary Society receive from the members of the Ohio Presbytery on their way to New Connecticut. Two of them, Joseph Badger and David Bacon, had already made transient visits to that inviting and destitute field, and more were soon to follow in their track, Ezekiel J. Chapman in the following year.

Meanwhile, several of the congregations connected with the Presbytery were visited by seasons of refreshing. There were revivals, some characterized by great power, in the churches of which McMillan, Patterson, Hughes, Brice, and Moore were pastors. On his way to his field of labor (November, 1800) in New Connecticut, Joseph Badger "passed through and near to twenty Presbyterian congregations," where from 1798 there had been "a pretty general serious awakening."[1]

---

[1] Conn. Ev. Mag., 1801.

Many hundred souls were converted. The revival extended nearly eighty miles from east to west. The new settlements northwest of the Ohio, to the very bounds of New Connecticut, were "visited in a special manner." The work was free from enthusiasm, but characterized by great power.[1]

By the commencement of the present century, "sixteen or seventeen very worthy and pious ministers" had been trained for their work in the "academic school" of Canonsburg. It was at first thought that it would be difficult to supply them all with fields of labor. But the revival "opened places enough." By September, 1800, there were three ordained ministers connected with the Ohio Presbytery in or near the Western Reserve.

CHAPTER XVI.

MARYLAND AND VIRGINIA, 1789-1800.

Although the Presbyterian Church in this country had been first planted on the Eastern Shore of Maryland, yet there were many obstacles to its spread both in Maryland and Virginia, which, until the close of the

---

[1] From 1781 to 1807, an extensive work of grace was experienced in the churches of Cross Creek, Upper Buffalo, Chartiers, Pigeon Creek, Bethel, Lebanon, Ten-Mile, Cross Roads, and Mill Creek, during which more than one thousand persons were converted. From 1795 to 1799, another series of gracious visitations was enjoyed by the churches of Western Pennsylvania, extending to the new settlements north of Pittsburg. Dr. McMillan received to his church one hundred and ten, and Thomas Marquis one hundred and twenty-three persons. Large additions were made to others.—*Humphrey's "Revival Sketches."*

Revolutionary War, effectually retarded its growth. Maryland was a Roman Catholic colony, and but a small proportion of its inhabitants would have been disposed to welcome Presbyterian missionary labor or Presbyterian institutions; while Virginia, settled by "Cavaliers," and with the Episcopal for the established Church of the colony, was long reluctant even to tolerate "Dissenters." The patriotic fervor of the Revolution, and the worldly and sometimes disgraceful conduct and character of the Episcopal clergy,[1] combined to effect a change in popular feeling and sympathy, and at the close of the war the field was open to Presbyterian effort.

The laborers, indeed, were few and far between. The eloquence of Davies, even, had been like the voice of one crying in the wilderness. His own heart was deeply burdened that he was left to toil almost alone. During the war, little could be done to supply spiritual destitution, and the single Presbytery of Hanover, feeble in numbers, though enterprising in spirit, was left to occupy and supply a region extending on every side hundreds of miles.

In Western Maryland the Presbyterian Church can scarcely be said to have had an existence until after the close of the war. Hagerstown and two or three other congregations were under the care of Carlisle Presbytery, and perhaps as many more feeble congregations existed between the Potomac and the Chesapeake. The Presbytery of Baltimore was formed, by a division of Donegal Presbytery, in 1786. At the meeting of the first General Assembly, it reported six members and twelve churches. Patrick Allison was at Baltimore, Isaac S. Keith at Alexandria, Stephen B. Balch at Georgetown, James Hunt at Bladensburg and Cabin

[1] Meade's Churches of Virginia.

John, John Slemons at Slate Ridge and Chance Ford, and George Lucky at Bethel and Centre; while Hopewell, Frederick, and Soldier's Delight were vacant.

The First Presbyterian Church of Baltimore dates from 1763. During the preceding year, a few Presbyterians from Pennsylvania had erected a log church edifice within the limits of the future city, which at that time could boast some thirty or forty houses and some three hundred inhabitants.[1] Allison, a graduate of the University of Pennsylvania, and a licentiate of the Second Presbytery of Philadelphia, was at the time connected with the Newark Academy, at which several young men from Baltimore were pursuing their studies, and, doubtless through their influence, he was induced for one or more Sabbaths to supply the pulpit. So acceptable were his services, that the congregation requested of the Presbytery that he might be appointed to supply them statedly on a salary of one hundred pounds per year. Declining a call to a larger church at New Castle, he accepted the appointment, and for thirty-five years continued in the pastorate of the First Church of Baltimore.

The congregation, small at first,—numbering, it is supposed, but six families,[2]—rapidly increased; the small edifice was pulled down for the erection of a larger one; this was subsequently enlarged; and at length, to accommodate the increased numbers, a large, expensive, and elegant structure was reared, worthy the enterprise of the growing city.

The personal appearance of Dr. Allison was highly commanding and impressive. Of medium height, but every way well proportioned, his manners combined, to

---

[1] Sprague, iii. 254.

[2] Baltimore was laid out as a town by Roman Catholics in 1729, and up to 1765 it contained but fifty houses.—*Eighty Years' Progress*, i. 183.

a remarkable degree, grace with dignity. With a proper self-respect, yet without ostentation, his bearing toward others was courteous and respectful. With a character above reproach, with intellectual gifts of a high order, which had been improved and expanded by more than ordinary culture, ever a diligent student, as well as a careful observer of passing events, he exerted a powerful and extensive influence throughout the community. Of exquisite literary taste, a master of history, ancient and modern, wielding a facile and yet a powerful pen, he stood ever ready to defend the cause of his country and the cause of religious freedom. During the Revolution, and after the close of the war, his pen was called into service, first to repel the arrogant claims of Episcopacy to state patronage, and afterward in defence of American Protestantism. His large foresight and liberal public spirit brought him forward on repeated occasions when the cause of education or the public welfare demanded an able champion. With Old-side sympathies strong to the last, he cannot be classed with such men as those who inherited the zeal of the Tennents or sympathized with the revival efforts of Whitefield; and yet it is possible that in the region where his lot was cast he was better fitted to accomplish the work that needed to be done, than he would have been with less learning and greater zeal. Until his death he was a leading member of the Presbytery. Of Baltimore College and Baltimore Library he was one of the original founders. In the judicatories of the Church, and in all public bodies in which he was called to take a part, he was especially eminent. His great sagacity, perfect self-control, and admirable command of thought and language marked him out as a leader, and warranted the estimate of him pronounced by President Samuel Stanhope Smith:—" Dr. Allison is decidedly the ablest *statesman* we have in the General Assembly." What Franklin was to the State, that, in large measure, he was to the Church; and a striking parallel might be drawn between the shrewd sagacity, perspicuity of thought and expression, freedom from impulse, and practical utilitarianism, by which the two men were characterized.

The church at Alexandria was probably formed shortly before the commencement of the Revolutionary War. In 1780, William Thom, who had supplied the congregation for several years, and perhaps been settled as pastor, was dismissed,[1] and Isaac S. Keith received "an affectionate and unanimous call"—to which "the inhabitants of every denomination echoed universal consent"—as his successor. The church was at the time in a feeble state, with a limited membership, and largely dependent for support on the co-operation of other denominations. Mr. Keith,[2] a native of Newtown, Pa., a graduate of New Jersey College, and a theological pupil of Robert Smith, of Pequa, was indeed the man for the place. An apt scholar, an elegant writer, fully devoted to the work of the ministry, unwearied in his endeavors to promote the cause of Christ, he originated, while at Alexandria, a plan for prayer and conference meetings, while as yet they were unknown, and endeavored to harmonize in effective co-operation the various religious elements of the community. For nearly a quarter of a century after his dismissal from Alexandria, he was the respected and beloved pastor of the Circular Church (Independent) of Charleston, S.C.; and rarely has any career been crowned with more honorable memories of use-

[1] William Thom was a licentiate of Donegal Presbytery in 1771 (Synod's Minutes, 1772), and was ordained in the following year. He probably commenced his labors soon after in Alexandria or its vicinity.

[2] Remains of Rev. Isaac S. Keith—Biographical Sketch.

fulness and devotion. An American edition of John Newton, revised and improved,—his letters, enriched with quotations from the "Olney Hymns," repeatedly remind us of the good sense and fervent piety of the friend of Cowper, Wilberforce, and Scott. The son-in-law of Dr. Sproat of Philadelphia, the correspondent of Dr. Green, a fast friend of missions, a principal founder of the Charleston Bible Society in 1810, extensively acquainted with the condition and wants of the country and the world, his life was one of uninterrupted and uniform effort in behalf of the cause to which he had devoted himself; and when, in the vigor of his years, he fell (1813) at his post, tears of unaffected grief from hundreds of mourning friends attested their deep sense of the loss which they had experienced.

His eight years' ministry at Alexandria was a period of peace and prosperity to the Church. Commanding the respect and confidence of the entire community, but especially the regard and attachment of his own flock, his resignation of his office was universally lamented, and the congregation felt it to be their duty earnestly to remonstrate against his removal. (Sept. 10, 1788.)

The successor of Mr. Keith, in the following year, was James Muir, whose ministry extended from 1789 to 1820.

The First Presbyterian Church of Georgetown (D.C.) dates from 1780.[1] In March of that year, Stephen Bloomer Balch entered upon this—at the time—most unpromising field. He had visited the place some months previous, on his journey with a view to missionary labor in the Carolinas. The people invited him to remain, promising him to build him a church; but, though encouraging them to hope for a compliance

---

[1] Sprague, iii. 411.

at some future period, he declined to abandon his present purpose.

The congregation was small and feeble; but in 1782, a few individuals interested in sustaining divine institutions joined in building a very plain house for public worship. Seven persons, including the pastor, were all who joined in the first celebration of the Lord's Supper. But with the increase of population and the growth of the place the church steadily increased in strength, until it was found necessary first to enlarge the church edifice, and at length (1821) to erect one more spacious and commodious.

The ministry of Dr. Balch at Georgetown extended over a period of fifty-three years, and was highly successful. His personal qualities endeared him to the people of his charge. Uniformly cheerful, and sometimes almost hilarious in his mirth,—even shaking the composure and ruffling the dignity of such a man as Dr. Ashbel Green,—he was not only a genial companion, and a favorite among his congregation, but an earnest and animated speaker, and of unquestionable personal piety. In the pulpit he never employed notes; and yet his discourses were evidently the fruit of mature thought. His death occurred September 7, 1833, and his successors were John C. Smith and R. T. Berry.

Among other members of the Presbytery were—John Slemons, a graduate of Princeton, a licentiate of Donegal Presbytery in 1762, ordained in 1765 by Carlisle Presbytery, and soon after, probably, commencing his labors in Maryland, but resigning his charge previous to 1798—George Lucky, a graduate of Princeton, ordained by the New Brunswick Presbytery in 1785, and settled over the churches of Bethel and Centre—and James Hunt (ordained by New Brunswick Presbytery in 1761), at Bladensburg, where his death occurred in 1793.

Shortly after the decease of the latter, Caleb Johnson was settled at Deer Creek, and Enoch Matson at Bermuda. Previous to 1798, Samuel Martin succeeded Slemons at Slate Ridge, while Adam Freeman had under his charge the three feeble congregations of Seneca, Cabin John, and Difficult; and Samuel Knox—received in 1795 from the Belfast Presbytery, in Ireland—was settled as pastor of the church at Frederick, which had been gathered there through the exertions of Mr. Balch soon after the settlement of the latter at Georgetown in 1780.[1] In 1799, William Maffit was pastor at Bladensburg, and John Brackenridge[2] had charge of a small congregation at Washington: the former, however, soon relinquished his post, and the latter, with little prospect of encouragement in the field, soon withdrew (1800), although destined to return to it at a later period.

At the time of the constituting of the General Assembly, the Presbyterian Church in Virginia was represented by the two Presbyteries of Lexington and Hanover,—the former with ten ministers and twenty-eight churches, seventeen of which were vacant, and the latter with seven ministers and twenty-one churches, of which eight were vacant.

In Hanover Presbytery, Richard Sanckey was at Buffalo Creek; John Todd[3] at Providence, Bird and Ford of Pamunky; William Irvine at North Garden, Rich Cove, Mountain Plains, and Dee Ess; John Blair Smith at Cumberland and Briery; James Mitchell at

---

[1] Sprague, iii. 412.

[2] Maffit and Brackenridge were both licentiates of the Presbytery. See Annual Reports to Assembly, 1791–1800.

[3] Died July 27, 1793.

Peaks of Otter; and John D. Blair at Hanover and Henrico. The churches of Cub Creek, Rock Fish, Concord, Hat Creek, Fauquier, Blue Stone, Lancaster, and Head of Smith's River were vacant. Within a few years the names of some of the most eminent ministers of the Church were to be found on the roll of this Presbytery,—Archibald Alexander, William Calhoon, James Turner, Drury Lacy, and James Robinson.

In a field where the name of Davies was a household word, and through which Whitefield had passed and repassed on his preaching-tours, there were now to be found men who, almost sinking under their accumulated tasks, labored nobly to stay the tide of irreligion which was sweeping over the land, and to which Virginia in an especial manner was exposed. The Episcopal Church was, as a body, in a most lamentable condition. She had not yet begun to feel that new impulse which, through the influence of Wilberforce, Newton, Scott, and others in England, and the labors of Bishops Madison and White in this country, was ere long to open before her brighter prospects.[1] The effects of the war, the spread of French politics and speculation, and the extensive apostasy of many from the zeal and devotion of the period preceding the war, demanded special effort on the part of the few Presbyterian ministers of Virginia. They were surrounded on every side by a missionary field. The churches were few and feeble, and the lot of the pastors was one of no little self-denial.

Glancing over the roll of the Presbytery, we find names well worthy of honorable mention:—Sanckey,[2] now an old man,—the patriarch of the Synod of which he was the first moderator, but still discharging his

[1] Meade's Churches of Virginia. [2] Webster, 457.

duties to the Buffalo congregation, who nearly thirty years before had fled from savage incursions to their present location, and who still clung to the pastor who had shared their lot; Matthew Lyle,[1] his successor at Buffalo, which he supplied in connection with Briery,—a man of sound judgment and sterling integrity, of uniform temper and devotion, honest, sincere, faithful, and in the pulpit discarding notes, but clear, forcible, and effective both in thought and utterance; John Durborrow Blair,[2] a son of John Blair of Fagg's Manor, subsequently principal of Washington Hall Academy, and in 1785 a licentiate of Hanover Presbytery,—a man who was esteemed by those who had listened to the eloquence of Davies fit to be his successor, and whose elegance of speech and manners was in keeping with his refined and exquisite taste; John Blair Smith,[3] who as yet had given but the earnest of that eloquence which was to thrill crowded assemblies, and whose intense earnestness and glowing piety seemed to lend a more than human energy and endurance to his enfeebled frame; and James Mitchel, whose ministry at the Peaks of Otter extended from 1786 to 1841, and whose force, animation, and startling earnestness in the pulpit fixed his words like arrows in the heart and conscience of the hearer.

Besides these, but at this time without charge, was another member of the Presbytery, whose fame will endure while literature cherishes the name of the author of the "British Spy." It may be that William Wirt allowed himself something of a poetic license in his description of the eloquence of the "old blind preacher;" but James Waddel was no ordinary man. Tall, slender, and erect in person, graceful and dignified in demeanor, with a long face, high forehead, Grecian nose,

[1] Sprague, iii. 629. [2] Ibid. iii. 459. [3] Ibid. 397.

blue eyes, and small mouth and chin,[1] his appearance was at once conciliating and commanding. His mind, richly stored and well disciplined, was at the same time well balanced; and, though he had never enjoyed the advantages of a collegiate education, yet at Dr. Finley's school at Nottingham, first as a pupil, then as an assistant teacher, and at length as an assistant in Robert Smith's school at Pequa, he diligently amassed those stores of learning which, whether by the fireside in familiar conversation, or in the pulpit, were so perfectly at command. On a journey to Charleston, he met Samuel Davies, then at Hanover, and through his influence was led to devote himself to the ministry. In April, 1761, he was licensed by the old Presbytery of Hanover; and such was the popular appreciation of his zeal and ability that at the October meeting five calls were put into his hands. He declined them all, however, intending to return to Pennsylvania. But representations of the spiritual destitution of the county of Lancaster so affected him that he consented to accept an invitation to the pastorate of Lancaster and Northumberland congregations.

Here he remained (1762–1776) for fourteen years, removing in 1778 to Augusta county and supplying for seven years the congregation of Tinkling Spring, and for the latter portion of the time that of Staunton. In 1785, he removed to Louisa, where he supplied several neighboring churches and engaged in the employment of teaching, yet without a stated charge.

It was here—at the little church about two miles from his residence, which he named Hopewell—that Wirt heard him. His sight was gone, and his limbs trembled from the effects of a stroke of palsy. But the cultivated taste of the statesman was captivated

---

[1] Sprague, iii. 239.

by the sublime simplicity and thrilling utterance of the "old man eloquent." As the latter closed his description of the crucifixion by the quotation from Rousseau,—"Socrates died like a philosopher, but Jesus Christ, like a God!"—it seemed to Wirt the climax of eloquence. "Whatever," he says, "I may have been able to conceive of the sublimity of Massillon, or the force of Bourdaloue, had fallen short of the power which I felt from the delivery of this simple sentence." "I had never seen," he remarks, "in any other orator, such a union of simplicity and majesty. He has not a gesture, an attitude, or an accent to which he does not seem forced by the sentiment he is expressing. His mind is too serious, too earnest, too solicitous, and at the same time too dignified, to stoop to artifice."

Under the eastern shadows of the Blue Ridge he had lived and died perhaps unknown to fame, but for the chance which brought William Wirt within the sound of his voice. And yet we have abundant testimony to confirm all the impressions that we gather from the report of the "British Spy." "I am satisfied," said William Calhoon, after having heard him on one occasion, "that I never witnessed such a torrent of eloquence before or since." In the course of a trial in Presbytery, an intelligent elder present, who had heard some of Patrick Henry's most successful pleas in criminal cases, but who now had the privilege of listening to Dr. Waddel, declared that this was the most perfect specimen of eloquence which he ever heard. Governor Barbour, of Virginia,—a pupil of Dr. Waddel,—shortly before his death, stated to a friend in Philadelphia that Dr. W. had spoiled him in regard to hearing other preachers.

Yet the eloquence of Dr. Waddel was not spasmodic, nor the result of any excessive development of any particular intellectual gift. His well-stored mind seemed without an effort to pour forth its treasures, and in full and graceful volume they flowed along a channel rich with native beauty and adorned with finished culture. And yet more precious than the charm of words was the spell which his own intense yet subdued feeling cast over his audience. He spoke from the depths of conviction. His hearers were not left to criticize his logic, or to admire his elegance of speech. No ostentatious display was allowed to obscure his theme, or present him in his Master's stead. Nor was the piety of the preacher confined to the pulpit. By the fireside, in the social circle, in affliction, on the sick and the dying bed, he was still the same intelligent, calm, trustful, hopeful servant of Him to whom he had consecrated his life. Till 1805 he was spared, occasionally to occupy the pulpit, and finally to crown a devoted life with the serene triumphs of a Christian faith.

The field of Lexington Presbytery, stretching from Northern Virginia near Winchester to the southwestern portion of the State, and covering the entire region west of the Blue Ridge, had but six settled pastors in 1789. Far to the extreme south, at New Providence, was John Brown, the patriarch of the Presbytery. Thirty-five years before, Samuel Davies, who preached his ordination sermon (at Fagg's Manor), spoke of him as "a youth of piety, prudence, and zeal;" and now, after a thirty-years pastorate at Newark, Dr. McWhorter could recall the searching discourse which from the lips of the youthful preacher had arrested his attention and led him to the Saviour. Till 1776, Mr. Brown was settled at Timber Ridge and Providence, retaining the latter till 1797;[1] and it may afford some

[1] His successor in 1798 was Samuel Brown, a licentiate of the Presbytery.

idea of the state of things among the seventeen vacant congregations of the Presbytery to know how the signers of the call, addressed to him more than the lifetime of a generation previous, had described their condition.

They spoke of themselves as having been "for many years past in very destitute circumstances for want of the ordinances of the gospel statedly among us, many of us under distressing spiritual languishments, and multitudes perishing in our sins for want of the bread of life broken among us; our Sabbaths wasted in melancholy silence at home, or sadly broken and profaned by the more thoughtless among us; our hearts and hands discouraged and our spirits broken with our mournful condition and repeated disappointments of relief in this particular."[1]

Lower down the Valley, in Augusta county, at Bethel and Brown's Church (Hebron), was Archibald Scott, a native of Scotland, a pupil of Finley, and a licentiate of Hanover Presbytery in 1777. Poor and friendless, without a relative on this continent, he had tasked his energies to secure an education, and, while he rested from his labors in the field, conned his Latin grammar, and familiarized the lesson while he followed the plough.[2]

Such diligence merited patronage, and received it. A worthy physician of Pennsylvania assisted to support him at Dr. Finley's school. While there, he was converted, and devoted himself to the work of the ministry. Removing to the Shenandoah Valley, he supported himself by teaching while he studied theology with Principal Graham, of Liberty Hall Academy. Licensed to preach, he had not far to go to find a settlement. For more than twenty years, and until his death, in

---

[1] Webster, 656. [2] Sprague, iii. 387.

1799, Hebron and Bethel continued to be his pastoral charge.

The parish was, in fact, a missionary field. It comprehended a district of country some twenty miles square. Yet, arduous as were the duties which the pastoral care of it imposed, the ability of the people did not suffice to support the pastor, and a scant salary was eked out by labors on a farm. Yet, by great energy and tireless devotion and perseverance, Mr. Scott was enabled to discharge his appropriate duties as a minister, without suffering himself to be diverted by secular interests. With the zeal of a patriot and the devotion and self-denial of an intelligent Christian pastor, he exerted himself to assist in laying deep the foundations of the Republic in religious truth, and prepare the rising generation to understand, appreciate, and preserve constitutional liberty.

Augusta Church—the mother-church of Presbyterianism in the Valley—had for its pastor William Wilson, ordained and installed two or three years previous, and destined to retain the pastorate for more than twenty years. At Mossy Creek and Cook's Creek (from 1780 until his death) was Benjamin Erwin, and at Winchester, with congregations at Opeckon and Cedar Creek, was John Montgomery; while John McCue had charge of Companion and Good Hope congregations. At Shepherdstown, where the religious state of things seemed quite unpromising, Moses Hoge, commencing his labors in the autumn of 1787, soon gathered around him a large congregation, of which he retained the charge until called to the Presidency of Hampden-Sidney College in 1807.

Besides these, the Presbytery had three members without pastoral charge,—William Graham, James McConnell, and Edward Crawford. But perhaps there was not within its bounds a single individual who was accomplishing a more important work than William Graham. He occupied in Lexington Presbytery a position not unlike that of S. S. Smith in Hanover.

Previous to 1800, several other names had been added to the roll of the Presbytery, mostly from the list of its own licentiates. Samuel Houston was settled at Falling Water and High Bridge, Benjamin Grigsby at Lewisburg and Concord, and Samuel Brown had succeeded John Brown at New Providence. In 1799, John Glendy, subsequently the pastor of the Second Church of Baltimore, but who at this time had just escaped—a refugee—from his native land, (Ireland) commenced his brief pastorate as the successor of Archibald Scott at Bethel and Brown's Church, including the congregation of Staunton. During the same year, George Addison Baxter succeeded, upon the death of William Graham, to the charge of Liberty Hall, while he ministered also to the congregations of New Monmouth and Lexington. Shortly after, Robert Logan commenced his labors at Sinking Spring and Roanoke.

Perhaps in no portion of the Church, save on the frontiers west of the Alleghanies, had the progress of the Church been more cheering for the twelve years which followed the establishment of the General Assembly than in the Valley of Virginia. The number of ministers had nearly doubled, and, instead of eleven, they had charge of twenty-eight congregations, while the vacancies had been reduced in number from seventeen to fourteen.[1] This growth was largely in excess of the proportionate increase of the population of the State. The latter had advanced at the rate of less than twenty per cent., while that of the churches of the Valley had been from sixty to eighty per cent.

In 1794, the Presbytery of Winchester was erected

---

[1] Assembly Minutes, 1802.

by a division of Lexington. It embraced those churches which lay at the northern extremity of the Valley, and in 1799 had under its care Shepherdstown, under the pastorate (1787) of Moses Hoge; Cedar Creek and Opeckon, the charge (1790) of Nash Legrand; Charlestown and Hopewell (or Berkeley), under William Hill (1792); South River and Flint Run, under William Williamson; Frankfort, Romney, and Springfield, for a short time under John Lyle; together with the vacant congregations of Concrete, Middletown, Back Creek, Lancaster, and Winchester, where William Hill in the following year commenced his pastorate of thirty-four years.

Of the pastors of the Presbyterian Church in Virginia in 1800, a large proportion had been educated at Hampden-Sidney College, and quite a number had been converted in the revivals of 1787–9. It is not too much to say that these revivals wrought an almost entire revolution in the prospects of the Church in this region. The names of Blythe, Hill, Allen, Reed, Calhoon, Lyle, Legrand, Alexander, and others are intimately associated with aggressive missionary effort, not only in Virginia but in the new fields at the West; and yet they belong to the class which at Hampden-Sidney or Liberty Hall were reached and brought into the ministry through the influence of the revival.

It is a significant fact that the revival commenced in connection with the institutions which the Synod had established for the education of young men for the ministry. At an early period, this subject had claimed the attention of the friends of Christian learning attached to the Presbyterian Church in Virginia.

Before the commencement of the Revolution, the Presbytery of Hanover had felt the importance of making suitable provision for an educated ministry. The College of William and Mary, at Williamsburg, was under Episcopal control, as well as expensive in its charges, and was noted, moreover, for the prevalence in connection with it of immoral and deistical influences. The University of Virginia—the pet project of the Sage of Monticello—was not yet in existence, nor, had it been, would it have answered the wants of the Presbyterian Church of Virginia. Princeton was too remote to suit the convenience or wants of those whose limited means forbade them to take the distant and expensive journey. The obvious policy of the Presbytery was to have institutions more accessible, and, moreover, under their own care. Two academies were therefore established,—one in the Valley, and the other in Prince Edward county. The last grew into Hampden-Sidney College, and the other was known by the no less significant title of Liberty Hall.[1]

The first President of Hampden-Sidney was Rev. Samuel Stanhope Smith, D.D., who, until his removal to Princeton in 1779, proved himself its able and efficient head. A better man could not have been selected for the post. He was the son of Rev. Dr. Robert Smith, of Pequa, under whom large numbers of young men already in the ministry had pursued their theological course. His mother was the sister of Samuel and John Blair, a woman of sterling piety and rare intellectual gifts. The son proved himself not unworthy of such a parentage. At a very early age his mind was seriously impressed, and at the same time richly stored with acquisitions worthy of more mature years. After completing his course at Princeton with high distinction, he engaged for a time in assisting his father in the con-

---

[1] For a history of this institution, known successively as Augusta Academy, Liberty Hall, and Washington College, see American Quarterly Register for November, 1837. The circumstances which led to Washington's donation are there stated.

duct of his school, but was soon recalled to Princeton to fill the office of a tutor in the college. After remaining here for two years, he was licensed to preach (1773) by the Presbytery of New Castle. For the benefit of his health, which had suffered from too severe application, he declined at first any permanent charge, and went forth as a missionary to the western counties of Virginia. Here he received a hearty welcome, and soon became a universal favorite. It seemed to many that the mantle of Davis had fallen upon the young preacher, by whose eloquence they were scarcely less entranced.

At this period the project for the academy or college was started. Smith was designated as the man to take successful charge of the difficult enterprise. The subscriptions were rapidly filled up. The anxiety to retain the services of such a man among them led the rich to give of their abundance and the poor of their poverty. The necessary buildings were erected, a charter was secured from the Legislature, and the new institution commenced operations under the most favorable auspices. Mr. Smith took upon him for several years the double and difficult task of principal of the seminary and pastor of the church.

But a single seminary was deemed inadequate to the wants of so vast a region as that which extended on both sides of the Blue Ridge to the south and the southwest. In 1774, another was opened, under the patronage of Hanover Presbytery, near the present site of Fairfield, in what is now Rockbridge county. It was known at first as Augusta Academy, and was placed, by the recommendation of Dr. Smith, under the care of William Graham, assisted in his duties by John Montgomery.

Graham was the son of a Pennsylvania farmer, and from early years was inured to the hardships of frontier life. In his boyhood he had been posted to defend the family with his loaded musket, and had learned to face danger without a fear. Of a vigorous and sprightly turn of mind, he quickly outstripped his associates in study, although he was late in commencing his academical course, and in 1773 was graduated at Princeton. In college he had come under the notice of Smith, and in the following year, at his recommendation, assumed the charge of the new academy.

He proved himself worthy of the trust reposed in him. Funds were necessary for the new institution, and he did much in collecting them. He travelled to New England to solicit benefactions; but the period proved unfavorable for his efforts. The war intervened with its discouragements, and Mr. Graham was forced to remove the school to his own house. Yet the plan was not abandoned. Even in its then humble condition the institution was doing a good work. The late Dr. Archibald Alexander received his training here; and this fact alone would have made the institution famous if it had not had a subsequent history. At length a frame edifice was erected for its accommodation, and in 1782 it was incorporated by an act of Legislature under the name of Liberty Hall. At a still later period it was endowed by a large benefaction from President Washington, and thenceforward bore his name. The humble school first known as Augusta Academy had grown into the more imposing institution of Washington College.

At a critical moment, and not, perhaps, in the exercise of a wise discretion, Graham resigned his post in connection with the college. But his usefulness was by no means at an end. He turned his attention now to the subject of theological education, and had, for several successive years, a class of from seven to eight under his instruction. Some of these rose to high distinction, and his school was, in fact, an "incipient theological seminary."

Between 1786 and 1788, both these colleges, which for a time seemed scarcely to give promise of fulfilling the hopes of their founders, were visited by a remarkable revival of religion. At Hampden-Sidney, then under the charge of Rev. John Blair Smith, who had succeeded his brother as President, religion was at a low ebb. At the time of Dr. Blythe's matriculation there was not another student in the college who made any serious profession. The celebrated Carey H. Allen was commended to him as one of the most sedate of his associates; but scarce had he formed his acquaintance before he was called to witness him in the act of burlesquing a Methodist preacher from the counter of a merchant's store. This initiatory specimen of college life augured badly for what was to follow; but, rebuked by the fearless avowal of Christian principle on the part of a classmate (William Hill) under serious impressions, he was recalled to the path of duty. And now there gathered round him a little band, nearly every one of them destined to subsequent and distinguished usefulness in the service of the Church. Among these were Allen himself, and William Calhoon, pioneer missionaries, along with Blythe to Kentucky, Clement Reed and William Hill, whose names will not soon be forgotten even beyond the immediate scene of their labors.

Great opposition was manifested by the other students to the revival. The praying and singing of the little band produced almost a riot. The evil-disposed gathered with hideous uproar, mingled with oaths and ribaldry, to drown the voice of prayer. But, in spite of opposition, the seriousness spread. Nearly half of the eighty students were brought under conviction. Prayer-meetings were held, marked with deep, silent, solemn feeling. President Smith himself seemed to preach with new life. Often the trunk of an old tree, fallen in the woods, served him for a pulpit, from which on repeated occasions he endeavored to deepen the impression that had already been made on the minds of those who attended him, or whom he overtook, in his walks. Two hundred and twenty-five persons were added to the churches to which he ministered, in the space of eighteen months; while the revival extended over Prince Edward, Cumberland, Charlotte, and Bedford counties to the Peaks of Otter.[1]

But the revival was fruitful in other than immediate results. Among the converted students, besides those already mentioned, were Nash Legrand, Drury Lacy, and William Williamson. The band of pious youth at this time gathered within the walls of Hampden-Sidney were destined to perform most important service in the cause of Christ.

The news of what had taken place in the institution under the charge of President Smith reached Graham, at Augusta. He scarcely needed the importunities of his friend as an inducement to hasten to his assistance. He went, accompanied by two of his students, Samuel Wilson and Archibald Alexander, to attend with Dr. Smith a three-days meeting at Briery Church, in Prince Edward county, a hundred miles distant. Their stay was protracted to a fortnight, and when they returned it was to communicate in the region of Augusta and the neighboring counties the spirit that had been already kindled in their own bosoms. Its influence was felt through Rockbridge county. Nash Legrand threw his soul, with all its ardor, into the work. A revival commenced in the Valley, and extended as far as Augusta. Several of the young men who had been intend-

---

[1] Davidson's Kentucky, p. 43; Pres. Quar. Review, vol. ii. 42–49.

ing to study for the bar were converted, and turned their attention to the ministry. Mr. Graham willingly consented to superintend their theological studies.

The result was that, under the patronage of the Synod of Virginia, a theological department was now added to Liberty Hall. In January, 1794, a building erected for the purpose was opened for the reception of students. It was the first theological school in connection with a college in America. But Mr. Graham's resignation, in 1796, gave it a serious, if not fatal, blow. The cause of theological education was reserved for future and more successful efforts.

CHAPTER XVII.

THE CAROLINAS, 1789–1800.

WHEN, in May, 1788, the Synod of New York and Philadelphia determined to constitute a General Assembly of the Presbyterian Church in the United States, it was necessary, as a preliminary step, that some new Synods should first be set off; and of these the Synod of the Carolinas was one. The Presbyteries which united to form the Synod had all grown out of the old Orange Presbytery. They were now known as the Presbyteries of Orange, South Carolina, and Abingdon.

The Orange Presbytery consisted of ten members, with about three times as many churches. The ministers were Patillo, Caldwell, McCorkle, Hall, whose names are already familiar to us, and Robert Archibald, James McRee, Jacob Lake, Daniel Thatcher, David Barr, and John Beck. In the Presbytery of South Carolina, besides Joseph Alexander and Thomas Reese, already mentioned, there were James Edmonds, John Harris, John Simpson, Thomas H. McCaule, James Templeton, Francis Cummins, Robert Finley, Robert Hall, and Robert Mechlin. The Abington Presbytery consisted of Charles Cummings, Hezekiah Balch, John Cossan, Samuel Houston, Samuel Carrick, and James Balch. The ministers of the entire Synod numbered twenty-eight.

These occupied a territory in which, forty years previous, there was to be found but a single Presbyterian minister. Quite a number of them had passed through the scenes of the Revolutionary conflict, and remained, as far as possible, faithful to their parochial duties. Amid civil discord and scenes of strife and battle, they had seen their congregations scattered, and the seeds of military vice and license spring up to a large harvest. But a better day had now dawned. Peace had returned. The congregations were again gathered, and new churches were rapidly organized. The Presbytery had grown to a Synod. The few missionary stations had multiplied to more than a hundred,—some of them flourishing churches. A broad field to the South and West invited to yet more abundant labors, and among the ministers of the Synod there were not a few that were equal, as far as human strength will allow, to the demands of the emergency.

The newly constituted Synod met at Centre Church, November 5, 1788. In the course of the two following years, the Presbytery of South Carolina had increased its number of members by the reception of Robert McCulloch, William C. Davis, John Springer, and Samuel Houston. The names of David Kerr, from the Presbytery of Templepatrick in Ireland, and of William Moore, from Hanover, were added to the list of members of the Orange Presbytery. One of the first measures of the Synod was action on an overture for the publication of Doddridge's "Rise and Progress of Religion" and his ten sermons on Regeneration. Its members felt the necessity of enlisting the press as an ally in their work.

A policy more important in its results was initiated in 1791. At its meeting in October of this year, the Synod took up the subject of Domestic Missions, and resolved to send out four missionaries to act in the destitute regions each side of the Alleghanies. A commission of Synod, to act during its recess, was to give them their directions; and their annual support was fixed at two hundred dollars. The first missionaries appointed for the service were James Templeton and Robert Hall, of South Carolina Presbytery, and Robert Archibald and John Bowman, of the Presbytery of Orange. The two first were to labor, each for four months, in the lower parts of South Carolina and in Georgia; the two last for three months each, in the lower parts of North Carolina. The most important rule which was given them was, "not to tarry longer than three weeks at the same time in the bounds of twenty miles, except peculiar circumstances may appear to make it necessary."

In 1792, the Presbytery of Orange reported three new members added by ordination, William Hodge, James Wallis, and Samuel C. Caldwell. To the first of these, reference has been already made. Wallis was born at Sugar Creek, educated at Liberty Hall, and a student for a time under Dr. Barr, at Winnsborough, S.C. His life was spent in the service of the Providence Church, and in the fierce contest with infidelity which prevailed around him soon after his ordination he bore a conspicuous part. Clear, strong, ardent, by some more dreaded than loved, he was unfaltering and unwearied in his course, and, while carrying his religious principles into his political creed, he asserted the unlimited control of the word of God in all matters pertaining to conscience. Condensing the arguments of Watson, Paley, and Leslie into a small pamphlet, he sent them forth to stay the prevalent tide of error that was desolating the community.

Samuel C. Caldwell was a native of Guilford, a grandson of Rev. Alexander Craighead, already mentioned as a pioneer in this field. At the early age of nineteen, he was licensed by the Presbytery of Orange to preach the gospel, and in 1792 was ordained pastor of Sugar Creek and Hopewell Churches. A revival followed almost immediately upon his settlement, and more than seventy young converts were united with the Church on a single sacramental occasion.

Modest, mild, and gentle in his whole demeanor, none could make a greater mistake than to suppose him pliant in principle. Clear in thought and utterance, plain and direct in speech, and never losing his self-command, he was a man to be respected as well as loved, and the kindness of his nature made his influence in behalf of the truth more decidedly felt. Not less effectively than Wallis did he act as the champion of revelation at a period when his namesake, Joseph (afterward President) Caldwell (1797), said, "Religion is so little in vogue, and in such a state of depression, that * * * every one believes that the first step he ought to take to rise into respectability is to disavow, as often and as publicly as he can, all regard for the leading doctrines of the Scriptures."

In 1793, Rev. Humphrey Hunter and Robert M. Cunningham were reported from the Presbytery of South Carolina as new members, and Lewis Feuilleteau Wilson, James McGready, Joseph Kilpatrick, Alexander Caldwell, and Angus McDermiad from the Presbytery of Orange. Some of these men are worthy of special mention.

The most noted among them all, at an after-period, was the Rev. James McGready, who already for some years had been laboring within the bounds of Orange Presbytery. In the subsequent revival of 1800, in Kentucky, he was the leading spirit. He was of Scotch-Irish descent, a native of Pennsylvania. At an early age his father removed with his family to Guilford county, N.C., within the bounds of the Buffalo congregation. From his earliest years young McGready was remarkable for sedateness and conscientious regard to his religious duties. An uncle of his conceived the idea of securing him an education for the ministry. There was no doubt, in the mind either of uncle or nephew, of the piety of the latter. The young man, exemplary in all his deportment, at the age of seventeen united with the Church. At a somewhat later period, a remark which he overheard from the lips of another, in which a doubt of his piety was expressed, first exasperated him, and then led him to serious self-examination. The result was the abandonment of his old hope. He at length, after a self-exposure which taught him to lay open the hiding-places of the hypocrite and the self-deceived, found peace in Christ.

His literary and theological course was pursued under the direction of Dr. McMillan, and he was licensed by Redstone Presbytery. On his return to Carolina, in 1788, he passed through the scenes of revival which then prevailed in that region, making some stay on his way at Hampden-Sidney College. His own heart was kindled to new zeal, and he resumed his journey prepared to speak with a fervor and boldness that had rarely been equalled in that region or period. At the time when he entered upon his labors, the evils which had resulted from the war or had been fostered by its feuds and license had attained their height. Within the sacred enclosure of the Church a fearful conformity to the world prevailed. Dancing, horse-racing, intemperance, and kindred mischief had become fashionable amusements; while they all found sufficient sanction in the popular infidelity which for some years past had been boldly advancing its claims.

McGready was not a man to regard these things with complacency or in silence.[1] He set himself fearlessly and promptly to stem the tide. His congregations were those of Haw River and Stone Creek; but his preaching was by no means limited to these. He visited the surrounding region, and left on many minds deep and abiding impressions. Solemn, earnest, direct, overwhelming in his appeals, and pungent in his dealing with the conscience, he was a man toward whom none could assume an attitude of indifference. They were either his warm friends or his bitter opponents. Whatever he said or did was with a practical object in view, to alarm the secure or convict the careless. Repeatedly were his visits to the neighboring congregations blessed. Revivals commenced in different places, and the tide of overflowing iniquity was arrested.

But the bold and almost defiant tone of McGready made him many enemies, and, after several years, he was constrained to remove to another field. That field proved to be one beyond the mountains, in Logan county, Kentucky.

Another of the new members of Synod, to whom we have referred as joining it at this period, was Lewis Feuilleteau Wilson. He was born at St. Christopher's, in the West Indies, and was the son of a wealthy planter. He was sent to England to be educated, but at the age of seventeen migrated with his uncle to New Jersey, and soon after his arrival became a member

---

[1] Davidson's Kentucky, p. 132; Foote's North Carolina.

of Princeton College. While in college, a revival occurred, of which he was a subject, and his attention was directed to the ministry (1773). He at first proposed to take orders in the Established Church of England; but, dissatisfied with its condition, he turned his thoughts to the medical profession.

For some time he was settled as a practising physician at Princeton, N.J.; but through the influence of James Hall, of North Carolina, with whom he had become intimately acquainted during his college course, and to whom he was ever after strongly attached, he was induced to remove to Iredell county, N.C., the scene of Mr. Hall's labors. Here his excellent qualifications for the ministry soon attracted attention, and the good people around him became urgent that he should change his profession. His intimate and influential friend Mr. Hall seconded the suggestion. After due deliberation, he concluded to yield to the advice, and was licensed by the Presbytery of Orange in 1791.

His pulpit-efforts were received with marked approbation, and several congregations at the same time sought to secure his services. He ultimately accepted the call of Fourth Creek and Concord Churches, and was installed in 1793. In the remarkable revivals which followed throughout the region, ten years later, he bore a conspicuous part.

Humphrey Hunter was a native of Ireland, but at an early age emigrated with his widowed mother to Mecklenburg county, N.C. He had scarcely passed his boyhood when he listened with patriotic enthusiasm to the proceedings of the Mecklenburg Convention, and in the years that followed, of Revolutionary strife, he bore an active part in the camp and on the field of battle. Some of the incidents of his career are of thrilling interest. He commenced his classical education at "Clio's Nursery," in Rowan county, under the instructions of James Hall. Dr. McWhorter subsequently became his teacher. In 1785, he entered as a student of Mount Zion College, at Winnsborough, in South Carolina, and in 1789 was licensed to preach by the Presbytery of that name. He first labored in connection with the congregations of Hopewell and Amwell, in South Carolina, subsequently at Unity and Goshen, in Lincoln county, and, finally, as pastor of Steel Creek Church. Earnest, though unassuming, and often eloquent, with a talent for refined sarcasm and a mind of much originality, he was loved by the good and feared by the evil, and in devotion to his work was surpassed by few of his contemporaries.

The name of (Dr.) Robert M. Cunningham is more familiar to us in connection with the history of the Presbyterian Church of Kentucky, in which the strength of his manhood was spent. He was a native of Pennsylvania, and a graduate of Dickinson College (1789). In 1792, he was licensed by the South Carolina Presbytery, and in the autumn of that year went to Georgia and organized a church in that part of Green county now called Hancock, and ordained elders to a church called Ebenezer. In this neighborhood he settled, preaching a portion of the time at the church at Bethany, twenty miles distant. Here he labored faithfully as one of the missionaries of the Synod. At the same time, James Hall and Samuel C. Caldwell were employed in North Carolina, John Bowman in North Carolina and Tennessee, and Robert McCulloch in South Carolina.

In 1794, there appear on the list of the Synod's members some names worthy of especial notice. Besides those of William Williamson and Robert Wilson, we find those of Moses Waddel and John Brown. Moses Waddel was born on the banks of the South Yadkin, in

1770. His mind was remarkably precocious. At the age of fourteen he was named by Dr. Hall as the fittest linguist educated at "Clio's Nursery" for a vacant tutorship in Camden Academy. For some years he taught in the neighborhood of Bethany, Ga., and afterward in South Carolina. He was graduated at Hampden-Sidney in 1791, and licensed by Hanover Presbytery in the following year. For the greater part of his life he was engaged in teaching; and under his instructions some of the most eminent civilians and clergymen of the South received their education. Among these may be mentioned John C. Calhoun, William H. Crawford, McDuffie, Legaré, Pettigru, Butler, Longstreet, Carey, &c. In 1819,[1] he was elevated to the post of President of the University of Georgia, which he continued to occupy for ten years. Few men, through their pupils, have wielded a more extensive influence over the country. Yet, while mainly employed as a teacher, he did not withdraw from the pulpit. Almost to the close of his life there was scarcely a Sabbath when he was not engaged in the duties of the ministry. A severe student, a high-minded, honorable Christian man, unremitting in his devotion to the cause of learning and religion, the Presbyterian Church has abundant reason to honor his memory.

John Brown was a native of Ireland, and while yet a child migrated with his father to Chester district, S.C. In the scenes of the Revolutionary conflict he was an active participant, sharing with his countrymen generally their sympathies for his adopted country.

He studied theology under Dr. McCorkle, near Salisbury, N.C., and was licensed to preach in 1788. For ten years he labored in the pastorate of the Waxhaw

---

[1] He was pastor of the Presbyterian Church at Wilmington, S.C., from which he was called to the Presidency of Georgia University.

church of South Carolina, and, while popular in the pulpit, rose to high literary distinction. In 1809, he was elected to a professorship in the University of South Carolina, and two years subsequently he was chosen President of the University of Georgia. Many of the citizens of these and of the adjoining States will long remember him with gratitude.

In 1795, the Synod was still further strengthened by the accession of new members. These were John Robinson, James Bowman, John M. Wilson, and John Carrigan, from the Presbytery of Orange, and Robert B. Walker, William Montgomery, and David Dunlap, from the Presbytery of South Carolina.

Robinson was the father of the Presbyterian Church in Fayetteville. A native of Mecklenburg county, he pursued his studies at Winnsborough, S.C., and was licensed by the Presbytery of Orange in 1793. Benevolent, humble, consistently and devotedly pious, he was firm in purpose, and possessed of an intrepidity that would quail before no danger. Striking anecdotes are told of his fearless courage. For more than forty years, as a missionary, as a teacher, and as pastor alternately at Fayetteville and Poplar Tent, his labors were abundant and largely blessed.

John Makemie Wilson, like Robinson, was a native of Mecklenburg county, and but one year his junior. At the age of twenty-two he was graduated at Hampden-Sidney with the highest honors, and then commenced the study of theology under Dr. James Hall. In 1793, he was licensed by the Presbytery of Orange, and sent out on a missionary tour through the lower counties of the State. For several years he resided and labored in Burke county, until, in 1801, he accepted a call from the congregations of Rocky River and Philadelphia. Many new churches had been gathered by his efforts, and those which before were weak had been strengthened.

His labors as a teacher were popular and successful. In 1812 he opened a classical school, which he continued twelve years. Fifteen young men from Rocky River congregation entered the ministry in about as many years, and twenty-five of his pupils became clergymen.

The Presbytery of Orange had now become so large and extended that a division of it seemed advisable. Accordingly, in 1795, the Presbytery of Concord was set off from it. Of this new body, McCorkle, Hall, McRee, Barr, S. C. Caldwell, Wallis, Kilpatrick, L. F. Wilson, A. Caldwell, J. M. Wilson, and Carrigan, were members. In the following year the Presbytery of South Carolina was also divided. The members living west of the Savannah River, John Newton, John Springer, Robert M. Cunningham, Moses Waddel, and William Montgomery, constituted the new Presbytery of Hopewell. The Presbytery of South Carolina reported, as new members, John Foster, George G. McWhorter, John B. Kennedy, Samuel W. Yongue, and James Gilliland, the last of strong and decided anti-slavery sentiments, and on this account, a few years later, leaving for a Northern field. His name occurs again in connection with the history of the Presbyterian Church in Ohio.[1]

At its meeting in November, 1796, the Synod was largely engaged in the consideration of questions pertaining to slavery. While an order was passed enjoining upon heads of families the religious instruction of slaves and teaching them to read the Bible, it was also decided to be inexpedient "to admit baptized slaves as

---

[1] Settled at Red Oak, Ohio, a few miles from Ripley, and a member of that Presbytery during the last years of his life.

witnesses in ecclesiastical judicatories, where others cannot be had." The case of James Gilliland was also brought to the attention of Synod. The Presbytery of South Carolina, of which he was a member, had enjoined upon him to be silent in the pulpit on the subject of the emancipation of slaves. This injunction he declared to be, in his apprehension, contrary to the counsel of God. The Synod took up his memorial for deliberation, and endorsed the action of the Presbytery, advising him to be content with using his utmost efforts in private to open the way for emancipation. It was of opinion that "to preach publicly against slavery, in present circumstances, and to lay it down as the duty of every one to liberate those who are under their care, is that which would lead to disorder and open the way to great confusion."

During the two following years the Synod was strengthened by the accession of several new members. George Newton and Samuel Davis had been ordained by the South Carolina Presbytery, and the erratic but eloquent William C. Davis had united with that body. The Orange Presbytery had added to its list of members the names of William T. Thompson, William Paisley, John Gillespie, Samuel McAdow, and Robert Tate.

It was under Paisley, the successor of William Hodge in the pastorate of Hawfields, that the great revival of 1802 commenced. For twenty years he was a successful laborer in this field. Tate occupied the sphere once filled by McAden, and under his ministry "Rockfish, Keith, and Hopewell sprang up, and opened the doors of the sanctuary to a large region of country." Black River congregation was long a sharer in his ministerial labors.

The Synod now (1800) embraced seven Presbyteries. In 1797, the Presbytery of Abington, west of the mountains, had been divided, and the new Presbytery of Union formed. The last consisted of but four members. That of Orange numbered fourteen, with four licentiates and eight candidates; that of Concord, fifteen ministers and one candidate. The Presbytery of South Carolina was most numerous, comprising eighteen ministers, three licentiates, and two candidates. In 1799, it was divided by the Synod, and out of it the First and Second Presbyteries of South Carolina were constituted. Broad River was made the dividing line. West of the mountains, in East Tennessee, the new Presbytery of Greenville was erected in 1800. The ministers composing it were George Newton, Samuel Davis, Hezekiah Balch, and John Cossan. Thus the Synod had increased, in the course of fifteen years, from the three original Presbyteries constituted of the members of the Presbytery of Orange, till it numbered seven. From the field occupied a half-century before by a single Presbyterian missionary, the bounds of the Church had been extended till they included the whole or portions of several States. In 1788, the Synod numbered twenty-eight ministers; in 1800, they had increased to nearly seventy,—considerably more than doubling in the course of thirteen years.

During nearly this whole period the missionary work of the Synod had been prosecuted with a good degree of energy. One of its original Presbyteries was beyond the mountains in East Tennessee, and it had already extended its field of effort till two new Presbyteries were formed out of it. Throughout the destitute portions of North and South Carolina, in the northern part of Georgia, and in the Mississippi Valley, missionaries bearing the Synod's commission were to be found. The leading members of the body did not themselves shrink from the self-denying duty of itinerant labor. Their names are repeatedly found on the list of those appointed both to near and to distant fields. From 1794 to 1800, we find James Hall, S. C. Caldwell, John and James H. Bowman, Robert McCulloch, Robert Cunningham, John M. and Robert Wilson, John Robinson, and others, engaged in this arduous service. It was thus that the bounds of the Church were extended, and the reports of the missionaries reacted upon the Synod to encourage them to new effort. In some cases these annual reports were so extended as to cover sixteen folio pages.

CHAPTER XVIII.

NEW YORK, 1789–1800.

At the time of the organization of the first General Assembly, the Presbyterian congregations in the State of New York numbered less than forty: of these, eleven were on Long Island, in connection with the Presbytery of Suffolk; nine were under the care of the Presbytery of Dutchess County; and nineteen under the care of the Presbytery of New York. Besides these, Sampson Occum, a member of Suffolk Presbytery, had mission-stations among the Oneida Indians at New Stockbridge and Brotherton.

Within the bounds of Suffolk Presbytery, the churches of Jamaica, Hempstead, and Smithtown were vacant. The first of these had been without a pastor since the dismission of Matthias Burnet (1785),[1] whose lack of patriotic zeal during the war had saved his church-edifice, but rendered him unacceptable to his parishioners. His successor, in 1789, was George Faitoute, whose min-

---

[1] Afterward settled at Norwalk, Conn.

istry here covered more than a quarter of a century (1815). Smithtown and Hempstead had for many years been supplied by Joshua Hart, but after his connection with them ceased they were long vacant,—Hempstead until the settlement of William P. Kuypers, June 5, 1805.[1] It serves to show the disastrous influence of the war, that when, after its close, measures were taken to re-gather the Hempstead church, ten members only were present at the communion administered by Burnet of Jamaica.[2]

At East Hampton was Dr. Samuel Buell (1746–1798), succeeded by Lyman Beecher in 1799–1810; at Aquabogue and Mattituck (Southold), Benjamin Goldsmith (1764–1810);[3] at Huntington, Nathan Woodhull (1785–1789), succeeded by William Schenk (1793–1817); at Brookhaven (Setauket), Noah Wetmore (1786–1796), succeeded by Zechariah Green; at South Haven (or Firplace), David Rose (1765–1799); at Southampton, Joshua Williams (1784–1789), succeeded by Herman Daggett (1792–1795) and David S. Bogart; at Bridgehampton, Aaron Woolworth (1787–1821); and at Westhampton, Thomas Russell (1787–1789), succeeded by Herman Daggett (1797–1801).

Previous to 1800, several other congregations had been taken under the care of the Presbytery. Joseph Hazard was installed at Southold, June 4, 1797; Daniel Hall at Sag Harbor, where a feeble church had long existed, September 21, 1797; Luther Gleson, successor of Joshua Hart (1774–1787), at Smithtown and Islip, September 21, 1797; Nathan Woodhull, who had been previously settled at Huntington, at Newtown, which was soon after transferred from New York to Suffolk Presbytery, in 1790, and who labored here for twenty years.

---

[1] Prime's Long Island, p. 283.
[2] Ibid. p. 262.
[3] At Mattituck his labors did not begin till 1777.

Of these men, the most memorable, if not the most able, was Samuel Buell. A native of Coventry, Conn., a graduate of Yale College in 1741, a friend of Brainerd, Whitefield, Bellamy, and the elder Edwards, he held preeminent rank among the preachers and theologians of his day. In 1743, he was ordained an evangelist, and in 1746 he accepted a unanimous call to East Hampton, where he remained as pastor for fifty-two years.

The most striking characteristics of his preaching were solemnity and fervor. He had been some time in the ministry when he made this entry in his diary:—"The first time I ever preached to an assembly where tears of affection under the word were not to be seen." Yet, with the zeal of a revivalist, he had neither the rashness of Tennent nor the fanaticism of Davenport. His sermons were rich with scriptural instruction, and in their delivery his hearers were made to feel that every word he uttered came from his inmost soul. A rich blessing attended his labors. In the revival of 1764, ninety-nine were added to his church on a single occasion. Other marked seasons of refreshing were enjoyed by his church, especially in 1785 and 1791. To extreme old age, with natural force scarcely abated, he devoted himself untiringly to his work, regarding with Christian anxiety not only the spiritual welfare of his own congregation, but that of the neighboring churches. On the day that completed his eightieth year, he rode fourteen miles, preached, and returned home in the evening. His closing hours were marked by the triumphant experience of the dying saint.

Of medium stature and somewhat slender frame, he had yet great physical vigor and elasticity. His cheerfulness, vivacity, inexhaustible fund of anecdote, sprightliness, wit, and gentlemanly manners made him a universal favorite. When the English forces occupied Long Island in the Revolutionary War, they left him—though he never concealed his strong Whig sympathies—unmolested, or even cheerfully granted the favors he requested. Yet his wit was combined with boldness in the cause of truth. An English officer told him that he had commanded some of the farmers of his congregation to appear at Southampton, twelve miles distant, on the next day, which was the Sabbath, with their teams. "So I have understood," said the doctor; "but, as commander-in-chief on that day, I have countermanded your orders;" and in consequence the project was relinquished. On one occasion he was invited by the officers to join them on a deer-hunt. He was tardy in making his appearance, and of one of them, evidently impatient, the doctor pleasantly asked, what portion of his majesty's troops he had the honor to command. "A legion of devils direct from hell," was the reply of the ill-humored officer. "Then I presume, sir," returned the doctor, assuming an attitude of profound respect, "I have the honor of addressing Beelzebub, the prince of the devils."[1]

His influence over his people was almost unlimited. They regarded him with the utmost love, respect, and reverence. A young British officer, recently arrived in the neighborhood, rode to his door, and said, "I wish to see Mr. Buell." The doctor soon appeared. "Are you Mr. Buell?" was the question. "My name is Buell, sir." "Then," said the officer, bowing with great respect, "I have seen the god of East Hampton." For many years Dr. Buell was the patriarch of the Presbytery. His remarkable self-control, quick perception, clear judgment, unquestioned piety, and devout prayerfulness gave him great influence. In his large, neat, white wig, with his dignified mien and serene aspect,

---

[1] Sprague, iii. 109; Prime's Long Island, 179.

on which the lines of firmness, decision, and fearless, ness were distinctly traced, he looked—as he was—the saintly Puritan. Such was the man of whom President Stiles once remarked, "This man has done more good than any other man that has ever stood on this continent."

Benjamin Goldsmith was a fit compeer of Dr. Buell. He was a man of sound mind and solid acquirements, plain and unostentatious in his manners, diffident of his powers, but of unfeigned piety. As a theologian he was well read. Edwards, Bellamy, and Hopkins were his favorite authors, and Henry's Commentary was his daily companion. His sermons were unusually well conceived, plain, scriptural, and instructive. In manner he was solemn and affectionate. His influence was that of a peacemaker, and his labors tended to promote the unity and edification of the body of Christ.[1]

Aaron Woolworth, of Bridgehampton, was a son-in-law of Dr. Buell. A native of Longmeadow, Mass., a graduate of Yale College in 1784, and a licentiate of the Eastern Association of New London county, he commenced his labors at Bridgehampton in 1787, while the church, subsequently Presbyterian, was yet Congregational. Of small stature, mild but prepossessing countenance, gentlemanly manners, sound judgment, deep and active piety, he was widely known as a "great, good, and useful man."[2] A more genial spirit was scarcely to be found. Erudite as a theologian, intellectual, discriminating, and argumentative as a preacher, though earnest in delivery and pungent and powerful in application, he was also eminent as a pastor, and by all classes was regarded with confidence, affection, and respect. Ever true to his own

[1] Prime's Long Island, 155. [2] Sprague, iii. 469.

maxim,—*Suaviter in modo, fortiter in re,*—his example enforced his precepts; and the epitaph on his gravestone, though written by the hand of friendship, and eulogistic in its praise, is said, by one whom we must pronounce a competent witness, to contain "not a word of fulsome flattery or empty compliment."[1]

Nathan Woodhull, a native of Setauket, and a graduate of Yale College in 1775, commenced his labors at Huntington in 1785, and at Newtown in 1790. Of fine personal appearance, gentlemanly and winning manners, and great vivacity in conversation, he easily won and retained a popularity fully justified by his purity of character, fidelity in pastoral duty, and power in the pulpit. To the last he possessed the undivided confidence and affection of his people.[2]

Other members of the Presbytery are entitled to honorable mention. William Schenk, though not eminent as a preacher, yet dignified and excellent as a man and successful as a pastor;[3] Herman Daggett, a native of Massachusetts, a firm Presbyterian, of sterling talent, scholarly attainments, spotless character, cheerful yet dignified,—a man who was "never known to laugh," and of whom one of his brethren said, "Brother Daggett is just a fit man to preach to ministers;" Zechariah Green, a soldier of the Revolution, and as such engaged in routing a company of British soldiers from the church in which he afterward preached for thirty-four years,[4]—a man of great natural vivacity, fearless, enterprising, of strong patriotic feeling and great public spirit; Daniel Hall, of Sag Harbor, converted from Universalism, and ever after a remarkably affectionate preacher, a son of consolation rather than a Boanerges; and David Rose, of Southaven, a

[1] Prime, 201.
[2] Riker's Newtown, 233.
[3] Prime, 255.
[4] Prime, 225.

physician as well as a preacher, and stated clerk of the Presbytery.

A noble band of men were these; and their liberal spirit and superiority to prejudice are testified by the circumstance of their adhesion to the Presbyterian Church after it was proposed to frame a Constitution and establish a General Assembly. Surrounded by Congregational churches, several of their own number trained as Congregationalists, with strong New England attachments, they felt little sympathy for any policy which would introduce upon these shores an ecclesiasticism of a rigid Scotch type; and in consequence of this, as well as in view of their comparatively isolated condition, they respectfully asked, in 1787, of the Synod of New York and Philadelphia, a dissolution of their union with that body. The letter presenting the request was kindly answered,[1] and a committee of the Synod was appointed to meet and confer with the Presbytery. This committee consisted of Drs. Rodgers and McWhorter, and Messrs. Roe, John Woodhull, and Davenport. The Presbytery were urged to reconsider their resolution and remain in union with the Synod. The subject was discussed "with the greatest freedom, candor, and amity," at a meeting of Presbytery held at Brookhaven, April 8, 1788; and the result was, that, after a full conference and satisfactory explanations on both sides, the Presbytery agreed to withdraw their request.[2]

The growth of the churches, though not rapid, was steady and cheering. The war had inflicted upon them serious injury. The membership, exposed to the virulence of Tory feeling allied with the forces of the enemy, were largely driven from their homes; and some of the pastors were forced to flee for their lives

---

[1] Minutes of Synod, 532. [2] Ibid. 544.

or to escape imprisonment. At Newtown, public worship was suspended; a few young Tories, by night, sawed off the steeple of the church, and the edifice, after having been used as a prison and guard-house, was demolished to make huts for the soldiers.[1] At Huntington, not only were the orchards cut down, the fences burned, and the scanty crops seized, but the whole town was given up to depredation. The seats in the church-edifice were torn up and the building converted into a military depot.[2] The bell was taken away, and so injured as to be thenceforth useless. The church-edifice at last was pulled down and the timber used for block-houses; barracks were erected in the grave-yard, where graves were levelled and tombstones used for fireplaces and ovens. Long after, there were those who could testify to having seen loaves of bread drawn from these ovens, with the reversed inscriptions of the tombstones of their friends on the lower crust.[3] At Islip, the church-edifice was torn down by the British soldiery, and its materials were carried away for military purposes.[4] Other congregations were less harshly dealt with, but many of them were reduced almost, if not quite, to the verge of extinction by the disastrous influence of the war. In several instances the membership had become so reduced as almost to necessitate a reorganization.

But with the return of peace the pastors resumed their labors. The Presbytery exerted itself to supply, or provide for, its feeble and vacant churches. A more hopeful aspect of spiritual prosperity cheered the hearts of laborers in this field. Here and there revivals were enjoyed, some of them characterized by great power, as at East Hampton in 1785, 1791, and

---

[1] Riker's Newtown, 198.
[2] Prime, 250.
[3] Prime, 251.
[4] Ibid. 263.

1800, at Bridgehampton in 1799, and at Huntington in 1800. The membership of the churches steadily increased. At the close of the war, few of them could number more than thirty members, and several fell short of this. Hempstead had but ten, Bridgehampton had but eleven, male members. Others were almost equally desolate. But before 1800, many of them had wellnigh recovered their former strength, and some of them had enlarged their borders.

The Presbyterian Church in the city of New York felt with peculiar severity the disasters of the war. Its two pastors and a large portion of its members had been forced to flee for safety. The church-edifices had been put to military uses. The Brick Church had been converted into a prison, and as such had been given up to all kinds of abuse and all manner of filth.[1] Of the Wall Street Church, the whole interior had been destroyed during the war, only the walls and roof, or rather the principal timbers of the roof, being left.

On November 26, 1783, the day after the evacuation by the British troops, Dr. Rodgers returned to the city. The numbers of the church had been greatly reduced by death and by removals, and the pecuniary resources of most had been impaired, and of some exhausted. With a considerable debt which had accumulated, and with both houses of worship in ruins, the prospect of the church was not encouraging. But in their houseless condition, and until their buildings could be repaired, the vestry of Trinity Church kindly invited them to occupy alternately St. George's and St. Paul's Churches, and the energy of the pastor accomplished the rest. By personal solicitation he raised the means necessary for repairing the church-edifices, and in the

---

[1] Life of Ethan Allen.

course of six months the Brick Church, which had been least damaged, was ready for occupancy. But so urgent was the demand for pews that it was felt imperative to expedite the repair of the building in Wall Street. At a cost of some ten thousand dollars, both structures were so far restored as to admit of occupancy; and, to secure a supply for both pulpits, James Wilson was called in 1785—after the dismission of Mr. Treat—as collegiate pastor with Dr. Rodgers.

In 1789, John McKnight, of Marsh Creek, Pa., was called to supply the place of Mr. Wilson, whose failing health forced him to seek another climate. In 1796, it became evident that another church was needed to accommodate the increased Presbyterian population of the city, and the Rutgers Street Church was established. The new building was completed in May, 1798, and a call was extended to Philip Milledoler, of the Third Presbyterian Church of Philadelphia, which he was induced to accept, to take charge of the congregation. The three churches, however, continued united until 1809.

Under the harmonious labors of the three collegiate pastors, the churches continued to prosper. The venerable character, sound judgment, eminent ability, and devoted piety of Dr. Rodgers commanded the respect not only of the members of his congregation, but of the whole community. Liberal in sentiment, prompt to respond to the calls of humanity and benevolence, eminently disinterested, animated and fervent in his pulpit ministrations, indefatigable as a pastor, and judicious in all his measures, his standing was such that in all his relations, whether to his own congregation, to the state, or to the Church at large, he exerted a powerful and beneficent influence. As the second moderator of the General Assembly, the voice of his co-presbyters ranked him next to the venerable Witherspoon; and a more sagacious and reliable counsellor in the emergency of the Church, when called to revise and adopt her permanent Constitution, was not to be found.

Dr. Milledoler was a faithful preacher and a highly successful pastor. His labors with Rutgers Street closed in 1813.

Dr. McKnight had been laboring in the ministry, in Virginia and Pennsylvania, for about fourteen years, when he was called to New York. His ministry here continued for twenty years, and was characterized by an earnest and faithful discharge of his duties as preacher and pastor. With much simplicity of character, he was graceful and dignified in manner, free and affable in social intercourse, and pleasant and instructive in conversation. Although by no means a pulpit orator, he was a lucid and logical writer and a pleasant speaker.

North of New York City, quite a number of churches, mostly in Westchester county, which had been hitherto connected with the Synod, declined to retain their connection with the Assembly; and the result was the formation of an Associated Presbytery, which, except that it was based upon the same principles with the Morris County Presbytery and stood in intimate relation with it, occupied an attitude of independence. More than a quarter of a century elapsed before they returned to their former connection. One principle which seems to have characterized their ecclesiastical platform was the unscriptural character of appeals in Church courts.[1]

The Presbytery of Dutchess County had, in 1789, six members and nine churches. Solomon Mead was at Lower Salem, where his pastorate commenced in 1752 and continued for nearly half a century; Wheeler Case was at Charlotte Precinct, better known as Plea-

[1] Minutes of Assembly, 1789.

sant Valley, and served also for some time as supply for Poughkeepsie; Ichabod Lewis, for a time colleague, and at length (1769) successor, of John Smith at "White Plains and Singsing,"[1] was at Philippi; Samuel Mills, who, like Lewis, was a licentiate of the Presbytery, was at Fredericksburg; John Davenport was at Bedford; while Pound Ridge, White Plains, West Fredericksburg, and Providence were vacant, and Blackleach Burritt was without charge.

In 1795, Hudson Presbytery was erected, and embraced under its care most of the churches of Dutchess County Presbytery, and those of New York Presbytery lying on the west side of the Hudson. From this date the churches of Fredericksburg, West Fredericksburg, and Providence, previously under the care of Dutchess County Presbytery, disappear from the rolls. This Presbytery had never greatly enlarged its original strength or bounds. Albany and Cherry Valley had been transferred to the Presbytery of New York. Samuel Sackett, of Hanover, afterwards of Crumpond, in 1768, declined their jurisdiction; and, though he is said to have sought a readmission, his name no longer appears on the list of the Presbytery. William Hanna (of Albany), of whom Bellamy from the first had an unfavorable opinion, and who was one of the early members of the Presbytery, was suspended from the ministry in the same year that Sackett withdrew.[2] The vacancies made by deaths or removals were barely made good by their own licentiates.

The members of New York Presbytery who were transferred to constitute the new Presbytery of Hudson were Nathan Ker, pastor at Goshen (1763–1804); John Close, who labored at New Windsor and Newburgh or vicinity (1773–1796); Jonathan Freeman, at

---

[1] Webster, 653. [2] Minutes of Synod, 378.

Hopewell (1.94–1797), and at Newburgh (1797–1805); Andrew King, at Wallkill (1777–1815); John Minor, at Union;[1] and Methuselah Baldwin, at Pleasant Valley.[2]

The congregation of Florida, long under the pastoral care of Amzi Lewis, and connected with the Morris County (Independent) Associated Presbytery, came under the care of Hudson Presbytery after his removal to North Salem (1787);[3] and on June 13, 1797, John Joline was installed its pastor,[4] in connection with Warwick. In the following year, Josiah Henderson succeeded to the vacancy occasioned by the resignation of Davenport at Bedford some time previous.[5] Meanwhile, Methuselah Baldwin had been dismissed from Pleasant Valley, and shortly after commenced his protracted pastorate at Scotchtown. In the report to the Assembly for 1799, the churches of Pleasant Valley, Franklin, Newburgh, New Windsor, Bethlehem, Fishkill, and Pound Ridge are mentioned as vacant.

The growth of the Church on the line of the Hudson was far from rapid. The attractions of the West drew away the strength of its natural increase to other fields. The labors of the pastors were largely missionary, and their own churches were for the most part feeble. Yet some of the most faithful pastors of the Church, although not specially distinguished as preachers, were to be found in this region:—Ker at Goshen,—a Whig of the Revolution, a volunteer chap-

---

[1] Somewhat uncertain.

[2] The Presbytery of Dutchess, in 1794 reduced to four ministers, report to the Synod the death of a member, April 8, 1793. The name is not given; but it was probably Mr. Wheeler Case; and Mr. Baldwin was his successor. Mr. Davenport, of Bedford, however, died at about the same time.

[3] Sprague, ii. 155. [4] Minutes of Assembly, 1798.

[5] Bolton, i. 22.

lain in the army, a man of well-balanced and cultivated mind, enlarged and liberal views, earnest piety, and extensive influence; Freeman at Hopewell and Deer Park, afterward of Bridgeton, N.J., a large contributor to several religious periodicals, a respectable scholar, a faithful pastor, and an acceptable preacher, possessed of a good share of mental vigor; King, of Wallkill, not specially learned or eloquent, but known in the Presbytery as "the peacemaker," and eminently successful in the work of the ministry; Mead, of Salem, the patriarch of the body, on whose gravestone might well be written, "Blest is the memory of the just;" and, well worthy to rank with them, the devoted and liberal Lewis and the venerable Davenport.

Some portions of the field embraced by the original Albany Presbytery had long been settled when the Presbytery was erected. Albany, Schenectady, Johnstown, Cherry Valley, and a few other places, had an ante-Revolutionary history. Albany, as a trading-post for the Dutch, dates from 1623, and was known successively as Beaverwyk and Wilhelmstadt until 1684, when it received its present name. Schenectady was settled in about 1661,[1] and in 1690, when it was sacked by the French and Indians, had a church and sixty-three houses.

The Dutch were the first occupants of the region. Even after the colony had passed under English jurisdiction, three thousand Palatines are said to have migrated to this country in a body, some of them settling in Schoharie county and parts adjacent.[2] Queen Anne (1702) offered lands to those Germans who were willing to settle on the frontiers; and large numbers yielded to the inducements thus held out. But soon afterward emigration began from Scotland, and, though

---

[1] New York Gazetteer. [2] History of Schoharie County.

checked by the troubles of the French and Revolutionary Wars, yet the names of many of the settlements north of Albany indicate the source from which the predominant part of the population was drawn. Among these we find Galway, New Scotland, and Breadalbane, as well as those which were derived from the names of the leading settlers.

The patent which included the town of Cherry Valley was granted in 1738. The name of the place, from the principal patentee and first settler, was Lindesay's Bush. In 1740, Samuel Dunlop accepted an invitation from the proprietor to procure a body of colonists, of whom he was to take the pastoral charge. A large portion of these, through his influence, were induced to emigrate from Londonderry, New Hampshire, whither they had first removed from the north of Ireland and Scotland.[1] Here, on the borders of civilization, and constantly exposed to Indian invasion, the pastor and his flock retained their mutual relations uninterrupted for more than thirty-five years. In 1763, the church was taken under the care of the newly-erected Presbytery of Dutchess County, of which Mr. Dunlop became a member. Its relations were subsequently transferred to the Presbytery of New York.

The quiet history of this little church was at length interrupted by one of the most fearful tragedies of Indian warfare. On November 11, 1778, the place was attacked by the barbarous foe, thirty or forty persons were murdered, others were retained as hostages or prisoners, and the houses of the settlement were burned. With the close of the war, the scattered inhabitants who survived returned to the scene of desolation. Their aged pastor was no more. The fate of his family involved his own. But, true to their early vows, they

---

1 History of Londonderry, p. 195.

again gathered for the ordinances of worship, and invited, in their feebleness, the compassion of the missionaries sent out by the Synod.[1] In 1788, they applied for supplies to New York Presbytery.

Johnstown, deriving its name from Sir William Johnson, was included, together with Kingsborough, in the original Kingsborough patent, granted June, 1753. In 1761, Sir William removed to the mansion still known as Johnson Hall, yet standing near the village.[2] The tenants upon his lands were numerous, and were strongly attached to him. For their accommodation he erected a church-edifice (1763), in place of which a larger one was built in 1767, in which he allowed ministers of all denominations to officiate. The Episcopalian and the Presbyterian met here upon equal terms, and the policy of the proprietor was simply to gratify the tastes or prejudices of his tenants. The approach of the Revolutionary conflict forced upon Sir William the alternative of loyalty to his native or his adopted country; but, while he hesitated in trembling anxiety, death relieved him of the stern necessity of a decision in either case critical to his fame and fortune. His heir sided with the mother-country; his estates were confiscated, and at the close of the war the State Legislature granted the church-edifice to the Presbyterians, reserving, however, to the Lutherans and Episcopalians their proportionate right to its use in case they applied for it. They were, from an estimate of their numbers, found to be entitled to it but for eight Sabbaths in the year,—four Sabbaths to each denomination: so that the congregation was virtually Presbyterian.[3]

The first minister whose services were secured after

---

1 Campbell's Tryon County. 2 New York Gazetteer.

3 Dr. Hosack's sketch of the church, on the files of the old Albany Presbytery.

the building was thus placed in their possession was James Thompson, a member of the Presbytery of New York. His course, however, was far from exemplary, and when he left, in 1787, quite a number of charges affecting his character were brought against him. At the request of the church, addressed to the Presbytery of New York, asking for a supply, Simon Hosack was sent them, and, October 8, 1790, he was dismissed from the New York to Albany Presbytery, and was settled at Johnstown, December 28.

In other places within the bounds of the Presbytery the settlers were from various quarters, quite a large number from New England. In 1761, a patent for thirty-one thousand five hundred acres of land, including the site of the town of Cambridge, was granted to sixty persons, most of them residents of Hebron, Conn. Of the six owners, one was Jacob Lansing, the founder of Lansingburg.[1] At an early period two congregations were formed, one Presbyterian (Associate, John Dunlop, pastor) and the other Congregational.[2] A portion of the former coalescing with the latter constituted a Presbyterian church, which placed itself under the care of the Albany Presbytery. In 1793, Gershom Williams, who had performed much missionary service in this region, and had repeatedly supplied them, was called as their pastor.

Salem was settled in 1761–6, by a mixed population,—some from New England, but a larger portion from the north of Ireland. In 1764, a patent was obtained for twenty-five thousand acres,—one-half owned by a company from New England, mainly from Pelham, Mass., and within the bounds of the Boston Presbytery; the other half, originally owned by two Government officials, was sold by them to a company of Irish and Scotch

---

[1] New York Gazetteer.

[2] Files of Albany Presbytery.

immigrants, who brought with them their minister, Thomas Clark.[1] The rivalry between the two companies led to rapid improvements. One party wished to call the place White Creek, and the other New Perth. The foreign party, who belonged to the Seceders, were too exclusive to suit the tastes of the New England men;[2] and the result was that the latter withdrew, and, in 1769, organized a church under the care of the Presbytery of New York. Three years later they commenced the erection of a house of worship, which was completed in 1774–5. But during the war (1777–8) it was burned to the ground. In spite of this discouragement, another was erected before the close of the war, and the congregation anxiously sought to procure a pastor. In May, 1787, John Warford, of New Brunswick Presbytery, sent out as a missionary to this region, agreed to supply them, and in July, 1789, he was installed as their pastor.

Ballston was organized as a town in 1788. It derived its name from Eliphalet Ball, who, with a portion of what had long been his pastoral charge at Bedford, Westchester county, removed in that year to this place.[3] Its earliest minister was William Schenk, who had previously been settled at Cape May. Galway was first settled by Scotch emigrants in 1774. Plattsburg was first recognized as a town in 1785, and the first sermon in the place was preached by Benjamin Vaughan in 1787. Stillwater was formed in 1788. Waterford was settled by the Dutch at a somewhat earlier date. Stephentown was formed in 1784; Troy was constituted a town in 1791. Lansingburg, founded about 1770, had a Reformed Dutch church organized in 1784, and in

---

[1] New York Gazetteer. [2] Files of Albany Presbytery.

[3] He had been appointed a missionary to this region as early as 1771.—*Synod's Minutes.* This was the case also with Mr. Schenk.

1792 it was reorganized as Presbyterian, and called Jonas Coe as its pastor.

In 1771, a Presbyterian congregation had already been gathered at Schenectady, and they were engaged in the erection of a church-edifice, for the completion of which they applied, through Alexander Miller, to the Synod[1] for assistance. Mr. Miller, a pupil of Rev. James Findley, a graduate of Princeton in 1764, and a student of theology under Dr. Rodgers, of New York, was licensed in 1767, and ordained in 1770, when he took the pastoral charge of the church. His ministry continued for about eleven years, when the perils of the war and the dispersion of his people led him to remove.[2] For some years the church appears to have been without a pastor or stated supply, and was doubtless greatly reduced in strength. Down to 1790, it was only able, in connection with Currie's Bush[3] and Remsen's Bush, to support a pastor,—John Young, whose stay in the field was a brief one, and who left in 1790–1, and was dismissed to Montreal Presbytery in 1793.[4] In 1796, he was succeeded by Robert Smith,[5] a graduate, probably, of Princeton in 1781; but his laborious zeal enfeebled his health, and in 1801 he accepted a call to Savannah. His successors within a few years were William Clarkson (before 1803, who left before 1809), Alexander Monteith (before 1814, who left before 1819), and Walter Monteith (before 1825).

In 1760, a very pressing application was made by English Presbyterians of Albany to the Synod for supplies,[6] and Hector Alison, recently dismissed from Drawyers, Del., and Abraham Kettletas, already on the point of resigning his charge at Elizabethtown, were directed to visit and supply them. In 1763, at the conclusion

[1] Minutes, p. 419.
[2] Christian Herald, vii. 97.
[3] Now Princetown.
[4] Records of Albany Presbytery.
[5] Dwight's Travels, ii. 489.
[6] Synod's Minutes.

of the French War, a church was organized, and shortly after, William Hanna was installed its pastor by the Presbytery of Dutchess County. He was, however, unfit for the position, and occupied it only for two years. After quite an interval, during which they were visited, at the Synod's appointment, by Dr. Rodgers, of New York, Andrew Bay, "a broad Scotchman," but "a highly talented and eloquent preacher," was called to the pastorate. For nearly twenty years previous, he had been settled in Maryland, and, at the request of the Synod, in 1768 he spent six Sabbaths in the vicinity of Albany and among the Scotch settlements in Washington and Montgomery counties. So acceptable were his services that he was called by the church at Albany, where he remained for five years, when he removed to Newtown, L.I.[1]

Previous to his settlement, a church-edifice had been erected; but a heavy debt had been incurred in its construction, and the congregation was in "a distressed condition." They applied to Synod for assistance (1763); but "sincere pity" was all the aid which the Synod could afford. In 1771, under Mr. Bay's ministry, they repeated their application. From their report of the case, it appeared that the edifice had cost nearly three thousand pounds, for more than two-thirds of which three persons only were responsible, one of whom had already paid out of his own pocket over one thousand pounds. The Synod "cheerfully and cordially" recommended them "to the assistance of all well-disposed charitable persons within their bounds." The recommendation undoubtedly answered its purpose; for we hear of no further application for aid.

The effect of the Revolutionary War, however, was to disorganize the church. For several years there was

---

[1] Riker's Newtown.

no regular religious service or administration of ordinances. In 1785, the pastoral labors of John McDonald were secured, and in the following year the church was reorganized.[1] Four elders and two deacons were appointed, and in 1787, when the first season of communion was held, one hundred and sixteen members were admitted to the church.

In 1796, a new church-edifice was erected. It was opened (Nov. 2) by a sermon from John Blair Smith, then President of Union College. In 1798, Eliphalet Nott was installed pastor. The sermon was by Dr. Smith; and several of the neighboring Dutch ministers joined in the imposition of hands.

Up to the time of the erection of Albany Presbytery, the Synod made repeated and urgent efforts to extend to this field the benefit of missionary labor, and quite a number of the early pastors were those who had gone forth as missionaries. This was the case, among others, with Schenk of Ballston, Warford of Salem, Condict of Stillwater, Williams of Cambridge, and Thompson of Hudson, the last of whom, with John Burton, had been received as a licentiate from Scotland, and with whom in 1787 he was sent into this field.[2]

The Presbytery of Albany was erected by the Synod of New York and New Jersey in 1790. Most of its churches were transferred to it from the Presbytery of New York. Of this number were Albany, Cherry Valley, Johnstown, New Scotland, Harpersfield, Ballston, East Ballston, Cambridge, Kingsbury, Schenectady, Currie's Bush, and Remsen's Bush. In 1788, all but three of these were vacant. William Schenk was at Ballston, John Warford at Salem, and John McDonald at Albany. In the course of the following year, Sampson Occum was received from Suffolk Presbytery, as

[1] Munsell's Albany.

[2] Synod's Minutes for the year.

his mission among the Oneida Indians fell more properly within the bounds of Albany Presbytery, John Lindsley commenced his labors—although not installed—at Harpersfield, and John Young entered upon his ministry at Schenectady in conjunction with Currie's Bush.

At Johnstown, Simon Hosack commenced his extended pastorate December 8, 1790. At East Ballston, William B. Ripley began to preach in March, 1791, and was installed January 10, 1792, his ministry closing September 12, 1797. At Stillwater, which he had previously visited as a missionary, and where he had organized a church, Aaron Condict was settled, after the delay of a year, January 15, 1793. At Charlton, Samuel Sturges was installed June 26 of the same year. At Cambridge, Gershom Williams, who afterward removed to New Jersey, was settled June 25, 1794. At Hudson, where a church had been organized but a few years previous, John Thompson, who had been sent out by the Synod as a missionary, commenced his brief pastorate July 23, 1794. At New Scotland, Benjamin Judd began his labors in September, 1795. At Plattsburg, the ministry of Frederick Halsey dates from February 29, 1796.

The establishment of the Presbytery was hailed with joy by the numerous feeble congregations in the process of formation within its bounds. It was flooded with applications for assistance. In September, 1791, Granville and Westfield asked for supplies. In February, 1793, the Congregational and Presbyterian congregations of Cambridge became united, and joined in a similar request, the result of which was the settlement of Mr. Williams. Stephentown, in a feeble condition likewise, made the same application. From Glen's Purchase, Royal Grant, and Spruce Creek a petition (Feb. 1793) was presented, asking to be taken under the care of Presbytery and to be furnished with supplies. In

1795, the Presbyterian congregation of Waterford was received, in spite of the earnest remonstrance of members of the Dutch Church, and Abraham Barfield, an English Dissenter, was allowed to labor with them as stated supply. In March, 1795, Cooperstown was received under the care of Presbytery. In the following year Schodack applied for supplies of preaching. Providence likewise presented the same request.

Meanwhile (1795), Thompson had been dismissed from Hudson, and the church was served by stated supplies for quite a period. McDonald of Albany (1795) had been deposed from the ministry, and Bogart, who had been called in his place, had declined, after a short period of service (1797). Young had left Schenectady (1791), and the church, supplied for a time by John Blair Smith, President of Union College, had called Robert Smith, of New Castle Presbytery. Judd had been dismissed from New Scotland (Sept. 1796), and Lindsley, who had left Harpersfield for Galway, where he remained till September 13, 1796, had been called to Kingsborough, where he was installed in April, 1797. At the same time, Sturges was dismissed from Charlton, to be succeeded, two or three years later, by Joseph Sweetman. Eliphalet Nott, received (Aug. 1797) as a licentiate from the New London County Association, had declined (Aug. 1798) a call to Cherry Valley, and accepted one from Albany, where he was ordained October 3, 1798. At the same date, Galway and Breadalbane gave a call to William Scott, and on November 13, 1798, John Arnold, from Carlisle Presbytery, was settled at New Scotland. In February, 1798, John Blair Smith was dismissed to accept the charge of the Third Presbyterian Church in Philadelphia, and Jonathan Edwards, his successor in the Presidency of Union College, was received in August, 1799. In February, 1800, Joseph Sweetman was called at the same time to

Charlton and Ballston, the former of which he chose to accept (Sept. 17). At the same time Lindsley was dismissed from Kingsborough. In August, Aaron J. Booge was called to Stephentown, and was installed November 11. In November, Robert Smith left Schenectady for his health, and his place was temporarily supplied by President Edwards.

In 1800, the Presbytery consisted of thirteen members, ten of whom had charges, besides which they had under their care fourteen vacancies, eight of which were able to support a pastor. The report of the following year showed that four members had been added to the Presbytery, making its number eleven pastors, and six without charge.

The early members of Albany Presbytery were largely from New York and New Brunswick Presbyteries, although some were from Scotland. To the latter class belonged McDonald, Thompson, and two or three others, none of whom were of any permanent value to the Presbytery. The sad fall of McDonald—deposed in 1795—did not alienate from him the sympathies of many of his countrymen, who long insisted on his restoration, and finally united to form another church, of which he became pastor. Of the other members of the Presbytery, there are several whose names are worthy of honor:—Coe, of Troy, a Christian gentleman, genial, judicious, and faithful as a man and devoted as a pastor; Hosack, whose long and successful ministry at Johnstown, where one of the strongest churches of the Presbytery was gathered, testifies to his fidelity and efficiency; Condict, of Stillwater, whose melancholy humors and dark forebodings could not hide his worth or repress his kindness and hospitality, and who was eminent for wisdom and humility; Schenk, of Ballston, not an orator, but a kind and faithful pastor, and who, like Warford, of Salem, had a heart enlisted in the cause of Christian philanthropy and missionary enterprise; Ripley, of East Ballston, a man of cool judgment and good sense, and who deliberately preferred his missionary task to more inviting fields; and to these we need only add the names of John Blair Smith, President Edwards, and Eliphalet Nott, to form a group worthy to hold their place as pioneers at the gateway of the young and growing West.

Union College, at Schenectady, was established in 1795. The plan of such an institution had been agitated as early as 1779. The inhabitants of the northern counties of the State were dissatisfied with the remote location, if not the management, of Columbia College, and demanded an institution of their own to meet their local wants. In the petition to the Assembly of 1779, Schenectady was designated as the site of the institution.

A favorable report upon the petition was made to the Assembly, and the petitioners were allowed to bring in a bill to answer their design at the next session; but the emergencies of the war diverted attention from a project which could flourish only in the atmosphere of peace. Several years passed by, and the only progress which had been made in 1791—when a petition for liberty to ask incorporation for a college was laid before the State Legislature—was the establishment of an academy on the site of the future college. The prayer of the petition was not granted, and it was not till four years later that a charter could be obtained.

The institution derived its name from the union of different religious denominations in its establishment. The Presbyterians and the Reformed Dutch were most active in their co-operation. John Blair Smith, a son of Robert Smith, of Pequa, was chosen its first President. For twelve years he had had charge of Hampden-Sidney College, in Virginia, and for four years had been pastor of the Pine Street Church in Philadelphia He was a decided Presbyterian, but of a liberal spirit and well fitted for the post which he was now called to occupy. He presided over the infant institution for three years with great credit and success; and to his influence in this prominent position the future ecclesiastical type of the new settlements in Western New York was largely due.

Soon after his inauguration as President, in the summer of 1795, a young clergyman, sent out by the Connecticut Society on a mission to the "Settlements," passed through Schenectady, and was invited by President Smith to spend the night at his house. Inquiring of the young man his views, objects, and proposed theatre of action, he found that he had been trained in the Congregational Church, that his sympathies were with it, and that his opinions were in favor of its form of church government. Without discussing at large the question of denominational forms, President Smith directed the attention of his visitor to the fact that the orthodox churches of New England held "substantially the same faith as the Presbyterian," and, "this being the case," he asked, "is it wise, is it Christian, to divide the sparse population holding the same faith, already scattered, and hereafter to be scattered, over this vast new territory, into two distinct ecclesiastical organizations, and thus prevent each from enjoying those means of grace which both might much sooner enjoy but for such division? Would it not be better for the entire Church that these two divisions should make mutual concessions, and thus effect a common organization on an accommodation plan, with a view to meet the condition of communities so situated?"[1]

The arguments used by President Smith were deemed

[1] Sprague's Annals, iii. 403.

conclusive by the young clergyman. They gave a new direction to his efforts, and led, through the influence of other Congregationalists whom he induced to co-operate, to the formation of numerous Presbyterian churches on the accommodation plan, and, finally, to the *Plan of Union.*

This originated, therefore, with the ex-President of Hampden-Sidney College, and was carried into effect largely through the influence of the young clergyman who had passed the night with him on his journey to his missionary field. That clergyman was Eliphalet Nott, who, through the influence of President Smith, was induced to accept the pastorate of the Presbyterian church of Albany in 1798, and in 1804 succeeded[1] to the post which the latter had occupied as President of Union College.

Thus, six years before the Connecticut General Association endorsed the "Plan of Union," it had been substantially sketched out and adopted by two men, one an unquestioned Presbyterian and the other a decided Congregationalist, each a fair representative of his own denomination; and, when it was introduced to the attention of the General Assembly in 1801, it was on the motion of Dr. Edwards, the then President of Union College, who was chairman of the committee to which the subject was committed.

And it was indeed time that some method should be devised for meeting an emergency that had never occurred before, of harmonizing the action and effort of two denominations differing only in their form of government and occupying the same field. The tide of emigration had begun already to set strongly toward the West. By the treaty of 1794 between the United

---

[1] Dr. Jonathan Edwards was the immediate successor of Dr. Smith, in 1799. Edwards died in 1801.

States and the Six Nations, the danger of depredations to settlers was removed, and a large and fertile region was opened to the surplus population of the Atlantic States. The Genesee Valley became an El Dorado to the youthful enterprise of the East, and the fame of its wheat-fields was scarcely less exciting than, at a later period, the report of California gold. The want of roads was no sufficient check to this newly awakened energy of purpose, refusing any longer to be pent up within the bounds of the older States. The inhabitants of Albany regarded the tide of emigration which passed through their city—the principal avenue to the Western country—in the winter of 1795, as a strange phenomenon. The old Dutch citizens were not a little surprised and astonished to see the loaded sleighs and ox-sleds go by. Twelve hundred of the former, loaded with men, women, children, and furniture, passed through the city within three days, and on the 28th of February five hundred were counted, on their way, between sunrise and sunset.[1]

At this gateway of the West, the young man who had become a convert to the views of President Smith was stationed at this critical period. The Connecticut pastors on their missionary tours would not pass without stopping on their way to consult and advise with their pioneer brother, who had traversed the region before them, and whose large heart and sound judgment were ever at their service. With nothing of ecclesiastical bigotry or prejudice to blind their views, with hearts all aglow with sympathy for the destitution which they had witnessed, with deep anxiety for the religious welfare of a young empire springing up in the wilderness, it was only natural that they should feel themselves, and endeavor to impress on others, the

---

[1] Munsell's Annals of Albany.

necessity of united effort to plant gospel institutions all over a broad waste, soon to be alive with men. The General Association of Connecticut, standing already on the semi-Presbyterian Saybrook platform, and with its leading members, like Dwight, Backus, and Strong, decidedly in favor of a nearer approximation to the Presbyterian system, felt that it was no recreancy to principle, and scarcely a compromise of feeling, to cheer on the efforts of Presbyterians in building up churches of their order in the new settlements. Hence, when the idea of a plan of union was once suggested to them, it not only met with no opposition, but was warmly favored. The Association readily accepted, therefore a plan, first suggested by a leading Presbyterian, then seconded by the experience of pastors and missionaries; and it was finally adopted, by both parties, without a dissenting voice. It is a noble monument of the liberal feeling both of the Congregationalists and the Presbyterians of that period; and the Exscinding Assembly of 1837 paid it no unmerited tribute when they admitted that it was "projected and brought into operation by some of the wisest and best men the Presbyterian Church has ever known."

In 1801, a committee was appointed by the General Association of Connecticut to confer with a committee to be appointed by the General Assembly on the plan of union to be adopted. The Committee of the Association consisted of the Rev. Messrs. John Smalley, Levi Hart, and Samuel Blatchford; that of the Assembly, of the Rev. Drs. Edwards, McKnight, and Woodhull, and Rev. Messrs. Hutton and Blatchford, the last of whom, as delegate from the Association, was also a member of the Assembly.

The result of their conference was the adoption of the Plan of Union,—a plan which for more than the lifetime of a generation secured the friendly and harmonious co-operation of two Christian denominations in a work whose magnitude and beneficence future centuries will record.

The rapid settlement and growth of Central and Western New York is one of the marvels of the present century. Before the year 1784,[1] when Hugh White, the father of the New England settlements in that region, removed his family from Middletown and planted himself in Whitesborough, there was not a single spot cultivated by civilized man between the German Flats and Lake Erie, except the solitary Stedman farm, near Niagara Falls; yet in 1810 this region contained 280,319 inhabitants.

At the commencement, therefore, of the present century, it began to attract the special attention both of the General Association of Connecticut and of the General Assembly. It was an opportune field for the exertions of the missionary societies that had been recently organized in New York and New England, and had no unimportant influence upon their formation. The Northern Missionary Society of New York, located in the neighborhood of Albany and embracing mainly the Dutch and Presbyterian churches in that region, was in the midst of a mission-field where all its energies were required. But still beyond, the destitution was far more extreme and urgent. The Military Tract, embracing the counties of Onondaga, Cayuga, Seneca, and Cortland, with portions of Tompkins, Oswego, and Wayne, was surveyed in 1789, and was now rapidly filling up with immigrants.

The Indian title to the Phelps and Gorham Purchase (still farther west) was extinguished in 1788. Geneva, Pittsford, and Richmond were settled before the close of 1790; yet in that year what was then the county of

[1] Dwight's Travels, iii. 530.

Ontario, including the whole Genesee country, contained only one thousand and eighty-one inhabitants. From this period, however, the growth of Western New York was unprecedently rapid: immigrants came pouring into it from all quarters. Some were from Pennsylvania, some from the Old World, but a very large proportion were from New England. By 1800, the population had increased to nearly sixty thousand, and in ten years more it had multiplied fourfold.[1]

The character of this immigration was one to excite alarm and apprehension. The first settlements were formed at the period when French infidelity had attained the largest influence which it ever possessed in this country. Even where pious families were to be found, they were as sheep without a shepherd, and were disheartened and discouraged by the prevalent irreligion around them. Some who had been members of churches in New England seemed to have left their religion behind them. In many places there was no one to be found to take measures for the establishment of public religious worship. "The habits of the people were loose and irreligious. The Sabbath was made a day of business, visiting, or pastime. Drinking and carousing were frequent concomitants." In other places, however, there were those to be found who were still mindful of the professions or the privileges of earlier days, and who longed for the enjoyment of the means of grace. Gathering their neighbors around them, they would endeavor to observe in their little assemblies the forms of public worship, and seek to edify one another in prayer, exhortation, and the reading of the Scriptures.

For some years after the settlement of the country commenced, not a minister of the gospel, Presbyterian

---

[1] See Hotchkin's Churches of Western New York.

or Congregational, resided within its bounds. There was not even an organized church. Nearly all the missionary labor that had been performed in the region had been performed by ministers appointed for short periods by the General Assembly. Yet, limited as the time of their efforts was—in their absence from their own charges—the reports of their labors and successes were pronounced by the Assembly of 1799 to be "favorable," and to "afford rational ground to believe that the appropriations of the voluntary contributions of our Christian brethren for the benevolent purpose of extending the means of religious instruction in those parts of our country will prove satisfactory to them, and encourage them to further assistances in that way."

Of the ministers sent out by the Assembly, Rev. Ira Condict organized a church in Palmyra in 1793; Rev. Benjamin Judd, one at Windsor, at nearly the same time; and Rev. Daniel Thatcher, in 1795, the three churches of Elmira, Lima, and Geneseo. Almost at the same time, Congregational churches were organized by missionaries from Connecticut,—one by Rev. Mr. Campbell at Sherburne, and another by Rev. Zadoc Hunn at East Bloomfield. Between 1796 and 1800, several other small churches had been organized. Rev. Reuben Parmele was installed at Victor in 1799; Rev. Timothy Field at Canandaigua in 1800; and Rev. Mr. Grover at Bristol in the same year.

But in 1800 more vigorous measures were taken by the General Assembly for the visitation and supply of this whole region. In 1798, Rev. Mr. Logan had traversed the country, and preached with so much acceptance that the settlers urgently requested his return. The request was approved by the Assembly, and additional laborers were appointed for different periods in this inviting field.

These measures were adopted in accordance with the established mission-policy of the Church, but they were prosecuted with enlarged vigor in consequence of the intelligence from Western New York. A letter of the late Dr. Williston, of Durham, N.Y., then a young missionary in the service of the Connecticut Missionary Society, was published in the New York "Missionary Magazine" early in 1800, and spread before the churches the cheering success of the previous year. That year, for a long period, was destined to be remembered throughout the region as the year of the *Great Revival.* One of the most prominent of the ministers who were connected with it was the late Jedediah Bushnell, of Cornwall, Vt. Six years before, while engaged in his tanning-mill at Saybrook, Conn., a stranger stepped in to inquire of him the way. Having obtained his information, he lingered long enough to ask his informant whether he was in the "way" of salvation. A few serious words were dropped, which led to the conviction and conversion of Mr. Bushnell. He immediately gave up his business, entered Williams College, was graduated in 1797, and in the following year was invited to Canandaigua to supply the pulpit of the infant church in that place. He went; but, not content with supplying his own people, he traversed the surrounding region as a missionary. Earnest, affectionate, discreet, and devoted entirely to his work, he won the affection and respect of all. A powerful revival commenced. Mr. Williston, who had completed his commission for the Military Tract, joined his friend Bushnell. On every side the work spread. Places could not be procured large enough to accommodate the crowds who pressed to hear the word. "It seemed as if there was scarcely anybody at home who could possibly get to meeting."

Intelligence of this state of things was given in Williston's letter. He wrote, moreover, "There is a great call for preachers in this county and in the other western counties of this State. There are scarcely any settled ministers in all this extensive, flourishing, and growing country." Rev. Walter King, who performed a missionary tour in the counties of Chenango and Tioga (1798), wrote, "While I have been a preacher, never did I enjoy a season, in so short a time, of so much Christian satisfaction or so high a probability of being really useful to the souls of men." In the winter of 1798 the work began. Through the spring and summer following it was characterized by a "wonderful display of divine power and grace in the conversion of sinners." Throughout the region "individuals appeared awakened in most places." Several churches were soon organized, although the missionaries said, "We are afraid to establish churches while there are no shepherds within call to feed and lead them."

The revival commenced at Palmyra; it soon extended to Bristol, Bloomfield, Canandaigua, Richmond, and Lima, and to other places in a less marked manner. Quite a number of churches were formed, and in 1800 the Association of Ontario was organized,—at first on strictly Congregational principles, but three years later its Constitution was so revised and altered as to give it jurisdiction over the ministers and churches to such an extent as to exclude them from the connection if found erroneous in doctrine or practice.

Here was already, almost contemporaneous with the adoption of the Plan of Union, a voluntary approximation by the Congregational body to Presbyterian principles. The circumstances in which ministers and churches in the new settlements found themselves, demanded a stricter discipline than was necessary in the towns and parishes of New England. There was thus on the part of Congregationalists themselves a disposition not to fall back on any favorite form of government, but to select that which was best adapted to the emergencies of the case.

At the close of the eighteenth century the institutions of the gospel had been extensively planted in Western New York; and it would be difficult to say whether the preponderating influence was on the side of Presbyterians or Congregationalists. It was a question which no one was disposed to raise, and the means of its solution are not readily to be obtained. The strength of the two denominations west of the Hudson seems to have been nearly equal, in case the Presbyterian leanings of the bodies Congregational in name be not taken into account. Nearly or quite twenty churches had been organized, although with scarcely an exception they were all in a feeble state. By 1793 the churches of Sherburne, Windsor, and Cazenovia had been gathered. In the course of the two or three years that followed, those of Auburn, East Palmyra, and Elmira were added to the list. Before or by 1800, the number was increased by those of Oxford, Bainbridge, Springport, Scipio First, Milan, Geneva, Ovid, Lisle, Naples, and probably some few others.

Thus the foundation was laid for the operations of subsequent years, and already the policy which was declared in the Plan of Union was initiated, and, with or without ecclesiastical legislation, the spirit of the leading ministers and missionaries was such as was sure to promote the results which the Plan was intended to secure.

CHAPTER XIX.

EARLY HISTORY OF THE PRESBYTERIAN CHURCH IN KENTUCKY, 1775-1800.

SOME estimate may be formed of the urgent claims of the great mission-field west of the Alleghanies and south of the Ohio, from the fact that the aggregate population of Kentucky and Tennessee had increased from little more than one hundred thousand in 1790 to three hundred and twenty-five thousand in 1800. A constant stream of immigration was pouring into it from the older settlements, at the rate of something like an average of twenty thousand a year. This was during a period when New England had scarcely begun to colonize west of the Hudson, and when Central and Western New York were in process of being surveyed. The pioneers were bold and hardy men, ready to brave the hardships of the wilderness and contend with the beasts of the forest or the scarcely less merciless Indian tribes. Their lives were full of strange vicissitude and romantic incident. Constant hazard and peril seemed to become at length the necessary stimulant to healthful energy.

Among such a people, the recluse scholar, with his logical, polished discourse read from the manuscript, was not needed. Erudition and refinement were not in demand. The hardy backwoodsman required a new type of preacher,—one who could shoulder axe or musket with his congregation, preach in shirt-sleeves, and take the stump for a pulpit. Men of this stamp could not be manufactured to order in colleges. They must of necessity be trained up on the field.

They were for the most part thus trained,—many of them after their arrival in the region; but it was wise and necessary that they should not despise learning. A happy influence was exerted over them by the pioneer missionary who laid the foundations of the Presbyterian Church in this part of the country. Rev. David Rice, better known as "Father Rice," at the mature age of fifty, crossed the mountains and found a home in Mercer county, Ky., as early as October, 1783. He was a man of education and ability and of most devoted zeal. He had pursued his classical studies in early life under the direction of the celebrated James Waddel, had been graduated at Princeton College under the Presidency of Samuel Davies, had studied theology with Rev. James Todd, been licensed by the Presbytery of Hanover, had labored as a missionary in South Virginia and North Carolina, and settled as pastor of the church at the Peaks of Otter. During the Revolutionary conflict he occupied a new and frontier settlement, and in that mountainous region and among a heterogeneous population acquired that experience which fitted him so well for his future field. Tall and slender in person, quiet in his movements, but with an alertness that continued to extreme age, he entered upon his work beyond the mountains with the energy and composure of one who knew the greatness of the task he had undertaken. Sagacious to discern the signs of the times, and quick to detect the character and dangers of the society around him, he was fully competent to expose the errors which were flooding the land, and lay solid the gospel foundations that should stay the rushing tide. His "Essay on Baptism" did good service in that Western region years before the opening of the present century, and when a printing-press to publish it could not be found west of the mountains. Of the cause of freedom he was a bold and consistent champion. "Slavery Inconsistent with Justice and Policy" was the title of a pamphlet issued by him in 1792. The views presented in it were forcibly urged by him in the convention that formed the State Constitution. Nor did the cause of education find in him a lukewarm friend. While a resident of Virginia, he had officially labored to promote the cause of liberal learning. He took an active part in the establishment of Hampden-Sidney College, and had an important agency in procuring its two first Presidents, Samuel Stanhope Smith and Robert Blair Smith. Kentucky needed such a man; and when the trustees of Transylvania University met, shortly after his arrival in that region, at Crow's Station, he was President of the Board, and was ever its steadfast friend. He felt that the School and the Church had a common interest, and that Kentucky must educate her own sons. To the ripe age of eighty-three he was spared to see new laborers gather around him, and the institutions he had planted rise to the promise of a blessed harvest.

Nor was he left long alone in this new field. In 1784, Rev. Adam Rankin, who settled at Lexington, and Rev. James Crawford,[1] who located at Walnut Hill, came to his support. Two years later, Andrew McClure, who took the first charge of the Salem and Paris congregations, and Thomas B. Craighead, of North Carolina, whose name is associated with that of the Shiloh Church, and of whom the Hon. John Breckinridge said that his discourses made a more lasting

---

1 James Crawford was a graduate of Princeton in 1777. Two years later he was licensed by the Presbytery of Hanover, and in 1784 removed to Kentucky, settling at Walnut Hill, where he gathered a flourishing church. His death occurred in 1803.

impression on him than those of any other man, joined the feeble band. These five ministers, with Rev. Zerah Templin, recently ordained an evangelist, constituted the first Presbytery, October 17, 1786. Twelve congregations were already at least partially organized.

In 1790, the first missionaries sent out by the Synod of Virginia, and in fact by the Presbyterian Church after the formation of the General Assembly, entered this field. These were Robert Marshall and the celebrated Carey H. Allen. The first was a licentiate of Redstone Presbytery. He was a native of Ireland, but in his twelfth year (1772) emigrated with his father's family to Western Pennsylvania. He was a wild youth, and at the age of sixteen enlisted as a private in the army, against the remonstrance of his mother. Strangely enough, his course now was more sober and moral than before. He abstained from all the vices of camp-life, and, when not on duty, retired to his tent and devoted himself to the study of arithmetic and mathematics. He was in six general engagements, one of which was the hard-fought battle of Monmouth. Here his locks were grazed by a bullet, and he narrowly escaped with his life. After the war he joined the Seceders, but was still a stranger to vital religion. It was under a searching discourse of Dr. McMillan that he was first brought to feel his guilt as a sinner. Now he was humbled in the dust: his self-possession deserted him, and he fell into a state of the deepest anguish. At length hope dawned upon him, and, with new views of duty, he devoted himself to the work of the ministry.

He pursued his academical studies at Liberty Hall. His theological course was completed under Dr. McMillan. For some months he labored as a missionary in Virginia, and at the close of 1790 set out under the commission of the Virginia Synod for Kentucky.

He was accompanied by Carey H. Allen. Allen was the son of a Virginia planter of Cumberland county. He was educated at Hampden-Sidney, and was one of the early converts of the revival of 1787. His disposition was gay and volatile; and such, to a great extent, it remained after his conversion. But his spirit was ever cheerful and his good nature imperturbable. "He was a mirthful, fun-loving, pleasant companion, and a great wit and satirist." Such was his humorous demeanor, and so odd and ludicrous his frequent conversation, that the Presbytery for some time hesitated to license him. But his strange sallies and eccentricities were overruled by his controlling devotion of purpose, and made, not unfrequently, the means of arresting the attention or exciting the religious interest of others.

The journey of the two young men to Kentucky was by no means one that could be considered safe or pleasant. There were but two routes to the Western settlements, and each was beset with great hazard and danger. One was by the Ohio, taking a boat at Redstone Old Fort,[1] and the other by a forced passage, with greater risk of Indian assault, through the wilderness. The last was tolerably safe for large bands of emigrants, but more dangerous for individuals. Marshall and Allen chose the river-route. While waiting for the company to be made up, they employed themselves in preaching among the neighboring congregations. In spite of the disaffection produced in some quarters by their use of Watts's Psalms and Hymns, a favorable impression was made, and a revival commenced. It was fairly in progress when they embarked, and continued after their departure.

The voyage was favorable, and they landed safely in Kentucky. They immediately entered upon their

[1] Brownsville, on the Monongahela.

missionary work. Marshall collected a congregation who chose him for their pastor, and he was soon settled over Bethel and Blue Spring Churches. Allen itinerated for six months with marked popularity and success. He preached almost daily, and frequently at night. Crowds followed him, many of them attracted by more than a mere idle curiosity. Seed was sown for the harvest of after-years.

In the spring of 1791, Allen returned to Virginia. A small party accompanied him. Armed with a rifle, and girded with a wampum shot-pouch which had been taken from a hostile Indian and given to him as a present, he looked more like a backwoods hunter than a clergyman. The journey was safely made, and Allen made his report to the commission of Synod. It was so interesting and encouraging that he was directed to return and continue his labors as an itinerant missionary.

William Calhoon, recently licensed by Hanover Presbytery, accompanied him as an associate. In some respects he was the reverse of Allen, but not less devoted. Sedate, unaffected, sincere, and conscientious from his very childhood, which had been spent in a pious home, he entered Hampden-Sidney at an early age, and was one of the converts of the revival of 1787. At the request of William Hill, a fellow-student, he brought back from his father's house the book—"Alleine's Alarm"—the perusal of which was the first occasion of serious inquiry among the students. Along with Allen, Blythe, Hill, and Read, he was associated in the meetings and efforts by which the revival was promoted and extended. On the 12th of May, 1792, he was licensed to preach, and a few months afterward set out with Allen on his trip to Kentucky. He was at this time only twenty years of age.

Both entered zealously upon their work. Both

travelled extensively among the infant and scattered settlements of Kentucky. Their several characters were strongly in contrast in some respects, but each was wellnigh unrivalled in his own sphere. Calhoon was more grave, but equally self-possessed. Calm, resolute, clear in thought and purpose, with a readiness and promptness of utterance that put him always at his ease, he was prepared for any occasion. Pleasing anecdotes are narrated of his perfect self-possession and quickness of retort. He wrote few sermons; but in his extempore efforts his thoughts were carefully meditated and arranged. His work, like that of his friend Allen, was faithfully and energetically accomplished. Dividing their labors between Kentucky and Virginia, they accomplished, each in his sphere, a vast amount of labor.

Meanwhile, feeble as were the beginnings of the Presbyterian Church in Kentucky, it was still further weakened by schism and secession. A large number of the Presbyterians who had settled in the region clung with a bigoted affection to the exclusive use of the old version of the Psalms. The Synod of New York and Philadelphia in 1787 allowed "that Dr. Watts's imitation of David's Psalms, as revised by the Rev. Mr. Barlow, be sung in the churches and families under their care;" while at the same time they disclaimed all disapproval of Rouse's version, leaving it to each congregation to judge and select for themselves.

This was, in the view of many, the toleration and *quasi*-encouragement of a dangerous innovation. But, in spite of opposition, it was rapidly gaining ground. The young preachers especially were decidedly in favor of Watts, and in some cases fanned a flame of prejudice against themselves by advocating the innovation. Old Mr. Finley was so apprehensive of the effects upon his own congregation of the use of Watts by Allen and Marshall during their brief stay in the neighborhood of Redstone fort, that he begged them to desist. "Never fear," said Allen: "God will bring order out of it." And he did. The young people and the great mass of the congregation had no special attachment to Rouse's version, and crowded to hear the young preachers. The powerful revival referred to above soon commenced.

But the most disastrous results of the change initiated were felt in Kentucky. Quite a large number of the Presbyterian settlers were from Scotland and strongly attached to the Associate Synod. They needed only a champion of Rouse, to give him a warm support.

This champion soon appeared; but his own character injured the cause he advocated, and gave occasion for sad divisions. Adam Rankin, born in Western Pennsylvania, was on his mother's side descended from one of the Scottish martyrs. In his childhood he had heard from her lips the terrible story of the massacre in which that ancestor had fallen a victim, and it never lost its impression. From the moment of his birth he was dedicated to the ministry. But his nature was a strange compound. He seemed to inherit all the stirring energy with no little of the disputatious spirit of the most impractical and theorizing of the martyrs of the Covenant. Obstinate and opinionated, nothing could control his headstrong purpose. With something of humorous sarcasm and acute reasoning on minor points, he was no logician, and made up for his lack in this respect by a Lutheran coarseness of expression. His opponents were "swine," "sacrilegious robbers," "hypocrites," "deists," "blasphemers." In his disposition there was a dash of enthusiasm, bordering on fanaticism. He believed in dreams: a dream led him to leave his native home; a dream was his warrant for opposing Watts's version of the Psalms. He met his death at the outset of his contemplated journey to Jerusalem,—a journey to which he had been impelled by a dream, or his visionary views of the prophecies.

In 1784 he was laboring in Augusta county, Va., when a call reached him from the Presbyterians of Lexington, who were endeavoring to secure the organization of the Mount Zion church. He repaired to the field to which he had been invited, and immediately found himself surrounded by a large congregation. On sacramental occasions, not less than five hundred communicants, it is said, sometimes participated. These scenes, somewhat approaching the character of the camp-meetings which were soon to be introduced, were congenial to Rankin's taste. They allowed full scope for his peculiar energies. His own sensibilities were intensely excited, and at length seemed to acquire a morbid character. But the question of psalmody was still paramount to all others. Before Transylvania Presbytery (1786) was constituted—at the Conference of 1785, when "Father" Rice was the only ordained minister present beside himself—Rankin, who had resided in Kentucky but a few months, brought the subject to the attention of the body. It was composed, besides two ministers, Rice and Rankin himself, of two probationers, Crawford and Templin, and twenty-three representatives of twelve different congregations. The harmony of the Conference was in great danger of being disturbed. The psalmody question at such a crisis could be regarded only as an apple of discord. But he stood alone in his views; and, while he regarded his ministerial brethren as latitudinarian, they were constrained to regard him as little less than a bigot.

The action of the Synod in 1787 greatly dissatisfied him. Instead of regarding the kind counsel of that body upon the subject, he was only irritated by it.

His indignation broke out in censorious invectives. The Presbyterian clergy he accounted deists and blasphemers, rejecters of Revelation and revilers of the word of God. From the communion of his own church he unceremoniously debarred all Watts's admirers.

Such was his zeal in the matter that he attended the first General Assembly at Philadelphia, in 1789, and, though he bore no commission, handed in an overture and a request to be heard upon the subject. His object was to obtain a repeal of the resolution of the old Synod, allowing the use of Watts in the churches. He was patiently heard and considerately and kindly advised; but the charity which the Synod recommended him to exercise accorded neither with his character nor his principles.

More vehement than ever, he shielded himself under the pretence of a divine warrant extended to him in dreams. Parodying the words of Christ, his reply on one occasion to a question addressed him was, "Tell me, was the institution of Watts of heaven or of men, and I will tell you by what authority I did these things." He would displace Watts to restore Rouse, yet gave his own night-visions a place above the authority not only of reason, but of the word of God.

His unwarrantable proceedings could no longer be passed over in silence by the Presbytery. A committee of prosecution was appointed to examine the allegations against him, and, if necessary, make arrangements for a trial. The result of their labors appeared in several formal charges and specifications. He was cited for trial, but, from reasons easily to be surmised, refused to appear. Precipitately withdrawing from the country, he remained absent two years. Rev. James Blythe was appointed to fill his pulpit, upon the request of his congregation for a supply.

Upon his return, the citations were renewed. The

trial came on, April 25, 1792. After a protracted investigation, he was found guilty of traducing his brethren, unwarrantably excluding applicants from the Lord's Supper, and narrating his dreams as revelations from heaven. When summoned to hear the opinion of the court, he refused to acknowledge his fault or make any concessions. "I appeal," he cried, "to God, angels, and men. I protest against the proceedings of this Presbytery, and will be no longer a member of the Transylvania Presbytery." Having said this, he withdrew, accompanied by his elder. For this open contempt of jurisdiction the Presbytery suspended him from the exercise of ministerial functions until the next stated session.

This, however, he was prepared to disregard. He had not taken the step without calculating his strength. No sooner had he pronounced his declinature, than a hundred of the spectators stepped forward and, giving him the right hand of fellowship, pledged themselves to sustain him. A general meeting of his followers was soon held, and measures were matured for a separate organization. Commissioners appeared, representing portions of twelve congregations and five hundred families. A narrative of events and declaration of principles was drawn up by Rankin. The Presbytery were forced to meet it by a counter-statement, and, in consequence of his contumacy, to depose him from the ministry and declare his charge vacant. Artful misrepresentations of the matter were spread abroad by Rankin's adherents. He was represented as a martyr to his adherence to Rouse's Version, and was thus commended to the sympathies of the Associate Reformed, with whom he united in 1793.

From this period his cause received no new accession of strength. In 1798, Armstrong and Fulton, missionaries from the Associate Church of Scotland, visited

Kentucky, and Rankin's followers left him to join them. His own church clung to him with devoted attachment, and, when he broke off from the Associate Reformed, became Independent. But his cause continued steadily to decline, till it became almost utterly insignificant. Its only effect had been to rend congregations in sunder, distract them with dissensions, and convulse them with disputes, disturbing the harmony of the Church and aggravating the difficulties of the field as a sphere for missionary effort.

These difficulties, and others disconnected with them, were to be met by fresh bands of Presbyterian missionaries. In 1792, Rev. James Blythe entered the field. He was a native of North Carolina, and of Scottish extraction. His education was acquired at Hampden-Sidney College, where for a time he was the only member who had made a profession of religion. His seriousness, however, vanished as he mingled with his thoughtless associates; nor was his careless course arrested till almost forcing his way into the room of a fellow-student, the late Dr. Hill, he found him reading the Bible. Attempting to sneer at this oddity in a fellow-student, he was stung by the reproof of the reply, and found no peace till he had retraced his steps and found peace in his neglected Saviour. From this moment he broke loose from the snares that surrounded him, and gave himself up without reserve to the cause of Christ.

After his graduation in 1789, he pursued the study of theology under Dr. Hall, of North Carolina. He was licensed by the Orange Presbytery, and visited Kentucky as a missionary in 1791. On July 25, 1793, he was ordained pastor of Pisgah and Clear Creek Churches. Like his brethren of this period in Tennessee, he carried his rifle and rode with his holsters, for fear of hostile attack from the Indians. For nearly forty years he labored in this field, mainly in connection with the Pisgah church. For a long period he was a professor, and for twelve or fifteen years acting President, of Transylvania University. Subsequently he was President of South Hanover College, in Indiana.

Almost at the same time with Blythe, or shortly afterward, Thomas Cleland, John Poage Campbell, and Samuel Rannells united with Transylvania Presbytery. Rannells was a native of Virginia, and a licentiate of the Presbytery of Lexington. Early in 1795 he visited Kentucky as one of the Synod's missionaries. For twenty-two years he continued pastor of the united churches of Paris and Stonermouth. Zealous and indefatigable, and remarkably gifted in prayer, his moderate abilities were made effective in conjunction with a devoted piety.

John P. Campbell was unquestionably the most brilliant, in point of intellect, of the whole pioneer band. At fourteen years of age he removed with his father to Kentucky, and was one of the first of "Father" Rice's pupils in Transylvania Grammar-School. He returned to Virginia to complete his studies, and at the age of nineteen took charge of an academy at Williamsburg, North Carolina. At this time he had, unfortunately, imbibed infidel sentiments; but he was afterward converted by the perusal of "Jenyns on the Internal Evidences of Christianity." From this time his views were directed toward the ministry. In 1790 he was graduated at Hampden-Sidney, and, after studying with William Graham and Moses Hoge, was licensed to preach in May, 1792. After laboring a short time in Virginia, he removed in 1795 to Kentucky, where his first charge was the churches of Smyrna and Flemingsburg, in Fleming county.

His subsequent labors were in the regions of Danville, Nicholasville, Cherry Spring, Versailles, Lexington, and Chillicothe. His life was at times one of severe hardship. His salary was small and insufficient; while his pride kept him from disclosing his necessities.

His eminent gifts forced him into the position of a controversialist in defence of the Church at a critical period of her history. For this post of distinction he was well fitted. He was an accurate and well-read theologian. His mind was acute and discriminating, quick to unravel the fallacies of the sophist and detect the weak points of an adversary. He was a man of fine taste; and his style was elaborate and elegant. No pen was so efficient as his in the subsequent conflict with the Arminian New Lights, led off by Stone. The Pelagianism of Craighead was soon exposed by his vigorous handling. His works on Baptism, although considered too learned for popular use, were not without their influence in settling the views of many. In the pulpit, a graceful and energetic elocution, a delivery not fluent, but animated, combined with solidity of matter and grace of style to give him reputation in his early ministry. His appearance was such as well became the orator. Tall and slender in person, his deep-set, dark-blue eyes, under strong excitement, flashed like lightning from under his jutting forehead. Competent judges pronounced him one of the most talented, popular, and influential ministers in the country. With the shining gifts, he had also the infirmities, of genius. His delicate nervous organization rendered him acutely sensitive and easily irritated. Repeatedly he changed his field of labor. Restless and aspiring, he bore with some discontent the poverty he was too proud to confess, and could not endure to yield where his honor appeared to be concerned.

Thomas Cleland was born in Maryland, and at an early age removed to Kentucky. His religious impressions were deepened under the preaching of Dr. Blythe, with whom he pursued his studies at Pisgah Academy. Although occasionally serving as an exhorter, it was not till 1801 that he entered upon the active labors of the ministry. From this period his efforts were largely blessed. Several revivals took place under his ministry, and in connection with the judicatures of the Church his name occupied a high rank.[1]

In 1795, Joseph P. Howe, from North Carolina, entered the field, and was ordained over Little Mountain (Mount Sterling) and Springfield. A devoted man, although of moderate abilities, he took a conspicuous part in the Great Revival of 1800. In 1796, he was followed by James Welch, a missionary of the Synod of Virginia, afterward ordained pastor of the Lexington and Georgetown churches. He was afterward appointed Professor of Ancient Languages in Transylvania University.

In 1797, John Lyle and Archibald Cameron brought a new accession of strength. Lyle was of Irish descent, and born in Rockbridge county, Virginia. He labored on the farm with his father, who, on principle, would not own slaves. When twenty years of age, he was converted, and became desirous of devoting himself to the ministry. Overcoming difficulties that would have discouraged others, he completed his studies at Liberty Hall in 1794, pursued his theological course with William Graham, and was licensed by Lexington Presbytery, April 21, 1796. For some years he labored as a missionary in Kentucky, and in 1800 took charge of the churches of Salem and Sugar Ridge, in Clark county. Subsequently he occupied other fields, but was eminently efficient in promoting the cause of education and checking the excesses of the

[1] See Life of Cleland, by his son.

Revival, which commenced almost contemporaneously with his removal to Kentucky.

Cameron was a native of Scotland, but removed with his father's family to Kentucky in 1781. His literary course was pursued at Transylvania Seminary and at Bardstown, and his theological under the charge of "Father" Rice. In 1796 or 1797, he was installed over the churches of Akron and Fox Run, in Shelby county, and Big Spring, in Nelson county. For several years his labors in this region were abundant. Many churches were organized and built up under his efficient instrumentality. With "a mind cast in the finest mould," and possessed of a ripe scholarship, he was also gifted with keen powers of satire, and in contending for the truth was remarkably direct and pungent. In his bluntness of manner he was a John Knox. He possessed great shrewdness and independence of thought. His extemporaneous address was characterized by method, chasteness, and beauty. In prayer, rich evangelical thought was blended with hallowed tenderness and devout elevation of heart. For nearly forty years he pursued his course of extended and hallowed labor.

In 1798, the number of laborers was increased by the installation of Robert Stuart, Robert Wilson, and John Howe. Stuart was a native of Rockbridge county, Va., and, like his kinsman Campbell, could trace back his lineage to that eminent Scottish divine, Rutherford. He was first awakened under the preaching of Dr. Alexander, at New Monmouth Church, studied at Liberty Hall, was licensed by Lexington Presbytery in 1796, and, after performing missionary service in Virginia, directed his course to Kentucky. In December, 1798, he was appointed Professor of Languages in Transylvania University, but resigned his post a few months later, to establish a private grammar-school in Woodford county. Quite a number of eminent men received their education under his training. In 1803, he preached to the Salem Church, and in 1804 took charge of the church of Walnut Hill, six miles east of Lexington, in connection with which he labored forty years. Discreet and prudent, and sometimes called a "Moses" for his meekness, he was capable, when occasion demanded, of keen antagonism to error; and the first publication which stung the Unitarian President of Transylvania University was from his pen.

Wilson, of Irish descent, was a native of Virginia. Like Stuart, he performed missionary labor in his native State before his removal to Kentucky. For nearly twenty-five years he was settled at Washington, near Maysville; and the neighboring churches were greatly indebted to his exertions.

John Howe was a native of South Carolina, but completed his studies at Transylvania Seminary. He studied theology with James Crawford, and was licensed in 1795. For several years he preached alternately at Glasgow and Beaver Creek Churches, subsequently removing to Greensburg, Green county. He was amiable, unostentatious, and useful and popular as a preacher. Fifty-three years of his ministry were spent in Kentucky. He then removed to Missouri, where he died in 1856.

From the date of this accession, the number of ministers multiplied rapidly, although not in proportion to the demand made by the increase of population. Before the formation of the Synod, in 1802, the Presbytery numbered on its list the names of Samuel Robinson, Samuel Finley, James Vance, James Kemper, Samuel B. Robertson, John Bowman, John Thompson, Matthew Houston, John Dunlavy, Isaac Tull, William Mahon, John Evans Finley, Peter Wilson,

William Speer, James Balch, John Rankin, Samuel McAdow, Samuel Donnell, Jeremiah Abeel, together with Robert G. Craighead, James McGready, and William McGee. The last three, with Bowman and Thompson, were from North Carolina; Houston, Vance, and Mahon, from Virginia; Tull, Robinson, Dunlavy, and McNemar, from Pennsylvania; and Finley, from South Carolina.

The field to be occupied was large and difficult. It extended over the whole region west of the mountains, with the exception of Tennessee and the field of Redstone and Ohio Presbyteries. Northward it extended beyond the Ohio, and to the east and west its respective boundaries were civilization and barbarism. A large population, in sparsely-settled districts, was spread over this vast area. The labor of reaching them was one of exceeding difficulty, and added new discouragements to itinerant missionary labor.

Nor was the moral aspect of the field at all inviting. The seeds of French infidelity had been sown broadcast over it. Societies affiliated with the Jacobin Club of Philadelphia were formed (1793) at Lexington, Georgetown, and Paris. Politically, they were violent and dogmatic; morally, they were corrupting, and in respect to religion utterly infidel. The nomenclature of towns and counties still attests the French sympathies of the first settlers. It is quite significant of the state of social morals that at this period French agents were able to enlist two thousand recruits within the bounds of the State to attack the Spanish possessions on the Mississippi.

Nor was this all. Years had passed in many settlements before they were visited by a single missionary, or were reminded, by his presence and words, of religious ordinances. A backwoods life created an irrepressible passion for excitement. Lawlessness largely prevailed. Family education and religion fell into neglect. The intense cupidity of the settlers, fed by constant speculation, and incited by land-jobbing, litigation, and feuds of various kinds, tended to social demoralization. The variety of religious bodies on the ground, each to some extent at variance within itself,—the Baptists wrangling between Regulars and Separates, and the Presbyterians convulsed by the question of Psalmody,—greatly aggravated the difficulty. Evangelical effort, instead of presenting an unbroken front, was torn with intestine feuds and weakened by division. The enemies of religion were not slow to take advantage of this state of things. Jeffersonian influence was as strong west as east of the mountains. In 1793, the services of a chaplain to the Legislature were dispensed with. The measure was mainly significant as showing the influences which were ascendant in high places. A revolution was effected at the same time in the Transylvania Seminary by placing at its head a disciple of Priestley, and thus virtually alienating with utter contempt the early friends who had toiled and endured so much to lay its foundation on the basis of Christian truth. An apostate Baptist minister was chosen Governor of the State. No public remonstrance was raised in consequence of these proceedings. Before the close of the century, a decided majority of the population of the State were reputed to be infidels. As might naturally be expected, vice and dissipation attended this influx of fatal error.

It was no easy task—and it required no ordinary boldness to venture—to stem the tide. It seemed to roll, with irresistible power over the whole region. The few who should have girded themselves for the work were divided among themselves. The last hope of recovering the ground lost appeared to be fast dying away. Yet it was at this very crisis that a reaction commenced. The Great Revival, which marks the opening of the present century, with all its extravagances and excesses, effectually arrested the universal tide of skepticism and irreligion. It began when religion was at the lowest ebb, and spread over a region that to superficial view was proof against its influence.

CHAPTER XX.

RISE OF PRESBYTERIANISM IN TENNESSEE, 1775–1800.

RETURNING now to the fountain-head of Presbyterian emigration in Virginia, we take note of another branch of the current, following the line of the Holston. In 1785, Abingdon Presbytery was erected by a division of the original Hanover Presbytery. It embraced the churches of Southwestern Virginia, and extended so as to include the new settlements on the Holston, in what is now Eastern Tennessee. In 1797, twelve years from its formation,—although Transylvania Presbytery was formed from it in 1786,—it numbered thirty-six congregations; while three others which had been under its care had become almost, if not quite, extinct.[1] Of these, eleven were within the State of Virginia, nineteen were in Tennessee, and seven were in the western part of North Carolina.[2] More than two-thirds of the whole number were at that time vacant,—viz.: New Dublin, Austinville, Graham's Meeting-House, Adam's Meeting-House, Davis's, Upper Holston or Ebbing

---

[1] Report to General Assembly, 1797.

[2] Nearly all, however, were within the limits of what is now the State of Tennessee.

Spring, Glade Spring, Rock Spring, Sinking Spring, Green Spring, and Clinch Congregation, in Virginia; Upper Concord, New Providence, New Bethel, Hebron, Providence, Chesnut Ridge, Waggoner's Settlement, Charter's Valley, Gap Creek Congregation, Pent Gap and Oil Creek Congregations, Hopewell, Shunam, Lower Concord, and Fork Congregation, in Tennessee; and Rimm's Creek Congregation, Mouth of Swananoa, Head of French Broad, Tennessee Congregation, and Grassy Valley, in North Carolina.

The pastors at that time were John Cossan at Jonesborough, Samuel Doak at Salem, Hezekiah Balch at Mount Bethel, James Balch at Sinking Spring, Robert Henderson at Westminster, Samuel Carrick at Knoxville, and Gideon Blackburn at Eusebia and New Providence.

The oldest of the Virginia congregations, that of Upper Holston, or Ebbing Spring, had been in existence for twenty-five years, the others for shorter periods, varying from seven to twenty. In Tennessee, those of Upper Concord, New Providence, Salem, Mount Bethel, and Charter's Valley were organized in 1780; New Bethel, in 1782; Providence, in 1784; Hopewell, in 1785; Chesnut Ridge, Sinking Spring, New Providence, Pent Gap, Oil Creek, and Westminster, in 1787; Fork Congregation, Shunam,[1] and Hebron, in 1790; Waggoner's Settlement and Lower Concord, in 1791; Gap Creek Congregation, in 1792; Knoxville, in 1793; and Jonesborough, in 1796.

Meanwhile, the Presbytery of Transylvania, formed from that of Abingdon in 1786, and consisting of five members only at the time of its erection, had outgrown the parent Presbytery, and was fast attaining the dimensions of a Synod. Its field embraced the

---

[1] Organized by Carrick perhaps a year or two later.

new settlements in Kentucky, and already extended across the Ohio River. Abingdon Presbytery thus marked the grand route by which the pioneer columns of the great Presbyterian army were moving on to take possession of the new settlements beyond the mountains.

At the commencement of the French War, about fifty families had located on the Cumberland River; but these were driven off by the Indians. About the same time the Shawnees, who had lived near the Savannah River, emigrated to the banks of the Cumberland and settled near the present site of Nashville; but they also were driven away by the Cherokees. In 1755, a number of persons removed to the west of the present bounds of North Carolina, and were the first permanent colonists of Tennessee. By 1773 the population had considerably increased; but in 1776 the Cherokees were incited by British agents to attack the infant and feeble settlements. Their incursions, however, were repelled, and during the war Tennessee colonists hastened to join their countrymen east of the mountains in repelling the attacks of the foe upon the Southern States.

At the close of the war, although the dangers of Indian warfare were still imminent and the settler stood in constant fear of savage ferocity, the vast territory sparsely occupied by the Cherokees was too inviting to be overlooked by pioneer enterprise; and the fair valley of the Holston was specially attractive. A wilderness of two hundred miles intervened between this region and the Kentucky settlements; but the grant of military lands brought into the bounds of what now constitutes the State not a few bold and hardy men, who had been schooled in peril, and to whom the trials of the wilderness were only a new spur to enterprise and strange adventure.

Those who were already on the ground—and they were largely composed of Presbyterians from the upper counties of Maryland and from Pennsylvania—were in constant danger from the hostile Indian tribes: yet, even thus, they had not been unmindful of the need of gospel ordinances. At Brown's Meeting-House, June 2, 1773, a call was presented to Hanover Presbytery for the services of Rev. Charles Cummings, by the congregations of Ebbing Spring and Sinking Spring, on the Holston. It was signed by one hundred and thirty heads of families. The call was accepted; and Mr. Cummings, who had labored for several years in Augusta, removed to his new field, as yet unoccupied by a single Presbyterian minister, beyond the mountains.

It was amid strange scenes that the early years of his pastorate in this region were passed. The Indians were very troublesome, and during the summer months the families were compelled, for safety, to collect together in forts. Once (1776) Mr. Cummings himself came near losing his life from a hostile attack. The men never went to church except fully armed and taking their families with them. Mr. Cummings did not fail to set an example of precaution. On Sabbath morning he was wont to "put on his shot-pouch, shoulder his rifle, mount his dun stallion, and ride off to church." There he met a large congregation, every man of whom had his rifle in his hand. Stripping off his military accoutrements and laying down his rifle, the speaker would preach two sermons, with a short interval between them, and the people would disperse. For more than thirty years this pioneer of Presbyterianism in Tennessee was known and revered as an exemplary Christian and a faithful pastor. He was "a John Knox in zeal and energy in support of his own Church." Beyond the bounds of his more immediate field he performed a great amount of missionary labor, the fruits of which yet remain.

With the return of peace the tide of immigration commenced anew. In 1782, Adam Rankin, whose name is more intimately associated with the history of the Church in Kentucky, was licensed to preach, and soon visited the region of Holston. But he had been preceded four years by a man whose name deserves a more permanent record. This was Samuel Doak, conjointly with Cummings the founder of the Presbyterian Church in East Tennessee. Of Scotch-Irish descent, in a humble but honorable condition of life, he early resolved to secure himself an education. With this object in view, he proposed to relinquish to his brothers his share in the patrimonial inheritance and devote himself exclusively to study. By great self-denial, he prepared himself for college, and in 1775 was graduated at Nassau Hall. After studying theology with Dr. Robert Smith, of Pequa, he accepted the office of tutor in the then new college of Hampden-Sidney. Here he continued his theological studies, and was licensed to preach by the Presbytery of Hanover, October 31, 1777. Almost immediately he directed his steps to the Holston settlements. The means of subsistence were very scarce, and he was under the necessity of going thirty miles in the direction of Abingdon for supplies. His family ran great risk of being cut off in the Indian War. Repeatedly he left his pulpit or his students to repair to the camp at some hostile alarm.

Throughout his life, Dr. Doak was the devoted friend of learning and religion. In 1784, he was a member of the convention that framed the Constitution of "the ancient commonwealth of Franklin," and secured in it the provision for a university. At Little Limestone, in Washington county, he purchased a farm, on which he built a log house for the purposes of education, and a small church-edifice, occupied by the "Salem congregation." This literary institution—the first that was ever established in the Mississippi valley—was incorporated in 1785 as "Martin Academy," and in 1795 it became Washington College. Till 1818, Dr. Doak continued to preside over it. Few men in the history of the Church were better fitted, by wisdom, sagacity, energy, and learning, to lay the foundations of social and religious institutions than Dr. Doak.

Early in 1785 he was followed by a man of kindred spirit, who was destined to exert a vast influence upon this growing region. This was Hezekiah Balch, a graduate of New Jersey College in the class of 1762. After teaching for some years, he was licensed to preach by the Presbytery of New Castle, and labored for several years as a missionary within the bounds of Hanover Presbytery, his field reaching from the Potomac indefinitely toward the Pacific. After having labored thus in various localities, mainly as an itinerant missionary, he directed his course to East Tennessee. Here for more than twenty years his labors were abundant; and Greenville College owes its existence to his exertions. In May, 1785, he joined with Messrs. Cummings and Doak in a request to Synod that a Presbytery might be formed embracing the territories of the present States of Kentucky and Tennessee. The result was that the Abingdon Presbytery was erected,—soon, however, to be divided to compose the new Kentucky Presbytery of Transylvania. Along with Doak, Cummings, and Balch, the two new members Cossan and Houston constituted the Presbytery of Abington after the division. The last of these (Houston) had in 1783 accepted a call from the Providence congregation in Washington county; but he labored in the field for only about five years.

A valuable and efficient co-laborer in the pioneer missionary work of East Tennessee was found in a young man by the name of Robert Henderson. He was one of Doak's pupils soon after Martin Academy, in Washington county, was opened. Here he pursued his course preparatory to entering the ministry. By Abingdon Presbytery he was licensed in or about 1788, and took charge of the two churches of Westminster and Hopewell, the latter the present county-seat of Jefferson county. Here he continued for more than twenty years; and few of his associates exerted a more extensive or permanent influence. His powers of address were great and varied. When, to use his own language, conscience said, "Robert Henderson, do your duty," it mattered not who composed his audience. No man was spared; and on one memorable occasion, when profanity was his subject, and most others would have been overawed by seeing some of the most notorious swearers in the State present, his delineations, lashings, and denunciations are said to have been absolutely terrific. When dealing with vice, he used a whip of scorpions. Yet his moods were various,—now overwhelmingly solemn, now witty and humorous, and again most severe and scathing. With a matchless power of mimicry, and a perfect command of voice, countenance, attitude, and gesture, his flashes of wit or grotesquely humorous illustrations would break from him in spite of himself, convulsing with laughter an audience just trembling under his bold, passionate, and at times awfully grand appeals. He was aware of his own infirmity, and strove against it; but it gave him a popularity and influence with the masses such as few others have ever possessed. Thousands of hearers on a single occasion would be subdued and overwhelmed by his melting pathos. A crowd was sure to gather where it was known that he was to preach; and his indescribable earnestness, emphatic tones, and bold and striking gestures were "perfectly irresistible." His longest sermons—and they were sometimes very long—were heard without impatience to their close. His influence was felt less upon a select few than upon the masses; and yet there were some whom he helped to train who occupy a distinguished place in the annals of the Presbyterian churches of the West. Among these was Gideon Blackburn.

In some respects the pupil surpassed his teacher. With less of the comic element in his nature, and holding it always under perfect control, Blackburn was none the less effective. He might be regarded as the best personification of *backwoods* eloquence. What he said to his pupils on the subject of rhetoric he seems to have practised himself:—"There is one rule, not laid down in the books, more important than all:—get your head, heart, soul, full of your subject, and then let nature have its own way, despising all rule." A better illustration of the application of the rule than he himself afforded could not be found. His words, tone, manner, were most solemn and impressive. Few men owed less to education or art. He was first a student under Doak at Martin's Academy, and afterward under the training of Henderson. Like the latter, he declined the use of notes in the pulpit, uniformly preferring the freedom and effect of extemporaneous effort.

Nurtured amid hardships, and early forced to self-reliance, he was exactly fitted to the sphere of life in which his lot was cast. He could preach in coat-sleeves or with his musket by his side, and with equal readiness in the pulpit or from the stump. Without a dollar in the world, and on the very outskirts of civilization, amid the alarms of savage invasions, forced to accept escorts of armed men from fort to fort, he began his work. But the young preacher was daunted by no fear, disheartened by no obstacle. In 1792, the Presbytery of Abingdon had granted him his license, and within a few months he had charge of the two congregations of New Providence and Eusebia, and had organized several other neighboring churches. Shortly after this, with Carrick, Ramsey, and Henderson, he was associated in the first Presbytery formed in the part of the country in which he labored.

Carrick was a pupil of Graham, at Augusta, Va., and labored for several years in that State. In 1791, he was dismissed to the Abingdon Presbytery, and for several years had the joint charge of the Knoxville and New Lebanon Churches. In 1800, he was chosen by the Legislature President of Blount College. In some respects he presented a contrast to his associates. He was of the old Virginia school of ministers, urbane, even courtly, in his manners, and in the pulpit grave, dignified, and solemn. His views of divine truth were clear and definite; and they lost nothing by his mode of exhibiting them.

The description that is left us[1] of his reception in the field which was thenceforth to be the scene of his active labors for many years, presents a graphic picture of the early settlements. Tradition reports that in the spring of 1789 a party of hunters and landmongers pitched their tent just where the Lebanon church-edifice now stands. The ancient forest still overhung the spot, in all its primitive beauty, undisturbed by the echoes of the woodman's axe. The oak, the poplar, and the elm lifted high above them their lofty branches, "while the aroma of the walnut and the hickory diffused around the camp their delightful fragrance." Cedars and other evergreens were not wanting to add to the finished beauty of the scene. Grape-vines, springing from the virgin soil, and encircling every trunk, spread themselves in lavish luxu-

[1] Presbyterian Herald, Feb. 14, 1861.

riance among the tree-tops, or, clustering together in beautiful festoons, formed a canopy and an arbor around the temporary abode of the backwoodsmen. The whole surrounding country was carpeted with verdure, and the woods were adorned with their richest foliage. With the "upland solitudes" and "the pensive beauty of the river-bottoms," "the scene was lovely in the extreme."

All west of the camp was one unbroken forest, in the midst of which the Father of Waters rolled his turbid tide. The pioneers had advanced beyond the last landmark of civilization, and before them lay the unbroken wilderness. Preparing to lay the foundation of stable and orderly government, their first step was the appropriation of lands. Schooled in the scenes of Revolutionary conflict, some of them active participants in the perils of the field, they yet retained on the outskirts of civilization their love of liberty regulated by law.

Here, then, they awaited the arrival of the surveyor. He lived in the older settlements, on Limestone, in Washington county. On his arrival, he received a cordial greeting and a hearty welcome to the civilities of the camp. He found the party all clad in domestic fabrics, the product of their own industry, each wearing the hunting-shirt and each armed with his trusty rifle. The first salutations over, inquiries were immediately made for the latest news from the older settlements, and, among others, what new settlers had come in. To the last inquiry the surveyor replied by enumerating the new emigrants, and among others mentioned the arrival on Limestone of a Presbyterian minister by the name of Samuel Carrick.

The little party were electrified by this intelligence, and clustered around their informant, manifesting by their demeanor the most exciting interest and intense curiosity. Most, perhaps all, of them were the sons of pious parents,—children of the Covenant,—in the older country had known the Sabbath and appreciated its privileges,—had bowed in prayer or swelled with their own voices the notes of praise,—had listened to the preached word and had been impressed by its truth. Yielding to the promptings of a restless spirit of enterprise and adventure, they had forsaken the altar and the fireside, and had thrown themselves amid the rough scenes and rude social elements of the Western frontier. Here, surrounded by heedless, if not vicious, associates, they had become habituated to Sabbath-desecration, if not to scenes of immorality and vice. Most of them were now heads of families, and identified with all the industrial and social interests of the new community of which they formed a part. Their children were growing up around them unbaptized, and in destitution of religious privileges. In these circumstances, the scenes of their own youth were revived with peculiar freshness; conscience was aroused, and memory recalled the Sabbath, the catechism, the school-house, the ministry, and the ordinances of other days.

Thus recalling the past, the enterprise and objects of the present—staff, compass, land-warrant, and entry—were for the moment forgotten, and they determined to appoint a day on which the strange minister should be invited to preach in these new settlements. The day was fixed; the spot was selected,—an Indian mound near the confluence of the two rivers,—the Fork. The surveyor bore back on his return the invitation to Mr. Carrick. He accepted it, and, by a strange coincidence, Hezekiah Balch chanced also to be present on the same occasion. To the latter, as the older man, Mr. Carrick courteously yielded the precedence, and, after the sermon, remarked that he had selected the same subject and the same text, and, as the subject was not and could not be exhausted, he would pursue the theme. Tradition reports that the text was, "We then are ambassadors for Christ," &c.

Attracted by the importance as well as the novelty of the occasion, an immense crowd attended this first religious meeting held in all the region. Some came from what are now Sevier and Blount counties, armed with guns to defend themselves from the possible attack of the Cherokees. Parents brought their children with them in order that they might be baptized. It was soon after this that Mr. Carrick—universally acceptable as a preacher—commenced his labors as a pastor of the Lebanon Church in conjunction with Knoxville.[1] The former he retained till 1803.[2]

Ramsey was the last of the little band composing the new Presbytery, to reach the Western field. He, too, was a pupil of Graham of Virginia, and soon after his licensure, in 1795, extended his missionary tour to the "Southwestern Territory."

As he went from house to house in the frontier settlements of Knox county, near which a brother of his had resided for several years, he found the people anxious to enjoy the privileges of the gospel. At each cabin a hearty welcome greeted him, and a cordial

---

[1] The first church in Knoxville was never regularly organized. Carrick, after preaching at the Fork, began to preach a part of his time in Knoxville (1793–1794), and at a later date to administer the ordinances. The elders of the Fork assisted, and subsequently acted as elders in Knoxville.—Dr. McCampbell, in the Presbyterian Herald, Feb. 1861.

[2] "The first Sabbath I spent in Tennessee," says Dr. John McCampbell, "was in the Fork Church, July, 1803. There was no minister present on that day. The exercises of public worship were as follows:—two sermons were read, one by Col. F. A. Ramsey, the other by Archibald Rhea. Four prayers were offered, with singing."

wish was expressed that the young man would remain in the country and organize churches in the wilderness. He went from fort to fort and station to station, preaching to multitudes who had not for years heard a Presbyterian sermon. Thousands came out to listen to the strange minister. They followed him from place to place, and hung in rapt attention upon his lips. Young Ramsey felt that he was not at liberty to neglect the Macedonian cry that followed him from the Western wilderness back to Virginia. In 1797, he returned to Tennessee, and settled at Mount Ebenezer, eleven miles west of Knoxville. Here he extended his labors over a vast surrounding region, ministering to several congregations, and tasking his powers to the utmost, till he sank under his burden. Gentle, winning, conciliatory, and prudent, he bound his people to himself by the strongest ties, while his whole course, eminently unselfish and self-denying, commanded universal respect.

Such were the men who led the way in planting the Presbyterian Church in Tennessee. Of varied gifts, untiring zeal, and entire consecration to their work, they were eminently successful. Under their eyes and by their hands the foundations of the Church were firmly laid in a new region, where it was to be widely extended.

Yet this early period was not without its peculiar trials. The Presbytery of Abingdon was connected with the Synod of the Carolinas; and the attention of the latter was repeatedly called to questions generating strife and division that had risen west of the mountains. Hezekiah Balch was a decided Hopkinsian. He had visited New England, and from the lips of the very author of the "New Divinity" had heard his views expounded. These views commended themselves to his own mind, and he was charged with saying that he was "fifty thousand times stronger" in his peculiar belief "than he was before he went away." His only objection to the charge was that it was not strong enough: the fifty thousand should have been five hundred thousand.

Some of his church, as well as of his ministerial brethren, were greatly dissatisfied. They complained of his Hopkinsianism and kindred errors, as they regarded them. All this, however, did not constitute his real crime. There were others who held Hopkinsian views, and some who were far more eminent in the Presbyterian Church than Mr. Balch. But he was indiscreet. His convictions were strong, his feelings ardent, and he acted often from impulse rather than judgment. In his own congregation some unwise measures had been adopted which brought him into variance with his Session. Suits at law were threatened against him. A new Session was constituted, and Presbytery and Synod had to interfere repeatedly to restore peace. Yet none could question the piety, or Christian spirit generally, of Mr. Balch. His labors were unremitting and efficient in promoting the cause of religion and learning. His journey to New England was more to collect funds for his college than to listen to the apostle of the New Divinity. But he had a strong propensity to overlook consequences; and it was not his nature to consult prudence.

CHAPTER XXI.

GENERAL ASSEMBLY, 1800–1815.

THE commencement of the present century opened a new era in the history of the American Presbyterian Church. A revived missionary spirit gave enlarged scope and increased energy to its operations. Almost simultaneously, in New York, Pennsylvania, and New England, missionary societies were formed to extend to the frontier settlements and among the Indian tribes the knowledge of the gospel. Of these the New York Missionary Society took the lead. It was formed Nov. 1, 1796. A few months later, the Northern Missionary Society, embracing the region in Northern New York, was organized. In May, 1797, the Connecticut General Association formed itself into a missionary society The Massachusetts Society was formed in the following year. Almost contemporary was the Berkshire and Columbia Missionary Society; and in 1802, the Western Missionary Society at Pittsburg commenced operations. But for the alarm occasioned by the presence of the yellow fever in Philadelphia, a kindred society would have been formed there in 1798.[1]

The effect of this newly-enkindled missionary zeal, extending to different denominations, was to promote fraternal feeling and hearty co-operation. The New York Society sustained for a period a Baptist missionary to the Indians of Central New York, whom the

[1] Dr. Green's letter, in the N. Y. Miss. Mag., i. 110.

churches of his own order were too feeble to support. In the plan for social prayer adopted (Jan. 18, 1798) by the directors of the society, the second Wednesday evening of every month was appointed to be observed as a season for concert of prayer, and the meetings were to be held in rotation in the Reformed Dutch, Presbyterian, and Baptist churches. The General Assembly partook largely of this fraternal and co-operative spirit. This is manifest in the "plan for correspondence and intercourse" between the Presbyterian, Reformed Dutch, and Associate Reformed Churches, which was adopted by the Assembly of 1799. In this, "the communion of particular Churches, the friendly interchange of ministerial services, and a correspondence of the several judicatories of the conferring Churches" were recommended, and the report favoring it was unanimously adopted by the Assembly.[1]

Nor was this all. The wants of the mission-field already opened to Christian effort in New York and Ohio demanded the united efforts of Presbyterians and Congregationalists. The Connecticut Association had resolved itself into a missionary society, and its missionaries were already to be found in friendly co-operation with the ministers sent out by the Assembly to itinerate through Central and Western New York. It was of the highest importance that there should be no denominational conflict or collision. The claims of missionary evangelization were felt by both parties to be paramount to all denominational interests. With a wise forethought, and "with a view to prevent alienation and promote union and harmony in these new settlements, which are composed of inhabitants from these bodies," the General Association of Connecticut proposed to the General Assembly of 1801 "A PLAN OF

[1] Rejected, however, by the other bodies.

UNION." This plan strictly enjoined "mutual forbearance and accommodation." It allowed a Congregational church to settle a Presbyterian pastor, reserving to him the privilege of appeal to Presbytery or to a mutual council equally composed of Presbyterians and Congregationalists. In case a Presbyterian church settled a Congregational pastor, he might (appeal to, or) be tried by his Association, or a mutual council equally constituted of both denominations. In a Congregational church, the body of the male communicants of the church constituted the virtual Session; yet here the appeal might be to a mutual council or to Presbytery, in which the delegate of the church should have the right to sit and act as a ruling elder.

Exception might have been taken to the irregular constitution of inferior judicatories in which these principles should be adopted and allowed to prevail; but no objection was urged. It was felt that the strictness of ecclesiastical forms should be held subordinate to the higher objects of Christian effort, and that to sacrifice the last to the first would be but to "tithe mint, anise, and cummin," against the "weightier matters of the law."[1]

---

[1] [There was no such diversity of views or ecclesiastical preferences as to justify collision or to excite mutual suspicions between the two bodies; and every Christian principle demanded just that co-operation which the Plan of Union secured. In proof of this, we quote the following statement of views and polity.

In 1799, the Hartford North Association of Ministers, composed of such men as Drs. Strong and Flint, of Hartford, and Dr. Perkins, of West Hartford, made the following declaration of their principles:—

"This Association give information to all whom it may concern, that the constitution of the churches in the State of Connecticut, founded on the common usages, and the Confession of Faith, Heads of Agreement, and articles of Church Discipline, adopted at the earliest period of the settlement of the State, *is not Congregational, but contains the essentials of the government of the Church of Scotland,*

It is a subject of gratulation that at this crisis in the religious progress of our country such liberal and Christian views prevailed. The next fifteen years were to

---

or [*the*] *Presbyterian Church in America;* particularly as it gives a decisive power to ecclesiastical councils; and a Consociation, consisting of ministers and messengers, or a lay representation from the churches, is possessed of substantially the same authority as Presbytery. The judgments, decisions, and censures in our churches and in the Presbyterian are mutually deemed valid. *The churches, therefore, in Connecticut at large, and in our district in particular, are not now, and never were, from the earliest period of our settlement, Congregational churches,* according to the ideas and forms of church order contained in the Book of Discipline called the Cambridge Platform. There are, however, scattered over the State perhaps ten or twelve churches (*unconsociated*) which are properly called Congregational, agreeably to the rules of church discipline in the book above mentioned. Sometimes, indeed, the associated Churches of Connecticut are loosely and vaguely, though improperly, termed Congregational. While our Churches in the State at large are, in the most essential and important respects, the same as the Presbyterian, still in minute and unimportant points of church order and discipline both we and the Presbyterian Church in America acknowledge a difference."] F.

The fact is also stated (Am. Quar. Reg., Aug. 1839) that in 1790, by the General Association of Connecticut, "a further union with Presbyterians was declared to be expedient," and a committee of correspondence was appointed for the accomplishing of this object.

For many years *after* the adoption of the Plan of Union, the disposition to favor the Presbyterian system continued. The action of the General Association in repeated instances is quite decisive on this point, to say nothing of the avowed sentiments of many of the leading ministers of the State. In 1812, the question of the mutual relation of pastor and people was brought up for discussion in connection with the subject of the frequent changes and removal of pastors; and among other conclusions was the following:—"that this scheme of settling a minister places the dissolution of the contract between him and his parishioners chiefly in the power of the contracting parties, and to a great extent removes it from under the control of an ecclesiastical council; that, in consequence of this fact,

decide grave questions in regard to the destiny of the country as well as the prospects of the Presbyterian Church. An unexampled emigration from the settled regions of the East was to pour westward, swelled on its course by heterogeneous elements from other lands. The combined influence and effort of all who loved the cause common to Presbyterians and the churches of New England was necessary to control the current, or direct it in the channels of sobriety and religion. With unprecedented rapidity, new cities and villages were to spring up in the forest and along the lines of traffic, for whose urgent necessities of missionary and pastoral labor both denominations united would be tasked to furnish a supply. The time of conflict had come. The great struggle of the century—to shape the future destiny of a growing nation—had commenced. It forbade all minor dissension, and demanded the hearty co-operation, on broad principles, of all who loved the common cause.

The very spirit of the occasion did much to win the battle. With the adoption of the "Plan of Union," a new vigor seemed to pervade the Church. On all sides there was progress. The very next year after the adoption of the Plan (1802), the General Assembly was

---

the bands of ecclesiastical discipline will (we think) be gradually loosened, and the solemn business of placing a minister over a congregation, and of committing them to his charge, be finally left in the hands of the contracting parties, in direct contradiction, as we apprehend, to the order of Christ's house."

In the following year it was decided that a member of Association dismissed from his pastoral relation was still responsible to the Association, and that "no dismissed minister shall be accounted at liberty of himself to lay aside the ministerial office, or to dissolve his connection with the Association." These are but specimens of the tone of ecclesiastical sentiment in Connecticut.—*Conn. Ev. Mag.*, 1812, 1813.

called to divide the Presbytery of Albany into the three Presbyteries of Albany, Columbia, and Oneida, which were in 1803 constituted the Synod of Albany. Two years later, the Presbytery of Oneida was divided and the Presbytery of Geneva was erected.

In 1807, the Synod of Albany expressed their readiness—with the approbation of the Assembly—to form as intimate a connection with the Middle Association (Congregational) of the Military Tract as the Constitution of the Presbyterian Church would admit, inviting them to become a constituent branch of the Synod, and assuring them of the disposition of the Synod to leave their churches undisturbed in the administration of their own government until they should be better acquainted with the Presbyterian mode and voluntarily adopt it. Delegates from the churches should be received as ruling elders, and they, as well as ministers, on "adopting our standard of doctrine and government," might sit and vote as a constituent part of the body. This plan was sanctioned by the Assembly of 1808; and the Middle Association, and Presbytery of Geneva, covering in part the same ground, were subsequently constituted, with some interchange of members, the Presbyteries of Geneva and Onondaga. The liberal spirit of the Assembly, accordant with the "Plan of Union," is evinced by their sanction of this kindred measure.

In obtaining an act of incorporation, which was secured in 1799, and which authorized the possession of property yielding not over ten thousand dollars annual income,[1] exclusive of annual collections and voluntary contributions, the Assembly had in view the importance of securely holding an amount of property which should suffice as a fund for missionary purposes. This

---

[1] Minutes of 1790-1820, p. 175.

project was first brought forward in the Assembly of 1791.[1] It was recommended that a permanent fund should be raised, and the several Presbyteries were enjoined to take effectual measures to secure annual collections from their churches for this object. The amount collected for several succeeding years exceeded what was required for the payment of the missionaries annually employed; and upon the examination of reports of agents for soliciting donations, it was found, in 1801, that the Assembly held to its credit the sum of twelve thousand three hundred and fifty-nine dollars and ninety-two and a half cents. This was, by the decision of the Assembly, to be regarded as capital stock, which should "at no time be broken in upon or diminished," but invested in secure and permanent funds. The *interest* of these, only, was to be employed for the support of missions.

In 1805, the Committee of Missions were recommended to publish, by subscription, a periodical magazine "sacred to religion and morals," and pay the profits into the funds of the Assembly, to be applied to missionary purposes.[2] The work was commenced, and the ministers within the bounds of the Church were repeatedly urged to contribute to its columns; but the project failed, and the publication of the magazine was suspended in January, 1810.[3]

The success of the Connecticut Missionary Society in carrying out a similar project led the Assembly to overlook the greater difficulties which they would have to encounter. That society, while diffusing religious intelligence by means of its "Evangelical Magazine," had secured annually, as profits of the enterprise, a sum ranging from thirteen hundred dollars to over two thousand dollars, which was devoted to the purposes

---

[1] Minutes, 1790–1820, pp. 38, 40. [2] Ib. 317. [3] Ib. 450.

of the society. With such economy and success was the plan managed, that the permanent fund in the course of a few years amounted to more than thirty thousand dollars; and in some years, when collections were not secured from the churches, the interest of the fund and the profits of the magazine sufficed to provide for the support of the missionaries employed. For several years the Assembly prosecuted a kindred policy; but the rapid extension of the mission-field soon baffled every attempt to supply it by means of the interest of a permanent fund.

There seemed more feasibility in the plan which the Assembly proposed (1800) in behalf of ministerial education. This was intended to secure a fund which should suffice to provide candidates for the ministry with the necessary means for a partial or entire support. In each Synod a theological professor might be appointed, to whom students should be at liberty to resort, and who should receive from the fund a moderate compensation.[1] But this plan was ere long deranged by the adoption of the Seminary system of instruction, which left only the support of the student in his course of study to be provided for.

In 1802, a change was made by the Assembly in its method of conducting its missionary operations. Experience had shown that to give to these system and efficiency it was necessary that they should be put in the charge of men who should not only be empowered to act during the intervals of meetings of Assembly, but who should give the subject careful attention and be so situated as to have frequent opportunities of mutual conference. It was therefore resolved that a committee be chosen annually, to be denominated the "Standing Committee of Missions." It was originally to con-

---

[1] Minutes, 1790–1820, p. 196.

sist of seven members,—four ministers and three laymen; but in 1805, on the suggestion of the committee itself, its numbers were increased by the addition of five more members from Philadelphia and its vicinity, and one member from each of the seven Synods constituting the Church. It was made the duty of the committee "to collect, during the recess of the Assembly, all the information in their power relative to the concerns of missions and missionaries;" to digest this information, and report thereon at each meeting of the Assembly; to maintain such a correspondence on the subject of missions as the cause might require, and make such suggestions or arrangements as should enable the Assembly to act intelligently in its appointments; and, in fact, to "superintend generally, under the direction of the Assembly, the missionary business." It was not till 1816 that the style of the committee was changed to that of the "Board of Missions" and it was authorized to act with a large measure of independence.

The appointment of the committee (1802) was contemporaneous with a revived zeal in the cause of missions throughout the bounds of the Church. The Synod of Pittsburg began its existence (1802) as a missionary body, assuming the name of the Western Missionary Society. Its attention was directed largely to the new settlements northwest of the Ohio, and to methods for christianizing the Wyandotte Indians. The latter portion of their project was interrupted by the war, and the burning of the mission-premises; but on the conclusion of peace the plan of an Indian mission was resumed, and for some years received aid annually from the funds of the Assembly. Among the new settlements lying properly within its own bounds or those of the Synod of Kentucky, its missionaries were diligently employed, sometimes, however, receiving their compensation from the Connecticut Missionary Society, who could secure funds more readily than men for the distant field.

The Synod of Virginia, at the same time, prosecuted the mission work within its own limits, but with a marked decline of energy after the erection of the Synod of Pittsburg within its original bounds. For several years it had only from three to five missionaries in the field,—one of these to its own black population.

In 1802, before the erection of the Synod of Pittsburg, its report showed that it had sent nine missionaries to the west of the Alleghanies, three of whom visited the Shawanese and other Indians about Detroit and Sandusky. In 1807, when the Indian Mission had passed under the care of the Pittsburg Synod, and the missionary zeal of the Virginia churches had somewhat abated, the Synod wished to resign their missionary business into the hands of the Assembly; but the latter declined to accept the trust.

In 1803, the newly-formed Synod of Kentucky stated to the Assembly that the missionary field on their frontier was "so extensive and promising that the Synod find themselves inadequate to the demand." They asked that the Assembly "take the business under their own care and direction." The request was granted, and the destitutions of the Synod thenceforth received the attention of the Assembly in its annual appointments.

The Synod of the Carolinas, from the time of its erection, had given special attention to the subject of missions. Among its ministers were some who rank among the foremost and most efficient in this field of Christian enterprise. The Synod continued its efforts till the amount of its own immediate destitution forced it (1812) to resign the charge of missions to the care of the Assembly.

Meanwhile, the New York Missionary Society had sent out missionaries among the Indians of that State, and Joseph Bullen was commissioned to labor among the Indian tribes at the Southwest, in Mississippi Territory. In 1803, Gideon Blackburn—in all probability imbibing his views, or kindled to greater activity by Mr. Bullen's zeal—determined to see what could be accomplished in behalf of the Cherokees. He had vainly sought (1799) to engage his Presbytery (Union) actively in the work, and he now presented the cause to the attention of the Assembly. It received their favorable notice. Appropriations were made for it for many successive years from the Assembly's funds; and the zeal of Blackburn, sustained by the recommendation of the Assembly, accomplished still more by individual application in the Eastern cities. Such was the foundation of the Cherokee Mission.

The Assembly's committee at first had their attention directed especially to the destitutions of Northern, Central, and Western New York. . But soon appeals for aid reached them from Ohio, Indiana, Kentucky, and Tennessee. The deficiencies of the Synods were supplemented by the Assembly's appointments, and Presbyteries applying for aid were repeatedly authorized to employ missionaries at the Assembly's expense. In 1803, the number of appointments made by the recommendation of the committee, independent of those employed by the Synods, was only five. The next year it rose to twelve. In 1807 it amounted to fifteen, while five hundred dollars were appropriated to the Cherokee Mission. In 1811 the number had risen to forty, and in 1814 to over fifty, exclusive of such as the Presbyteries or Synods were authorized to employ at the Assembly's expense,—the Pittsburg Synod also receiving aid, during a portion of the period, for its Indian missions.

To sustain this extended and still extending plan of

operations, the Assembly was forced to make repeated appeals to the churches for aid. Presbyteries were urged (1811) to send out "their members, either by pairs or individually, to act as missionaries in the country contiguous to their residence;" and, as some of them failed to send in their annual missionary collections, they were directed to take "the most prudent and effectual measures" to forward "an annual contribution to the treasurer of the Assembly."

A great and beneficent work was thus accomplished. In 1810, the Assembly stated, as evidence of progress, that in the space of the preceding eleven years the number of ministers in the western parts of the State of New York had increased from two to nearly fifty. In other regions the growth of the Church had been less rapid; but there had been a steady and healthful advance. Much good had been accomplished, doubtless, by subsidiary agencies. Local societies of various kinds —missionary, tract, and Bible—had heartily co-operated with the Assembly in missionary efforts; and this co-operation was (1811) gratefully recognized. Each Synod (1809) was recommended, in view of the great and increasing good that had accrued to the Church "through the distribution of small, cheap religious tracts," to take measures for "establishing as many religious tract societies, by association of one or more Presbyteries," as might be convenient for the purpose. Books were purchased (1802) by the funds of the Assembly for distribution in the frontier settlements. They were put (1805) into the hands of individuals and Presbyteries to distribute, or missionaries were supplied with the means to procure them for the fields in which they labored. In 1806, it was resolved that one hundred dollars should be appropriated annually—if the funds of the Assembly would allow—toward procuring and distributing religious books. Among those which received the commendation of the Assembly were Vincent's Exposition of the Shorter Catechism, and Andrew Fuller's "Gospel worthy of all Acceptation,"—the last a work appropriate for circulation in this country, in which Brainerd and Eliot—through the reading of whose lives and labors Fuller was led to adopt the sentiments it presents—had accomplished their noble work.

But the advance of the Church during the period under review was largely due to the powerful revivals which pervaded almost every portion of the land. The movement had commenced in Kentucky in 1797, and for several years it continued to spread and deepen, till society was shaken to its foundations. But the tares sprung up with the wheat, and the simple work of the gospel was marred by ill-regulated and fanatic zeal as well as illustrated by most remarkable conversions. In 1799, the revival commenced in the feeble and sparse settlements of Central and Western New York, and continued to extend during succeeding years. In 1802, the great revival of Western Pennsylvania was almost contemporary with the erection of the Pittsburg Synod, and resulted in supplying it with not a few of its future missionaries. In North Carolina and a portion of South Carolina, in Western Virginia and in New Jersey, the opening years of the present century were characterized by most remarkable outpourings of the Spirit. In repeated instances the face of society was changed. Churches almost extinct were restored to vigorous life.

The General Assembly made glad and grateful mention of "the very extraordinary success" which in many places had attended the ordinances of the gospel. "From the East, from the West, from the North, and the South, the most pleasing intelligence" had (1802) been received. In 1803, there was "scarcely a Presbytery under the care of the Assembly from which most pleasing intelligence had not been announced;" and from some of them communications had been made which displayed illustriously "the triumphs of evangelical truth and the power of sovereign grace." In most of the Northern and Eastern Presbyteries, revivals had prevailed, but free from "bodily agitations or extraordinary affections." At the South and West there had been a more remarkable awakening, but characterized by some features "of the origin and nature of which" the Assembly declined to express its opinion. In 1804, there had been a marked advance in nearly all parts of the Church, the exceptional features of revival which objectors had magnified having been limited to a single portion of the field. The report of 1805 was of a more varied character, and called attention to the excesses of the revival,—remarking that "true religion is a most rational and Scriptural thing." In 1806, while the Assembly felt constrained to bear testimony against Socinian error and reprehensible attempts to counterfeit the work of God, they could yet speak of the pleasure with which they had heard of the general extension and prosperity of the Church throughout the land. The narrative for 1807 speaks rather the language of apprehension and admonition than of gratulation. The reaction of the revivals of preceding years had produced its effects. But in 1808, although the Assembly found abundant "cause of sorrow and humiliation," and felt constrained, in view of the aspect of public affairs, to appoint for the observance of the churches a day of fasting and prayer, there was yet not a little which cheered them in the review of the year. At Newark a most powerful revival of religion had prevailed, under the labors of Dr. Griffin. The Synod of Albany had been also highly favored.

In 1813, after three or four years of steady growth,

but characterized by few extended revivals, the Assembly was cheered by the report of "scenes resembling those of Pentecost," in various parts of the Church. Revivals had prevailed in the Presbyteries of Jersey, Hudson, Onondaga, and Albany, and to a considerable extent elsewhere. It was found that in four years the membership of the Church had increased nearly twenty-five per cent.,—from about twenty-eight thousand in 1809, to thirty-four thousand six hundred and twenty-four in 1813.[1]

The influence of the war, although deleterious, and bearing severely upon certain portions of the Church, was less disastrous than might have been anticipated. During its continuance, a day of fasting and prayer was annually appointed by the Assembly, and marked outpourings of the Spirit did not wholly cease. The Assemblies of 1814 and 1815, while constrained to speak in warning tones of the spread of intemperance and kindred vices, could recount also special favors enjoyed by the Church in various portions of the land.

It is more than possible that the mention of intemperance in this connection was due less to any unprecedented development of the evil than to the fact that public attention had recently been called to it in a special manner. For several years individuals in different parts of the country had been reflecting anxiously upon the subject; but in 1811, by a concert of action, the General Assembly and the General Associations of Massachusetts and Connecticut were led to appoint a committee from each of their several bodies to co-operate in devising measures for preventing the numerous and

---

[1] Probably these numbers as reported are much below the actual membership. The additions in 1813 were unusually large, amounting to three thousand seven hundred and twenty-one.—*Panoplist*, ix. 93.

alarming evils of intemperance. In the same year, one thousand copies of a pamphlet by Dr. Rush, entitled "An Enquiry into the Effects of Ardent Spirits on the Human Body and Mind," were given (or presented) to the Assembly, to be divided among the members and by them distributed among the congregations. In 1812, the committees appointed by the General Association of Connecticut and by the Assembly made their reports. The committee of the former body admitted the alarming evils of intemperance, but confessed that they did not see that any thing could be done. Dr. Beecher, who was present, and who at recent ordinations of ministers had witnessed the extent to which the drinking-usages of the times had been sanctioned by ministerial example,[1] rose at once to propose the appointment of a committee who should report at that meeting the ways and means of arresting the tide of intemperance. As chairman of this committee, he penned their report,—"the most important paper," as he declared nearly half a century later, that he ever wrote. It glowed with the earnest eloquence characteristic of its author, and far and near produced a deep effect.

The report adopted by the General Assembly was less extended, but was alike pertinent and practical. It sounded the note of alarm, which echoed abroad over the land and gave a powerful impulse to the cause of reform. It recommended to ministers "to preach as often as expedient on the sins and mischiefs of intemperate drinking, and to warn their hearers, both in public and private, of those habits and indulgences which may have a tendency to produce it." It enjoined special vigilance on the part of Sessions, the dissemination of addresses, sermons, and tracts on the subject, and the

---

[1] At the ordinations of Mr. Hart, of Plymouth, and Mr. Harvey, in Goshen, Conn.—*Autobiography of Dr. L. Beecher.*

adoption of practical measures for reducing the number of places at which liquors were sold. It was in the light of facts which several years of observation had spread before the community, that the Assembly felt warranted to speak as they did of the alarming evils of intemperance.

Other matters pertaining to the cause of sound morals claimed the attention of the Assembly. The death of Hamilton, who fell in a duel with Aaron Burr in 1804, thrilled the nation with horror. In the Synod of New York and New Jersey, Dr. Beecher—against strong political influences—secured the solemn condemnation of any indulgence or toleration of the "code of honor." The Presbytery of Baltimore instructed its commissioners, in 1805, to endeavor to engage the Assembly to recommend to its ministers to refuse to officiate at the funeral of any one who was known to have been concerned in a duel or had given or accepted a challenge. The Assembly, in reply, expressed its utter abhorrence of the practice of duelling, pronounced it "a remnant of Gothic barbarism," "a presumptuous and highly criminal appeal to God as the Sovereign Judge," "inconsistent with every just principle of moral conduct," "a violation of the sixth commandment," and a thing to be utterly discountenanced. They complied fully, moreover, with the request of the Presbytery of Baltimore, and recommended that no one who had been concerned in a duel, unless he had given unequivocal proof of repentance, should be admitted to the distinguishing privileges of the Church.[1]

In the Assembly of 1815, the slavery question, which

---

[1] In 1805, several slight amendments—mainly verbal—of the Form of Government, which had been submitted to the Presbyteries by the Assembly of the previous year, were found to have been approved by a majority of the Presbyteries, and were, consequently, adopted.

had been left undisturbed for twenty years, was again introduced. It was brought to the notice of the Assembly by the petitions of certain elders who entertained conscientious scruples on the subject of holding slaves, and of the Synod of Ohio, asking a deliverance of the Assembly upon the subject of buying and selling slaves. The report on the subject, after being read and amended, was as follows:—

"The General Assembly have repeatedly declared their cordial approbation of those principles of civil liberty which appear to be recognized by the Federal and State Governments in these United States. They have expressed their regret that the slavery of the Africans and of their descendants still continues in so many places, and even among those within the pale of the Church, and have urged the Presbyteries under their care to adopt such measures as will secure at least to the rising generation of slaves, within the bounds of the Church, a religious education; that they may be prepared for the exercise and enjoyment of liberty when God in his providence may open a door for their emancipation." The petitioners are then referred to the action of the Synod of 1787, republished by the Assembly of 1793, and to the action of the Assembly of 1795. To the first petition this was considered a sufficient answer; but as to the second, from the Synod of Ohio, "the Assembly observe that, although in some sections of our country, under certain circumstances, the transfer of slaves may be unavoidable, yet they consider the buying and selling of slaves by way of traffic, and all undue severity in the management of them, as inconsistent with the spirit of the gospel. And they recommend it to the Presbyteries and Sessions under their care to make use of all prudent measures to prevent such shameful and unrighteous conduct."

One of the most perplexing matters which during this

period was brought before the Assembly was the policy to be adopted with reference to the Synod of Kentucky. The powerful revival which had prevailed for some time within the bounds of that Synod was without a precedent in the history of the Church. From a state of almost hopeless decline, the churches were aroused to unexampled activity. The power of a hitherto prevalent infidelity was paralyzed. The spell of worldliness was broken. The hardened, the blasphemer, the skeptic, the atheist, were smitten with conviction; and hundreds, if not thousands, were added to the membership of the churches.

But the work was characterized by extraordinary manifestations, of which the more conservative ministers could not approve. The "Bodily Exercises," of various kinds, began to prevail as the work progressed, till in some minds they came to be regarded as its inseparable adjuncts. The enthusiasm of some, and the fanaticism of others, carried them beyond the limits of discretion. Uneducated but zealous men began to exhort, and at length to assume the work of preachers. The demand for their labors—increased by the revival—perplexed the Presbytery. To license them might flood the Church with inexperienced men, who would do mischief. To refuse them license or approbation as catechists or exhorters might be not only regarded as invidious, but as opposing the progress of the revival. "Father" Rice wrote a letter to the Assembly (1804), asking advice. The reply was cautious and discreet. It pointed out the dangers to be apprehended from introducing uneducated men hastily into the ministry, yet allowed the Presbytery to sanction catechists and exhorters, if men of sound judgment, over whom the Presbytery was to keep careful watch and supervision.

But the mischief apprehended had already taken place. The Presbytery and the Synod were divided into two parties in reference to the question; and to such an extent had they been carried in their zeal that friendly co-operation was no longer possible. Messrs. Blythe, Lyle, and Stuart, members of the Synod, applied to the Assembly (1804) for advice as to the course to be pursued for healing the breach. In response, Drs. Hall and Green and Rev. Mr. Marquis were appointed a committee to meet and confer with the Synod at their next meeting. The report of this committee in the following year showed that the grievances of the seceding brethren consisted in what they regarded as the violation of their own rules by the majority of the Synod, and the fatalism taught in the Confession of Faith. In their own defence the Synod had addressed themselves to their churches in their own vindication, exposing the inconsistency of those who would reject the use of creeds and disregard the authority of the judicatories of the Church.

The Assembly approved of the course pursued by the Synod, as "firm and temperate;" but it was felt—whether justly or not—that the evil had already gone too far to be reached by any measure which might be adopted either by the Synod or Assembly. Yet in the following year (1805), the "Presbytery of Cumberland" addressed the Assembly a letter of complaint, which the latter characterized in their reply as "respectful and interesting," while they disclaimed any intention to cast reproach on the revival or upon those who were connected with it. But the irregularities of the Presbytery on several points invited the reprehension of the Synod; and the latter, by extraordinary measures, endeavored to put a stop to these irregularities. To some of these measures the Assembly took exceptions (1807), and advised the Synod to review them. In reply to the aggrieved members of Cumberland Presbytery, the Assembly could only say that, had their case come up before them properly by way of appeal, the desired relief might perhaps have been afforded.

But already the hope of reconciling the parties at variance had vanished. The Assembly itself was not unanimous in regard to the policy to be pursued. Some—and among them Dr. Dwight—were strenuous in vindication of the cause of the Synod. Others—like Dr. Wilson, of Philadelphia—felt that a judicious combination of leniency and decision might have healed the breach and prevented the Cumberland secession. But as the latter became conscious of their own strength, and were largely sustained by popular sympathy, they became less and less disposed to seek a restoration to the communion of the Presbyterian Church. At length, in 1814, the Assembly, in response to the inquiry how those who had belonged to the late Presbytery of Cumberland, but who upon its dissolution had erected themselves into a new one, should be treated, replied that they should be viewed as "having derived no authority from us for the exercise of discipline, &c.," and that "our regular members cannot treat with them as a body, but only as individuals." Such was the origin of the Cumberland Presbyterian Church.

Notwithstanding all the adverse influences exerted by the fanaticism, extravagances, and irregularities of the Kentucky revival, and the effects of the war, with the political passions and party zeal which preceded and accompanied it, the period under review was for the Presbyterian Church in this country one of steady and even rapid progress. It was characterized to a remarkable extent by a spontaneous missionary activity. Local as well as more general societies for the distribution of Bibles, tracts, and religious books, or for sending out missionaries to the destitute, were organized. New York and Philadelphia had each a city missionary society, the first organized in 1809, and the latter in

1807-8. The Church Session of Savannah, under the labors of the gifted Kollock, generously made provision (1810) for the support of two missionaries—one the Rev. Mr. Storrs, of Massachusetts, who had just completed his theological course at Andover—in the interior of the State of Georgia. In all parts of the land there was more or less of this disposition to volunteer missionary effort. In New Brunswick (1810) a Sabbath-school was established for the gratuitous instruction of poor children in moral and religious truth; and the fact was deemed so important as to be made a subject of grateful mention by the Assembly of 1811. The devoted Patterson of Philadelphia heard of it, and introduced the system of Sunday-schools into his own church; and in a few years more it had become general throughout the land.

The evidence of progress was evinced also by the increase in the number of Presbyteries, the organization of new churches, and the constant increase in the aggregate membership. In 1801, the four Synods numbered twenty-eight Presbyteries, with probably not far from two hundred and twenty-five ministers, and four hundred and fifty churches. In 1815, there had been an increase of nearly one hundred per cent. In 1801, Erie Presbytery was erected. In 1802, Columbia, Oneida, and Cumberland; in 1805, Geneva; in 1808, Hartford and Lancaster; in 1809, Jersey and Harmony; in 1810, Cayuga, Onondaga, West Tennessee, Muhlenberg, and Miami; in 1811, Northumberland; in 1812, Fayetteville; in 1814, Grand River and Champlain; and in 1815, Louisville and Mississippi, were successively erected; and the summary for the latter year embraced forty-one Presbyteries, five hundred and twenty ministers, eight hundred and fifty-nine churches, and thirty-nine thousand six hundred and eighty-five members. A full report would doubtless have added at least five per cent. to the number of ministers, churches, and members.

This was certainly a most rapid growth; but it had not overtaken the wants of the mission-field. As the circle of light expanded, it was encompassed by a still more extended circumference of darkness. The explorations of Messrs. Mills and Schermerhorn, who in 1812 and 1813, under the patronage of the Massachusetts and other missionary societies, visited the Western and Southwestern frontier of the field, afford us some feeble idea, at least, of the destitutions which prevailed. They went prepared to examine and to report back to the Eastern churches the necessities of the region they traversed, and the measures to be adopted for its supply. The statistics which they gave constituted the most eloquent appeal for enlarged effort.

In Pennsylvania west of the Alleghanies there was a population of about two hundred thousand inhabitants, and one hundred and one Presbyterian churches. In Ohio, with a population of three hundred and thirty thousand, there were seventy-eight Presbyterian and Congregational churches and forty-nine ministers. In Virginia, with a population little short of a million, there were about seventy Presbyterian churches and forty ministers. Old Virginia, as it was called,—the portion of the State lying on the seaboard,—was represented as in a deplorably destitute condition. Three-fourths of the entire State exhibited "an extensive and dreary waste." West of the Alleghanies it had but twelve Presbyterian churches and three ministers. Kentucky, with a population of four hundred thousand, had ninety-one Presbyterian churches and forty ministers. Three infidel publications were issued from the press in Lexington. Of the two hundred and ninety-three Baptist societies in the State, quite a large number were Arian or Socinian. Tennessee, with a population of more than two hundred and sixty thousand, had seventy-nine Presbyterian churches and twenty-six ministers. At its two colleges, one at Knoxville and the other in Green county, several students were preparing for the ministry. Here also was organized the only missionary society west of the Alleghanies, except the Synod of Pittsburg. The State of Louisiana, with a population of seventy-seven thousand whites and thirty-five thousand blacks, had not a single organized Presbyterian church. This was the case also with Missouri Territory, with a scattered population of twenty-one thousand. At New Orleans, Mr. Schermerhorn preached to a congregation of two hundred persons, and regretted that he could not accept their invitation to remain and labor among them.

Mississippi Territory, with a population of fifty-eight thousand, had but six Presbyterian churches and four ministers. "The state of society" was "deplorable." It was believed "that more innocent blood was shed in this Territory and in Louisiana in one year than in all the Middle and Eastern States in ten years!"

Indiana Territory was in no better condition in respect to religious destitution. With twenty-five thousand inhabitants, it had but one Presbyterian church and minister. Illinois Territory, with thirteen thousand inhabitants, could not lay claim to be represented by a single church or minister of the Presbyterian denomination.

This whole region thus surveyed was, for the most part, one great missionary field. It did not contain two-thirds as many ministers, Presbyterian and Congregational, as were to be found in the single State of Massachusetts. In some portions of it the Baptists and Methodists were quite numerous; but many of their preachers were utterly unqualified for their work, and in some cases their influence was disastrous rather than otherwise. Yet it was in these destitute fields that the largest future advance of the Church was already anticipated. In many of the older portions of the country there had been not only no positive increase, but in some there had been in fact an actual loss. In Virginia quite a number of the early churches were falling to decay. Too feeble without aid to support a pastor, they sank for years into a gradual decline. "I think the state of religion in this country," says Dr. Rice, in a letter to Dr. Alexander (Jan. 1810), "worse by some degrees than when you left it. Presbyterian congregations are decreasing every year, and appear as if they would dwindle to nothing." This was also the case, to a considerable extent, on the Eastern Shore of Maryland, and in Delaware. Central Pennsylvania was depleted by emigration; and some of the oldest churches were reduced to great feebleness. New Jersey was steadily but yet slowly gaining; while in Western Pennsylvania the growth was rapid. In Western New York, Ohio, Kentucky, and Tennessee, the Church received large accessions.

The funds at the command of the Assembly were scant indeed. The annual expenditure during this period for missions rarely exceeded two thousand five hundred dollars, and sometimes came far short of it. Yet the funds were judiciously applied. The salary of the missionary was sometimes thirty-three dollars per month, at others one dollar per day and his expenses. At length, forty dollars per month was allowed: yet it was not always accepted. It is impossible to peruse the reports of missionaries to the Assembly without a deep impression of the self-denying generosity of men who for the merest pittance were willing to brave all the hardships of the wilderness, and exposure to storm and fatigue, in order to accomplish their missionary work. There is more than is expressed to the eye in such statements as these:—that Mr. Chapman (of Geneva) "received forty-five dollars and thirty-two cents, travelled two thousand miles, and preached above one hundred sermons;"—that John Lindley, absent for four months, "baptized eleven children, preached ninety-six times, and received twelve dollars and fifty cents;"—that Mr. Coe (of Troy) "served as a missionary for six weeks, and received three dollars and seventy-five and a half cents;"—that James Hall, missionary to the Mississippi Territory, "served on his mission seven months and thirteen days, and received eighty-six dollars." Behind the dry statistical facts of the committee lie hidden whole chapters of welcome hardship, of heroic self-denial, and of results achieved enduring yet, the history of which no human pen can fairly trace, but whose "record is on high."

There was an urgent demand during this whole period for an increase in the number of ministers. The field was white for the harvest, but the laborers could not be procured. This lack of men fitted for pastoral and missionary work was felt to be a serious and growing evil. In 1805 it was brought before the Assembly by an overture from the pen of Dr. Ashbel Green. "Give us ministers, such"—it declared,—"is the cry of the missionary region; Give us ministers, is the importunate entreaty of our numerous and increasing vacancies; Give us ministers, is the demand of many large and important congregations in our most populous cities and towns." Weak and illiterate ministers could not supply the want or meet the emergency. Pious but educated men were needed; and a problem of the first importance was, How can they be secured?

The first thing proposed was an effort, by means of increased salaries, to remove discouragements of a temporal kind, especially the fear of inadequate support, which prevented young men from entering the ministry.

The other was a plan to be adopted by the Assembly for requiring the Presbyteries to do what lay in their power in the way of seeking out and assisting proper candidates. The overture was laid over till another year, and recommended to the attention of the Presbyteries. In 1806, their replies were received; and the general unanimity which they manifested warranted the Assembly in earnestly recommending, to every Presbytery under their care, increased endeavors on their part to bring forward a larger "number of promising candidates for the holy ministry." They were to urge the subject upon the attention of the congregations. Parents of pious youth were to be exhorted to educate them for the Church, and the youth themselves were to be persuaded "to devote their talents and their lives to this sacred calling." Vigorous exertions were to be made to raise funds for their support, and reports of their success were to be annually forwarded to the Assembly.

A letter from the trustees of the College of New Jersey was also (1806) recommended to the attention of the Presbyteries. It stated that they had "made the most generous provision for the support and instruction of theological students." They might pursue their studies at Princeton "at the moderate charge of one dollar a week for board, and enjoy the assistance of the President and Professor of Theology, without any fee for instruction."

The overture of Dr. Green may be perhaps regarded as the germ of the project which issued in the establishment of Princeton Theological Seminary. Nothing, however, was publicly spoken with direct reference to such an institution until it was mentioned in the opening Assembly of 1808, by Dr. Alexander. Encouraged by the favor with which the suggestion was received, the Presbytery of Philadelphia, at the instance of Dr.

Green, brought the subject, by overture, to the attention of the Assembly of 1809. It is probable that the success of the institution at Andover, which had been recently established, and which already numbered thirty-six students, was a weighty argument in favor of the project. The Assembly, after mature deliberation, determined to submit to the Presbyteries three plans for the promotion of theological education, and to adopt that which the reports of the following year should designate as preferable. These plans were—first, the establishment of "one great school" in some central position; secondly, the establishment of two, one for the Northern and the other for the Southern portion of the Church; and thirdly, one for each Synod. The reports made to the Assembly of 1810 showed that the first of these plans was preferred; and steps were immediately taken for carrying it out. A committee was appointed to draft the constitution of the proposed seminary; and upon Dr. Green, as the chairman of the committee, the task of doing it devolved. Adopted by the Assembly (1811) with slight alterations, vigorous measures were taken to endow the institution. The first meeting of the directors was held June 30, 1812, and the corner-stone was laid September 26, 1815.[1]

---

[1] After adopting this plan of the Seminary, the General Assembly which met in 1811 did little more than take measures for collecting funds for the proposed institution, by appointing a number of agents in all the Synods for that purpose. They also appointed a committee to confer with the trustees of the College of New Jersey, at Princeton, respecting any facilities and privileges which the said trustees might be disposed to give to a theological seminary if located at Princeton.

At the meeting of the next Assembly (1812) the location of the Seminary was fixed at Princeton, a board of directors was elected, and Dr. Alexander was appointed Professor of Didactic and Polemic Theology. The first meeting of the directors was held at Princeton, on the last Tuesday of June. On August 12, Dr. Alexander was

But the institution had already commenced its sessions. Early in 1814, the number of its students amounted to twenty-four: yet its state was pronounced to be "at once promising and critical," and its friends were exhorted to continue their efforts for its endowment. Year after year the attention of the Assembly was directed toward measures for procuring funds, and the ablest and best ministers of the Church were engaged in the task of soliciting contributions. The cause met with general acceptance, and even favor, and from every direction contributions were received. The amount for the year closing May, 1813, was not far from twenty-four thousand dollars.

A survey of the Church at the close of this period (1815) will bring to view some of the leading minds by which its policy was shaped and its success promoted. In New England were Samuel Taggart, a member of the Londonderry Presbytery, and pastor of Coleraine, Mass., for many years a member of Congress, a man of most remarkable memory and rigid logic; Dr. Daniel Dana, of Newburyport, and Morrison, of Londonderry, the last a model pastor, strict without austerity, and fervent without enthusiasm, sound in judgment, independent in thought, searching as a preacher, and as impressive in his sermons as in his prayers. In New York were Dr. Samuel Blatchford, of Lansingburg, trained as an English Independent, respectable as a scholar, kindred in spirit with Dwight

inaugurated. At this time, on the opening of the institution, the number of students was *three*. In May of the following year (1813) it was eight. The Assembly then elected Dr. Miller, of New York, Professor of Ecclesiastical History and Church Government, and he was inaugurated September 29. The seminary was now located permanently at Princeton. In the autumn of 1817, the edifice for the students was first occupied. It was of stone, one hundred and fifty feet long, fifty broad, and four stories high.—DR. MILLER, in Am. Quar. Register, x. 35.

and Edwards, with whom he was for years associated, of a large Christian heart, the friend of learning, philanthropy, and missions, and instructive and sometimes powerful in the pulpit; Jonas Coe, of Troy, great in *character* rather than in intellect, wit, or eloquence, pure-minded, judicious, and the model of the Christian gentleman; David Porter, of Catskill, eccentric, but kind, tender-hearted, of exquisite sensibility, a man of sharp discrimination, original thought, clear judgment, and a master in theology; President Nott, of Union College, then in the zenith of his fame and the vigor of his powers, eminent as a scholar, an orator, and a teacher; Aaron Woolworth, of Bridgehampton, L.I., discreet, benevolent, modest, but with heart and lips that amid revival scenes seemed as if touched by "a live coal from off the altar," and with a daily life that in the fragrance of goodness was "as ointment poured forth;" and M. L. Perrine, Gardiner Spring, and John B. Romeyn, of New York City; the first "the beloved disciple," "wise as a serpent and harmless as a dove;" the second in the flush of youthful enthusiasm, but faithful to the purpose which diverted him from the bar to the pulpit and has now crowned his age with the memories of a successful pastorate; the latter, with rich stores of knowledge, a sprightly, active intellect, a ready utterance, but with an earnestness of tone, manner, and gesture which dissipated all doubts of his sincerity, and gave to the tide of his discourse the force of a torrent.

In New Jersey were Richards and Griffin, of Newark, —the former practical, sagacious, discreet, carrying his unfeigned piety with him into every sphere, a safe guide, a trusted counsellor, and devoted pastor, the latter physically and intellectually a giant, just returned from his battle with the Anakims of Boston Unitarianism; Ashbel Green, President of New Jersey College, of sound rather than sprightly intellect, sternly conscientious even if wrong-headed, persistent in purpose, with theories that were convictions, and with convictions that were acts,—grave, dignified, courteous, leaving no man in mistake as to his aims, opinions, or positions, however objectionable, and with a pride of character and standing that none might call in question; Archibald Alexander, lovely in mind and person, idolized alike as pastor and teacher, in the pulpit fascinating rather than impressive, and destined for more than thirty years yet, as theological professor at Princeton, to shape the views, character, and destiny of hundreds of the pastors of the Church; and Samuel Miller, the Christian gentleman, the model of urbane and dignified deportment, with a consistent piety, a sound judgment, and a balance of character which exempted him alike from the brilliancy and the infirmities of genius, yet fitted him admirably to serve as the compeer of Alexander in training up an educated ministry.

In Pennsylvania were Wilson, Janeway, Skinner, Potts, and Patterson, of Philadelphia; the first liberal in spirit, profound in scholarship, unanswerable in argumentation; the second, of fair abilities and careful culture, a faithful pastor and discreet preacher; the third, just entering upon a ministry of long-continued and extended usefulness, and already giving earnest, in his "pungent appeals," of the force of truth pressed home by a clear logic and a glowing heart; the fourth, a practical worker, pastor of a church built up by his own efforts, kindly, judicious, sympathizing, and liberal-minded; the last, all this and far more,—a man who in dealing with sin and proclaiming the terrors of the law might almost be said to speak thunder and gesticulate lightning, and who seemed to draw his vital breath in the atmosphere of revival; F. A. Latta, of Chesnut Level, a poet, a classical scholar, and an orator; Wm. Paxton, of Lower Marsh Creek, modest, affectionate, untiring in pastoral duty, his tall, manly frame a fit index to his large heart; Henry R. Wilson, of Carlisle, as pastor or professor, ever active, energetic, enterprising; Samuel Porter, of Redstone Presbytery, the Patrick Henry of the pulpit, a man who had the boldness, tact, and eloquence that enabled him successfully to confront the Whiskey insurrectionists of 1794 on their own ground, and who with the advantages of early culture might have taken his place among the foremost metaphysicians and scholars of the age; Andrew Wylie, President of Jefferson College; John McMillan, of Chartiers,—the patriarch of the Presbytery, the father of Canonsburg Academy and Jefferson College, impetuous and almost irresistible in his appeals and denunciations; Matthew Brown, successively President of Washington and Jefferson Colleges, if impetuous and hasty, yet never shrinking or timid; Macurdy, of Cross Roads, intensely practical, but intensely devoted to his work, the friend of missions, and a powerful revivalist; Marquis, "the silver-tongued," of Cross Creek, whose voice was music, and whose art of persuasion was wellnigh perfect; and James Hughes, a faithful pastor, a scholar, a philanthropist, for years a superintendent of the Indian missions, and finally President of Miami University.

Returning eastward of the Alleghanies, we find at Wilmington, Del., Thomas Read, none the less venerable that he retains the manners, dress, and even wig of the olden time,—an example of hospitality, sympathizing with every form of benevolence, a pastor and yet a missionary, retaining still the sympathies of his youth, and as devoted to the Church as he had been to his country; at Baltimore, Inglis and Glendy, the first a most accomplished orator, charming every listener by the elegance—sometimes excessive—of his rhetoric, and the grace of his utterance, but falling short of that higher standard which Cowper commends;

the last, an Irish exile, and in every sermon betraying his national relationship to the Irish orators represented by Counsellor Phillips, and in his daily intercourse, and even in the pulpit, venting his Irish wit and humor, yet never forgetful of the character and manners of a Christian gentleman; at Georgetown, the humorous but sensible, shrewd, and genial Balch; at Alexandria, James Muir, with his staid Scotch gravity and dignity, kind-hearted, studious, Biblical in his preaching, spotless in reputation, and called, in reference to his stature as well as his meekness, "the little Moses."

In connection with the Synod of Virginia, we find Moses Hoge, President of Hampden-Sidney and Professor of Theology,—in the pulpit ungraceful and even uncouth in manner, but with a mind of uncommon vigor, well disciplined and richly stored; James Mitchel and his youthful colleague James Turner, at the Peaks of Otter, the first animated, fervent, sometimes quaint in the plans of his discourses, but suffering nothing to divert his aim from the heart and conscience; the latter, master of "soul-stirring, tear-drawing eloquence;" John H. Rice, at Richmond, with his varied scholarship, fervent piety, practical talent, and lovely spirit; George A. Baxter, President of Washington College, and pastor of Lexington and New Monmouth, a man as modest as he was great, with an understanding comprehensive, profound, clear, and logical, a memory wonderfully retentive, a judgment that rarely erred, and a fervent emotion which it needed but the occasion to evoke; Conrad Speece, of Augusta, with all his wit and drollery, a giant in intellect as well as person, and insatiable in his thirst for knowledge; and, besides these, not a few who had caught the spirit of the great revival at Hampden-Sidney, or had been converted under its influence.

Still farther to the South, we meet with the venerable

David Caldwell, long a patriarch among the churches of North Carolina,—learned, pious, patriotic, a Revolutionary whig, a genial friend and trusty counsellor as well as successful teacher and able preacher; Robert H. Chapman, President, and Joseph Caldwell, Professor, of the State University, both from New Jersey, and men of sterling worth; James Hall, of Bethany, a man of rare gifts, and, with his magnificent person and his hoary head,—"a crown of glory,"—the beau-ideal of nature's nobleman,—untiring in missionary zeal, and shrinking from no hardship; Andrew Flinn, of Charleston, as attractive in the pulpit as unwearied in his pastorate, winning not only by the charm of his eloquence, but by his grace of manner; Moses Waddel, of Willington, eminent as a teacher, subsequently President of Georgia University, a man whose prayerful, beneficent, and useful life well earned him the epithet "blessing and to be blessed;" Francis Cummins, to whom the people for hundreds of miles around looked as their missionary pastor,—a profound theologian, an original thinker, and in the pulpit impressing on every hearer his own deep reverence; and, eminent among many others, John Brown, for several years Professor in Oglethorpe University, and pastor at different periods of several churches,—humble, unassuming, confiding, with the law of kindness on his tongue, and called by some of his parishioners "our Apostle John,"—opening his lips to pour forth a clear, silvery stream of evangelical instruction, rich with the stores of ample learning and personal experience.

Beyond the mountains, and in the new States of the West, there were men who had been, or eventually were to be, heard of on the Atlantic slope,—men like Blackburn, Henderson, Coffin, Ramsey, and Anderson, of Tennessee, Rice, Cunningham, Balch, Blythe, Nelson, Stuart, and Cleland, of Kentucky, and Hoge, Gilliland, and the Wilsons, of Ohio.

Such were the men who held, in the concluding portion of the period under review, the foremost place in directing the councils and carrying into effect the policy of the Church. We may indeed regard them as representative men. Not a few of their co-presbyters, in humbler spheres or more remote fields of labor, were full as worthy, full as gifted as themselves; and possibly more self-denying. An obscure parish could enjoy then, with less fear of molestation than now, the gifts and graces of their favorite pastor. Hence, in quiet country neighborhoods, or perhaps supporting themselves in part by labor on the farm or in the work of instruction, many were to be found whose names might have graced a more resplendent record than the Session-book or the list of Presbytery, but whose work has proved not less valuable, enduring, or important, that the only star that hovers over their names is that which college catalogues affix in token of the dead.

Yet the men who have been enumerated, while some of them, of course, take rank above their less distinguished brethren in natural gifts, intellectual culture, and the graces of eloquence, were fair representatives of the liberal spirit, enlarged policy, and consecrated aims of the Church. These were the men whose wisdom framed and whose energy executed the plans which resulted in equipping the Church more fully for her mission, enlarging, or perhaps new-creating, the means of ministerial education, and perfecting measures for aggressive evangelical effort. They were by no means fully accordant on all theological points; but they were kindred in spirit and harmonious in effort.

CHAPTER XXII.

PENNSYLVANIA, 1800-1820.

At the commencement of the present century, the Presbyterian Church in Pennsylvania was represented by the six Presbyteries of Philadelphia, Carlisle, Huntingdon, Redstone, Erie, and Ohio,—the three last connected with the Synod of Virginia. The Presbytery of Philadelphia consisted of eighteen ministers and about twenty churches; that of Carlisle, of eighteen ministers and twenty-nine churches; that of Huntingdon, of twelve ministers and thirty-seven churches; that of Redstone, of about twelve ministers and thirty churches; that of Erie, of about eight ministers and thirty churches; while that of Ohio numbered[1] eighteen ministers and over thirty churches. The aggregate within the bounds of the State amounted to not far from eighty-two ministers and nearly one hundred and eighty churches. Of these, in repeated instances, two or three were united to form a single pastoral charge; while nearly half the number were vacant.

For several years the principal growth of the Church was in the western portion of the State. Immigration was multiplying the new settlements, while the eastern and central portions were depleted of their natural increase to swell the tide that was drifting toward Ohio and the regions South and West, and furnishing on the frontier "the seeds of new congregations."[2] The population of the State increased from 1800 to 1810 at the

[1] N. Y. Miss. Mag., 1801. [2] Minutes for 1807, p. 382.

rate of thirty-three per cent., and from 1810 to 1820 at the rate of twenty-five per cent., amounting at the last date to a little over one million of inhabitants.

The increase of the Church was not greatly disproportioned to that of the population. The ministers had increased from eighty-two to one hundred and thirty-five, and the congregations from nearly one hundred and eighty to two hundred and eighty. The growth had been most rapid in the region around Pittsburg. Western immigration, spreading along the Ohio valley and the lines of the tributaries of that river, had begun to develop the vast resources of the West; and the southwestern portion of Pennsylvania shared in the impetus thus given to industrial and commercial enterprise.

In 1820, there were nine Presbyteries, mostly within the bounds of the State. Of these, Philadelphia, Carlisle, Huntingdon, and Northumberland were connected with the Synod of Philadelphia, while Redstone, Ohio, Erie, Steubenville, and Washington were connected with the Synod of Pittsburg. To these was added in 1820 the Presbytery of Alleghany.

The Presbytery of Philadelphia, which in 1800 had eighteen ministers and twenty congregations, had now twenty-six ministers and thirty-seven congregations.[1] At Fairfield (N.J.) was Ethan Osborn, whose pastorate here was already one of more than twenty years,[2] and was to continue some fifteen years longer. At Bridgeton and Greenwich (N.J.), Jonathan Freeman, who had been settled at Newburgh (N.Y.) for eight years, commenced his labors as pastor in 1805, and remained in the pastorate until his death in 1822.

---

[1] The report for 1819 in the Assembly's minutes is the authority on which I have had mainly to rely for the following year.

[2] Settled previous to 1795.

His predecessors in the pastorate were George Faitoute[1] and William Clarkson.[2] At Allen's Township (Allentown) was Robert Russell, who succeeded Francis Peppard in the pastorate previous to 1800, and who had been laboring here, therefore, for more than twenty years. At Deep Run[3] and Doylestown was Uriah Dubois, a descendant of Louis Dubois, a Huguenot refugee who settled at New Paltz in Ulster county, N.Y., in 1660. He was himself a native of New Jersey, a graduate of the University of Pennsylvania in 1790, a theological pupil of Dr. Ashbel Green, and in 1796 a licentiate of the Presbytery of Philadelphia. He was installed, Dec. 16, 1798, as pastor of the churches of Deep Run and Tinicum; but, resigning the latter in 1804, he removed from Deep Run to Doylestown, where he became Principal of a large and flourishing school, and where also he established a Presbyterian congregation, to which, in connection with that of Deep Run, he continued to minister to the close of his life, Sept. 10, 1821. He was a man of great energy and industry, an excellent classical scholar, an accomplished instructor, and an earnest and attractive preacher.[4] His successor for a short period was Charles Hyde.

At Great Valley and Charlestown was William Latta, the successor of John Simonton and John Gemmil. He was a son of James Latta, and a graduate of Pennsylvania University in 1794. In 1799[4] he was installed, and his pastorate continued until February, 1847, when he had nearly completed his fourscore years.[5] He was a fine scholar and a graceful writer.

In the city of Philadelphia, the pastors of the Pres-

---

[1] Assembly's Minutes for 1789.

[2] Assembly's Minutes for 1800.

[3] James Latta was pastor here from 1761 to 1770.

[4] Sprague, iii. 200.

[5] Sprague, iii. 205.

byterian churches in 1820 were Drs. Wilson, Janeway, Ely, Potts, Skinner, and Neill; while John Gloucester had charge of the African Church. The pastorate of James Patriot Wilson over the First Church extended from May, 1806, to the spring of 1830. Dr. Ewing had died in 1802, and John Blair Linn, who was settled in 1799 as co-pastor with him, closed his ministry with his life, in August, 1804, at the early age of twenty-seven.

Dr. Linn was a son of Dr. William Linn, one of the pastors of the Reformed Dutch Collegiate Church of New York. After his graduation at Columbia College, in 1795, at the age of eighteen, he commenced the study of law with the celebrated Alexander Hamilton. But this pursuit was far from a congenial one. His taste for poetry and elegant literature revolted from dry legal technicalities, and his mind, under the serious impressions made upon it by more mature reflection, was drawn to the Christian ministry. Under Dr. Romeyn, of Schenectady, he pursued his theological studies with great ardor, and after his licensure, in 1798, the popularity of his first pulpit efforts gave brilliant promise for his future. But the severe duties of his pastorate were too much for a constitution at best feeble, and anxiety, care, and intellectual effort told with speedy effect upon his sanguine temperament, his exquisite sensibilities, and his delicate frame. He had the brilliant gifts, but he had also the infirmities, of genius. A fancied slight destroyed his composure; and he dwelt more on the dark than the bright side of the picture of life. His poetic inclinations were perhaps too freely indulged, and he was too ready to draw upon the strength that should have been reserved for the more plain and prosaic duties of life. His published poems, for one so yoüthful, were quite numerous; and one of them was republished in England. Nor did he shrink from the arena of controversy. His reply to Dr. Priestley indicated vigorous intellect and extensive research.[1] But, while with years his mind became more equable, he was still haunted by gloomy fancies. He doubted his adequacy to the duties of the ministry; he scrupled his right to salary for such services as he could render; he looked upon his spiritual state with frequent and deep distrust. In August, 1804, the frail tenement which had been racked by too exquisite sensibilities and imprudent efforts gave way, and the hopes inspired by his early attainments were finally blighted.

His successor, Dr. Wilson, was, at the time of Dr. Linn's death, pastor of Lewes, in Delaware, his native place, where his father had for many years labored in the ministry. Graduated at the University of Pennsylvania in 1788, he had fitted himself for the bar, entered upon the practice of law, and attained a reputation unsurpassed perhaps in his native State. The skepticism of his earlier years was disturbed by a series of distressing afflictions, and he was finally brought, by reflection and examination, not only to a conviction of the truth of Christianity, but to a full and hearty acceptance of it. He at once relinquished the honors and emoluments of his profession, and devoted himself to the ministry. After ten years' labor in Delaware, he entered upon the pastorate of the First Church in Philadelphia, where he remained for about a quarter of a century.

Few names in the history of the Church are entitled to more honorable mention than that of Dr. Wilson. His was one of the leading minds of the denomination. Of tall stature, with a countenance grave rather than animated, his features bore the stamp of kindly feeling

[1] Sprague, iv. 212.

and high intelligence. Uniformly urbane and obliging, fastidiously modest, of a truly catholic and liberal spirit, he was the model of a Christian gentleman. His learning was thorough and extensive. Almost a recluse in his habits, he devoted himself to study, and was perhaps the only clergyman in the country of whom it might be said that he not only had read all the Greek and Latin Fathers, but that "he almost literally lived among them."[1] Yet he was by no means a mere pedant or bookworm. Few men have ever so thoroughly digested their laboriously acquired knowledge. His mind was disciplined to its tasks; and, though he never used a note or read a line in the pulpit, the logic of his argument was clear, concise, consecutive, and conclusive. On a blank leaf of the Tract by Ware on "Extemporaneous Preaching" he left the following testimony over his own signature:—"I have preached twenty years, and have never written a full sermon in my life, and never read one word of a sermon from the pulpit, nor opened a note, nor committed a sentence, and have rarely wandered five minutes at a time from my mental arrangement previously made."

His piety was in keeping with his simplicity and humility. His convictions of the truth of what he preached were firmly grounded in his own experience.[2] His sermons, if rarely imaginative, were replete with lucid exposition or solid instruction. He sought to bring forth the real meaning and to elucidate the teachings of the Scriptures. Erudite, and usually un-

---

[1] Sprague, iv. 359.

[2] He once sent to Dr. Green a Hopkinsian work, together with a note expressing his views of it. "The first dissertation," he says, "would require me to change my prayers; the second would invert the order of my conceptions; the third, alter my Bible; the fourth, make me abandon God's justice and frustrate his grace in Jesus Christ."

impassioned, none would mistake him for a brilliant, but all would admit him to be an able, man.

His eccentricities might many of them excite a smile, but they were never assumed for effect, and they threw light on his generous, noble, kindly, or modest bearing. He did not like to be put under obligation to any one. He was even proudly independent. For mere forms he had no relish, and for mere authority no reverence. A rigid Presbyterianism was by no means to his taste. His dislike of all egotism was attested by a sometimes almost ludicrous use of the regal plural,—*we*. His sensitiveness to any thing indecorous was extreme. But one who had ever listened to his familiar, instructive, and edifying conversation, or who had ever felt the impress of his warm, loving heart, or who had followed him in his clear and forcible presentation of the sublime truths of revelation, would have felt that all his peculiarities were lost from view, like spots on the disk of the sun.[1] His impetuousness when engaged in debate or controversy—so unlike his ordinary manner—was studiously checked; and when he feared that he could not master it he would absent himself from the place of meeting.

The pastor of the Second Presbyterian Church—till 1812 the colleague of Dr. Green—was Jacob J. Janeway, whose long term of public service has made his name familiar in the annals of the Church. A native of New York City, a graduate of Columbia College in 1794, and a student of theology under Dr. Livingston, of the Re-

[1] Dr. Ely states that he once heard Dr. Ashbel Green say of himself and Dr. Wilson that they were both proud men. "But I am proud," said Dr. Green, "and know it; he is proud, and is ignorant of it." Dr. Green doubtless pronounced him proud, because he had too much independence to be the satellite of any man, even of Dr. Green. One who knew him intimately has pronounced him remarkable for humility.

formed Dutch Church, he was ordained as colleague pastor of Dr. Green in 1799. Here he remained till called in 1826 to the Theological Professorship in the Western Seminary at Alleghany City. This post he retained but a short time, and from 1830 to 1839 was connected with the Reformed Dutch Church, as pastor in New Brunswick (1830–32) and Vice-President of Rutgers College (1833–39). His closing years were devoted to the promotion of the various benevolent enterprises of the Church, in connection with its Boards. At the age of eighty-four, after a gradual decline, he died at New Brunswick.

Neither remarkably profound nor brilliant, he was yet a man to inspire respect and confidence: conservative in council, discreet, yet prompt in action, he was ever ready for every good cause and work. By his influence and example he contributed largely to the prosperity of the Church and her institutions. His liberality was marked, and on principle he gave away in charity one-fifth of his annual income. Kind, affectionate, easy of access, he was venerated and loved by all who formed his acquaintance.

In the Third Church, as successor to Dr. Alexander, was Ezra Stiles Ely, son of Rev. Zebulon Ely, of Lebanon, Conn., where the father was settled and where the son was born. His first settlement was in Westchester parish, in the town of Colchester, Conn.; and at that time his course was scarcely such as his later years would approve. But a change at length took place, and the rash fancies or ill-regulated humor of youth gave place, at least to a great extent, to a genuine devotion to the work of the ministry. Zealous in behalf of the vital doctrines of the gospel, he believed them to have been assailed by Hopkinsian error; and forthwith he placed himself at the head of its opponents, and through the press and in the ecclesiastical assemblies sought to smite it down. His octavo volume in which various heresies are ranged in parallel columns is a literary, or perhaps we should say a theological, curiosity. Time, however, cooled his anti-Hopkinsian zeal, or rather it subsided into a genial and kindly recognition of the Christian character and worth of those whom he found upon acquaintance to be, in spite of every prejudice, his brethren in Christ.

A man of his active mercurial temperament could not be idle. He was identified with all schemes of benevolence, constantly engaged in works of charity for the poor and suffering, and in all projects of Christian enterprise stood ready, both by word and example, to endorse and commend them. His house was ever open to all who loved his Master, and ministers and students shared his Christian hospitalities, not niggardly bestowed. His literary ability placed him in the front rank of those who exerted influence by the tongue or pen. While preaching to his own charge, and attending to the duties of a pastor as well as a preacher, he was also editor of the "Philadelphian," and proved himself ready as a writer as well as skilful in argument. The journal of his experience during his labors in New York, where he was residing when called to Philadelphia, was reprinted in England, under the title of "Visits of Mercy." In 1828, he published his "Collateral Bible, or Key to the Holy Scriptures," and subsequently a memoir of his father. His labors showed him to be a man of determination and enthusiasm, more than of cold calculation. Quick and clear, rather than profound, his sermons were enriched with frequent illustrations; and, gifted with a voice musical and distinct, and a full enunciation, and possessed of a self-reliance that never gave way, he moulded his audiences at will.

From 1825 to 1836 he was stated clerk of the General

Assembly, and in 1828 he was chosen its moderator In 1834, he conceived the plan of establishing a college (Marion) in Missouri, and in connection with it a theological seminary; but the financial crisis of 1837 overwhelmed the project with defeat, and in 1844, after his return to Philadelphia, he resumed his ministerial duties as pastor of the First Presbyterian Church, Northern Liberties, where with unabated zeal he labored till struck down by paralysis in 1851. His mind was thenceforth a wreck: yet for ten years longer he lingered, manifesting at intervals the religious sympathies of his heart.

The pastor of the Fourth Church was George C. Potts,[1] an emigrant from Ireland in the stormy times of 1797–98. A native of that country, he had been educated at the University of Glasgow, and licensed to preach by the Presbytery of Monaghan. But the zeal with which he espoused the cause of his country's independence rendered his longer residence in Ireland unsafe, and he directed his course to this country. After preaching for some time to vacant churches in Pennsylvania and Delaware, he removed to Philadelphia. Here, with the sanction of the Presbytery, he undertook to gather a new congregation in the southern part of the city; and his labors were crowned with success. In June, 1800, he was installed pastor of the church, which from small beginnings became large and flourishing. Popular as a preacher, faithful in the discharge of pastoral duty, distinguished for sound judgment and kindly and liberal spirit, he was spared to complete a pastorate of thirty-six years over the same church. His death occurred September 23, 1838.

The Fifth Church was under the pastoral care of

---

[1] Father of Dr. George Potts, pastor of the church in University Place, N.Y.

Thomas H. Skinner, who had commenced his labors in Philadelphia, some years previous, as co-pastor—upon the dismission of Dr. Green—of Dr. Janeway, of the Second Church.[1] With this Second Church the First Church of the Northern Liberties was connected, the two constituting a single pastoral charge under Messrs. Janeway and Skinner. But it was thought that the interests of religion would be best promoted by surrendering the Church of the Northern Liberties to a single pastor, who should devote to it his whole time and energies. James Patterson, of Bound Brook, N.J., was accordingly called to take charge of it, and was installed January 11, 1814. For one year longer the pastors of the Second Church continued to preach once on each Sabbath at Northern Liberties; but after this the new church was left to the care of the pastor alone.

Meanwhile, in hearty co-operation with Mr. Patterson in revival efforts, and through an enlarged acquaintance with the New England divines, the views of Mr. Skinner on some theological points had become more decidedly Edwardian, and his preaching gave evidence of the fact. He was indeed on this account—although unjustly—charged with holding Hopkinsian tenets, and a portion of the Second Church became disaffected toward him as colleague pastor. Such was the feeling of opposition that charges of heresy were brought

---

[1] Dr. Skinner is said to have been awakened under the preaching of Benjamin H. Rice, while the latter, laboring as a missionary of the General Assembly, was itinerating in North Carolina. Mr. Rice preached two sermons at Edenton, on a certain Sabbath, and among his hearers (1811–12) was Dr. Skinner, then a student of law. He went to hear, not without strong prejudice both against the preacher and the truth; but his prejudices were overcome, and the sermons were made instrumental in his conversion.—*Obituary Sermon on Dr. Rice, by W. E. Schenk.*

against him, and a request was presented to Presbytery that his pastoral relation to the church might be dissolved. The injustice of the charge was manifest to the Presbytery; and so long as it was not withdrawn, Mr. Skinner persisted in opposing the request of the disaffected portion of the congregation. But upon its withdrawal and the adoption of a compromise which secured his own rights and those of his friends, he felt it expedient and desirable that his pastoral relation to the church should cease. It was accordingly dissolved by Presbytery (Nov. 5, 1815), and, together with the portion of the congregation which still adhered to him, he withdrew, accepting a call to the Fifth Church, which occupied a small house in an uninviting locality in Locust Street.

This church had been gathered in 1810 by James K. Burch, a native of Albemarle county, Va., and a graduate of Washington College at Lexington. He was licensed and ordained by Orange Presbytery in 1807, and, after preaching for some time at Newbern and afterward at Washington, was, through the influence of Dr. Alexander, introduced to the pulpit of a Reformed Dutch congregation then worshipping in the Fourth Street Academy, Philadelphia. It was his desire to have them connect themselves with the Presbyterian Church, and, when they declined to do so, he left them, and, with a colony that was organized as the Fifth Presbyterian Church, commenced his pastorate, which, with varied experience, was continued till a short time previous to Mr. Skinner's dismissal. A man of more than ordinary eloquence, but greatly lacking in stability, he was quite unfitted to secure the confidence in himself or his measures which was necessary to build up a prosperous congregation.

The church was at the lowest point of depression when Mr. Skinner took charge of it; and for seven years, until his call to New Orleans in 1822, his labors in its behalf were devoted and unremitting. But, although not without result, his efforts were not prospered as in other circumstances they might have been; and at this juncture it was resolved by his friends, as the only method of retaining him in the city, to seek out a new locality. This was found in Arch Street, near Tenth. Here a large and commodious house of worship was soon erected, and it was not long before crowded assemblies testified to the popularity and success of the new enterprise. The clear, forcible, logical, earnest presentation of truth[1] from the lips of the youthful pastor produced a deep impression, and ere long the prosperity of the church was fully assured. For many years Dr. Skinner remained in the pastorate of the church,—at a later period filling posts of honor in the Seminaries of Andover and New York, and in the pastorate of the Mercer Street Church, gathered by his labors in the latter city.

The Sixth Church was organized in 1815–16,[2] and its first pastor was William Neill. A native of Western Pennsylvania (1778), he was exposed in early years to the hardships of frontier life, and, while yet a child, both his parents were killed by the Indians. Thrown thus as an orphan upon the kindness of generous friends, he was placed by them in a store at Canonsburg, where he enjoyed the pastoral oversight of Dr. McMillan. Here he was converted, and immediately resolved to devote himself to the ministry. Completing his preparatory

---

[1] Dr. J. W. Alexander, in his Letters, vol. i. p. 75, speaks of "the unanswerable arguments of Dr. Wilson, and the pungent appeals of Mr. Skinner."

[2] The Sixth Church grew out of a division of the old Pine Street Church, of which Dr. Alexander was pastor when called to Princeton in 1812. On the settlement of Dr. Ely, soon after, the division took place, and the Sixth Church was formed.

studies at the Old Academy, he directed his course to Princeton, where he was graduated in 1803. Engaging subsequently as tutor in the college, and prosecuting at the same time his theological studies, he received in 1805 a call to the church at Cooperstown, where he labored till 1809, when he was called to the charge of the First Presbyterian Church of Albany. Here he remained until his removal to Philadelphia.

In 1824 he was called to the Presidency of Dickinson College, which he retained till 1829, when he became Secretary and General Agent for the Board of Education. After two years' service, he relinquished the position, and commenced his labors with the Germantown church, which had maintained for some years a somewhat precarious existence, and which he found in a deplorable condition,—broken down, peeled and scattered, with few symptoms of spiritual life. In 1842 he left this field, and ceased from the active duties of the pastorate. He survived, however, in the gradual decay of his vital powers, till 1860.

Active, devoted, and useful, he stood ever ready to meet the calls of duty and supply others' lack of service by extra diligence of his own. His preaching was lucid and replete with gospel truth, and persuasive and tender in appeal. As a pastor, he was exemplary in looking after the interests of his flock. His successors were John H. Kennedy, and subsequently S. G. Winchester.

The Seventh Church was established in 1820–21, occupying the building—Ranstead Place—which had been erected for the use of an Independent church some years previous. The latter church was organized in 1810–11, mainly through the exertions of a Mr. Hay, from London, and in 1812 he was succeeded in the pastorate of the church by the Rev. John Joyce. Upon the failure of the enterprise, the building was purchased by Messrs.

Ralston and Henry of the Second Church, and devoted to the use of the congregation under Rev. Wm. E Engles, which assumed the name of the Seventh Church

The Eighth or Scots' Church had been in existence for some years, but first came into connection with the General Assembly upon the union with it of the Associate Reformed body in 1822. In the following year, William L. McCalla was installed pastor, and remained in this connection till 1835, when he was succeeded by Alexander Macklin. Fiercely orthodox, Mr. McCalla's zeal was sometimes excessive; acute, chivalrous, generous, fearing not the face of man, it was to his praise that he never failed to acknowledge that he feared God. His construction of the constitution of the Church was rigid, and he made no concealment of his sentiments, however obnoxious. His pulpit talents are said to have placed him in the front rank of the clerical orators of his day, and under his ministrations the church became large and influential. Mr. McCalla was dismissed from his people at his own request, though parting from them with strong regret. After an absence of two or three years, during which he travelled at the South, and is said to have extended his journey to the wilds of Texas, he returned to Philadelphia, and gathered a congregation—composed in part of members of his former charge—which met in a building at the corner of Fifth and Gaskill Streets.[1]

The Ninth Church was organized about the year 1823, and in 1825 reported a membership of a little over one hundred, but in 1828 had fallen to forty-three. Subsequently Wm. J. Gibson was installed as pastor; and in 1836 the membership had increased to three hundred and sixty-six.

---

[1] Reported (1837–8) as the Fourth Church.

In 1828–29, the Tenth, Eleventh, and Twelfth Churches are first named in the minutes of the Assembly. Shortly after, Thomas M'Auley was called to the pastorate of the Tenth, John L. Grant to that of the Eleventh, and Thomas Eustace to that of the Twelfth. Meanwhile (previous to 1836) the churches of Germantown (gathered about 1818 by the labor of a devoted layman, afterward licensed, by the name of Magoffin), Southwark, and the Second of Northern Liberties, had been gathered, of the former of which James Rooker was pastor, and of the second of which Truman Osborn was stated supply,—succeeded soon after by Charles Hoover,—while of the third James Smith was pastor. The Second Church of Southwark, first reported in 1827, with a membership of twenty-seven, had William Ramsey for some years as stated supply, succeeded in 1830–31 by Samuel Bertron, soon after which the church disappears from the roll of Presbytery.

Upon the death of Joseph Sanford, who had succeeded Dr. Janeway (1829–31) in the pastorate of the Second Church, the Central Church was organized by a colony, and Dr. McDowell was called from Elizabethtown to the pastorate of it. In 1836, the Western Church, with twenty-six members, and "Arch above Tenth," with ninety-two members, are reported.

The First African Church, founded in 1807, owed its existence, and for many years its continued support, largely to the "Evangelical Society of Philadelphia," organized upon the recommendation and through the influence of Dr. Alexander.[1] Its first pastor, although never installed, was John Gloucester, a slave of Dr. Blackburn, of Tennessee. He had attracted the attention of the latter, under whose preaching he was converted, by his piety and natural gifts, and by him was

---

[1] Semi-centenary Discourse, by Rev. W. T. Catto, pastor.

purchased, and encouraged to study with a view to the ministry. After having been licensed and ordained by Union Presbytery, he was in 1810 received from that body by the Philadelphia Presbytery, and, under the patronage of the "Evangelical Society," continued in charge of the African Church until his death in 1822. The house of worship, located on the corner of Shippen and Seventh Streets, was completed in 1811.

Mr. Gloucester first commenced his missionary efforts by preaching in private houses; but these were soon found insufficient to accommodate his congregations. A school-house was procured near the site of the future edifice; but in clear weather he preached in the open air. Possessed of a strong and musical voice, he would take his stand on the corner of Shippen and Seventh Streets, and while singing a hymn would gather around him many besides his regular hearers, and hold their attention till he was prepared to commence his exercises. Possessed of a stout, athletic frame, and characterized by prudence, forbearance, and a fervent piety, he labored with unremitting zeal, securing the confidence and respect of his brethren of the Presbytery, and building up the congregation which he had gathered. His freedom was granted him by Dr. Blackburn, and by his own application he secured the means in England and this country to purchase the freedom of his family. He is said to have been a man of strong mind, mighty in prayer, and of such fervor and energy in wrestling supplication that persons sometimes fell under its power, convicted of sin.

On March 23, 1814, the First Presbyterian Church of Kensington was organized, with only seven members. Its first, and for nearly half a century its only, pastor, was George Chandler, a native of Middletown, Connecticut, a graduate of Yale College, and in 1813 a licentiate of Huntingdon Presbytery. He had preached for a short time at Newark, when he was called to take charge of this feeble congregation. Its prospects were far from promising; but he proved to be a devoted minister and a hard worker, attending conscientiously and faithfully to his own duties, and in other respects almost secluding himself from public notice. Not great, but good, soundly orthodox, but liberal toward those who differed from him, a warm friend of revivals, and employing unhesitatingly all lawful means to lead sinners to Christ, his ministerial life for forty-five years was one of quiet usefulness. He received to the communion of his church, during his protracted ministry, between thirteen hundred and fourteen hundred members. Spared to baptize, marry, and bury successive generations, he commanded to the last increasing respect and affection. Kensington Church was the home of his heart. He had no ambition for fame or ecclesiastical eminence. Lively, fluent, earnest, sincere, and intelligent as a preacher, he sought only success in his Master's work. Every good cause found in him a warm and steadfast friend; and in the habitual exercise of a meek and quiet spirit he discharged his long, laborious, and successful ministry, leaving behind him a name, example, and memory worthy of lasting honor. He died in 1860, and on his marble monument is the just inscription, "He was the representative of Christianity in its purity."

At this period the First Church, Northern Liberties, had for its pastor a man who seemed to combine the pungency of a Baxter with the zeal of an apostle. His church, which for some years had been a portion of the charge of the two co-pastors of the Second Church of the city, in 1813 unanimously called James Patterson—who, since 1809, had been settled at Bound Brook, N.J.—as their pastor. He was installed Jan. 11, 1814, and entered at once upon a difficult and hitherto neglected field. It was by no means an inviting sphere of effort for one who consulted his ease or thirsted for human distinction. Among its rapidly increasing population ignorance and vice abounded. The sanctuary and the institutions of religion were but lightly regarded. The feeble organization numbered only fifty-three members, and most of these were by no means efficient; while the congregation was composed almost exclusively of the poorer classes.

It was not long until there was a marked change. The half-filled house had become crowded with eager listeners. It was necessary to enlarge it. The pastor's visits to the lanes and alleys revealed to him scenes of vice and degradation, and his heart was moved by witnessing the hundreds of poor and neglected children that swarmed the streets and seemed hopelessly abandoned to courses of indolence and crime. He had heard of a lady of New Brunswick who had gathered a number of poor children at her house on the Sabbath for instruction; and this sufficed to prompt his own enterprising philanthropy to a similar experiment on a larger scale. "The Sabbath-School Association of the Northern Liberties" was the result. One hundred children were immediately gathered for instruction, and many more were soon added to the number. The success of the enterprise led to the formation of similar institutions, until at length the churches of the land, generally, availed themselves of their advantages.

Nor was this all. Prayer-meetings were established,[1]

---

[1] Mr. Patterson's first prayer-meeting was held in a little frame house, with the aid of two apprentice boys,—lads of sixteen or seventeen years of age. His people soon "laid hold of the thing," and "it went well." In the course of a few years he had in his church forty-four meetings of this kind every week, and four thousand persons were brought under religious instruction, besides those in the church. The meetings were held in the lanes and

enlisting the co-operation of the members of his church, whose efficiency and usefulness he endeavored to promote. The "lay preaching"—as it was denominated by some—which was thus introduced was viewed by some of his co-presbyters as an unwarranted innovation, and for some time was the subject of warm discussion in the Presbytery. The general current of sentiment was against it, and Mr. Patterson was left to stand alone, except as he was countenanced by Drs. Wilson and Skinner, and perhaps one or two others. Some of his measures may have been imprudent; but none could question the philanthropy or piety by which they were dictated.

His position was peculiar, and called, possibly, for peculiar instrumentalities. He was among a people who had enjoyed nothing worthy the name of religious education, and who in many cases combined the hardened features of civilized depravity with the ignorance, waywardness, and undisciplined moral feeling of heathenism. To attract their attention, to hold them together, to present the truth to their minds in the most impressive manner, and to train them, when brought to repentance, to habits of intelligent Christian activity, required a rare combination of tact, talent, and devotion.

Yet this was the task which Mr. Patterson accomplished. The forcible exposition and stirring appeals of the pulpit were seconded by the fidelity and vigilance of pastoral duty. Revival followed revival, through a ministry of nearly a quarter of a century, with rare frequency and power. Scores upon scores were re-

alleys of the city, some of them two, three, or four miles off. At every communion, from fifteen to forty were added to the church. The circulation of printed matter by the prayer-meeting agents—the matter being furnished by Mr. Patterson—led to the establishment of the "Philadelphian."—*Patterson's Pamphlet*, 1836, pp. 8, 9.

ceived, successively, at single seasons of communion. His influence was felt not only in his immediate neighborhood, but throughout the city, and even to distant places. His labors in Alexandria, in Washington City, and in other regions, were remarkably blessed.

And yet Mr. Patterson was not a *great* man, intellectually. He had, indeed, far more than average ability. He had a mind well stored and disciplined. But his devotion to his work supplied the place of genius, or, rather, it was something higher and better than genius. It put to their most effective use the advantages which nature had supplied. It gave, in his utterance of searching truth, a more commanding aspect to his tall, slender, but erect, dignified, and well-proportioned frame. It gave a more penetrating glance to his black and piercing eye. It kindled his intellect to a more untiring activity and a loftier grasp, and it roused to ardor all the emotions and sympathies of his soul. He was ever engaged in his Master's service. He would become "all things to all men, that he might gain some." Affable and kind, he won the love of the children; faithful and affectionate, he commanded the respect and confidence of all.

If not studiously original, he was never commonplace. He spoke for effect upon the heart and conscience; and an imagination more fertile than chaste supplied him with ready and striking, rather than elegant, illustrations. His nervous Saxon words fell like the blows of the stalwart arm upon the anvil, and under their crushing weight the convicted soul was little disposed to criticize one who could handle the sledge-hammer better than the scalpel. Measured by the ordinary standards of pulpit eloquence, Mr. Patterson came short; and tried by the rules of decorum and ministerial propriety, he could scarcely have secured a verdict in his favor. But his ministry, notwithstanding, was remarkably successful, and to the last his zeal, devotion, and self-denial were unabated. If Horace Walpole would have sneered at him, or Chesterfield have called him a ranter, Baxter would have admired him.[1]

The pastorate of James Boyd at Newtown and Bensalem, which commenced before 1789, continued for more than twenty years; and his successor at Newtown was Alexander Boyd. In 1814, John F. Grier,—a son of James Grier, of Deep Run,—a graduate of Dickinson College in 1803, and a teacher for several years at Pequa and at Brandywine Academy, commenced his labors as pastor at Reading, where he continued until his death in 1829. Solesbury had Thomas Dunn (in 1814 at Germantown) as pastor previous to 1819. At Pittsgrove,[2] N.J., G. W. Janvier, whose pastorate continued for many years, commenced his labors previous to 1814. Cape May, which had been united with it as a pastoral charge under John Jones (previous to 1803), had previous to 1819 Isaac A. Ogden as its pastor,—although for a short time preceding it seems to have been united with Penn's Neck, under the pastoral care of David Edwards. In 1811, shortly after the death of Wm. M. Tennent, pastor of Abington, Norristown, and

---

[1] In 1837, the Presbyterian churches of Philadelphia were:—the First, Albert Barnes, pastor; Second, Dr. C. C. Cuyler; Third, Thomas Brainerd; Fourth, Wm. L. McCalla; Fifth, Thomas Waterman; Sixth, S. G. Winchester; Seventh, S. D. Blythe; Eighth, Alexander Macklin; Ninth, Wm. J. Gibson; Tenth, H. A. Boardman; Eleventh, John L. Grant; Twelfth, *vacant;* Central, John McDowell; First Kensington, George Chandler; Second Kensington, *vacant;* First Southwark, Albert Judson; Second Southwark, *vacant;* First Northern Liberties, James Patterson; Central Northern Liberties, *vacant;* Germantown, Wm. Neill, stated supply; First African Church, Charles S. Gardner; Second and Third African Churches, *vacant.*

[2] Several of the churches of New Jersey were under the care of Philadelphia Presbytery.

Providence, he was succeeded by William Dunlap at Abington. Norristown and Providence were at a later period under the charge of Joseph Barr, whose ministry, commencing previous to 1814, extended to a date subsequent to 1819. Frankford, which in 1814 had John M. Doak, had before 1819 Thomas J. Biggs as pastor; and his ministry continued to a date later than 1825. The death of Nathaniel Irwin, March, 1812, left Neshaminy vacant; but in the following year Robert B. Belville commenced, as his successor, his extended pastorate.

The vacant churches of the Presbytery in 1819 were —Abington,[1] the young and feeble churches of Moyamensing, Springfield, Ashton, and Middletown, Deerfield, Germantown, Cohocksing, Bensalem, Tinicum, Alloway's Creek, Durham, and Millville.

Central Pennsylvania, including the Susquehanna Valley, was in 1800 included within the bounds of Carlisle and Huntingdon Presbyteries. The aggregate membership of the two Presbyteries was thirty. In 1811 the Presbytery of Northumberland was erected; and in 1819 the three jointly numbered thirty-eight ministers and had under their care eighty congregations.

The growth of the Church in this region, during this period, was slow. The ministers had increased in numbers more rapidly than the churches. Emigration overleaped this field for the more inviting regions north and west of the Ohio. The powerful revivals which prevailed among the churches of the Pittsburg Synod soon after its formation in 1802 do not seem to have

---

[1] John Steel was pastor in 1825 of Abington, John Smith of Ashton, James Rooker of Germantown, while John W. Scott was stated supply of Bensalem, and Francis G. Ballantine had been settled at Deerfield.

extended to this field. The churches were depleted by removals, and largely robbed of their natural increase.

In 1819, there were ten vacant churches in the Presbytery of Carlisle. These were Harrisburg,—of which W. R. Dewitt was the same year installed pastor,—Greencastle, Waynesburg, Great Cove, Bedford, Cumberland, Monaghan, Petersburg, Lower West Conococheague, and Williamsport. Of these, the four last were unable to sustain a pastor; and of the whole number four only had enjoyed a settled ministry during the period of twenty years. At Paxton and Derry, N. R. Snowden (1793–96) was succeeded by Joshua Williams (1791–1801) and James Sharon.[1] At Harrisburg, which had formed part of the charge of Mr. Snowden, James Buchanan—who had charge also of Middle Paxton—was installed in 1809. He was dismissed in 1815, and in 1819 was succeeded by Wm. R. Dewitt, the present pastor. Bedford had Alexander Boyd for its pastor from 1808 till 1815, and Jeremiah Chamberlain from 1819 till 1822. Their successors were Daniel McKinley (1827–31), Baynard R. Hall (1832–38), Elbridge Bradbury (1839–41), and Wm. M. Hall. Monaghan and Pennsborough were left vacant by the death of Samuel Waugh in 1807, but had subsequently John Hayes (1809–15), after whose dismission the church was dependent on supplies for many years.

Of the pastors of the Presbytery in 1800, six only remained in 1820. These were John Linn at Sherman's Valley, James Snodgrass at Hanover, Robert Cathcart at York and Hopewell, William Paxton at Lower Marsh Creek, David Denney at Upper and Lower Path Valley (1793–1800) and at Chambersburg (1800–38),

---

[1] Died April 18, 1843.—*Nevin's Churches of the Valley.* He was settled previous to 1809. See Assembly's Minutes.

and Joshua Williams at Derry and Paxton (1799–1801) and at Big Spring (1802–29).

The ministry of Mr. Linn closed in 1820. Of manly form, vigorous constitution, and great powers of endurance, his disposition was social and cheerful, and his presence in every circle was cordially welcome. His sermons, delivered *memoriter*, with a voice of remarkable clearness, were uttered with great solemnity and impressiveness; while his discharge of his pastoral duties was unremitted and exemplary. The pastorate of Mr. Snodgrass at Hanover was protracted till 1845, and that of Dr. Cathcart at Hopewell till 1835, and at York till 1837. Mr. Denney was pastor at Chambersburg till 1838.

Upon the removal of Dr. McKnight to New York, he was succeeded at Lower Marsh Creek and Tom's Creek by a young man who, without a collegiate education, had, by great diligence and application, fitted himself for the work of the ministry. This man was William Paxton, a native of Lancaster county, the son of a farmer; and he had devoted himself, till twenty-four years of age, to agricultural pursuits. But his thirst for knowledge led him to seek the advantages of education, and his warm piety induced him to prepare himself for the work of the ministry. In 1792, he was called to succeed Dr. McKnight; and for forty-nine years Lower Marsh Creek enjoyed the labors of a pastor whose diligence, promptitude, and fidelity could not well be surpassed. Of large stature, full six feet in height,—of a manner solemn, dignified, commanding, and graceful,—dispensing in the pulpit with the use of notes, yet never failing to make full and careful preparation,—he was as a preacher highly interesting and acceptable, while as a pastor he was faithful and affectionate. Spared till 1845, he departed in the eighty-sixth year of his age, a patriarch indeed, his memory crowned by his friends and admirers with honors which his own modesty forbade him to seek.

Joshua Williams was pastor of Big Spring from 1801 till 1829. His preceding ministry at Derry and Paxton had lasted less than two years. He had pursued his studies, preparatory to college at Gettysburg, under Rev. Alexander Dobbin, and even then was distinguished for uncommon skill in debate and great fluency in extemporaneous speaking. In 1795, he was graduated at Dickinson College, and pursued his theological studies under Dr. Robert Cooper.

Dr. Williams was accounted "an able and profound theologian."[1] His intellect was of a high order, and distinguished for acuteness and power of discrimination. As a preacher he was highly instructive and evangelical,—although his style was more philosophical than colloquial. In manner he was grave and dignified, earnest but not vehement. Though fond of debate, his nervous temperament unfitted him for the conflicts of ecclesiastical bodies; yet in private company or the social circle his conversational gifts were of a rare order. His piety was not fitful or spasmodic, but accorded with the character of his mind,—solid, deliberate, and perhaps more than usually inclined to severity.

A classmate of his at Gettysburg and at Dickinson College, although in age considerably his junior, was David McConaughy, for nearly thirty-two years pastor of the churches of Upper Marsh Creek and Great Conewago. His ministry here commenced in October, 1800, and continued till 1832, when he accepted a call to the Presidency of Washington College, which office he sustained until 1849. His death occurred some three years later, when he had reached the seventy-

---

[1] Sprague, iv. 199.

seventh year of his age and the fifty-fifth of his ministry.

The congregation of Upper Marsh Creek removed in 1813 to Gettysburg, the county seat.[1] Their new house of worship was not completed and ready for occupancy till 1816. But the congregation after its removal retained not only its name, but its connection with Great Conewago. The people of both were devotedly attached to their pastor. Kind, sympathizing, faithful, and affectionate, he was an object of universal love, esteem, and confidence. Above all his titles—and he was "doctorated to the highest point"—his distinction was that of "*a good man.*"[2] At college he bore off the highest honors of his class; and in the positions he subsequently occupied he proved himself equal to the emergency. His discourses, both in matter and style, bore marks of careful preparation. Rich in evangelical truth, they were characterized by a classic elegance of style, and delivered in an earnest and persuasive, if not altogether attractive, manner.

Of superior natural endowments, careful culture, extensive and accurate scholarship, his unswerving integrity, dignity of deportment, kindness of heart, and anxiety for the welfare and improvement of his pupils, admirably fitted him for the post of President of Washington College, which he filled, with honor to himself and profit to others, for the space of seventeen years.

---

[1] The Associate Reformed Church in this neighborhood was under the charge of Dr. McLean. Dr. Charles G. McLean was born in Armagh county, Ireland, March 11, 1787. Emigrating to this country, he studied theology under Dr. John M. Mason, having first been graduated at Pennsylvania University. In 1812, he was ordained pastor of the Presbyterian church near Gettysburg, Pa., where he preached for twenty-nine years. He died at Indianapolis in 1860.

[2] Sprague, iv. 202.

The monument of his fidelity and ability is the record of the college itself.

Robert Kennedy, a graduate of Dickinson College in 1797, commenced his pastorate at Welsh Run (or East and West Conococheague) in 1802,[1] resigning his office in 1816, but resuming it, after a nine-years residence in Maryland, in 1825, and continuing to discharge the duties until his death in 1843.

At Silver Spring, which, together with Monaghan, was left vacant by the death of Mr. Waugh in 1807, Henry Rowan Wilson was settled in 1813. He too, like Williams and McConaughy, was a pupil of Mr. Dobbin and a graduate of Dickinson College. In 1802, soon after his licensure, he removed to Bellefonte, Centre county, and commenced preaching. The Presbyterians had as yet no organized church and no house of worship. But, securing the use of the court-house, and devoting himself to his work, he soon gathered a congregation, and a church was organized. At Lick Run, twelve miles distant, another was formed through his exertions. Of these congregations he was installed pastor; and, as there was no church-edifice in the region, and no private house sufficiently capacious, the exercises were held in the woods.

For four years he retained the pastorate, but in 1806 was called to the Professorship of Languages in Dickinson College. Here he remained for seven years, assisting Dr. Davidson in the pulpit on the Sabbath. After this, he commenced his labors at Silver Spring. The church, which since Mr. Waugh's death had been in a languishing state, began ere long to revive, and in the seven years of Mr. Wilson's ministry the membership was more than doubled. His successor, after his dismission in 1823, was James Williamson.

---

[1] Successor of Thomas McPherrin.—*Assembly's Minutes*, i. 101.

Dr. Wilson was a man of remarkable activity and untiring usefulness. His personal appearance was prepossessing. All his movements indicated manly strength and vigor; while his manners were dignified and gentlemanly. Honest and open-hearted, he could not always disguise his scorn of any thing bordering on duplicity, even when prudence would have dictated reserve. As a preacher, he was able, energetic, and popular. Rich blessings attended his labors; and he was the instrument of bringing many souls to Christ.

Upon leaving Silver Spring, he removed to Shippensburg, where his devotion to his work would have done honor to the zeal and enterprise of a frontier missionary.[1] He was accustomed regularly to open the Sabbath-school in the morning with reading, singing, prayer, and a short address, preach at ten o'clock, and again at twelve, then mount his horse and ride four or five miles into the country, to preach in some school-house or dwelling-house, then return and preach at night in his church,—making four sermons, in addition to the Sabbath-school service,—and riding on horseback—often under hot suns or in severe storms—from eight to ten miles. He had four preaching-places in the four corners of his congregation, at one of which he preached every Friday. Neither bad roads, unfavorable weather, nor slight indisposition, prevented him from fulfilling his appointments. His ministry at Shippensburg closed in 1838, and from 1842 to 1848 he was Bellville's successor at Neshaminy. His death occurred in 1849.

At Upper and Lower Path Valley, David Denney succeeded Samuel Dougall in 1793; but, resigning his charge in 1800, he was in 1802 succeeded by Amos A. McGinley, who retained the pastorate till 1851. Within

---

[1] Sprague, iv. 301.

about thirty years after Mr. McGinley's settlement, his church had attained a membership of between four and five hundred.

At Middle Spring, John Moody succeeded Dr. Robert Cooper, after an interval of several years, during which the church was reported vacant. His pastorate commenced in 1803; and in 1833 this church, which he still continued to serve, had a membership of nearly three hundred. His pastorate closed in 1853–4.

At Upper West Conococheague, the successor of the venerable Dr. John King, whose resignation took place shortly before his death in 1811, was David Elliott, subsequently professor in the Alleghany Theological Seminary. At Rocky Spring, Francis Herron commenced his labors, as successor of John Craighead, in 1800; but in 1810 he resigned his charge of the church, and his place was supplied by Dr. McKnight, who had retired from New York to this vicinity, and who, except for the short interval during which he filled the post of President of Dickinson College, continued in charge till his death in 1823.

Piney's Creek and Tom's Creek, vacant in 1800, had for their pastor, previous to 1803, Patrick Davidson, who remained till subsequent to 1809, and, after a vacancy of some years, Robert S. Grier, who was still pastor of the church in 1862.

The church of Carlisle had been left vacant, by the death of Dr. Davidson at the close of 1812; but in 1816, George Duffield[1] was called to the pastorate, and remained in charge of the church until his removal to Philadelphia in 1835.

In 1800, the Presbytery of Huntingdon numbered twelve ministers, of whom four—John Hoge, Asa Dunham, Hugh McGill, and James Johnston—were without

---

[1] Now the venerable Dr. Duffield, of Detroit.

charge. Of the others, David Bard was at Frankstown, Matthew Stephens at Shaver's Creek, John Johnston at Huntingdon and Hart's Log, Hugh Morrison at Buffalo and Sunbury, John Bryson at Chillisquaque and Warrior Run, David Wiley at Spring Creek, Isaac Grier at Pine Creek, Lycoming, and Great Island, and Samuel Bryson at Spruce Creek and Sinking Valley. More than twenty vacant churches were under the care of the Presbytery.

Of the pastors in 1800, John Johnston and John Bryson were the only ones who continued to retain the pastoral charge till 1820, the latter remaining at his post till subsequent to 1825. Previous to 1803, James Johnston was settled at Dry Valley and East Kishacoquillas, and was still pastor in 1820. This was the case also with William Stuart at Sinking Creek and Spring Creek, and with John Coulter at Lower and Middle Tuscarora, both of them continuing in the pastorate of these churches till about 1834. At Mahoning and Derry John B. Patterson commenced his labors previous to 1803, and his pastorate continued, in connection with Derry, for nearly forty years. At Buffalo and Milton, the pastorate of Thomas Hood, which began previous to 1809, continued till 1834–35. For a portion of his time Washington formed a part of his charge. At Mifflintown and Lost Creek, John Hutchinson commenced his labors, as the successor of Matthew Brown, previous to 1809; and here he labored as pastor till 1834–35. At Bellefonte and Lick Run, where congregations had been gathered in 1802 by Dr. Henry R. Wilson, subsequently at Shippensburg, James Linn was settled as his successor (1813), and continued in the pastoral charge for more than twenty years, the united churches numbering nearly four hundred members. After the resignation of Isaac Grier, who had charge of Northumberland, Sunbury, and Shamokin, in

1809–14, he was succeeded by Samuel Henderson at Shamokin, with which Bloomsburg and Brier Creek were made a joint charge, and at Northumberland and Sunbury by Robert F. N. Smith. Isaac Grier had previously been settled, as successor of James Martin, at Piney Creek and Great Island, of which, after a vacancy of some years, John H. Grier became pastor, remaining in charge some twenty years.[1] Samuel Henderson remained from about 1817 until near 1829 at Bloomsburg, Brier Creek, and Shamokin, and in the last-mentioned year was stated supply at Shamokin, New Columbia, and Holland Run. Previous to 1819, James Galbraith was settled at Frankstown and Williamsburg, his pastorate continuing till 1834–35; at nearly the same period, Nathaniel R. Snowden was settled at Millerstown and Liverpool, his pastorate closing previous to 1825. This was likewise the case with William Kennedy at Lewistown and West Kishacoquillas, William A. Boyd at Spence Creek and Sinking Valley, and James Thompson at Shaver's Creek and Alexandria.

In 1811, the Presbytery of Northumberland was erected, the pastors of it, transferred from the Presbytery of Huntingdon, being Asa Dunham, John Bryson, Isaac Grier, John B. Patterson, and Thomas Hood. It embraced the churches of Warrior Run, Chillisquaque, Northumberland, Sunbury, Shamokin, Mahoning, Derry, Buffalo, Washington, Milton, Lycoming, Pine Creek, Brier Creek, Greenwood, and Catawissa. No other churches seem to have been added to the list previous to 1820.

The Synod of Pittsburg was erected in 1802. It consisted of the Presbyteries of Redstone, Ohio, and Erie,—all previously connected with the Synod of Vir-

---

[1] Isaac Grier—but probably another person than the one mentioned above—was subsequently (1816) pastor at Washington.

ginia. The Presbytery of Erie was formed from the two others in 1801, and a portion of its churches were within the bounds of the State of Ohio,—several on or near the Western Reserve. At the time when the three Presbyteries were constituted a Synod, Redstone Presbytery had eleven ministers and thirty-five congregations, Ohio Presbytery had sixteen ministers and thirty-four congregations, while Erie Presbytery had five ministers and forty congregations. The aggregate was thirty-two ministers and one hundred and nine congregations, of which not more than ten or twelve were outside the limits of Pennsylvania.

Of Redstone Presbytery, the members were James Power (1779–1817) at Mount Pleasant, Joseph W. Henderson (1799–1824) at Bethlehem and Ebenezer, Jacob Jennings (1792–1811) at Dunlap's Creek and Little Redstone, John McPherrin (1790–1803) at Salem, Samuel Porter (1790–1825[1]) at Congruity, George Hill (1792–1822[1]) at Fairfield and Donegal,[2] William Swan (1793–1818) at Long Run and Sewickley, David Smith (1798–1803[1]) at Rehoboth and Round Hill, James Adams (1795?–1814) at George's Creek and Union, James Dunlap (1782–1803) at Laurel Hill, and Francis Laird (1799–1831) at Poke Run and Plumb Creek.

The accessions to the Presbytery in the following years were William Speer at Unity and Greensburg (1803–29[1]), Robert Steel at Pittsburg (1803–10[1]), Thomas Moore at Salem (1803–09), William Wylie at Rehoboth and Round Hill (1805–17), James Guthrie at Laurel Hill and Tyrone (1805–50), James Graham at Pitts Township (afterward reported as Beulah) (1804–32), N. R. Snowden at Pittsburg, Second Congregation (Oct.–Dec. 1805,) James Galbraith at Harmony (1805–12) and

[1] Died in the latter year.

[2] In later years, Fairfield and Ligonier.

Gilgal (1805–17),[1] Robert McGarrough at New Rehoboth and Licking (1807–22),[2] John Boggs at Pittsburg, Second Congregation (Dec. 1807–April, 1808), Thomas Hunt at Pittsburg, Second Church (1809–18), Francis Herron at Pittsburg, First Church (1810–50), Robert Lee at Salem (1813–19), William Johnston at Dunlap's Creek (1813–39) and Brownsville (1813–41), Robert Johnston at Rehoboth (1817–32) and Round Hill (1817–31), John Reed at Indiana and Gilgal (1818–29), John Ross at Somerset (1817–19), Ashbel G. Fairchild at Morgantown and George's Creek, Asa Brooks at French Creek and Buchanan (1819–27), Elisha P. Swift at Pittsburg, Second Church (1819–33), William Swan at Long Run (1819–22), William Wylie at Uniontown (1819–24), Aretus Loomis at Tygart's Valley (1820–23), David Barclay at Jefferson, Lower Plumb Creek, Glade Run, s. s. (1820–28), and A. O. Patterson at Mt. Pleasant and Sewickley (1821–34).

In 1802, Redstone Presbytery had under its care thirty-eight congregations supplied with pastors, and seventeen vacant; in 1808, with sixteen pastors, eleven of its thirty-eight congregations were vacant; in 1815, with eighteen pastors and the same number of congregations as in 1808, ten were vacant. In 1820, it numbered nineteen ministers and thirty-eight congrega-

[1] According to Wilson's "Historical Almanac," James Galbraith was born in Adams county, Pa., in 1780. His academical course was pursued at Jefferson College, and his theological with Dr. King. In 1807, he was ordained by Redstone Presbytery over Mahoning and Indiana Churches. In 1828, he preached for Frankstown and Williamsburg Churches, in Huntingdon Presbytery. In 1841, he supplied Middle Sandy Church, New Lisbon Presbytery, in 1843, Weathersfield and Rehoboth; but at length he declined any stated charge, preaching occasionally as his strength permitted. He was a man of sterling integrity, faithful in the discharge of his duties. He sank under the infirmities of age, March 28, 1858.

[2] Transferred to another Presbytery.

tions, of which nine were vacant, and six unable to support a pastor.

The venerable Dr. Power, the patriarch of the Presbytery, was spared till 1830, and died in his eighty-fifth year. A strange transformation of the wilderness to the fruitful field, and of the haunts of savages to smiling cities and villages, had been wrought before his eyes. There were scores of churches scattered over the region which, when he first traversed it, was little more than a hunting-ground for barbarous tribes. The place which he selected for his field of labor was far from any of the beaten tracks of civilization. It lay beyond the mountains, one hundred and twenty miles from the settlements of white men. No macadamized road, canal, railroad, or navigable stream led to it. The only route to the "backwoods" was a horse-path over rocks, precipices, and marshes, or through the shadows of the deep and tangled forest. Parties of hostile Indians hovered about the more frequented tracks, armed with their tomahawks and scalping-knives. The very nomenclature of the towns along the route—"Burned Cabins," and "Bloody Run"—indicated the experience which the traveller had to dread. No hotel, no settler's cabin even, stood convenient to welcome him after the fatigues of the day. And when he had reached the "backwoods," he found himself surrounded with evidences of pioneer hardship and primitive destitution. Iron had to be tediously transported over the mountains. Salt cost five dollars the bushel. Mills for grinding had not yet been erected, except at remote points; while the terrors of Indian warfare brooded over the scattered and feeble settlements.

There was not in the whole region a church-spire to greet the traveller's eye. Except in inclement weather, nature furnished temples in her forests, and "the aisles of the dim wood" rang with the "hymns of lofty cheer" with which the sturdy emigrant sent up his praise to God. And when the rude log structure was reared for a shelter to the worshipping assembly, there was no saw or plane to shape the rude logs, nor a hammer to strike, nor a nail to drive.[1] The clap-boards of the roof were bound down by logs. The doors, also made of clap-boards, were fastened by wooden pins to cross-bars projecting far enough on one side to form part of the hinge. The windows were small openings in two adjacent logs, and were glazed with oil-paper or linen. The floors, if any were laid, were of cleft logs, smoothed by the axe. Sometimes the church was in shape a parallelogram,—sometimes cruciform; but the twelve sides and the twelve corners were not accounted symbolic.

Yet in such structures as these, scenes of deepest interest occurred. These rude piles of logs were witnesses to pentecostal seasons; and often did the breathless silence, the deep sigh, the falling tear, or the agonizing cry for mercy, attest the thrilling power of the preacher's appeal. Nowhere on the globe was the gospel preached with greater force or with more simplicity and purity. Churches were gathered which it tasked the missionary pastors to supply, and a Christian civilization, fast pressing on the track of the pioneer, supplied structures for worship of which the older settled portions of the country need not have been ashamed. It was no longer necessary,—as in early times,—if a stream was swollen so that it could not be forded, that the pastor, unable to cross to parties who wished him to unite them in the marriage relation, should stand on one side, while they stood on the other, as the ceremony was performed. The Pitts-

[1] Sprague, iii. 329.

burg region, including the original field of Redstone Presbytery, embraced at the time of Dr. Power's death, in 1830, six Presbyteries, with nearly one hundred ministers and more than one hundred and seventy churches.

Samuel Porter was another veteran in this field. His ancestry were Covenanters; but after his privilege of listening first to the preaching of Dr. King, of Upper West Conococheague, and afterward to that of Dr. Joseph Smith and Dr. McMillan, he united himself with the Presbyterian Church. By their advice, he was induced to prepare himself for the ministry. Without a regular education, but with a vigorous intellect and a somewhat extended acquaintance with theology, derived from reading and reflection, he applied to Redstone Presbytery for licensure in 1789. In the following year he was installed pastor of the congregations of Poke Run and Congruity, the former of which he retained only till 1798, remaining with the other, however, till the close of his life, in 1825.

In several respects his career finds a parallel in that of Patrick Henry. Both were remarkably gifted by nature; and the statesman was scarcely a more consummate orator than the divine. Neither had enjoyed the advantages of academical or extended preparatory education, and each was *surprised*, as it were, into his profession. Like Patrick Henry, Mr. Porter proved himself equal to every emergency. In the Whiskey Insurrection of 1794, he gave a most striking proof of the power of his eloquence in his successful attempt to restrain the passions, calm the excitement, and expose the prejudices of the insurgents. Strange stories are told of his mastery over the minds of his hearers, of his ready wit, sometimes bordering on levity, his startling imagery, his graphic descriptions, and his overpowering appeals. A competent judge who once listened to him[1] while he addressed the assembly in a beautiful beech-wood grove, speaks of his holding "the large assembly for two hours in breathless attention, while a torrent of sweet celestial eloquence poured from his lips with a rapidity and pathos that dissolved a large portion of the assembly in tears." He speaks of the impression made as one of a moral and intellectual greatness which he had "never before attached to any human being."

Another veteran pioneer in this region was James Dunlap. He was a native of Chester county, Pennsylvania, and was a graduate of New Jersey College in 1773. From 1775 to 1777 he was a tutor in the institution, pursuing his theological studies at the same time under the care of Dr. Witherspoon. In the autumn of 1782 he united with Redstone Presbytery, and became pastor of Dunlap's Creek and Little Redstone. In 1789 he accepted a call to Laurel Hill, where he remained until he accepted the invitation to the Presidency and Professorship of Languages at Canonsburg Academy, now (1803) transformed into Jefferson College.

In 1812, on account of his health, he resigned his office, and removed to New Geneva, about thirty miles distant, where he labored as a teacher. In the following year he removed to Uniontown, to take charge of the academy (now Madison College) of that place. In 1816, he recrossed the mountains, to spend his remaining days with his son William, pastor at Abington; and two years later his death occurred.

As a preacher he was distinguished for faithfulness and eloquence. Himself a living example of Christian humility, his daily life was a constant sermon. But as

---

[1] Dr. David Elliott. A judge quite as competent as Dr. Elliott pronounces the account given above greatly exaggerated.

a classical scholar, and as an instructor, he stood preeminent. It is praise enough for him to say that he was accounted above others the fittest man to succeed the accomplished Watson at Canonsburg. His extreme sensibility no doubt impaired his usefulness. At times he was the victim of melancholy, induced perhaps in part by his enfeebled health, and indisposing him to active effort. His amiable temper, though never yielding to an implacable spirit, was in his later years subject to irritability; but a moment's reflection was enough to restore him to himself. His abstracted mood and his tendency to a brooding meditation disqualified him for that measure of social converse which would perhaps have proved as beneficial to himself as to others; but it was not inconsistent with a ready disposition to assist and sympathize with those who claimed his regard.

Still another of this group of pioneers in Western Pennsylvania was John McPherrin,[1] a native of Adams county, Pa., a pupil of Robert Smith of Pequa, and a graduate of Dickinson College in 1788. In September, 1790, he was installed pastor of Salem and Unity congregations. In 1800 he resigned the latter, and in 1803 the former, and removed to Concord and Muddy Creek, in the bounds of Erie Presbytery, in connection with which we shall meet him again.

The founder of the church in Alleghany was Joseph Stockton,[2] born near Chambersburg, educated at Canonsburg, and a theological pupil of Dr. McMillan. In 1801 he was installed pastor of Meadville and Sugar Creek, where he remained till 1810, when he became Principal of Pittsburg Academy, supplying at the same time the churches of Pine Creek and Alleghany. Resigning his academical post in 1820, he devoted his whole time to these churches till 1829, when he resigned his

[1] Sprague, iv. 242; also, Old Redstone. [2] Sprague, 243.

charge at Alleghany, and for the three remaining years of his life had charge of the church at Pine Creek. He was one of the first instructors in the Western Theological Seminary, and had much influence in securing its location at Alleghany.

George Hill, another member of the Presbytery, was settled for thirty years (1792–1822) at Fairfield and Donegal, in connection for his first years with Wheatland, and subsequently with the new church at Ligonier (1798). He was a faithful and laborious pastor, shrinking from no personal exposure in the discharge of his duties.[1] In times of high water, he has been known to swim the Conemaugh on horseback, preach in his wet clothes, recross the river, and return to his own house,—a distance of ten miles,—the same day. But such was the vigor of his constitution that he experienced no ill effects. Exceedingly humble and modest, and with great sensibility, he had yet acuteness of intellect and firmness of character, and, when duty called him to the defence of truth, he did not shrink from it.

Upon the death of Robert Steel, in 1810, Francis Herron[2] was called to succeed him as pastor of the First Church of Pittsburg. He was at this time thirty-six years of age, and had already made full proof of his ministry. Of Scotch-Irish descent, he was born near Shippensburg, Pa., and was graduated at Dickinson College in 1794. The prayers of his pious parents were answered in his conversion, and after studying theology under his pastor, Dr. Robert Cooper, he was licensed by Carlisle Presbytery, October 4, 1797.

He entered at once upon the ministerial work, travelling as a missionary to what was then the Western frontier, the town of Chillicothe,—where the first land-office north of the Ohio had been opened but three years

[1] Old Redstone, 415.

[2] Wilson's Presbyterian Almanac.

before,—preaching on his way. His journey led him through Pittsburg, then a small village; and at Six-Mile Run, near Wilkinsburg, he was prevailed upon by the people to delay till the following Sabbath, when, in the lack of a house of worship, he preached to them under the shade of an apple-tree. Resuming his journey the next day, he pushed on to his destination, with a frontier settler for his guide, and directed on his way through an almost unbroken wilderness by the "blazes" on the trees. Two nights he encamped among the Indians, then numerous near what is now the town of Marietta, Ohio.

On his return from Chillicothe, he stopped at Pittsburg. The tavern-keeper with whom he lodged was an old acquaintance, and, at his request, the young minister consented to preach. Notice was sent around, and a congregation of about eighteen persons assembled in the evening in a rude log structure occupying the site of the present First Presbyterian Church. Such was the primitive style of that day that the swallows, nested in the eaves, flew among the congregation.

After preaching for Dr. McMillan, and participating in the scenes of the revival then prevalent in the region, he received a call from Buffalo Church; but an invitation awaited him from Rocky Spring, in the vicinity of his home, and this he concluded to accept. Here he was installed, April 8, 1800.

After a successful pastorate of ten years, he was called to Pittsburg; but here for many months the prevalent coldness and indifference to religious things seemed to impose a barrier to success. He proposed to hold prayer-meetings; but the project was opposed. In concert with Thomas Hunt, of the Second Church, he persisted, and, to avoid objection, the meetings were held in the room occupied by Mr. Hunt as a day-school. The first meeting consisted of the two pastors, one layman, and six women, and for eighteen months there was no addition to their number. Indifference at length grew into downright hostility, and husbands and fathers prohibited their wives and daughters from attending. Dr. Herron was told that the meetings must be stopped. "Gentlemen," said he, "these meetings will not stop: you are at liberty to do as you please, and I also have liberty to worship God according to the dictates of my conscience, none daring to molest or make me afraid." From this time a change was manifest. Several gay and fashionable persons gave evidence of conversion, and a deep and healthful impression was made upon the whole community.

Combining practical tact with devotion as a preacher and loveliness of character as a pastor, Dr. Herron succeeded in relieving the church from the incubus of debt, and thenceforward its prospects brightened. The house was crowded. The congregation and the membership of the church rapidly increased. The church-edifice was enlarged, and from this time his ministry was blessed with successive and powerful revivals. In 1850, when he had reached his seventy-sixth year, he pressed his resignation upon a reluctant people; but their gratitude followed and cheered his succeeding years, till he rested from his labors at the ripe age of eighty-six.

Warm hearted and sincere, his heart was enlisted in every cause which promised good to man or glory to God. His public spirit, his sincerity, and his zeal were acknowledged by all. Missionary enterprise secured from him warm sympathy and efficient co-operation. He was the fast friend of sound learning. Patriotism was a part of his religion, and his heart was alike true to his country and to his God. He knew the worth of human liberty, and believed that these United States are a peculiar heritage of freedom.

In 1825, when the General Assembly had resolved to found a Western Theological Seminary, Dr. Herron, in concert with Dr. Swift, urged the claims of Alleghany City. Successful in securing the location, he entered with his whole heart into the enterprise of sustaining the institution. He seemed to rejoice in superabundance of toil in its behalf; and to no one man does the seminary owe more for its present position and success than to Dr. Herron.

The Second Presbyterian Church of Pittsburg dates from 1803.[1] It originated with those members of the First Church who could find "no kind of spiritual advantage" from the ministry of the pastor, Rev. Robert Steel. The Synod sanctioned the enterprise, but for many years it gave but feeble promise. Messrs. Snowden (1805) and Boggs (1807) were settled over it,—each dismissed after a few weeks; but in 1810 Thomas Hunt took charge of it, eking out a scanty salary by laboring as teacher of a day-school. A church-edifice was erected; but the debt incurred, reaching at length the sum of ten thousand dollars, bore heavily upon the small and feeble band. At times the prospect seemed absolutely cheerless, and, amid the financial prostration that followed the close of the war, it was felt that the enterprise must be abandoned.[2] Other Presbyterian churches, but in a different connection, had already been gathered in the city, which now numbered from seven to eight thousand inhabitants.[3] But in 1819, Elisha P.

---

1 Minutes of Pittsburg Synod.

2 Dr. Swift's Historical Discourse.

3 Rev. Dr. Black was ordained in 1800, in the Old Court-House, pastor of the Reformed Presbyterian Church recently organized, and Rev. Dr. Bruce in 1807 was settled over the First Associate Church, where he remained till 1846. The death of Dr. Black occurred three years later. In 1816, Rev. Dr. McElroy, now of New York, gathered the First Associate Reformed Church of Pittsburg.

Swift was called to succeed Mr. Hunt in the pastorate; and under his ministry the prospects of the church became brighter, until at length it was established on a firm basis. Till 1835, when he resigned his charge to accept a professorship in the Western Theological Seminary, he continued successful and abundant in his labors as pastor of the Second Church.

In 1832, in connection with a revival in the First Church, seventy-three persons were added to its communion on profession of faith. As the result, a new congregation was formed, which for some months was supplied by Henry A. Riley. In March (19), 1833, the Third Presbyterian Church was organized, consisting of thirty-six members. Steps were taken for the erection of a church-edifice, which was completed in the following year. Meanwhile (January, 1834), David H. Riddle, called from Winchester, Va., had been installed pastor. This relation he continued to sustain till, at his own request, he was dismissed, in 1857, soon after which he was succeeded by Dr. Henry Kendall.[1]

The Fourth Church—known till after the erection of the Third as the First Church of Northern Liberties—reported in 1832 a membership of fifty, and at that time had succeeded in obtaining as pastor Allan D. Campbell. In 1836, the pastors of the four churches were Dr. Herron, Joseph W. Blythe, successor of Dr. Swift, David H. Riddle, and Dr. Campbell.[2]

---

[1] Presbyterian Historical Almanac, 1861.

[2] The Fifth Presbyterian Church of Pittsburg was organized about the year 1840. In 1846, it was vacant, with a membership of one hundred and twelve. In 1849, under the pastorate of Nathaniel West, it withdrew from the Presbytery of Pittsburg and joined that of Ohio.

The Sixth Church was organized about the year 1851. In 1852, Thomas B. Wilson was installed pastor, and remained in the office till 1855.

At the time of Dr. Swift's settlement at Pittsburg, in 1819, the observer might have seen, north of the Alleghany and Ohio Rivers, a beautiful tract of land, with thirty or forty dwellings interspersed among meadows, fields, and orchards, destined in less than forty years to be the site of a city of nearly fifty thousand inhabitants.[1] When it was resolved by the General Assembly to establish a Western Theological Seminary, this was the place selected for its location, and here it commenced operations in 1827. It was not, however, till February, 1830, that the First Presbyterian Church of Alleghany was organized, with fifty-four members. Until the settlement of Dr. Swift in the pastorate, in 1835, it enjoyed the ministry of Joseph Stockton, John Joyce, and Job F. Halsey, whose pastorate extended from 1831 to 1835.

William Wylie, settled successively at Upper and Lower Sandy and Fairfield (1802-05), Rehoboth and Round Hill (1805-16), Uniontown (1819-23), Wheeling and West Liberty (1823-32), and at Newark, O. (1832-54), was a native of Washington county, Pa., where he was born July 10, 1776. He studied first with Thaddeus Dod, and afterward at Canonsburg, removing upon the conclusion of his classical course to Kentucky, where, after engaging as a teacher for some years, he was licensed by West Lexington Presbytery. His experience at the West fitted him for the hardships of pioneer life. At Uniontown, Pa., he preached in the court-house and in the orchards and groves in the vicinity, and thus worked zealously and faithfully, until, when he left, there were the elements out of which was shortly gathered a vigorous and growing church, with a house of worship, and a strong Presbyterian influence pervading the whole community. His death occurred in his eighty-second year.

---

[1] Dr. Swift's Historical Discourse.

Dr. James Hervey, in 1814 ordained pastor of the Forks of Wheeling and Wheelingtown, and remaining in charge of the former (1814–59) for more than forty years, was a native of Virginia, and in 1810 a graduate of Jefferson College. A humble, consistent Christian man, and a faithful minister, he commanded high respect and esteem.[1]

Dr. Andrew Wylie, a younger brother of William Wylie, was elected President of Jefferson College at the early age of twenty-three, and only two years after he had received as a graduate the highest honors of his class. Successively President of Jefferson (1812–16), Washington (1817), and Indiana (1829) Colleges, he still was diligent in the work of the ministry, preaching on the Sabbath, sometimes almost gratuitously, to feeble congregations. Of somewhat impressive and imposing exterior, with a countenance rather intellectual than benignant, he was a man who upon acquaintance conciliated esteem as well as commanded respect. Notwithstanding his naturally strong passions, it was rarely that the provocations of college discipline overmastered his self-control. If waggish students were apt to chalk "dignity" on his vacant chair, it betrayed less of jest than of just apprehension of the man. His pupils in later years pronounced him incomparable as a teacher. On every subject—languages, history, and philosophy—his conceptions were clear, comprehensive, and profound. Aristotle was his special favorite. With the ancient classics and the old English authors he was perfectly at home. Simple in life and manners, while not unconscious of his own powers, he combined a proper respect for himself with that just respect which others might claim. He could not tolerate

---

[1] Dismissed from the congregation of Wheelingtown, April 17, 1827. Wheeling Second Church was organized May, 1826.

a falsehood, and of meanness he could not and did not wish to disguise his scorn. Without dogmatism, he was yet fixed and definite in all his views and opinions. He would not needlessly offend, but he would not demean himself to conciliate, where truthfulness or justice had given provocation.

But under all the outward sternness of the man, and notwithstanding the frequent bluntness of his expressions, he possessed a heart that glowed with Christian charity. Amid all the measures which, from the time of his removal to the West, he saw tending to the division of the Church, his voice was raised for peace. His plea was for toleration. He preached as well as felt that "sectarianism is heresy." While the work of division was going on, he was charged with "sitting on the fence." "And what," asked one, "will he do when the fence is burned down?" "He will sit down," said Dr. W., "and weep in the ashes."[1] The answer was more sad than sportive, and the influences which resulted in his closing years in leading him to seek a connection with the Episcopal Church, originated doubtless in the impressions made upon his susceptible spirit by the conflicts which rent the Presbyterian Church in twain.

The Presbytery of Ohio at the time of the erection of the Synod of Pittsburg, and after the ministers and churches constituting Erie Presbytery had been set off for that purpose, consisted of sixteen ministers and thirty-four congregations. In 1819,[2] it had increased to twenty-eight ministers and forty-five congregations.

At Chartiers, the venerable Dr. McMillan continued in the pastorate for over fifty years, and in his eightieth year retained the vigor of a hale and hearty old age. More dependent than formerly on his notes, he could yet, he said, "bawl almost as loud as ever." Revival

[1] Sprague, v. 788. [2] Minutes of Pittsburg Synod.

after revival had crowned his labors, and even yet, after relinquishing his charge, his heart was in the work to which he had devoted his life, and in his visits to the churches and his occasional discourses he still manifested the fervor of a veteran apostle. Self-denying, unostentatious, simple in his tastes and manners, with no object but to glorify his Master in winning souls, he accomplished an amount of labor and exerted an extended influence, the result of which must long endure. His death occurred in 1833.[1]

Joseph Patterson's labors at Raccoon closed in 1816, when he was succeeded by Moses Allen (1817–38). Practical, indefatigable, fearless in the discharge of duty, habitually spiritual-minded and serious, yet possessed of an inexhaustible fund of genial humor, he was remarkably successful in his efforts, binding others to himself by his affability, his social affections and sympathies, and forcing them to feel the singleness of aim and purpose by which he was animated. The sixteen years during which he was spared, after the failure of his health compelled him to resign his charge, were not idly spent. Removing to Pittsburg,—then a thoroughfare for emigration,—he labored as a colporteur, or city missionary, amid the afflicted and destitute, while he gave cheerful counsel and aid to such as he met on their way to a new home in the West.

The pastorate of James Hughes over the churches of Short Creek and Lower Buffalo, Va., which commenced in 1790, extended to 1814, when he took charge of the Indian Mission in and about Lewistown, removing three years later to Oxford, to assume the office of Principal of what is now known as Miami University. After three years of service in this posi-

[1] His successor was Samuel F. Leake.

tion, his death occurred, May 2, 1821. As an earnest and faithful preacher and a zealous promoter of the cause of missions, his name is entitled to distinguished mention. His successor at Short Creek was Joseph Anderson, and at Lower Buffalo, after an interval of some years, Jacob Cozad, a licentiate of the Presbytery in 1818.

The pastorate of John Brice over the churches of Three Ridges and Forks of Wheeling, which commenced in 1790, closed in 1807, when, after an interval of two years, he was succeeded by Joseph Stevenson. The latter, however, shortly afterward relinquished his charge at the Forks, and it was united under a single pastoral charge with Wheeling, that had long been vacant, but over which James Hervey was settled in 1814.

The ministry of Thomas Marquis at Cross Creek extended from 1794 till 1826, when the infirmities of age compelled him to resign his post. His labors at Upper Buffalo, which commenced also in 1794, closed in 1798, and he was succeeded here in 1801 by John Anderson, whose pastorate closed in 1833. Few men on the field accomplished so much or left behind them so enviable a reputation as Thomas Marquis, "the silver-tongued." He was at once a pastor and a missionary, a laborer himself and a judicious director of the labors of others. Below the middle stature, but of compact build, and somewhat corpulent, he retained to his last years a remarkable degree of activity and vigor. His features were small, but finely formed, and the lines of thought were traced deeply on his forehead. Mild and frank in common intercourse, courteous yet dignified in his demeanor, he never repelled by austerity or offended by levity those with whom he was associated. As he rose in the pulpit, evidently under a deep sense of the solemnity of his office, calm and composed, as well as earnest, there was a sweet benignity in his tones. that charmed every ear and attracted every eye. As he warmed with his subject, he bore his audience with him on the tide of his own emotion, and sometimes their intenseness of feeling seemed to outvie his own. As he proceeded in his discourse, it was manifest that—master of his theme—he had full control of his audience. Logical in arrangement, perspicuous in expression, "a running brook upon a silvery bed could not show more clearly the pebbles in its path than do his sentences the exact shade of idea in his mind."[1] With a voice remarkably musical and under perfect control, and a power and delicacy of emotion ever exhibited in the speaking features or tearful eye, he was a master of the arts of persuasion, and his appeals were almost irresistible. On some occasions, hundreds of strong men were to be seen weeping like children, under his preaching. By Dr. Matthew Brown, President of Jefferson College,—who indulged, indeed, at times, in too great latitude of expression,—he was pronounced the most effective orator to whom he had ever listened. To a remarkable extent he combined "solemnity with vivacity, mildness with earnestness, affection with authority, and a Christ-like pungency" in the application of truth "with the holy unction which it belongs to the Spirit alone to impart." Many of the Presbyterian congregations in Ohio had their foundations laid by colonies from his church.[2]

The pastoral labors of Thomas Moore at Ten-Mile

---

[1] Sprague, Annals, iv. 88.

[2] It is said that Dr. Ashbel Green, after hearing Mr. Marquis in his own pulpit in Philadelphia, was so deeply affected by the matter and manner of his discourse that he resolved to abandon his own method and adopt that of Marquis.—*Old Redstone*, p. 434.

closed in 1803, upon his removal to Salem, and his successor was the son of his gifted predecessor, Thaddeus Dod. His dismission, and the installation of Cephas Dodd, took place at the same meeting of Presbytery, Dec. 14, 1803. Although it was mid-winter, the services connected with the ordination and installation were held in Joseph Riggs's "sugar-camp, with the open canopy of the heaven for a temple, the snow for a carpet, and the wind whistling through the leafless branches of the trees as an accompaniment to the solemn music, as it pealed forth from a choir consisting of hundreds of voices."[1]

The pastor was the honored son of an honored father. He possessed a clear, strong mind, enriched by manly culture and varied learning. His character, in which practical wisdom, a tranquil and uniform piety, and the sympathies of a loyal and enduring friendship were combined, was singularly complete, harmonious, and symmetrical. A good scholar, a sound divine, a prudent counsellor, he was also a tender and faithful preacher. In addresses on sacramental and funeral occasions, he greatly excelled. Perhaps his deficiency in doctrinal preaching, of which complaint was made, was due in part to Mr. Moore's excess. About the year 1816, he relinquished the charge of Upper Ten-Mile, where he was succeeded by Thomas Hoge (1817–19), Andrew Wylie (1819–21), Boyd Mercer (1821–22), Ludovicus Robbins, Cornelius Laughran, Jacob Lindley, and subsequently, among others, James M. Smith and Nicholas Murray. At Lower Ten-Mile, or Amity, Mr. Dodd continued in the pastorate until increasing infirmities compelled him to resign his charge (1855), after a ministry of over half a century. His death occurred in 1858.

---

[1] Wines's Historical Discourse, 18.

The pastorate of Samuel Ralston at Mingo Creek and Williamsport—now Monongahela City—continued at the former place for forty and at the latter for thirty-five years (1794–1829). Till fourscore years of age, he would not relinquish his sphere of active service, and for the remaining fifteen years of his life his mind still retained much of the vigor of earlier years. His career closed in 1851, when he had reached his ninety-fifth year.

At Bethel and Lebanon, William Woods was called to the pastorate on the decease of his venerable predecessor, John Clark, in 1797. Of the former he retained the pastoral charge for thirty-four years (1797–1831), resigning the other after a period of nearly twenty-five. His successor in the first was George Marshall, and in the last, Thomas D. Baird. Mr. Woods was a native of Lancaster county, and a graduate of Dickinson College. He studied theology in part with Dr. Smith of Pequa, and in part under Dr. Witherspoon. For some time preceding his acceptance of his call to Lebanon and Bethel he labored as a missionary in the surrounding region.[1]

At Mill Creek and the Flats, George M. Scott was settled about 1801, and his pastorate continued till April, 1826,—from 1819, when Washington Presbytery was erected, as a member of that body.

At Upper Buffalo, John Anderson commenced his ministry in 1801, and resigned his charge, on account of declining health, in 1833. Plain, candid, sincere, and straightforward in all his intercourse, he had little taste for display; and his quick, keen discrimination of character was almost sure to penetrate any disguise. There was in his manner a deep solemnity and earnestness, which was not made less effective by his

---

[1] Old Redstone, 354.

slender form, thin visage, cadaverous complexion, and small, dark eye which kindled responsive to his quick emotions. As a preacher he was searching and pungent, and his discourses were well digested and logically arranged. Eminent as a theological teacher, a warm friend of missions, a self-denying and devoted pastor, he holds a high rank among the pioneer pastors of the Church. For several years preceding his settlement within the bounds of the Presbytery, he itinerated in Kentucky and Tennessee, crossing over repeatedly into Ohio and Indiana.

At Pigeon Creek—for some time a part of Dr. McMillan's charge—Andrew Gwin was settled in 1800, and his pastorate, which included also the congregation of Pike Run, was continued till Oct. 7, 1819. Upon his dismissal, Dr. Andrew Wylie served some years as stated supply.[1]

Miller's Run, three miles distant from Canonsburg, was supplied by John Watson, who had charge of the institution at the latter place from the time of his licensure in 1798 till his death in 1802. Dr. James Dunlap, who succeeded him as President of what had now become Jefferson College, succeeded him also as pastor of the church until his resignation of the Presidency and his removal to New Geneva, in 1812. His successor at Miller's Run, as well as in the Presidency of the

---

[1] The succeeding pastors were Dr. W. C. Anderson, 1832–36; E. S. Graham, 1836–44; and James Sloan. Communicants in 1854, three hundred and seventy.

Andrew Gwin occasioned no little trouble to the Presbytery; and his case was finally carried up to the Synod and General Assembly. Dr. McMillan at first took his part, but finally was convinced that his judgment had been too favorable. The records of the General Assembly reveal little of the character of the difficulty. The Presbytery suspended him from the ministry; and when the Synod had reversed the decision, the Assembly sustained the Presbytery. This was in 1819.

college, was Dr. Andrew Wylie (1812–16), upon whose resignation as President, William McMillan, a son of the venerable Dr. John McMillan, was elected to the vacant post, and succeeded him also at Miller's Run. The resignation of President McMillan took place in 1822. The church was subsequently for many years under the care of William Smith, professor in the college, while the newly-organized church at Canonsburg enjoyed the services of Dr. Matthew Brown, the successor of McMillan in the Presidency.

At Washington, which had been vacant many years,[1] President Brown was settled in the spring of 1805. Here he labored in the double capacity of pastor, and Principal of the Washington Academy, chartered in 1787, but originated largely through the enterprise of that pioneer of Redstone Presbytery, Thaddeus Dod. In the spring of 1806, a year from the time when Dr. Brown took charge of the institution, it was merged into Washington College; and he retained the Presidency until difficulties which occurred led to his resignation in 1816. Although urgently invited to other spheres of effort, he retained the pastorate of the church until his acceptance of the Presidency of Jefferson College in 1822. His successor at Washington in the Presidency was Dr. Andrew Wylie, and in the pastorate of the church Obadiah Jennings, subsequently of Nashville, and son of Jacob Jennings of Dunlap's Creek.

At Richland, Ohio, Short Creek (West Liberty, Va.), and Cross-Roads, Joseph Anderson, a licentiate of Ohio Presbytery in 1799 or 1800, commenced, shortly after, a pastorate which was continued at Short Creek and St. Clairsville for about thirty years, and in connection with Steubenville Presbytery after its erection

---

[1] See Assembly's Minutes for 1799 and 1803.

in 1818. His successor at Short Creek was Benjamin Mitchel in 1830, and at Cross-Roads[1]—united with Three Springs under one pastoral charge—Elisha Macurdy in June, 1800.

Few men have accomplished more for the cause of Christ than Mr. Macurdy. With no brilliant or striking qualities, he was distinguished by sound practical judgment and strong common sense. Of medium size, sandy hair and complexion, with nothing peculiarly marked in his features, the ordinary observer would have discovered nothing in his appearance to attract special attention. But his sagacity in the discernment of character, and the readiness with which he could adapt himself to different types of intellect and feeling, conjoined with an uncommon constitutional ardor, which was hallowed by an unreserved consecration to his Master's work, made him remarkably effective in the spheres of labor which he was called to occupy. Nothing could daunt his resolution. Difficulty fired rather than taxed his energy. As a preacher he was direct, earnest, and bold, never daubing with untempered mortar, or softening down the truth of God to make it palatable to squeamish consciences. With little of literary taste or refinement, his uncompromising plainness, his manifest sincerity, his deep-toned piety, and the strictly evangelical character of his utterances, supplied every minor defect. In the revivals which occurred during the early period of his ministry in Western Pennsylvania, he took a leading part; and his labors in the cause of missions, both by itinerating among the new settlements and in visiting the Synod's missions to the Indians, attest his persevering ardor in the great work

---

[1] It is possible that the Cross-Roads of Anderson's is not the same with that of Macurdy's charge.

to which he had devoted his life. In the fall of 1823, in consequence of enfeebled health, he was constrained to resign his charge of Three Springs, and in 1835 that of Cross-Roads. At the former, in conjunction with the Flats, he was succeeded by Samuel Reed, and at the latter by L. R. McAboy. His death occurred July, 1845, in his eighty-third year.

At Steubenville and Island Creek, James Snodgrass, a candidate under the care of the Presbytery in 1799, commenced his labors in 1802. To this field he was sent as a missionary by the Presbytery.[1] In (October) 1816 he was dismissed, and at Steubenville was succeeded first by Obadiah Jennings, who subsequently (1822) removed to Washington, and, after his dismission, by Charles Clinton Beatty (1823–37). In 1838–39, the Second Church, gathered by Dr. Beatty's labors, called him as its pastor (1838–47). Crab Apple and Beech Spring congregations appear to have been gathered shortly after 1802; and of these John Rhea had for many years the pastoral charge. At Crab Apple his successors were Thomas Clark (June, 1811–1820),[2] Solomon Cowles (1822–30), and subsequently Jacob Coon (1831) and Moses Allen; while his pastorate at Beech Spring continued for nearly fifty years.

Two Ridges and Yellow Creek (Richmond) became the pastoral charge of William McMillan in 1806. In 1812 he was dismissed, subsequently accepting the Presidency of Jefferson College. After a vacancy of some years, his successor (1819) was Thomas Hunt, whose pastorate continued till near 1840.

---

[1] Minutes of 1803. From 1819 to 1825 he was pastor of Island Creek. His successor here was John E. Tidball.

[2] Nottingham became a part of Mr. Clark's charge as early as 1817. A year or two later, Fairview was joined with it; and in 1822, William Wallace became pastor of both.

To complete the list of the pastors of the Presbytery from 1800 to 1819, it is only necessary to add that in 1812 Michael Law was settled at Montour's Run (as successor of J. McLean, dismissed 1808) and Hopewell; in 1809, Joseph Stevenson at Three Ridges and Wheeling, Andrew McDonald in 1810 at White Oak, the Flats, and Flagerty's Run (1810–23); and Thomas Hoge (1818, s. s.) at East Buffalo, and three or four years later at Claysville.[1]

The churches vacant and unable to support a pastor were, in 1803, Jefferson, Waynesburg, Charlestown, Grave Creek, Yellow Creek, and Long's Run; in 1819, Concord, Hopewell, Cross-Roads, and Charlestown. At the latter date, Pigeon Creek, Lower Buffalo, Short Creek, New Providence, and Jefferson were vacant, but able to support a pastor.

The Presbytery of Erie, erected in 1801, embraced the northwestern portion of the field covered by the two Presbyteries of Redstone and Ohio, out of which it was formed. A portion of Eastern Ohio—and at length the Western Reserve—was embraced within its bounds. Its original membership consisted of five ministers,—Thomas E. Hughes at Salem (till 1808) and Mount Pleasant (till 1839), William Wick at Hopewell and Youngstown (1799–1814), Samuel Tait at Upper Salem (1800–06) and Cool Spring, subsequently at Mercer (1807–11) and Salem (1814–20), Joseph Stockton at Meadville and Sugar Creek (1800–10), and Robert Lee (till 1807) at Amity and Big Spring.

In the course of the following year the Presbytery was strengthened by the accession of James Satter-

---

[1] In 1814, James Hervey was settled as pastor of Wheeling Town and Forks of Wheeling. Mr. Stevenson (dismissed from Three Ridges in 1825) was succeeded in 1828 by John McClusky.

field,[1] settled at Moorfield and Upper Neshanock (1803–12), William Wylie at Fairfield and Upper and Lower Sandy (1802–05), John Boyd at Union and Slate Lick (1803–10), and Abraham Boyd at Bull Creek (1803–20), Middlesex (1803–21), and subsequently (1817–21) Deer Creek. The vacant churches of the Presbytery, including Erie, Oil Creek, Poland, Warren, and several more on the Reserve, numbered twenty-one.

In 1803, Mr. Badger wrote, "Twelve ministers are now settled north of the Ohio waters in Pennsylvania. These, with Mr. Wick and myself in this county,[2] form the Erie Presbytery. There are sixteen congregations newly formed within the bounds of this Presbytery, who are seeking for supplies, and several for candidates to settle with them; but there are not more than two or three licentiates on this side of the mountain. Several congregations will be formed in this county within another year."

During the year (1803) William Woods was settled at Centre (1803–08) and Plain Grove (1803–16); Alexander Cook at Slippery Spring and New Castle (1803–09), and James Patterson at Upper and Lower Greenfield (1803–05). In 1804, Robert Johnston was settled at Bear Creek (1804–07) and Scrub Grass (1803–11), Nicholas Pittenger at Westfield (1804–08) and Poland (1804–10), and John McPherrin, whose pastorate at Salem, in connection with Redstone Presbytery, closed in 1803, commenced his labors at Concord and Muddy Creek,—Concord and Harmony (1809–14), and subsequently Concord and Butler forming his charge till shortly previous to his death in 1822.[3]

---

[1] Satterfield and Wylie were original members of Erie Presbytery. Satterfield died in 1857,—a member at that time of Beaver Presbytery,—aged ninety years.

[2] Trumbull county, or the Western Reserve.

[3] Over the congregation of Butler, which he is said to have

In 1807, Benjamin Boyd[1] was ordained and installed pastor of Beulah, Trumbull, and Pymatuning (1807–09); and Samuel Tait, dismissed from Upper Salem, was settled at Mercer (1806–41) and Cool Spring, subsequently Salem. In 1808, Cyrus Riggs was settled at Fairfield and Mill Creek (1807–12); Reed Bracken at Plane and Nebo (1808–19); Johnston Eaton at Springfield and Fairview (1808–15), taking charge in 1815 of Fairview (1815–47), Erie, and North-East, demitting the charge of North-East after 1817, and of Erie after 1822; and James Boyd at Newtown and Warren (1808–13).[2]

In 1808, the Presbytery of Hartford was formed from that of Erie, by setting off to it eight ministers with their congregations, covering the region of the Western Reserve. In 1810, John Matthews was settled at Gravel Run (1810–14) and Waterford (1810–17). In 1811, Robert Johnston was settled at Meadville, Sugar Creek, and Conneaut Lake (1811–17). In 1814, Cyrus Riggs was settled at Scrub Grass (1814–23) and West Unity (1814–21), and Ira Condict at Fairfield and Big Sugar Creek, retaining the former—in connection for a period with Georgetown and Cool Spring—for many years. In 1815, John Reddick was settled at Slate Lick and Union (1815–21), and in 1818, John Munson at Plain Grove and Centre, where he remained during an extended pastorate. In 1819, Phineas Camp was settled at Westfield—formerly Chetauque Cross-Roads—(1819–21), and Reed Bracken at Middlesex. In 1821, John Vanlieu commenced his pastorate at Meadville.

The vacant churches of the Presbytery numbered twenty in 1802; and of these twelve were unable to

---

gathered, he was installed in 1813.—*Records of Synod of Pittsburg*, p. 106.

[1] Ordained in 1801. Labored in later years in Kentucky and Indiana. Died at Newport, Ky., in 1859.

[2] His death occurred in 1813.

support a pastor. In 1808, the nine ordained ministers of the Presbytery had increased to nineteen, and the congregations had risen from thirty-nine to sixty-five, of which thirty-seven were vacant,—twenty-six being unable to support a pastor. Hartford Presbytery—known as Beaver after 1833—numbered in 1815—seven years after its erection—thirteen ministers, and forty-one congregations, of which fifteen were vacant. In 1820 the Presbytery of Alleghany was formed from that of Erie, the latter numbering in the following year seven ministers and twenty-nine congregations.

Of the members of Erie Presbytery—occupying for several years after its erection one of the most arduous posts of frontier missionary service—we should welcome a more extended record than any that has been left us. Nearly all of them were, in fact, primitive bishops. Groups of churches have sprung up within what were once the bounds of a single parish. Yet the pastors of the Presbytery often extended their preaching-tours to regions far distant, devoting from one-fourth to one-half of their time to strictly missionary labor, and in many instances absenting themselves from home for months, in order to visit the stations among the Indian tribes.

Among these men were Thomas E. Hughes, the first minister of the gospel who settled north of the Ohio River, laboring for more than thirty years as the pastor of Mount Pleasant congregation, and rewarded by the fruits of repeated revivals,—a man whose dying testimony, "I feel unworthy to use such strong language as I might in truth, in speaking of the rich enjoyment the Lord permits me to experience," was worthy of his life; William Wick, a native of Long Island, a theological pupil of Dr. McMillan, the first settled minister on the Reserve, and ever the missionary and the friend of missions; Samuel Tait, whose sound sense and unswerving integrity were proverbial, and of whom his pupil and successor remarked, "His spiritual children I find wherever I go throughout the Presbytery;" Joseph Stockton, already mentioned, eminent as a teacher as well as for usefulness in the pulpit, whose name is ever identified with the Western Theological Seminary; William Woods, a native of Lancaster county, a graduate of Dickinson College, under whose labors nearly one thousand persons were added to the church; together with others like Satterfield, Wylie, Cook, Johnston, Pittenger, and the Boyds, the proper monuments of whose labors are to be sought, not in the minutes of Presbyterial reports, but in the foundations of society itself.[1]

---

[1] The vacant churches of the Presbyteries constituting the Synod of Pittsburg were, in 1802, Pittsburg, Greensburg and Unity, Pitt's Township, McKeesport, Morgantown and Middletown, New Providence, Uniontown, Tyrone, Sandy Creek, Crossings, Clarksburg, Tygart's Valley, Somerset, Turkey Foot, Wheatfield and Stony Creek, in Redstone Presbytery; Washington, Lancaster and Rush Creek, Jefferson, Waynesburg, Charlestown, Grave Creek, Yellow Creek, and Long's Run, in Ohio Presbytery; and Warren, Breakneck, Thorn's Tent, Concord, Franklin, Big Sugar Creek, Oil Creek, Gravel Run, Middle Brook, Power's Mill, Crossings of Cossawaga, Pymatuning, Slippery Rock and Lower Neshanock, Westfield and Poland, Upper and Lower Greenfield, and Erie.

As the Presbyteries extended, new congregations came under their care, not only in Western Pennsylvania, but in Southeastern Ohio and in the region of the Western Reserve. The new congregations reported are (1803) Quenmahoning (Redstone Presbytery); Conneaut Lake, Muddy Creek, Springfield, Mount Pleasant, Salt Springs, Beulah, Trumbull, Broken Straw, Franklin, Plain Grove, Centre (Erie Presbytery); Moorfields, Upper Neshanock, and Washington (Ohio Presbytery); (1805) Monongahela Glades, Cowanshawanick, Cherry Hill (Redstone Presbytery); Pit-Hole, Outlet of Conneaut, Waterford, Congruity, and Mt. Nebo (Erie Presbytery); Crab Apple and Beech Spring (Ohio Presbytery);

Meanwhile, the Presbyteries of Steubenville and of Washington had been formed (1819) from that of Ohio,

---

(1806) Fairview, Upper and Lower Sugar Creek, Mill Creek, Portland, Little Sugar Creek, Connewango, Beavertown, Harmony, Mercer (Erie Presbytery); (1807) Plain, Newton, Rocky Spring and Amity, Hartford, Smithfield, Upper Salem, Vienna, Bristol, Palmyra, Mesopotamia, Miles Settlement (Erie Presbytery); White Oak Flats, Hopewell, Will's Creek, Mine Run, Federal Creek, Athens, Leading Creek, Gallipolis, Kanawa, Middle Island, Centre, Salem, Pickaway Plains, New Lisbon, and Long's Run (Ohio Presbytery); (1808) Beulah, Indiana (Redstone Presbytery); Clinton, Frederick, Ebenezer, Springfield, Worthington, Crooked Creek, Federal Creek, Middle Island, Greenville, Clear Creek (Ohio Presbytery); East Unity, Boardman, Austinburg and Morgan, Indiana (Erie Presbytery); Vernon, Brookfield, Hubbard, Richfield, Hudson, Talmadge, Burton, Canfield, Westfield, Trumbull (Hartford Presbytery); (1809) West Unity (Erie Presbytery); (1810) Warren, McMahon's Creek (Ohio Presbytery); Chetauque, Mayville, Beech Woods (Erie Presbytery); Newton and Warren, Ellsworth, Euclid, Harpersfield, Upper Salem, Green, Columbiana (Hartford Presbytery); (1811) Red Bank, Glade Run (Redstone Presbytery); Grey's Station (Ohio Presbytery); North-East, Chetauque Cross-Roads,—subsequently Westfield (Erie Presbytery); Aurora, Hudson, Cool Spring (Hartford Presbytery); (1812) Williamsport, or Horse-Shoe Bottom, Sardis (Ohio Presbytery); Brookfield, Canton, Henderson, Mantua (Hartford Presbytery); (1813) Cherry Run (Redstone Presbytery); (1814) Alleghany and Pine Creek, Brownsville, Highland, Upper Plum Creek (Redstone Presbytery); Cherry Tree, Toby's Creek, Sandy Lick, Butler (Erie Presbytery); (1815) West Liberty, Clarksburg, French Creek, Bethany (Ohio Presbytery); Deer Creek (Erie Presbytery); Kinsman, Rootstown, Hamden, Nelson, Sharon, Talmadge (Grand River Presbytery); (1816) Richland (Erie Presbytery); Benton, Harpersfield, Painesville, Mantua, Dover, Madison, Green, Johnston (Grand River Presbybytery); Boardman, Yellow Creek, Scotch Settlement (Hartford Presbytery); (1817) Hopewell (Erie Presbytery); Brickville, Williamsfield (or Wayne), Kingsville, Ashtabula, Beuville, Bristol, Bloomfield, Wheatsborough (Grand River Presbytery); (1818) Gun's Cross-Roads, Hagerstown, Brushy Fork of Stillwater (Ohio Presbytery); Titeaute, Lottsville (Erie Presbytery); Stow, Harris-

—the first with eight ministers, Lyman Potter, Joseph Anderson at Richland and Short Creek, James Snodgrass at Island Creek, John Rhea at Beech Spring, Thomas Hunt at Two Ridges and Richmond, Obadiah Jennings at Steubenville, and Thomas B. Clark; the last with nine ministers, Thomas Marquis at Cross Creek, George M. Scott at Mill Creek and Flats, John Anderson at Upper Buffalo, Elisha Macurdy at Cross-Roads, Cephas Dodd at Lower Ten-Mile, Joseph Stevenson at Three Ridges, Andrew Wylie, President of Washington College, James Hervey at Forks of Wheeling and Wheelingtown, and Thomas Hoge stated supply at East Buffalo and Claysville.

The Presbytery of Grand River, formed from that of Hartford in 1814, and the Presbytery of Portage, formed from that of Grand River in 1818, although lying within the bounds of Ohio and covering the region of the Western Reserve, were in connection with the Synod of Pittsburg. In 1820, the Presbyteries consti-

---

ville, Black River, Florence (Grand River Presbytery); (1819) Armagh, Morgantown and George's Creek, French Creek and Buchanan (Redstone Presbytery); Wellsburg (Ohio Presbytery); Cossawaga, Red Bank (Erie Presbytery); Morgan, Huntsburg, Thompson, Andover, Charden, Braceville, Grearsburg, Westfield, Mesopotamia, Salem, Bainbridge, Farmington (Grand River Presbytery); Deerfield (Hartford Presbytery); Burrell's Settlement, Wadsworth, Sandusky City, Harrisville, Brooklyn, Margaretta, Palmyra, Brownhelm, Fitchville, Shalersville (Portage Presbytery); (1820) Bethesda (Hartford Presbytery); Rome, Kirtland, (Grand River Presbytery); Lyme, Strongsville, Norwalk, Granger, Medina, Atwater, Randolph, Palmyra, Franklin, Thorndyke (Portage Presbytery).

Some of the congregations were organized a considerable time before they were reported to the Presbytery. A large part of them were within the bounds of Ohio; and a glance at the Presbyterial connection of those above named will show the change of locality in the growth of the Synod for the first twenty years of the century.

tuting this body were the Presbyteries of Redstone, with twenty-one ministers and forty congregations; Erie, with thirteen ministers and forty-nine congregations; Hartford, with ten ministers and twenty-two congregations; Grand River, with twelve ministers and twenty-three congregations; Portage, with nine ministers and thirty-three congregations; Washington, with ten ministers and nineteen congregations; Steubenville, with seven ministers and twelve congregations; and Ohio, with not far from twelve ministers and eighteen congregations,—making an aggregate of about ninety-four ministers and two hundred and sixteen congregations, an increase in eighteen years of nearly three hundred per cent. in the ministry and nearly two hundred per cent. in the churches on this field.

The cause of learning and the cause of missions were not neglected by the Synod of Pittsburg or its constituent Presbyteries. The Canonsburg Academy —changed to Jefferson College in 1802, contemporaneously with the erection of the Synod—was for some time under Presbyterial supervision, and has ever been dependent on the support and patronage, while it has retained the sympathies, of the Presbyterian Church. The school at Washington—subsequently developed into Washington College, and in some respects a rival to the one at Canonsburg—was yet under the supervision and control of Presbyterians; while the first President of Alleghany College at Meadville was Timothy Alden, a member of the Presbytery and pastor of the church.

When the project of establishing a theological seminary at Princeton was adopted by the Assembly, it was cordially endorsed by the Synod, and measures were taken to secure funds to aid in its endowment. It was not long, however, until the special wants of the Western field became obvious. As early as 1819, the plan of establishing a seminary within the Synod's bounds was agitated. It was confidently anticipated that a union of Washington and Jefferson Colleges might be effected, and the buildings of the former secured for the Seminary. Perhaps in anticipation of this, Dr. McMillan was elected Professor of Theology at Canonsburg, and contributions of books were made with a view to secure a theological library. Upon the failure of the project, it was proposed to unite with the Synods of Ohio and Kentucky in the establishment of an institution; but the discordant views of the local bodies resulted in its defeat, and the Synod of Pittsburg resolved upon the establishment of the Western Theological Seminary within its own bounds.

In connection with the organization of the several local missionary societies among the Eastern churches at the close of the last and the commencement of the present century, a warm interest was excited in behalf of the aborigines of this country. Each local society, for the most part, with its other fields in view, directed particular attention to the Indian tribes. The General Assembly, in drawing up, in 1800, its list of objects entitled to special attention, placed at the head of it, and in precedence of plans for ministerial education, "the gospelizing of the Indians on the frontiers of our country."[1] The scheme of missionary effort was to be connected with a plan for their civilization, the want of which had occasioned, it was believed, the failure of former efforts.

The Assembly could not readily command the means for carrying its scheme into execution; and the Synod of Pittsburg resolved to supply—to some extent, at least—its lack of service, and assume the

[1] Minutes of Assembly for 1801.

burden itself. With a vast region around it, rapidly filling up with immigrants, and with calls from new communities and feeble churches which might have absorbed all its energies, it still looked to the regions beyond, and determined, carrying out the plan already initiated by the Synod of Virginia, to prosecute at the same time its mission to the white population of the Northwest and its mission to the Indian tribes.

The measures taken to execute the latter project gave flattering promise of success.[1] The Wyandotte Indians, in the neighborhood of Sandusky, seemed prepared to welcome missionaries whose efforts should be directed at the same time toward their religious instruction and the introduction among them of the arts of civilized life. They were repeatedly visited by members of the Synod, who remained with them for a brief period; but in the summer of 1805[2] the Synod sent out three missionaries, who remained among them "for two months or more," and were well received. The necessity, however, of a permanent mission, demanded that some one should be located and resident among them; and Joseph Badger was employed by the Synod for this purpose. He arrived at the settlements of the Indians in May, 1806,[3] and met with a hospitable reception.

---

[1] This statement is not intended to apply to the earliest efforts of the Synod. At the very session during which the society was formed, Joseph Patterson was appointed to visit the Shawanese Indians and to continue among them for five months; and Alexander Cook, a licentiate of the Presbytery of Ohio, was to visit and labor among them at Sandusky for the same period. Both visited their respective fields; but the reception they met was not what they expected, and both returned in less than two months. The Synod, however, did not abandon their project. Subsequent visits of the missionaries were better appreciated by the Indians.

[2] Minutes of 1806.

[3] Appendix to Minutes of 1807. Elliott's Life of Macurdy.

The plan proposed was to combine religious instruction with initiation into the arts of civilized life. Especial attention was to be given to agriculture, in order that the Indians might be induced to adopt a settled mode of life and industrious habits. For this purpose, Mr. Badger was accompanied by three laborers, who were to give practical instruction to the Indians, to aid them in fencing, ploughing, raising corn and other kinds of grain, as well as to assist them in erecting comfortable dwellings. A missionary farm was to be cultivated as a model for native imitation. From the beef, pork, corn, and vegetables that might be produced, the missionary family was to be supplied; while the Indian children were to be fed, lodged, and clothed at the expense of the society.

The plan was carried out to a considerable extent, although opposed by the Indian traders. A small dwelling-house and a school-house were erected upon the Reserve, opposite the Indian village at the lower rapids of Sandusky. The mission was furnished with a team of two horses, two yoke of oxen, ploughs, chains, &c. The Rev. Joseph McLean, sent by the Board of Trust to assist the mission, procured some live stock on the Scioto—mainly through the liberality of the people of that region—and conveyed them to Sandusky. Fields were laid out and fenced and put under cultivation, and several of the Indians began to devote themselves to agricultural pursuits. In the course of one or two years, twenty acres of ground were fenced. Crops of corn, oats, flax, turnips, and potatoes, as well as many garden-vegetables, were produced. In the fall of 1809 the missionary stock on the farm numbered twenty-six head of cattle. Intoxication was utterly unknown among the Indians who had been brought under missionary influence; many of the natives had been induced to attend regularly upon the preaching of the gospel, and several gave good evidence of genuine conversion.[1]

But the mission had many obstacles to encounter. There were no mills to grind the grain, and the Indians had to pound it in a large mortar. Farming-tools could be procured only with great difficulty. Plough-irons and other kinds of smith-work could not be procured within a distance of one hundred miles. In these circumstances, Mr. Badger determined to see what could be done at the East in aid of the cause.

In November, 1808, he set out for New England. He told the story of what he had attempted, what he had accomplished, and what he designed to do. At Boston and in the vicinity he raised over one thousand dollars in behalf of his mission. Returning to his field of labor, he devoted himself anew to his work. But domestic afflictions—first the death of a daughter, and then the loss by fire of the dwelling occupied by his family—called him back repeatedly to the Reserve. Discouragement thus followed discouragement; and finally, in 1810, he abandoned the mission, and removed with his family to Ashtabula, where he labored for many years as a settled pastor.

The Synod, however, did not relinquish its purpose to prosecute the mission. Quite a number of its members had repeatedly visited it, and took the deepest interest in its continuance and success. From 1805, the Synod applied for, and received from the Assembly, the sum of from one hundred to five hundred dollars annually, to enable them to sustain it. The mission continued, in a hopeful state, till the War of 1812, when, the buildings having been burned and the improvements destroyed by the enemy, it was suspended.[2]

---

[1] Conn. Ev. Mag., April, 1809.

[2] It is said that through Mr. Badger's influence the Indians were kept from joining the enemy during the war.—*Green's Pres. Mis.*

Few missions, even to heathen tribes, have ever been conducted under more discouraging circumstances than this mission to the Indians about Sandusky. Their condition in almost every respect was most pitiable and degraded. They were contaminated by the white man's vices, while their own superstitions were by no means weakened by contact with such civilization as they witnessed in the Indian traders.

Mr. Macurdy, during Mr. Badger's absence in New England, took the sole charge of the mission for several months; and his journal unfolds to view a scene of degradation which would have put to flight in a moment the brilliant fancies of Rousseau. "Their houses," he says, "when they have any, are wretched huts, almost as dirty as they can be, and swarming with fleas and lice; their furniture, a few barks, a tin or brass kettle, a gun, pipe, and tomahawk. Such is their ingratitude that whilst you load them with favors they will reproach you to the face, and construe your benevolent intentions and actions into intentional fraud or real injury. They will lie in the most deliberate manner, and to answer any selfish purpose."

Even this picture Mr. Macurdy pronounces far short of the reality. Among such a people must the missionary live. The dangers, difficulties, and perplexities of such a life must be his daily experience. Surrounded with them he lies down to sleep, oppressed by them he seeks repose, confronted by them he goes forth to his daily task, without an earthly friend to give him counsel, to share his burden, or to listen to his griefs. Well might he say, "No honor or emolument that this world can confer can compensate a man for the sacrifices he must make and the trials he must endure" in such a lot.

Yet among these Indians the results attained seemed to encourage a renewal of the mission at the close of the war. In 1818, it was determined to resume the work among the Ottawas, on the Maumee River. But difficulties intervened, and the work was not prosecuted till 1822. A few years later, after a mission had been established, and afforded good hopes of success, it was transferred to the care of the American Board.

Meanwhile, a mission had been planned to "the Indians in and about Lewistown."[1] James Hughes, in 1814, resigned his pastoral charge of Short Creek and Lower Buffalo, in order to prosecute it. For three years he continued to labor at Urbana (Ohio) as missionary and stated supply, receiving annually from the Assembly four hundred dollars toward the support of the mission.

The sympathy of the Synod not only for the cause of missions, but in behalf of ministerial education, tract-distribution, Sunday-schools, colonization, temperance, Sabbath-observance, and the monthly concert, as well as sound doctrine, is sufficiently attested by its records. To promote its objects, a magazine was established (in 1803), of which Messrs. McMillan, Moore, and Anderson were managing editors, and the profits of which, paid into the treasury of the Synod's Board of Missions in 1807, amounted to over three hundred dollars. Upon the failure of the enterprise, no further effort seems to have been made to sustain a religious periodical till 1821, soon after which the "Pittsburg Recorder" was established, succeeded, however, a few years later, by the "Spectator" and the "Christian Herald."

The powerful revival enjoyed by the churches under

---

[1] The mission at Lewistown seems to have been abandoned on Mr. Hughes's acceptance of an invitation to take charge of Miami University, in 1818.

the care of the Presbytery of Ohio,[1] during this period, commenced under the labors of Rev. Elisha Macurdy, at Three Springs, where he was settled as pastor. For some months previous the church had not been without signs of the divine favor; but on the last Sabbath in September, 1802, in connection with a sacramental season, the work began in earnest. On Monday evening the meeting should have been dismissed; but those who were assembled were unwilling to leave the ground. They remained together all night, and until near noon the next day. Some of the features which had characterized the revivals in Kentucky, Tennessee, and the Carolinas, were witnessed here. Numbers sank down in their distress, and gave evidence of great concern and anguish of spirit. Five or six were supposed to have found peace before the close of the meeting.

Two weeks later, a sacramental season was observed by the church at Raccoon, under the charge of Mr. Patterson. The occasion was deeply solemn. Bold and hardened sinners were awakened and reduced to deep distress. Such was the state of things that it was determined to appoint the last Sabbath in October for an extra meeting and communion.

On this occasion a great multitude was on the ground. Families came in wagons, bringing their provisions with them. The meeting was at the Cross-Roads,—another station where Mr. Macurdy labored. Ten ordained ministers and four licentiates were present. Between seven and eight hundred communed; and the exercises, which commenced on Saturday, continued till Tuesday morning,—by night as well as by

---

[1] Conn. Ev. Mag., Feb. 1803, letter of Rev. James Hughes, West Liberty, Short Creek, Ohio county, Va. Quite an extended account of the revival is given in Elliott's Life of Macurdy.

day. The cries and groans of the distressed were almost incessant. Sometimes, indeed, the speaker was interrupted by them in his discourse. The number under conviction continued steadily to increase. On Monday, sermons were preached at the same time in three different places, sufficiently remote from each other to avoid mutual disturbance,—one of them in the meeting-house.

But, as the assemblages were preparing to disperse, the joy of those who had been converted found expression in acclamations and songs of praise. Strangely mingling with the groans and cries of distress from others, they added a new feature to the "solemn, awful, and pleasing scene." "Some very young were enabled to speak, recommending Christ, and inviting and warning sinners, in a manner truly astonishing."[1]

Another extra meeting was appointed for the fol-

---

[1] In a letter to the "New York Missionary Magazine" for 1802, the writer mentions other features of this occasion, not contained in the narrative from which the above statements are derived. He says, "On the Sabbath and Monday after the sacrament, not less than fifty were sometimes lying at once, crying for mercy, complaining of the hardness of their hearts, and pleading for pardon. They met every day or night—and frequently both—all that week. They remained in church all Sabbath night: some suppose sixty, others a hundred, were lying at once: the ministers exhorted and prayed alternately most of the night. Every age and sex are the subjects of this work, *Christians* and *ministers* not excepted. Many of them fall instantaneously, without discovering the least symptoms before; some appear affected, and after some time fall; others lie down and become helpless; some weep, some sigh and groan, others scream out violently; some fall but once, some a number of times; one has fallen five times, and yet received no comfort; some get ease in an hour, and speak to those around them in an astonishing manner. . . . The ministers say they are ashamed to speak after them. A very wild young man ridiculed the work, went away, shortly returned, fell instantaneously, lay there hours, got ease, and spoke about three hours or more *with power and eloquence almost divine.*"

lowing Sabbath at Upper Buffalo congregation, of which John Anderson was pastor,—"a very central place,"—to accommodate the multitude who were expected to attend. The number present was estimated at "not less than ten thousand." Twelve ministers attended. The exercises were prolonged as before, and from first to last as many as two thousand were "affected." "The distressed," of whom there were several hundred at the same time, "appeared to have awful apprehensions of their sins. Their cries, generally, were, Oh! my sins! Oh! my hard heart! Oh! what shall I do for Christ? O Jesus, take away my hard heart."

On the first of these occasions, before any precedent had been afforded by any churches in this region of country, the "bodily exercises" commenced. There were "such scenes of distress as exceeded any description." There were about fifty persons whose bodily strength was so far overcome that they were unable to stand without support. On the next occasion, the exercises of the first day of the meeting continued for "about four hours and a half, without intermission." During the day they were held in the open air, and in the evening a third service was held in the church, which was crowded to its full capacity. Numbers fell, crying out in distress and anguish.

On this occasion, Joseph Badger, of the Western Reserve, who had just returned from the meeting of the Synod of Pittsburg, was present. He noticed those who fell, and states that "they very nearly resembled persons who had just expired from a state of full strength. For a considerable time, pulsation could not be perceived. Their limbs were wholly unstrung, and respiration was scarcely perceptible: yet they retained their reason, and knew what was said within their hearing." Gradually, their strength returned; they opened their eyes and looked around them, but spoke in a low and feeble voice. When asked the occasion of their distress, they said it was the apprehension they had of the sinfulness of their sins, as committed against a holy God, and their soul-destroying nature. Their views of their own guilt were scriptural, and their salvation, they confessed, must be of sovereign grace. Five ministers and five hundred people continued in the meeting-house all night; and yet, except for the interruption produced by sighs and tears, there was nothing in the scenes disorderly or unbecoming.

The revival extended to other congregations.[1] The ministers who attended on these occasions returned from them to find their own people more anxious to hear the gospel. In the course of a year from the commencement of the work, it had extended over the whole region covered by the Synod of Pittsburg; and of the eighty or ninety congregations under its care, there were not more than five or six which had not been more or less affected.[2] The Rev. Thomas Robbins, sent out by the Connecticut Society to the Western

---

[1] By the close of December the work had spread from Mr. Macurdy's congregation to those of Messrs. McMillan, Patterson, Marquis, Anderson, Ralston, Gavin, and Moore. In November, forty persons were received into Mr. Macurdy's church, the youngest twelve years of age, the oldest over one hundred.—*New York Miss. Mag.* iv. 113.

[2] Connecticut Ev. Mag., 1804, letter of Mr. Robbins. At Valley Mills, in Luzerne county, a revival commenced soon after the remarkable scenes in Ohio Presbytery had occurred. The writer of a letter to the "New York Missionary Magazine," under date of February 23, 1803, says, "The two weeks past I would not exchange for a former seven years." "We find no difficulty now in getting people to meeting: the want is room to contain them. Many stout-hearted sinners are unexpectedly bowed down in tears to the earth. On Thursday evening, at my house, fifteen of this description came forward."

Reserve, was arrested on his way by the interest excited by these scenes of revival, so unlike any thing that had been experienced east of the Alleghanies. Yet he testifies freely to the genuineness of the work. "I conceive it," he says, "in many respects to resemble the revival of religion in New England in 1740-1742. In extent of territory it exceeds that. In its diffusion to almost every town and society it also exceeds that. With respect to the number of subjects in the several societies where the work is, I believe the present hardly equals the former. The opposition, the ridicule and reproach, which the present work receives, is not less than did the work of the same Spirit sixty years ago. The only difference is, opposition is not now conducted with the same external violence, it not being the custom of the day. The manner of the minister's preaching is also much as it was then,—Calvinistic in sentiment, serious, earnest, and pathetic. The state of society in these back-countries is in some respects similar to what it then was in New England. In the general attention and commotion which is produced among all classes of people, the two cases are quite similar. If there were any excesses among ministers who were great instruments in that work, it was doubtless owing to the violent opposition they experienced. In the present revival I have not known any thing of the kind. But they appear to conduct with great moderation and propriety. People at a distance may say what they will, but, when they come to be eye-witnesses, every reasonable man is effectually restrained from declaring it to be any thing but the mighty power of God."[1]

[1] The report of the revivals in Western Pennsylvania did not meet with a very approving reception from some of the ministers in the region of Philadelphia, especially those who retained the traditions and prejudices of the Old Side. Patterson, of Philadelphia,

He freely admitted that the work was "in many respects mysterious and extraordinary." Some things about it "could not be understood." "But there are things to be seen which are not to be described. After all that could be told or written, your conceptions would be far short of the reality, or of what they would be if you could be an eye-witness."

The bodily exercises, as they came under his observation, extended to most of those who were the subjects of the work. From two-thirds to three-quarters fell when under the force of their convictions. But others, of the genuineness of whose conversion none could doubt, were not thus affected. Those who fell usually did so repeatedly. Even after they had attained a Christian hope, they continued to fall. Persons who had long been members of the Church, and even ministers in some instances, were similarly affected. Elders of the churches, serious men, the aged and middle-aged, as well as the young, were among the number.

The falling took place, likewise, on all occasions,—most generally, however, at the public meetings. Yet instances occurred at family prayer, in solitude, and even "in merry company," or during the prosecution of ordinary business.

The degrees of bodily affection were quite various, although all alike were described as *falling*. Yet there was every grade of agitation, from the least

---

says, "In 1805, Marquis and Macurdy were commissioners from the Ohio Presbytery. I saw them when they returned home, and heard them tell what a time they had in the Assembly about those revivals, and how furiously some of the ministers in this region did oppose them. And they remarked, that if there had not been some little yielding and paring down, so as to unite, as there was toward the last in the Assembly, they never would have seen the ministers west of the Alleghany Mountains in the Assembly again."—*Patterson's Pamphlet*, 1836.

nervous to the most violent, or even "to a death-like weakness and inaction." Some could sit who could not stand. Some could sit when in part supported, who could not otherwise. Some, however, needed to be held "as much as infants," some as much "as persons in high convulsions." "Nervous affections and convulsions" were more frequent than a loss of strength and animal powers. In the latter case the subject was silent; in the former he sighed, or sobbed and groaned, in proportion to the degree in which he was affected.

The duration of the "exercises" was various,—in some cases only for a few minutes, in others for hours, and sometimes for days. Yet no after-inconvenience was occasioned by it. Though apparently deeply distressed, they experienced no bodily pain. Rarely was any one sensible of any injury received through his fall, either at the time or afterward.

One feature in the experience of those affected is especially noted. "They never lost their senses." Their minds appeared, indeed, to be then more active than ever, and all their powers "intent upon the things of religion and the interests of eternity." Their perceptions were remarkably clear, and their memories uncommonly retentive. Many would speak "in broken accents and half expressions," begging for mercy, deprecating wrath, groaning under sin, calling upon perishing sinners, or giving glory to God.

When they recovered, the impulse to speak seemed irresistible. Some would speak for quite a time, and "speak to admiration." "It seems," says Mr. Robbins, "almost—not from the manner, but from the truths they utter—as if they had been to the invisible world."

Yet the people were carefully instructed that there was no religion in the mere falling, or in the bodily exercises. Against this idea they were repeatedly put upon their guard. It received no encouragement from the ministers; and even among those who had ridiculed the phenomena, who had pronounced them delusions or mere excitement, some were affected. That the work was genuine, and that it could not be explained on any known principles, all alike, friends and foes of the revival, were finally agreed.[1] The witness, fully competent, whose testimony has been so freely adduced, closes his observations with the remark, "I firmly believe this to be a conspicuous and glorious work of divine grace, and that thousands of

---

[1] One gentleman who attended upon one of the sacramental occasions declared to the ministers and others that he could account for all the extraordinary exercises by his medical skill and on philosophical principles. He said none but weak women and persons of weak nerves were made to fall; but if some stout, healthy, brawny-built man should fall, he should think it something above human art. It was so ordered that he had the most fair trial. Some time in the meeting, he found himself alarmed from his security, and, instead of philosophizing on others, was constrained to attend to his own soul. His strength was so far gone that he could not rise; and he asked help to be carried out. But when beyond hearing of the preacher, "Oh, carry me back!" he called out: "God is here: I cannot get away from God. I know now that I am in God's hands: this is God's work." Subsequently, when others came to speak with him, he said, "Oh, I have lived forty-seven years an enemy to God. I have been in some of the hottest battles, and never knew what it was to have my heart palpitate with fear; but now I am all unstrung. I have cut off limbs with a steady hand; and now I cannot hold this hand still if I might have a world. I know this is not the work of men. I feel that I am in God's hands, and that he will do with me just what he pleases." Mr. Badger met this man a few weeks later, when he said to him that "he thought at some times he could see a little how God could save, through Jesus Christ, such a sinner as he was; but most of the time he was in total darkness."—*Conn. Ev. Mag.*, Sept. 1804.

immortal souls, the subjects of it, will adore the riches of divine mercy through eternity."[1]

It was during the first weeks, the opening scenes, of this powerful revival, that the Synod of Pittsburg met at Pittsburg and organized themselves (October, 1802) into the Western Missionary Society. The field which they felt called to occupy was suddenly expanded, and emphatically—beyond all that they could have anticipated—was white for the harvest. The laborers already employed were tasked almost beyond measure; and yet they flagged not in their efforts. Others were needed to aid them; and not a few—as the result of this revival and the efforts of the Synod—were brought forward to their aid. The excesses of the revival—if indeed they can be so termed—passed away, and ere long were wellnigh forgotten, overshadowed, at least, by the more remarkable phenomena of the Kentucky revival; but the results that followed have their lasting monuments in the churches scattered over the broad region swept by the revival.

---

[1] As to the leading features of the work, the testimony of Rev. Mr. Badger (Conn. Ev. Mag., Sept. 1803) is coincident with that of Mr. Robbins. In speaking of the impression made upon his own mind while participating in one of the large gatherings during the revival, Mr. Badger says, "The sweet and lovely frame Christians appeared to be in, the meekness and humbleness of mind, exceeded any thing I ever saw before. It helped me to get some faint ideas of what the saints will enjoy when they come to see the King in his beauty and be present at his table, without sin or flesh to intercept their sight."

CHAPTER XXIII.

NEW JERSEY, 1800–1820.

In 1800, there were in connection with the Presbyterian Church in New Jersey, and under the care of the two Presbyteries of New York and New Brunswick,[1]—which covered the field,—thirty-two ministers, twenty-seven of whom had pastoral charges, while there were also thirteen vacancies. The number of all the Presbyterian churches in the State was, thus, but about forty.

During the first twenty years of the present century, there was a steady and healthful growth. In 1809, the Presbytery of New York was divided; and from the portion of it lying within the bounds of New Jersey the Jersey Presbytery was erected. In 1817, the Presbytery of New Brunswick was likewise divided, in order to form the Presbytery of Newton. In 1820, there were thus within the bounds of the State the three Presbyteries of Jersey, New Brunswick, and Newton. The thirty-two ministers of 1800 had increased to fifty-four, the twenty-seven pastors to forty-three; while the churches had advanced from about forty to sixty-seven, or at the rate of about seventy per cent.

The Presbytery of Jersey embraced the churches in the northern part of the State. The First Church of Newark, through the influence of the great revival of 1807–08, and under the labors of Dr. Griffin, received

---

[1] Other churches were connected with Presbyteries of other States.

large accessions,—ninety-seven on a single occasion, and one hundred and seventy-four in a period of six months. A membership of two hundred and two was in the course of eight years increased to five hundred and twenty-two, and the result was that, shortly after Dr. Griffin's removal to the Park Street Church in Boston, a Second Church was formed.[1] In 1815, this church, then vacant, extended a call to Dr. Griffin, which he felt it his duty to accept,—the First Church, meanwhile, having enjoyed the pastoral labors of Dr. James Richards.

Among the distinguished ministers of the age, Dr. Edward Dorr Griffin occupied the foremost rank. Nature had been munificent in the gifts which she had lavished upon him. His large and well-proportioned frame and commanding presence impressed the beholder at a glance; and his intellectual endowments were in keeping with his person. A native of Connecticut, and a graduate of Yale College in 1790, he pursued his theological studies under the younger Edwards, and for several years after his licensure preached in different places in his native State, until his call to New Hartford in 1795. A revival of considerable power followed almost immediately upon his settlement; and three years later, one still more remarkable attested and crowned his fidelity to his work.

In 1801, he was called to Newark, as the colleague of Dr. McWhorter. Here he remained for eight years, and for the last two or three his church enjoyed an almost continuous revival. Such was his reputation

---

[1] The churches of Newark date as follows:—Second, 1810; Third, 1824; Fourth (of short duration), 1831; African Presbyterian, 1831; Free Church (since Congregational), 1837; Central Presbyterian, 1837; Park Presbyterian, Sixth Presbyterian, and High Street Presbyterian, 1848; German Presbyterian, 1852; South Park Presbyterian, 1853.

that he was called first to a professorship in Andover Seminary, and subsequently to the pastoral charge of the Park Street Church in Boston. He had already entered upon the duties of his professorship when the claims of the Park Street Church were pressed upon his attention. But the post of a defender of the faith in a city which had become the stronghold of Unitarianism was one which, with all its responsibilities and difficulties, did not long allow him to hesitate. In the capital of New England, where evangelical truth had become unpopular and odious, and where intellectual culture and social respectability had attempted to frown it down, he stood forth as its undaunted, uncompromising, eloquent, and powerful champion.

In the spring of 1815, he was recalled to Newark, to the pastorate of the Second Church. Here, among faithful friends and among old revival-associations, he devoted himself with exemplary fidelity and characteristic energy to his pastoral duties. The benevolent institutions of the day found in him a warm and trustworthy friend. He was one of the original founders of the Bible Society. The United Foreign Mission Society was not a little indebted to his agency; while he zealously promoted the interests of the school established by the Synod of New York and New Jersey for the education of Africans. In 1817, he published his work on the Extent of the Atonement. In 1821, he was invited to the Presidency of Danville College, but ultimately declined the overture,—accepting, however, a similar invitation soon after extended him from Williams College.

His course in this matter undoubtedly saved the institution from extinction. Its continued existence was doubted even by its friends. By his exertions it was eventually placed upon a solid basis and its prosperity was assured. To the close of his active life he continued at its head; and, when increasing debility debarred him from the privilege of further service, he returned to Newark (1836), to die among his friends.

The majestic presence of the man, his solemn mien, his manifest sincerity, his deliberate and emphatic utterance, the simplicity of his thoughts, and the force and beauty of his language, marked him as the orator. The pulpit was his throne. There he maintained an indisputable pre-eminence. The tones of his powerful voice now rang forth in thrilling appeal and now subsided to a melting pathos. His hearers were convinced, overawed, electrified. His reading of the Scriptures seemed to evolve a meaning and richness unthought of before. He threw his soul into his utterance. His manner was simple, natural, and yet dignified; while his gesture was governed by the impulse of thought and feeling. The tide of his own emotions swept along with it the hearts and sympathies of his hearers; and those who had once been permitted to listen to his bursts of luminous, impassioned utterance would be sure never to forget them.

But the themes and doctrines of the gospel system were those upon which he most delighted to dwell. Tolerant of non-essential differences, he was tenacious of all that was vital and cardinal to the glory of redemption. His sympathies were broad enough to embrace all who loved Christ, but not blind enough to strike hands with those who betrayed him with a kiss.

No one was more anxious to witness the success of the gospel, or to promote the interests of religion by all proper methods. His zeal for the conversion and salvation of souls would, in one less magnificently and symmetrically endowed, have amounted to a passion; but with him it was prompted by intelligent conviction, and guided, rather than restrained, by judgment. His sermons were—many of them—written in the midst of revival scenes, and he aimed so to write them that they might be used in revivals. Indeed, it was only when the minds of others around him were most deeply stirred by the power of eternal things that he found himself in a sphere most congenial to the highest effort. The result of his labors and his prayers was what might have been reasonably expected. "The history of his life," it has been well said, "seems little else than one unbroken revival; and it would perhaps be difficult to name the individual in our country, since the days of Whitefield, who was instrumental of an equal number of hopeful conversions."

But, with all his ardent emotion, he was never the victim of irregular zeal. The spirit of fanaticism was not allowed to usurp the place of reason, and no erratic or extravagant measures could secure his endorsement. With a keen sense of propriety, with a just discrimination between the proper excitement of truth and the excesses of feeling, but, above all, with clear apprehensions of what was requisite to the new life of the soul and what was essential to its healthful life, he would extend his approval to nothing which experience, sound reason, or Scripture had not already endorsed.

Such was the man who for years stood at the head of the Presbyterian ministry in New Jersey, and, indeed, throughout the land. He was not, it is true, an extemporaneous speaker, except on less imposing occasions. He read his sermons; but he read them as perhaps no man had ever read before. His look, tone, manner, were independent of the manuscript trammels by which many are bound, and he used his manuscript to make them more free. Perhaps in this he erred; but, if so, the error, with so much to atone for it, was venial; and he will long be remembered as among the princeliest of pulpit orators.

It required no ordinary man to fill the place vacated by Dr. Griffin in the First Church in 1809. Almost any one might have hesitated long before consenting to accept the post of one "the splendor of whose gifts and the power of whose eloquence had elevated him to the highest rank of American preachers." But since 1794, for a space of some twelve years, there had been preaching at Morristown a young man who, without a college education, had risen to such distinction that when but thirty-seven years of age the General Assembly chose him as its moderator. His early years betrayed an insatiable thirst for knowledge, but the circumstances of his family forbade him to cherish the hope of a liberal education. At Newtown, Conn., at Stamford, and, it is said, at New York, he labored, as his feeble health would allow, as a cabinet- and chair-maker. In the midst of his gayety, he was struck under conviction. He was converted, and resolved to devote himself to the ministry. But ill health, weak eyes, and the lack of means to prosecute his studies, thwarted his plans. Yet even thus he resolved to persevere. Gathering up what he could earn by teaching school, he studied with one and another of the ministers near his place of residence (New Canaan), among others, securing the aid of Dr. Dwight. His diligence was untiring, and his improvement was worthy of the best advantages.

Licensed to preach in 1793, he supplied for short periods the churches at Wilton, Ballston, Shelter Island, and Sag Harbor. Here he became acquainted with Drs. Buell and Woolworth, who recommended him to the church at Morristown, vacant by the resignation of Dr. Johnes. This venerable man was made the umpire to judge of the fitness of the youth who had been recommended as his successor.[1] Sitting in his own dwelling,

---

[1] Sprague, iii. 17.

under the burden of almost fourscore years, he listened to the discourse which was to determine the acceptableness of the candidate. The decision of the veteran pastor was, no doubt, favorable, and James Richards entered upon his labors at Morristown. A few weeks passed away, and his predecessor, surviving long enough to know that his place was to be filled by one not unworthy to wear his mantle,—like aged Simeon,—could utter his *nunc dimittis*, and lie down to die.

Dr. Richards was not what a very refined taste would call a finished, or even a graceful, orator. He was by no means the equal, in powerful and impassioned utterance, of Dr. Griffin. His genius, his brilliancy, his graces, might all be summed up in a single expression, —good sense. He never committed a blunder or an indiscretion. He neither said nor did a foolish thing. With sound judgment he combined a most kind and genial spirit, and a rare power in the discernment of character. He read human nature, as it came under his observation, almost by intuition. Yet, in spite of its foibles, he never derided its weakness or repulsed its claims to sympathy. His self-possession and his tact were perfect. His humor was not exuberant, but it was exceedingly good-natured. His smile was benignant, and his portrait would answer to Goldsmith's limning of the country parson.

In the pulpit he was instructive, solid, and impressive. He was ever full of his theme; and his earnestness, if rarely impassioned, was grave and sincere. Above all, his piety was uniform and ardent. It shone with a constant, steady light. With a noble Christian liberality, he was yet a decided Presbyterian. Christ was the centre of his system; and rarely did he preach a sermon in which the cross was not exhibited. His labors at Newark were signally blessed. Powerful revivals were enjoyed in 1813 and 1817; and during his fourteen years' pastorate of the church about five hundred were added to its communion, two-thirds of the number on profession of faith. In 1823, he accepted a call to the Professorship of Theology in Auburn Theological Seminary, and died, in the discharge of its duties, in 1843.

A genial associate and close friend of Griffin and Richards was Asa Hillyer, of Orange. His pastorate extended from 1801 to 1833; and even till his death, in 1840, he did not fail to devote his waning strength to his Master's service. A graduate of Yale College in 1786, and a theological pupil, first of Dr. Buell, of East Hampton, and afterward of Dr. Livingston, of New York, he supplied for a time the church of Madison, and in 1798 performed a missionary tour of nine hundred miles in the new settlements.

With a fine person, a countenance open and genial, and bland and winning manners, Dr. Hillyer was a model of Christian and ministerial dignity, consistency, and loveliness. Kind and considerate, social and urbane, he reminded one of "the disciple whom Jesus loved." Respectable as a preacher, he was devoted as a pastor. His sensibilities were keen, and in him his people found, both in their joys and their sorrows, a sympathizing friend. In the house of affliction, by the bedside of the sufferer, and amid the grief of desolate homes, he was a son of consolation. The anxious and inquiring found in him a faithful guide and a tender counsellor. Under his ministry, his church became one of the largest and most influential in the State.[1]

At Mendham the pastoral services of Amzi Arm-

[1] The church of Wardsesson, or Bloomfield, was organized as the Third Presbyterian Church, in the township of Newark, in 1794. For many years it had no settled pastor. Previous, however, to 1814, Cyrus Guildersleeve accepted the charge. He left previous to 1819, and in 1820 was succeeded by G. N. Judd.

strong extended from 1796 to 1816, a period of twenty years. Though not a college graduate, he was a diligent student, and, before and after the close of his pastorate, was distinguished as a teacher. With an open countenance, eyes bright and piercing, courteous and gentlemanly manners, he occupied a high place in the esteem of his brethren and the affections of his people. In his perceptions he was quick, sagacious, and clear; and his lucid exposition of matters under debate won for him the facetious *sobriquet* of "the snuffers of the Presbytery." In the pulpit he dispensed with manuscripts, and spoke with great force and self-possession. In social life he was urbane and genial, with a ready flow of wit and a remarkable command of good-natured sarcasm. He was of an uncommonly happy disposition; and the mirthfulness of his spirit enlivened his intercourse, especially with his more intimate friends. Removing at the close of his pastorate to take charge of the school at Bloomfield, he gave place to his more illustrious successor, Samuel Hanson Cox.[1]

At Morristown, after the vacancy occasioned by the resignation of Dr. Richards, a call was extended to Dr. Wm. A. McDowell, who had been settled for a short time (1813–14) at Bound Brook. For nine years his ministry at Morristown was characterized by great acceptableness and usefulness. The failure of his health forced him to remove to the South; and for nine years he was pastor of a church in Charleston, S.C. He was subsequently chosen Secretary of the Board of Do-

---

[1] After a brief pastorate at Mendham, Dr. Cox was succeeded by Dr. Philip C. Hay. The latter was a native of Newark, a graduate of Nassau Hall, and a licentiate of Jersey Presbytery (1820). He was called soon after to Mendham, where he remained till invited to succeed Dr. Griffin at Newark. He subsequently labored at Geneva, N.Y., and died in 1860. He had studied law before entering the ministry.

mestic Missions, and continued in the discharge of its duties till 1850.

Of a kindly spirit, an even temper, and unassuming manners, he was a friend to be prized and loved. His sermons were more solid than brilliant, characterized by logical acumen rather than excursive imagination. In prayer he was eminently gifted, and in pastoral duty singularly faithful. The partial failure of his voice interfered with his usefulness and circumscribed his efforts. Never imperious, with a heart glowing with benevolence and characterized by childlike simplicity, he won many and lost no friends.

At Rockaway, which had been vacant for several years previous, Barnabas King commenced his labors in 1806. In October, 1807, he divided his time between Rockaway and Sparta. His first intention, after his graduation at Williams College in 1804 and his licensure by the Berkshire Association in the following year, had been to seek a missionary field in the new settlements of Western New York; but in the region around him he found enough of missionary labor to task all his powers. The church at Rockaway was wellnigh extinct, and his labors were truly in a new and hard field.[1] From Powerville to Berkshire, and from Walnut Grove to Stony Brook, could be collected only thirty-five church-members. Of these twelve were widows; and of the whole number only three men were found who prayed in public. But soon after he began his labors a general seriousness was observed to prevail, which ere long deepened into a revival. Before the close of 1808, eighty converts were added to the church as the auspicious beginning of his ministry. On December 27th of that year, he was ordained and installed pastor of the church.

---

[1] Tuttle's Funeral Sermon, p. 9.

Frail and feeble in appearance, and supposed by all to be consumptive, he was spared to the discharge of a long and useful pastorate. In labors he was abundant. He catechized the young, visited the schools, preached from house to house, and with simplicity and godly sincerity sought the salvation of souls. For forty years there was but one communion-season in which some were not added to the church. In 1818, one hundred and fifty-one professed their faith in Christ.

But, while faithful to his special charge, he did not neglect the missionary field around him. With the best men of Jersey Presbytery he bore his full share in itinerant evangelization, going from Powles Hook to the Delaware to tell the destitute of Christ. The monuments of his success were scattered around him far and near. One of the most eminent of his contemporaries remarked that he knew "of no minister whose walk and labor and success had been so admirable as those of Mr. King, of Rockaway;" and another thought it might be said, with truth, that "the grace that was bestowed upon him was not in vain, for he labored more abundantly than they all."

His great ambition was to win souls. His one book was the Bible. As a preacher he was simple and scriptural; and his whole course was characterized by good sense, consummate judgment, earnestness of purpose, and devotion to his work. Usefulness he preferred to eloquence or learning. Yet his utterance was always manly, and at times fervent. One of his most critical hearers remarked that "he never said a foolish thing."

Amid fragrant memories, and the rich harvests of the usefulness he coveted, he descended to the grave in a ripe and beautiful old age. The wrinkles of more than fourscore years were on his brow, but there was no wrinkle on his heart. His closing hours were marked by peace and cheerful hope, and when called to depart he was ready for the summons. The death of Dr. King occurred April 10, 1862.

The labors of Aaron Condict commenced in Hanover in 1796, and extended to Oct. 6, 1831. Under his ministry more than seven hundred were admitted to the communion of the Church, and he was permitted to witness nine or ten distinct revivals of religion. His wisdom, humility, benevolence, and hospitality, his interest in whatever pertained to the prosperity of the Redeemer's kingdom, and the fact that four of his sons entered the ministry, some of whom have risen to high usefulness and distinction, entitle his name to honorable mention.

At Perth Amboy, where a church had been formed previous to 1809, Josiah B. Andrews—for a time a missionary of the Connecticut Society—was settled some six or eight years later; and his ministry continued till 1825. At Elizabethtown the gifted and eloquent Henry Kollock, in 1800, commenced his ministry, removing, however, after three years, to Princeton, where he labored, as pastor of the church and professor in the college, until his settlement at Savannah in 1806. His successor at Elizabethtown was Dr. John McDowell, whose name is a treasured one in the history of the Church, and during whose ministry a Second Church was formed (1820), which has enjoyed from its origin the pastoral labors of Dr. David Magie.[1]

---

1 The church was organized, and Dr. Magie commenced his labors, in the fall of 1820. The membership of the church was forty-one,—all, with a single exception, from the First Church.—*Dr. Magie's Fortieth Anniversary Sermon.*

The Third Church, under the pastoral charge of Robert Aikman since its organization, was formed in 1851, reporting a membership of ninety-one in the following year. In the First Church the successor of Dr. McDowell was Dr. Nicholas Murray.

The successor of Dr. Roe, of Woodbridge, upon his death in 1815, was Henry Mills (ordained and installed July 12, 1816), subsequently professor at Auburn, who in turn was succeeded by William B. Barton. At Rahway, Buckley Carll (settled in 1804) continued as pastor till about 1825, and his death took place in 1842. At Paterson, where a church had been formed previous to 1814, Samuel Fisher commenced his somewhat extended pastorate a few years later. At South Hanover (or Chatham), Dr. Perrine, who removed to New York in 1811 to take charge of the Spring Street Church, was succeeded by John G. Bergen. John Ford, for more than forty years pastor at Parsippany, commenced his labors there about the year 1816.

The other ministers of Jersey Presbytery in 1820 were Henry Cook at Woodbridge Second, where e had been settled for nearly twenty years; Stephen Thompson, who previous to 1809 had succeeded Elias Riggs, at Connecticut Farms; Mr. Riggs, who had removed to take charge of New Providence; Jacob Green at Succasunna, and John E. Miller at Roxbury, where they had succeeded Lemuel Fordham, whose charge had extended to both churches. Besides these, Amzi Armstrong, Noah Crane, Humphrey M. Perrine, and Edward Allen were without charge; while the churches of Bloomfield,[1] Westfield, Springfield, Hardiston, Jersey, Ramapo, Newfoundland, Stony Brook, and Long Pond were (1819) vacant.

In the New Brunswick Presbytery, Dr. Woodhull was still at Freehold; his son, George S. Woodhull, had been many years at Cranberry, where he was succeeded by S. C. Henry, Aug. 8, 1820. Joseph Rue was still (1785–1826) pastor of Pennington and Trenton First; while John Cornell was settled at Allentown and Not-

---

[1] G. N. Judd was installed at Bloomfield Aug. 2, 1820.

tingham, where he had succeeded Joseph Clark previous to 1803. At Trenton, S. B. How, successor of J. F. Armstrong (1787–1816), and subsequently settled at New Brunswick, was pastor; at Bound Brook, John Boggs (1816–28), who had succeeded David Barclay (1794–1805), S. S. Woodhull (1805–06), James Patterson (1809–13), and Wm. A. McDowell (dismissed 1814); and at Kingston, David Comfort. At Lawrenceville a church had recently been organized, of which I. V. Brown was pastor. New Brunswick, after having successively Walter Monteith and Joseph Clark (1797–1813), was under the pastoral charge of L. J. F. Huntington;[1] and Princeton—which after the dismissal of Kollock in 1806 had called William C. Schenk, who remained for several years—was vacant. Middletown Point, Shrewsbury, and Shark River were likewise vacant, but unable to support a pastor.

At Princeton, where the Theological Seminary had meanwhile been established, were Drs. Green, Smith, Miller, Alexander, and Lindsley, all without pastoral charge, but members of the Presbytery. Dr. Samuel Stanhope Smith, for many years President of the college, had become by disease disabled from active service. But his life hitherto had been one of incessant activity and extended usefulness. A son of Robert Smith, of Pequa, a graduate of Princeton, a tutor in the college, a missionary in Western Virginia, where he was hailed as a second Davies, then President of Hampden-Sidney College, which was built and endowed that he might be placed at its head, he was invited in 1779 to the chair of Moral Philosophy at Nassau Hall, and accepted the appointment. The state of the college was most unpromising. Given up to the uses of the army during the previous year of the war, the

---

[1] He died May 1, 1820, and was succeeded by J. P. Jones.

building was in ruins, the students were dispersed, and, through the necessary absence of Dr. Witherspoon to serve in the councils of the nation, the operations of the institution had ceased. By the vigor, wisdom, and generous self-devotion of Dr. Smith, these were revived; and the subsequent prosperity of the college was largely due to his unceasing vigilance, earnest efforts, and distinguished ability. Upon the death of Dr. Witherspoon, he was elected to fill his place. Meanwhile, his reputation as a pulpit-orator had spread far and near. Persons were known to come from New York and Philadelphia—a distance of some forty miles—to listen to his Baccalaureate discourses.

In the spring of 1802, the college-edifice was destroyed by fire. The libraries, furniture, and fixtures of every description were consumed. The charter, the grounds, and the naked walls of brick and stone, were all that was left. But the trustees, recovering from the stunning blow, resolved to proceed at once to the work of renovation. Dr. Smith went on a *begging* tour to the Southern States, and returned with one hundred thousand dollars. Liberal collections from other parts of the country added to the sum, and the institution soon attained more than its former prosperity. This was his crowning achievement. His physical system, repeatedly prostrated before,—for he had been disabled by blindness and hæmorrhage,—at length began to feel the weight of years and protracted service, and, in 1812, repeated strokes of palsy warned him to desist from active service. He resigned his post as President, and after seven years, in which he was scarcely capable of mental labor, died, Aug. 21, 1819, in the seventieth year of his age.

In the Middle and Southern States, where he was best known, Dr. Smith was regarded as the most learned and eloquent divine of the age. Men that had listened to Davies and felt the power of Patrick Henry were enthusiastic in his praise. The highest expectations of him excited by his fame were realized. It seemed natural for him "to put proper words in proper places," and to select the most expressive. He eschewed all affectation, mannerism, and formality. His sincerity and uprightness could not be questioned. Firm, resolute, decided, courteous, and dignified in his deportment, his very presence commanded respect and overawed turbulence and mischief. In the college, in Presbytery, Synod, and General Assembly, as well as before a promiscuous audience, he was perfectly at ease and master of himself. His intellectual resources, which were rich and varied, were ever at his command. The purity of his life, his humble faith, his cheerful temper, his habitual meekness, sympathy, and charity, were in keeping with his venerable figure, saintly aspect, and benignant smile. One who knew him well in his later years[1] speaks of his life then as "a bright, blessed, glorious vision, such as we dream of but never realize. It seemed as if all the Christian graces and virtues, freed from every human imperfection, had now clustered around him, and blended together, like the colors of the rainbow, into a living form of chastened, hallowed, radiant loveliness."

The man who succeeded to the post made vacant by his resignation was of a quite different stamp. He was as clear-headed, not less practical, quite as energetic, but with little of the peculiar grace of manner and eloquence which invested the name of President Smith with lustre. Ashbel Green was a shrewd and able man. The impression of his presence was that of one born to command. His comprehension of truth was acute, logical, mathematical. In the pulpit he

---

[1] President Lindsley.

might convince, but he kindled no man to rapture. None of his hearers so far forgot themselves as to imagine that they were anywhere else than under the sound of his voice. Dr. Caldwell, of Philadelphia,[1] with his keen appreciation of Fisher Ames, could not relish him,—pronounced him dull, and chose to hear some other preacher. And yet he was a man of power. He knew his object, and took the most effectual method to attain it. He never surrendered to a weak sympathy, or compromised with what he accounted error. His blows were direct, premeditated, hearty. If he wished to rebuke a sin, he did it,—and did it with a boldness and fearlessness which struck terror into the victim. Yet he was not wanting in kindness and charity. If never surprised into emotion, he was not without warm feelings; and his pulpit-labors testified to his zeal for souls as well as his zeal for truth. In any sphere or calling he would have held a high rank. As a statesman, he would have shaped the policy of his party, if not of the country. As a general, he would have maintained the power as well as the title of his office, nor would he have lacked sagacity or energy; or, if his lot had fallen upon times which made it a duty and necessity, he would, like Samuel, with iron nerve have "hewed Agag in pieces before the Lord."

Such was the man who was called to succeed to the Presidency of the College of New Jersey. For more than twenty years he had been settled over the Second Presbyterian Church in Philadelphia, and had been one of the leading members, and for some time stated clerk, of the General Assembly. Thoroughly identified, in all his views, sympathies, and opinions, with the Presbyterian Church, an able administrator, and a rigid disciplinarian, some would have pronounced

---

[1] See his Autobiography.

him a bigot; but the nature of the man made him unbending in purpose, and his devotion to the interests of what he deemed truth and righteousness was supreme. Whatever he took in hand he did with his might, and, in whatever sphere he moved, he left behind him the impression of his activity and energy.

Of Dr. Alexander it is enough to say that, when the General Assembly determined to establish a seminary at Princeton, he was the man selected before all others to occupy the post of Theological Professor. At the age of forty, he was called from his pastorate in Philadelphia to occupy this position. Artless, frank, unassuming, and transparent in simplicity and integrity, he commanded love, as well as confidence and respect. His keen susceptibility and warmly sympathetic nature, his cheerful vivacity,—which never forsook him, even to the last,—his ready utterance and perfect command of all the resources of clear exposition, of appeal and persuasion, combined to place him in the front rank of pulpit-orators. In the professor's chair he shone with equal distinction, and was never found wanting in any emergency. But his deep and ardent piety crowned his rare intellectual gifts and attainments with peculiar lustre; and the reverence and affection of hundreds of his pupils have long supplied the place of eulogy. In a ripe old age, beautiful as the cloudless sun at its setting, he went down to the grave, leaving behind him a memory fragrant with precious and hallowed associations.

Dr. Miller was called, in 1813, to the chair of Ecclesiastical History and Church Government in the seminary. For twenty years he had labored as an acceptable, influential, and popular pastor in New York With little about him that would be called brilliant, he was yet an easy, graceful, and dignified speaker. Of a remarkably fine person, with bland and attractive manners, and, from the first, master of an uncommonly polished style, his pulpit-performances were not only uniformly unexceptionable, but admirable. One familiar with the old Puritans would have been reminded by him of "the silver-tongued Bates." His intellectual and moral character was in keeping with the symmetry of his person. Never bold or startling, his attitudes in the pulpit were extremely dignified, not to say precise; his voice, though not strong, was pleasant; his utterance was deliberate, and his enunciation distinct. His thoughts, if neither remarkably versatile, original, nor striking, were always appropriate, and never commonplace. He might not thrill, but he rarely failed to convince. If he did not startle, he yet commanded assent; and in all his intercourse he manifested the traits of the perfect Christian gentleman. Even toward an adversary, and in the warmth of controversy, he could not be other than bland and courteous; and the superior moral qualities of his nature were moulded by grace into an exalted specimen of Christian excellence. A student, but not a recluse, a pleasant companion, but not forgetful of the proprieties of his sacred office, a teacher who could be genial and yet command respect, he filled for a period of nearly thirty years the post of honor and responsibility to which he had been elected by the suffrage of the Church.

At the time when Dr. Miller commenced his labors as professor at Princeton, a young man then twenty-seven years of age, who had been—although not consecutively—for three years a tutor in the college, was appointed to the Professorship of Languages. He was a native of Morristown, successively a pupil of Robert Finley, a graduate of Nassau Hall, and a licentiate of the New Brunswick Presbytery. He studied theology under Dr. Smith and Dr. Perrine, and, although subsequently ordained, *sine titulo*, devoted himself to academical pursuits. This young man was Philip Lindsley. He sought no honors; but honors were heaped upon him. So late as 1855, on being asked if he would serve as commissioner to the General Assembly, his significant and characteristic reply was, "I have never sought any appointment; and when God has placed upon me a duty, I endeavor to discharge it." In September, 1817, he was elected Vice-President of the College of New Jersey. On the resignation of Dr. Green, in 1822, he was for one year the acting President. Early in 1823, he was chosen President of Cumberland College, Tennessee, and, a few months later, President of the College of New Jersey. Both appointments he declined, as well as a subsequent overture to accept the Presidency of Ohio University.

Urgent application led him to reconsider his refusal to accept the Presidency of Cumberland College. He was inaugurated Jan. 12, 1825; and the institution, under the name of the University of Nashville, enjoyed his labors for more than a quarter of a century. At least ten colleges, some of them repeatedly, invited him, during his public career, to become their President. But his ambition grasped at usefulness rather than distinction; and the cause of piety and learning will ever number him among its greatest and most efficient benefactors.

As an instructor, Dr. Lindsley had few rivals, and perhaps no superior, in the land. He communicated to his pupils his own enthusiasm. In the lecture-room—where his style was conversational—he is said to have been perfectly fascinating. The rich treasures of his well-stored mind were poured forth without apparent effort. The force and beauty of his language and the richness of his thought borrowed a new charm from his fine personal appearance. "With a form perfectly erect and symmetrical, with features chiselled after the finest Grecian mould, a spacious dome-like forehead crowned with full black hair, a dark penetrating eye that flashed with indescribable emotion as he spoke, a peculiar play of expression about the mouth which no painter's art could ever catch, and a voice rich and musical alike in its highest and lowest notes, he possessed, aside from his rare intellectual gifts and attainments, every outward attribute to make him attractive in conversation and eloquent as a public speaker." On some occasions he was not merely graceful, elegant, or dignified; he was majestic. The admiration of his pupils was expressed by the classic epithets applied to him of "Hector" and "Achilles."

Precise, accurate, and thorough as a scholar, profound and often original as a thinker, fascinating, powerful, and impressive as a preacher, he devoted himself with untiring energy to the cause of sound and Christian learning; and all his varied excellences were combined to advance and extend the influence of truth and promote the interests of morality, Christian education, and pure religion.

The name of Robert Finley is one that deserves honorable mention. His father was a personal friend of Dr. Witherspoon, and the son prosecuted his early studies under Ashbel Green while the latter was yet an under-graduate at Princeton. His inquiring and acquisitive mind, as well as his exemplary sobriety and stability of character, even before entering college, gave promise of a future which was not belied by experience. In his sixteenth year he was graduated at New Jersey College, and for eight years—two of which were devoted to his tutorship at Princeton—he was engaged in teaching. In 1795, he took charge of the congregation of Baskingridge, and in 1803 a revival of great power prevailed among his people. His active mind was incessantly employed in devising new and increased means of usefulness, and the cause of Christian philanthropy found in him a warm and devoted friend. In 1815, he suggested the idea of communicating religious instruction by means of Bible-classes, and, after putting his theories to the test in his own congregation, secured their endorsement and recommendation by the General Assembly. For several years—partly through his residence in Charleston as a teacher—his attention had been called to the condition of the free colored people in this country, and, in the spirit of a broad philanthropy, he conceived the plan of colonization. Early in December, 1816, he visited Washington to excite the interest and secure the co-operation of leading members of Congress in the formation of a society designed to carry out his plan. His efforts were not without success; and within the month a society was organized, of which Bushrod Washington was elected President. The result was not accomplished without encountering a large measure of indifference and prejudice. Meanwhile, he received a call to the Presidency of Georgia University, which he felt it his duty to accept. Undaunted by the difficulties of the situation,—for the institution, he found, was at its "last gasp,"—he set himself vigorously to the task before him, perfecting the organization, or begging funds for the institution. A Presbyterian church, moreover, through his exertions, was organized in the place (Athens), and he became its stated supply. But the burdens he had assumed, combined with the debilitating influence of the climate, prostrated his strength, and the disease which supervened brought his life to a close in October, 1817. Exemplary as a pastor, faithful and earnest as a preacher, a friend of revivals, a man above every thing like duplicity or disingenuousness, he was yet more distinguished for his public spirit and his thorough devotion to the cause of Christian philanthropy. The Church has few brighter names on her list of true and noble men than that of Dr. Robert Finley.

Newton Presbytery, erected in 1817, numbered in 1819 fourteen members and had under its care twenty-five congregations. Holloway W. Hunt, after a pastorate of nearly twenty years, was still at Bethlehem, Kingswood, and Alexandria. William B. Sloan, for several years pastor of Greenwich and Mansfield, retained the former congregation; while Jacob A. Costner was settled over the latter. The late Dr. William C. Brownlee had recently been settled in place of Dr. Finley at Baskingridge. Dr. Joseph Campbell for ten years had been pastor of Hackettstown and Pleasant Grove. Jacob Kirkpatrick had succeeded (June, 1810) Thomas Grant at Amwell First and Second, his pastorate continuing for about forty years. Joseph L. Shafer had taken the place of John Boyd at Newton (subsequently to 1809), and Horace Galpin had succeeded him at Lamington. John F. Clark was at Flemington, which had remained vacant several years after the close of Thomas Grant's[1] pastorate. David Bishop was settled at Easton,[2] in place of David Barclay, who in 1809 had charge of this place together with Mt. Bethel and Oxford. Jehiel Talmage was pastor at Knowlton; while Oxford, Harmony, German Valley, Fox Hill, Upper and Lower Mt. Bethel, Smithfield, Marksborough, Hardwick, and Amwell First[3] were vacant. John Boyd and Symmes C. Henry were without charge.

The career of William C. Brownlee is mainly identified with the history of the Reformed Dutch Church, which he served, in the capacity of one of the pastors of the Collegiate Church, New York, for many years;

---

[1] Died March, 1811. [2] In Pennsylvania.

[3] So stated in the Minutes; while Kirkpatrick is located at Amwell First and Second.

but he was, as pastor at Baskingridge, one of the early members of the Newton Presbytery. Joseph Campbell, at Hackettstown, was a native of Ireland, but emigrated to this country in 1797, at the age of twenty-one years. For a short time he taught school at Cranberry, studying himself with Mr. Woodhull, and subsequently opened an English and classical school at Princeton, where he studied theology,—probably under President Smith. Having been licensed by New Brunswick Presbytery in 1808, he accepted a call in the following year to Hackettstown, where he continued to labor, with great acceptance and success, for nearly thirty years. His congregation, small at first, became under his ministry large and flourishing. With great energy of character, he was a faithful pastor and a popular preacher, devoted to the cause of Christian philanthropy, and prompt, judicious, and efficient in the ecclesiastical bodies of the Church.

John F. Clark was the son of Dr. Joseph Clark, pastor at New Brunswick from 1796 to 1813. In 1807, he was graduated with high honors at the College of New Jersey, where subsequently he was engaged as tutor. Soon after this he was settled at Flemington and Amwell, where he remained for twenty years. He was afterward settled at Paterson, then at Cold Spring, N.Y., and finally at Fishkill. His death occurred in 1853.

The new churches reported in connection with the Assembly within the bounds of the State, during the period under review, were Hanover,[1] Woodbridge Second, Middletown Point, Hackettstown, Flemington, and Hardwick, previous to 1803; Roxbury, or Black River, Jersey (City), Pleasant Grove, Easton (Pa.), and Harmony, previous to 1809; Newark Second, Pater-

[1] See note next page.

son, Ramapo, Fox Hill, and Smithfield, previous to 1814; and Parsippany,[1] Newfoundland, Stony Brook, Long Pond, Scott's Mountain, German Valley, Lawrenceville (Maidenhead), and Marksborough, previous to 1819.

There were numerous revivals during this period among the churches of the State; but the influence of the great revival in Kentucky was not so perceptible here as in some other places, although it was not without effect. At Bloomfield, forty-seven were added to the Church at one time, and before 1802 the number was increased to about one hundred. In several other congregations there were powerful revivals; but none of those "general meetings" which were common in Kentucky and the Carolinas were held in New Jersey until June, 1803. By a concert among the ministers of two adjoining counties, one was held at Bottle Hill (Madison), where Robert Finley was settled as pastor. Twenty-three ministers were present, and an immense concourse of people was in attendance. The meeting commenced on Tuesday, and closed on Wednesday evening. The venerable Dr. McWhorter, of Newark. presided. The people were formed into two large assemblies, one in the meeting-house and the other in the fields. The exercises were characterized by a deep and solemn interest. The appearance of the assemblies was described as that of "an army with banners." Among the ministers were McWhorter, Finley, and the gifted and eloquent Kollock, and probably also Griffin, Perrine, King, Hillyer, Armstrong, and Richards,—men of rare natural gifts, "their hearts glowing with devo-

---

[1] Parsippany—as was the case with Hanover—was organized a long time previous. It was under the care of Morris County Independent Presbytery till 1816, and on the dissolution of that body and the settlement of Mr. Ford its relations were with the churches of the Assembly. Aaron Condict was pastor of Hanover from 1796 to 1831.

tion, their minds with eloquence, and their tongues as the pens of ready writers." "They appeared as tongues of flame." "Among the saints there was a peculiar trembling of holy fear, and, at the same time, childlike confidence with respect to the issue." Their hopes were not disappointed. "Many sinners were manifestly touched with the arrows of conviction."[1]

At the close of the day, when the congregation was about to be dismissed, Mr. Finley arose with a heart swelling with emotions too strong to be uttered. After he had labored a short time to express a few broken sentences, his tongue was loosed, and he broke out in a strain of such impassioned eloquence as Mr. Kollock declared he had never heard before.[2] The whole congregation was powerfully affected, and, after the benediction was pronounced, remained sobbing and overwhelmed. A powerful revival of religion followed in the congregation. At Baskingridge congregation, under the care of Mr. Finley, seventy persons were received on a single occasion to the Church; and other neighboring congregations were largely blessed.[3]

The most remarkable scene of revival, however, during this period, was in connection with the congregation of Rev. Dr. Griffin, at Newark. Early in 1807,

---

[1] N.Y. Miss. Mag., iv. 438. [2] Sprague, iv. 267.

[3] An account of the revival at Newark in 1817 is to be found in the "Christian Herald," vol. ii. pp. 320 and 382.

In 1817-18, there were revivals of considerable power in the congregations of Rockaway, Perth Amboy, Jersey City, Newfoundland, North Hardiston, and Second Congregation of Woodbridge. To the latter one hundred and fifteen persons were added during the year; to that of Rockaway, one hundred and twenty-two; to that of Jersey City, numbering previously but ten, twenty-one were added. Newfoundland was organized August, 1818, as the fruit of the revival, with thirteen members, to which an addition of twenty more was expected. More than ordinary interest prevailed also at Kingswood, Bethlehem, and Alexandria.—*Christian Herald*, v. 558.

there were marks of unusual seriousness The death of Dr. McWhorter in July "made a great impression on the congregation," and, a few weeks later, Gideon Blackburn, then on his Northern tour to collect funds for the Cherokee Mission, visited Newark. He preached there several times "with great zeal and energy." It was at this period that the work really commenced. All "appeared still around;" but secret anxieties were preying upon many.

In connection with two neighboring churches, a day (September 4) was set apart for fasting and prayer. It was marked by unusual stillness and solemnity. At the close of the services of the next—the sacramental—Sabbath, there could be no doubt that a revival had indeed begun. The scenes that followed were truly pentecostal. It was sometimes difficult to dismiss the assemblies. Multitudes might be seen weeping and trembling around their minister, while others stood gazing, astonished spectators of the scene. Even the children were deeply affected. On one occasion, after catechetical instruction, "not less than a hundred were in tears at once."

"The work, in point of power and stillness," wrote Dr. Griffin to Dr. Green, "exceeds all I have ever seen." The number of conversions was from two hundred to two hundred and fifty. The subjects were of all ages, from nine years old to more than threescore and ten. Among them were to be found some who had been most abandoned characters,—drunkards, apostates, infidels, and malignant opposers. Even the "poor negroes" were included, "some of them hoary with age." Three students of law were among the number, one of whom, at least, will not soon be forgotten.

END OF VOL. I.

www.ingramcontent.com/pod-product-compliance
Lightning Source LLC
LaVergne TN
LVHW021221110826
845150LV00002B/217

* 9 7 8 1 4 2 5 5 6 4 4 6 9 *